Consecrating S

Consecrating Science

Wonder, Knowledge, and the Natural World

———

Lisa H. Sideris

UNIVERSITY OF CALIFORNIA PRESS

University of California Press, one of the most distinguished university presses in the United States, enriches lives around the world by advancing scholarship in the humanities, social sciences, and natural sciences. Its activities are supported by the UC Press Foundation and by philanthropic contributions from individuals and institutions. For more information, visit www.ucpress.edu.

University of California Press
Oakland, California

Library of Congress Cataloging-in-Publication Data

Names: Sideris, Lisa H., author.
Title: Consecrating science : wonder, knowledge, and the natural world / Lisa H. Sideris.
Description: Oakland, California : University of California Press, [2017] | Includes bibliographical references and index.
Identifiers: LCCN 2017003514| ISBN 9780520294974 (cloth : alk. paper) | ISBN 9780520294998 (pbk. : alk. paper) | ISBN 9780520967908 (e-edition)
Subjects: LCSH: Environmental ethics. | Religion and science.
Classification: LCC GE24 .S54 2017 | DDC 201/.65—dc23
LC record available at https://lccn.loc.gov/2017003514

25 24 23 22 21 20 19 18 17 16
10 9 8 7 6 5 4 3 2 1

To Robert and Ridley, with love and gratitude

CONTENTS

ACKNOWLEDGMENTS

A pleasant upside of spending several years writing a book is that it leaves you with many people to thank. This project began several years ago with a fellowship at the Rachel Carson Center for Environment and Society in Munich, Germany, and has evolved quite a bit since that time. I am deeply grateful to the Carson Center and its director, Christof Mauch, for providing me the time and resources to think through what this project aimed to do, and for the opportunity to pursue my research in the company of a truly interdisciplinary, international collection of environmental scholars. Special thanks for intellectual, material, and moral support to Carson affiliates and alumni Kim Coulter, Lawrence Culver, Stefan Dorondel, Stefania Gallini, Agnes Kneitz, Cheryl Lousley, Katie Ritson, Alexa Weik von Mossner, and officemate extraordinaire Emilian Kavalski. I learned much from this brilliant and fun crew. The Carson Center experience opened up a new world of ideas to me, and it continues to be one of the brightest spots in the environmental humanities.

I owe a major debt of gratitude to my colleagues in the Department of Religious Studies at Indiana University. I am thankful for the abiding congeniality and intellectual diversity of the department I have called home, as a student and faculty member, for much of my life. Several colleagues read and responded to chapters and article spin-offs of the book in departmental colloquia and seminars, and some waded through early drafts in their entirety. Were it not for Constance Furey, my partner in writing accountability, I would still be digging out from under an avalanche of words and ideas. She is like a bodhisattva of the book-writing world who, as she nears the end of her own project, journeys back to help suffering colleagues cross the threshold. Winni Sullivan provided steady encouragement and excellent, and sometimes lawyerly, advice whenever I encountered adversity and intrigue of various sorts.

Graduate and undergraduate students in my "God Species" seminar in Fall 2015 at Indiana University helped me steer a path through the ever-growing mountain of literature on the Anthropocene, and allowed me to grasp the relationship of that scholarship to the movements and ideas I discuss in this book. I am grateful to them for taking on the challenge of the course with me, and for humoring my preoccupation with that dark topic, even when readings were ponderous and voluminous. Jacob Boss, Rachel Carpenter, Olivia DeClark, Jen Kash, Sarah Kissell, Jonathan Sparks-Franklin—my heartfelt thanks for your insights and stamina. My gratitude also extends to the IU Office of Sustainability for providing financial support for that seminar, and thereby supporting this project indirectly. Thanks also to the Institute for Advanced Study at IU for providing research funds in the latter stages of writing and editing. To Jonathan Sparks-Franklin and Carl Pearson: thank you for your fabulous editorial assistance and dedication to detail. Paul Tyler, my copy editor at the University of California Press, was prompt and meticulous, and very pleasant to work with.

Several portions of this book were presented publicly in one form or another, at one time or another. I can't recount them all here, but I especially wish to thank Jeanne Kilde for a workshop at the University of Minnesota that significantly shaped what is now chapter 7. Penny Edgell, Alan Love, and Dan Philippon, among others, were generous and valuable interlocutors. A number of lectures delivered at Creighton University ended up as portions of this book. I am grateful to Ron Simkins and John O'Keefe for many productive conversations about religion, nature, theology—the relative merits of "new stories" and "old stories"—and for their continuing friendship.

Several friends and colleagues read and commented in detail on the entire manuscript in its near-final stages. A very special thanks to Whitney Bauman, Sam Deese, Sarah Fredericks, Constance Furey, Michael Northcott, Kevin O'Brien, Clare Palmer, Michael Ruse, Winni Sullivan, and an anonymous reviewer for their critical acumen and careful feedback. Certainly, I did not heed every word of their advice—so much the worse for me—but I am sure the final product is much stronger for their insights. I am also grateful to Clive Hamilton for fruitful exchanges about the Anthropocene and anthropocentrism—even if I remain rather unmoved in my general indictment of anthropocentrism. I owe a particular debt of gratitude to Bron Taylor, whose express commitment to "taboo-free zones" within the field of religion / nature / ecology made it possible for me to engage with a veritable phalanx of critics in the *Journal for the Study of Religion, Nature, and Culture*. I am also sincerely grateful to Eric Schmidt at University of California Press for championing a project that made more than one academic editor a little skittish.

On a personal note, I thank my parents, Nancy Hatton Sideris and Homer Geri Sideris, for the countless ways in which they have shaped my particular view of the world. To my mother: Thank you for passing on to me your sense of wonder, as well as your survival instincts. To my father: There are many things about which we disagree, but I can't help thinking that all that Presbyterianism left its mark on me, generally for the better. To my aunt Maria Sideris Chapis: Thank you for your positivity and broadmindedness, and for your faith in me.

Book-writing is an elaborately selfish undertaking, made possible through the indulgence of others who pick up the slack. This book is dedicated to my husband Robert and my son Ridley. Robert: Thank you for allowing me space and time to pursue my obsessions and fixed ideas—academic and otherwise—in my over-serious fashion. Ridley: I hope one day you'll understand what all my talk of wonder was about, and why so much of it has to do with you.

Introduction

The Return of Mythopoeic Science

The sciences have an important role to play in the formulation of environmental ethics, and no less so in religious environmental ethics. The lack of coherence between religious environmental ethicists' vision for nature and the realities of Darwinian science has been the subject of my own research.[1] I have argued that ecological theologians, as well as many secular environmental ethicists, tend to ignore, or make selective use of, scientific—particularly Darwinian—information about the natural world. Darwinian perspectives allow us to appreciate that processes of suffering, strife, and competition for finite resources are not only regular features of the natural world but integral to healthy natural systems. Ethical proposals aimed at eradicating or redeeming natural suffering and strife often put ecotheology at odds with the science of natural systems, and may even treat natural processes as symptomatic of a fallen state that needs to be radically transformed. In short, because these ethicists and theologians fail to take science seriously, they support values and ethical guidelines for the natural world that are largely incompatible with evolutionary processes.

And yet, I have become increasingly troubled by a growing constellation of movements within religious and secular environmentalism that takes science rather *too* seriously. The new cosmology, as I refer to this constellation of movements, cedes too much territory and authority to science and its alleged mythic potential. Proponents of this new cosmology see cutting-edge scientific knowledge as the primary vehicle for restoring enchantment, wonder, meaning, and value to the natural world. The new cosmology goes by a variety of names, including the Epic of Evolution, the Universe Story, the New Story, the Great Story, or Big History. In its various iterations, it proffers a grand narrative of cosmogenesis—the unfolding of the universe from the Big Bang to the present—as a sacred story, a common creation myth for the modern world and for all people. Science, in this movement, offers a wondrous new revelation, an updated sacred scripture. The claim is that only with the recent emergence of this big picture from science has it become possible to narrate a common story. Awe at the unfolding story of the universe, it is hoped, will confer a shared sense of belonging and obligation for the natural world. At the heart of this book is a detailed analysis of the ethical implications of these movements whose impacts are felt in a variety of disciplines and well beyond the academy.

This book does *not* aim to flesh out an alternative environmental ethic, particularly in an applied sense. I will not, for the most part, be sorting through claims about rights or duties inhering in or owed to particular organisms or entities in the natural world. Although I assume a moral stance that is largely nature-centered and *anti*-anthropocentric, I will not devote space to developing the contours of an ecocentric ethic, as I have previously done. Rather, I start from the assumption that an overtly human-centered and human-exalting worldview is inimical to genuine appreciation, wonder, and concern for the natural world not just because I believe this to be true (which I do), but because that is where my interlocutors start. In other words, the new cosmologists set out to create a "new story" to supersede the flawed anthropocentric, dominionistic, controlling attitudes they believe to characterize the traditional faiths. Their objective is to craft a new scientific myth that avoids these arrogant pitfalls. In this effort, as my recurring focus on the anthropocentric, anthropic, and (for want of a better term) *Anthropocenic* dimensions of these narratives illustrate, the new cosmology fails.

That said, I do promote an anti-anthropocentric perspective in a more indirect and subtle way, via the lens of wonder. Wonder that exalts the human species or the human mind as a supreme object of reverence is not only a debased and mistaken rendering of what it *means* to wonder. It is also a danger to the natural world and—I suspect—to our moral well-being and grasp of *reality* (reality being a favored, operative word in the new science-based religions). Wonder is not true wonder that takes the human as its object. Nor, I believe and will argue, is true wonder a wonder that revels in cataloguing all that is *known*. Readers may well take issue with my staking out a particular version of wonder as genuine or authentic (historically? empirically? by definition?), and my answers may not settle the issue. But I hope my readers will come to appreciate, as I have in studying these movements closely, that the wonder they celebrate is largely complicit with the forces that have created our crisis-ridden, human-dominated planet. Indeed, the wonder enshrined in these movements is a likely *driver* of these crises. I develop these and many related claims in the pages that follow. My focus, then, is less on applied ethics than on fundamental attitudes, dispositions, habits of mind, moods, and orientations toward the world around us. Above all, the orientation that interests me—and my interlocutors—is wonder. Like them, I am keenly interested in the *placement*, the *positionality* of "the human" vis-à-vis the universe. Unlike them, I reject the proposition that there exist clear answers to questions about our "role" in the universe, and that science can provide such answers.

This book, then, is also an extended meditation on wonder, influenced by my longtime engagement with the life and work of Rachel Carson, who celebrated wonder as a salutary and enduring orientation on the world. Informed and inspired by Carson's account, I regard the appeal to wonder in these movements with some skepticism and sobriety. What is, or ought to be, the relationship between wonder and environmental values? How do we recognize and define appropriate and inappropriate forms of wonder that perennially emerge at the intersection of science, religion, and nature?[2] How do science and technology contribute to wonder and when do they become an enemy of wonder and a threat to nature's well-being? How do we achieve a proper balance between techno-scientific powers—advances that may improve human life, enlarge our body of knowledge, and expand our imaginations—and values inhering in the natural environment and more-than-human life? These are questions that Carson's work calls us to reflect upon, and they are more important today than ever. I critically examine a constellation of science-based ecospiritual movements with an eye to wonder's long history, shifting meanings over time, and ethical significance. Profoundly impoverished forms of wonder have come to inhabit a significant segment of contemporary discourse in religious environmentalism, science and religion, and a handful of other disciplines caught up in a kind of creeping scientism. These questionable forms owe some of their currency to arguments aggressively disseminated by a few prominent (one might say, celebrity) scientists and science writers—notably, Richard Dawkins and E. O. Wilson. In setting the contentious terms and tone for much of our contemporary science-religion discourse, they have also strongly shaped—I would say, *warped*—our understanding of wonder. In various ways, the new cosmology, and its attendant consecration of scientific knowledge as a new myth, provides a case in point of distorted, deracinated wonder. Thus, I am also concerned with the way these movements understand the relationship between science and religion, and between the humanities and the sciences. I find troubling the hubristic, quasi-authoritarian, and intolerant attitudes that are sometimes expressed or encouraged by exponents of the new cosmology toward the nonexpert, the nonscientist, and members of other faith communities, generally. As I see it, the full range of issues and concerns I raise throughout this book can be traced back, ultimately, to questions of appropriate or inappropriate wonder.

THE NEW COSMOLOGY

Prominent advocates of the new myths include the cultural historian, former Passionist priest, and "geologian" Thomas Berry (1914–2009) and his protégé, the mathematical cosmologist Brian Thomas Swimme; religion scholars Mary Evelyn Tucker, John Grim, and Loyal Rue; Big Historian David Christian; astrophysicist and science educator Eric Chaisson; biologist Ursula Goodenough; science writer Connie Barlow; and Christian pastor and popular author Michael Dowd. Many other scholars and popular writers could be listed here as well. In chapters that take up the new cosmology, I deal primarily with thinkers and projects having a notable impact on the discipline of *religious studies* (rather than, say, history), and within it, the subfields of religion and ecology and religion and nature, specifically.[3] That said, the book canvasses a number of debates that will likely be of interest to scholars in fields beyond my own immediate area of research, such as science and technology studies, history and philosophy of science, environmental history and environmental studies, to name a few. I would hope that all scholars concerned about interdisciplinarity or the future of the humanities will find something here to intrigue or provoke them, one way or another.

Contributions to "mythopoeic" science and defenses of the new cosmology have long been warmly received by many science-religion scholars (and their academic outlets) as well as numerous scholars within the field of religion and ecology. These movements have inspired books, films, YouTube videos, websites, podcasts, and—increasingly—university course offerings. Beyond the academy, they appeal to audiences with atheist, humanist, and religiously liberal sensibilities.[4] Some versions display elements of therapeutic or self-help spirituality, as with Dowd and Barlow, who offer web advice on how to "evolutionize" your life. Still others in the movement—Goodenough and Rue in particular—represent a trend toward atheistic religious naturalism or "dark green religion," i.e., nature- and science-oriented spiritualities that eschew and often critique the supernatural worldviews and values of traditional faiths, notably the Abrahamic traditions.[5]

The individuals cited above and throughout this work frequently reference one another's work and involvement in the new cosmology. While there are certainly differences of emphasis among them (which I spell out), they understand themselves as a fairly like-minded group, inspired by and contributing to a common vision and project of narrating the cosmos. Some, though not all, within this group take inspiration from the work and worldviews of Dawkins and (especially) E. O. Wilson.[6] Those most influenced by an evolutionary paradigm tend to invoke the phrase "Epic of Evolution," while those inspired by Big Bang cosmology refer to a "Story" or "Journey" of the Universe; however, Tucker and Swimme also deploy "Epic" terminology and Dowd and Barlow use a variety of terms interchangeably, including "Big History." Whatever terms they use, all of these movements fit the description of "epic science," as characterized by physicist-turned-philosopher Martin Eger: the turn to science for a new narrative of cosmic evolution and a fresh moral vision. "The grand evolutionary epic begins at the beginning—with the big bang—and, after various stages of cosmic and terrestrial evolution, ends understandably with the advent of human culture," according to Eger. "More significant even than the chronological sequence is the characteristic stance of the narrator— that omniscient, omnipresent subject . . . [who] speaks authoritatively, revealing the ultimate story in its ultimate form as an essentially finished product," even while pointing to things yet unknown and calling for additional investigation.[7]

These narratives define humans as the part of the universe that has become conscious of itself. Humans' dawning geological consciousness, combined with empirical knowledge of nature, will enable us to guide the future unfolding of the cosmic process, allowing our species to live in greater intimacy and harmony with the Earth. A new story is urgently needed, the argument typically goes, because "our" culture[8] is in the throes of a crippling condition of modernity known as *amythia:* "we" lack a functional cosmology, a serviceable myth that will orient us to what is real and important.[9] Stories we have inherited, especially from the tradi- tional faiths, are no longer plausible or relevant in light of modern science and our global environmental crisis. The conviction that stories determine our conception of reality and shape our fundamental values has deep roots in the philosophy of Berry, whose work exerts significant influence over many within the new cosmol- ogy. Our environmental crisis is "all a question of story," Berry famously argues.[10] Heeding this call, the new cosmology offers a "functional cosmology"—a better story—allegedly made possible by recent developments in science, ranging from the discovery of the Big Bang, to a deeply held belief in the unity of the sciences (what Wilson terms "consilience").

Some advocates, as I have noted, draw less from Big Bang cosmology than from an evolutionary paradigm that provides a coherent framework for human origins and destiny. For these thinkers, sociobiology and evolutionary psychology are par- ticularly germane to the creation of a new sacred myth. Evolutionary biology, they believe, both explains our need for religious myth *and* provides the raw materials from which a new, and superior, myth can be crafted. Evolutionary psychology, for example, posits a human brain hardwired for narrative coherence. In making their case for an evolutionary epic, these thinkers often find inspiration in reductionist biology and sociobiological pronouncements about human nature, even if they themselves move beyond reductionism.

Thus, Wilson and Dawkins call for *mythopoeticized* science: the recasting of scientific information as a consecrated narrative or poetic vision. This commit- ment to the creation and dissemination of mythopoeic science is key to Wilson and Dawkins's influence on the new cosmologists (in varying degrees for different individuals in the movement) and, more generally, it is one of the links between a certain mode of scientism and the narrative projects of religion scholars and reli- gionists that I examine throughout this work. Chapters 2 and 3 focus attention on Dawkins and Wilson, respectively, *not* because I take their views to be representa- tive of scientists generally (though neither are they wholly anomalous), but because their worldviews have inspired the forms of religious naturalism and science-based spirituality examined in subsequent chapters. Scientific materialism provides a satisfying *alternative mythology* to religion, Wilson argues. Belief in consilience similarly suggests that the disciplines will unite to tell a comprehensive narrative of the unfolding of evolutionary and human history. Wilson proclaims the evolutionary epic "probably the best myth we will ever have."[11] This claim is celebrated by a wide range of Universe Story and Epic of Evolution devotees.

For his own part, Dawkins has long argued for the superiority of scientifically clarified—"real"—wonder vis-à-vis wonder at perceived mysteries, puzzles, or miracles. Science banishes mystery and the miraculous, but the knowledge it returns is *itself* a thing of wonder and the stuff of magic. These claims receive enthusiastic support from some proponents of the Epic of Evolution. Self-styled "evolutionary evangelists" Dowd and Barlow endorse the Epic as a "religion of reality" and hail Dawkins as its courageous prophet. Converts to this religion of reality are not believers but "knowers."[12]

A distinctive celebration of knowledge-based wonder runs through these movements as a whole. The new cosmology calls on us to respond with awe and wonder to what is deemed most authentically real. Scientific information—if presented in sufficiently rich poetic and mythological language—is seen to fulfill many of the functions of a religious cosmology, while also orienting us toward deeper connection with and concern for the natural world. And yet, the wonder generated in these myths seems largely reserved for science and the scientific narrative first and foremost, and for nature only secondarily (if at all). Why this is so becomes clearer when we examine (particularly in chapters 2 and 3) how these dominant forms of wonder sit uneasily with a wondering response to and concern for the natural world.

A word about "science" and the "sciences" as discussed here: When I invoke science, the misuses of science, or the inappropriate reverencing of science, I do not envision the sciences as pernicious and threatening, nor do I indict scientists or scientific perspectives in some wholesale fashion. In fact, the vast majority of figures who appear in these pages are not scientists at all, though many are science enthusiasts of a sort.[13] (I too am a science enthusiast, though perhaps of a different sort.) I do not take science to be a monolithic activity or a seamless and bounded entity independent of other human activities. On the contrary, it is the scientific mythmakers who frequently deploy generic and uncritical categories of science, as when they insist that modern discoveries in cosmology or evolutionary biology point to some particular or objective meaning, purpose, or value in the universe or for human life generally. In fact, I believe that a more fine-grained analysis and nuanced understanding of the sciences and of scientific methodologies actually undermines the very *possibility* of an integrated, unified narrative of the universe or of human evolution, while opening up genuine options for wonder. I understand science to be an important but (necessarily, even virtuously) fallible human activity that is by its very nature incomplete and ongoing, even as it enables us to apprehend, manipulate, and make predictions about a "real world"—a reality that is simultaneously "out there" in some sense *and* coextensive with our mental and social constructs. A unified, integrated science composed of a handful of general laws, like a vision of a thoroughly graspable, neatly patterned, purposeful universe, is just that—a *vision*, a *dream*.

To the new cosmologists, this is a beautiful dream. To others like me, it may feel forced and confining in its wishful or willful human-centeredness and unwarranted sense of its own certainty. The unified vision is not itself "science" but rather a selective use of particular scientific claims and discoveries, carefully arranged and narrated so as to support meanings and messages desired by some. Moreover, and despite their fascination with deep time, a kind of chronological snobbery inflects these narratives in their belief that cutting-edge science has now revealed a grand and coherent reality that eluded previous, unenlightened generations. The new cosmologists are not sufficiently aware of (or sufficiently forthcoming about) the extent to which their narrative, and its forms of wonder, are manufactured from appealing pieces of a sprawling and diverse "body" of scientific knowledge.

My critique, then, is aimed not at science per se, but at scient*ism*. It is intended as an ideology critique, in the spirit of writer and social critic Curtis White who suggests that big, flashy stories told by Big Science are, at root, efforts to gain our consent to some particular version of reality.[14] More specifically, my target is the *consecration* of science. By the consecration of science, I refer to practices and rhetoric that invest science with sacred meaning and purpose, sometimes to the point of conflating science and religion, or making science *into* a religion. I do not mean science consecrated in the service of something *else* deemed supremely valuable or inherently sacred, as a person might consecrate herself to God so as to serve *God*'s purposes. Consecrated science is not science that is obviously in the service *of* nature and its goods; nor is it science made sacred primarily through association *with* sacred nature—though some of its practitioners do desire to serve the good of nature and / or deploy terms like "sacred" in reference to it. Because it invests science with sacredness, consecrated science often emerges as a rival and competitor not only with other religions, but with nature itself. And yet, as Weber famously argued, science in and of itself cannot answer the key question of whether the knowledge it produces is worth having; for such assessments, we must reflect on "our ultimate position towards life."[15] Similarly, wonder that is closely and narrowly bound to knowledge production is ill positioned to determine whether or not the knowledge at which it wonders *should* be produced. Consecrated science is science too enchanted with itself to make these judgments wisely.

Reflections on the nature of science, or philosophy of science, do not comprise a major theme in the book (though see chapters 3 and 7 for elaboration). However, I maintain that an accurate and clear-eyed appraisal of what the sciences are, how they operate, and what they can reliably tell us about the world effectively pulls the rug out from under mythopoeic renderings of science and the overarching meanings imputed to these cosmological stories. More positively, such appraisal might also open up a genuinely fruitful and egalitarian dialogue between scientists and humanities scholars, and between science and religion. These dialogues are critical to environmental studies. Contrary to the mythopoeic project, reality is not the purview of science alone, and the humanities do not—and should not be expected to—earn their keep by dispensing truths formally ratified by the sciences. This is not to say that science can make no claims to truth or reality, but that its truths and realities are not the only ones worth celebrating. Humanists are right to reject the faux interdisciplinarity of a consilient agenda that denigrates humanities as the poorer cousin of science, or as a treasure chest to be looted by intrepid explorers under a banner of consilience. The humanities are not failed attempts at science-like "explanations" of the world, nor is their disciplinary role that of poeticizing, prettifying, or otherwise publicizing the real world revealed by science (see chapter 3).

In what follows, I also stress sensory engagement with the natural world not as a *substitute* for scientific knowledge gained through more abstract theorizing and high-tech tools, but as a crucial component of our affective engagement with the (also) real worlds we know and inhabit. When I critique a confining, knowledge-based form of wonder, I am not claiming that wonder at scientific knowledge is (always) inappropriate and problematic or (generally) irrelevant for the cultivation of wonder for nature. My claim is that the elevation of abstract, expert knowledge above our lived experience of the world cuts us off from the strongest source of our felt connection to the more-than-human world. It calls us away from much of what it is to be human: a living, breathing, bodily, earthbound—and ultimately death-bound—creature, surrounded by and enmeshed with other living and dying beings whose own worlds and realities remain somewhat opaque and mysterious to us. At times, we may yearn to be called away from embodied existence—our own and that of others—in all its messiness and tragic finitude, its vulnerability and suffering with which humans are deeply complicit.

At such times we might indeed turn to the universe—to the wonders of deep space and time, to our species' emergence from such mysterious depths—with a powerful sense of relief. For there is something awesome about our ancient and infinite cosmos and we are right to feel gratitude for scientific discoveries that allow us to contemplate it. But the scale of the universe is not a human scale, and the overriding message of our global environmental crisis is that there is *no escape* from Earth or from ourselves as earthbound.[16] We cannot have, and should not seek, a grand narrative emanating from "nowhere, from space, or from the species."[17] The universe is not the scale on which we can meaningfully connect and interact with our worlds. Perhaps sensing this alienation, the new cosmologists attempt to recast the universe as a distinctly *human* drama, a story in which we comfortably feel "at home." But this move is also the wrong one, for it collapses an unfathomably vast and alien cosmos into something far less wondrous. It encourages a mood of self-aggrandizement, a kind of cosmic smugness that is contrary to wonder and, I think, demonstrably unscientific. The cosmic story *as* human drama too easily naturalizes and normalizes our entrance into the so-called Anthropocene epoch—a new stage of cosmic and geological unfolding in which our species assumes a managerial and directorial role. The generally anthropic modes of wonder underwritten by mythopoeic science are well positioned to *applaud* the ascent of the human in the Anthropocene age, and rather powerless to critique planetary dominance (chapter 5). If epic science directs our wondering gaze toward the human species and its immense journey, the Anthropocene provides the perfect backdrop. Put differently, the new cosmology *is,* quintessentially, paradigmatically, an Anthropocene narrative—and a problematically upbeat one at that.

In pointing out these "problematic" implications, I am not insisting that these authors necessarily endorse them. On the whole,[18] these scholars do not *intentionally* promote hubristic or anthropocentric or dominionist (or technophilic) attitudes. I take them at their word that they mean to promote quite the opposite set of values. But they fail to make a convincing case that the environmental and human values they claim to privilege are in fact supported by the narratives they dispense. Moreover, the new cosmologists likewise fail to engage in a sufficiently critical way with many of the concepts and thinkers they endorse (or who endorse them). There are, I think, two factors potentially at work that exacerbate the new cosmology's lack of critical engagement. One is that in attempting to create the big tent movement, they fail to develop, or they overlook, important distinctions between their own stated goals and those of their various constituents. Put differently, the desire of new cosmologists to create a large, unified environmental movement (or at least the appearance thereof) engenders a lack of critical reflection and an avoidance of conflict and disagreement. The second possible factor is a pronounced tendency among some of these practitioners to identify very strongly, and stubbornly—and often over the course of decades—with particular beloved figures: Thomas Berry, Teilhard de Chardin, Julian Huxley, and others. This almost hagiographic devotion to pioneers and projects also discourages and deflects critique and critical exchange. It leads scholars to invest too much in one particular agenda, and one type of "answer" to the problems that confront us. I have some sympathy with these moves. I too identify with and admire certain thinkers—notably, of course, Rachel Carson (an exalted figure in her own right, and one very rarely critiqued by environmental scholars; more about Carson in the final chapter). But I worry that these investments prove unhealthy and unproductive when they foster scholarly entrenchment or resistance to new ideas, or when they shield preferred projects and figures from critique.

WHAT IS AT STAKE?

How did we arrive at narrowed and impoverished articulations of wonder, and what, more precisely, do we stand to lose when we accept their terms? The first question is one I take up in chapter 1. I suggest answers to the second question in a variety of ways throughout the book as a whole, but it may be worthwhile to explain at the outset some of the reasons why I believe there is much at stake in how we define wonder vis-à-vis nature, science, and religion, and how we go about delineating its proper objects.

Proponents of knowledge-based wonder often portray science and religion as occupying the same explanatory slot, as if religions were nothing but inferior propositional statements about the world. Donovan Schaefer has noted a distinctly American tendency among critics of religion to posit religion as a deficient form of rationality, a "misbegotten science in need of correction or elimination."[19] Something similar inflects the new cosmology's quest for an overarching story with scientific credentials. Wilson, in this vein, argues that a great epic needs to be universal, spiritually compelling, and "above all, truthful."[20] On this account, the "accurate" materials that science furnishes for the myth-making enterprise result in a superior narrative that satisfies the intellect as well as the emotions. A scientific mythology, Goodenough claims, has the power to unite all of humanity because "it happens to be true."[21] Brian Swimme respects "the stories of the past," but insists that "they don't actually give us a careful, accurate depiction of the universe," such as the New Story offers.[22] Loyal Rue believes that the traditional religious stories are not sufficiently "competitive" according to empirical standards set by those invested in the competition. Each of the existing religious narratives "lacks the objectivity it would take to make the competition—whether an internal variant or an external alternative—look implausible or irrelevant."[23] On these accounts, the truth of the story is inseparable from its assumed universal appeal, the operative (and, it seems, unfounded) assumption being that people are bound to believe stories that are empirically and verifiably true.

The tendency to compare scientific and religious "explanations" of the world—and to find religion wanting—is facilitated by a slippery understanding of the term cosmology, where cosmology encompasses scientific explanation (think Big Bang cosmology) and overarching metaphysical frameworks that confer sense and meaning to the world. Tucker, for example, defines cosmologies as focused descriptions of "reality" or "explanations of the universe (mythical or scientific) and the role of humans in it."[24] Though this view sometimes allows that scientific cosmologies explain how things are but *not* how things ought to be or what has meaning (the purview of religious cosmology), the fact is that the new cosmology conflates the two. The scientific story provides all we need—not only "how things are" but "which things matter."

Religions, and their contingent narratives, are thus easily displaced by science's "real world" credentials. Appeals to the superior charms of science illustrate that science and religion are cast not simply as competing explanations for the physical world but as competing discourses of wonder. "Material reality, discovered by science, already possesses *more content and grandeur* than all the religious cosmologies combined," Wilson insists.[25] These pronouncements conjure images of modern mythmakers equipped with something like a "grandeur meter"[26] that can determine objectively and decisively that epic science offers more wonder than its mythic competitors.

Oddly, the superior wonder, magic, or grandeur said to infuse the new narratives is a function of the systematic *displacement* of abiding mystery, and the questioning impulse, with wonder at confident knowledge. The new narratives are demonstrably lacking in what Keats called negative capability: an ability to dwell in doubt, mystery, and ambiguity and to resist the categorization of all phenomena and experience into a system of knowledge.[27] Ambivalence toward uncertainty and mystery—expressed at times as outright hostility by Dawkins and Wilson— runs through these projects. The new scientific myth is often presented as something all-comprehending and omnicompetent. The story of the universe is thus poised to provide answers to humans' most enduring questions: "Where did we come from? Why are we here? How should we live together? How can the Earth community flourish?"[28] Wilson, bolstered by faith in consilience, maintains that "when we have unified enough certain knowledge, we will understand who we are and why we are here."[29] This form of displacement reaches toward the eradication of wonder itself.

Not surprisingly, alignment of wonder with an accurate rendering of physical reality also valorizes the disciplines most directly engaged in the production of scientific knowledge, while demoting other disciplines and ways of knowing. Enter consilience, Wilson's term for a gathering-together of all the disciplines into a single body of totalizing knowledge. The new cosmology—like the consilient project with which it is sometimes conjoined—presents itself as a grand interdisciplinary venture in which all forms of knowledge and human creative expression play a vital role. Science provides rich and accurate content; the arts and humanities supply the requisite metaphors or images that ennoble the content and lend it a mythic aura. Indeed, it often appears that the essential, and delimited, role of the humanities is to infuse science with religious appeal—perhaps even transform it into a religion by delivering some of religion's key assets right to the door of science. "The Epic of Evolution requires art if it is to attain the position of Myth," as former *Zygon* editor Philip Hefner observes.[30] The "true evolutionary epic" becomes a *religious* epic when "retold as poetry."[31]

The heady promise of consilience is inspiring a new wave of scholars who are eager to see evolutionary biology, evolutionary psychology, or neuroscience confer order and coherence to humanities disciplines in presumed disarray.[32] These critics typically portray the humanities as vacuous, obscurantist, and irrelevant. Advocates of the new cosmology are among those pushing hard for educational reform of college curricula in light of the evolutionary epic and consilient ambitions.[33] An examination of the current spread of consilient ideas in the academy is thus an additional focus of this project (particularly chapter 3). Universe Story proponents who look to Thomas Berry and insights of Big Bang cosmology similarly understand the story of the universe as radically reorienting all education and wisdom. "Both education and religion need to ground themselves within the story of the universe as we now know it through our empirical ways of knowing," Berry insists.[34]

These narratives suggest that the natural world as humans normally encounter it—without the aid of sophisticated instruments or facility with the latest scientific concepts—is neither fully real nor especially valuable. Wonder becomes the bailiwick of the expert who grasps the abstract knowledge that eludes the layperson. Once displaced from lived experience of the world to abstract realms accessible to experts, wonder becomes at best a vicarious experience; the natural world, at best, a derivative reality. In other ways, too, the new cosmology may foster dislocation and disconnection from nature. The vast cosmic scope and sweep of the Universe Story cultivates global—literally, *cosmopolitan*—sensibilities that have little to do with humans becoming strongly attached to and responsible for their particular environments. From the standpoint of the *universe as a whole,* the fate—immediate or long term—of one particular planet in an obscure corner of an infinite cosmos seems rather inconsequential. How are normative obligations and affective attachments to nature justified by the narrative? The promise that "wonder will guide us" remains unfulfilled—and unfulfilling. What we want to know is: Where is it guiding us, and why should we go there?

Whether or not wonder leads us astray depends very much on the objects toward which it is oriented and the dispositions and attitudes it engenders. Wonder's proper objects, and (especially) its attendant dispositions and attitudes, are what interest me here. The natural world, I believe, is a worthy object of enduring wonder and reality in a way that science—a human enterprise—is not. The mythopoeic impulse and its celebration of the human enterprise becomes a liability when it gravitates toward motifs of hubristic trespass or forbidden knowledge. Epic pioneers like Wilson embrace myths not as cautionary tales against overweening pride and reckless curiosity, but as *justifications* for intrepid pursuit of knowledge and eradication of mysteries. "Let us see how high we can fly before the sun melts the wax in our wings."[35] This is not the sort of dictum we should heed if it is nature—not merely ourselves—that we cherish and hold within our wondering gaze. In order to reclaim some of what has been lost through these diminished accounts of wonder, I turn (in chapter 7 and elsewhere) to insights from Rachel

Carson's life and work and to an older tradition of nature study that her work carried forward.

As the Anthropocene lens zooms out to take in the largest possible picture of our species, our planet, deep time, and the cosmos, the reigning assumption seems to be that our stories must also scale up dramatically. The idea seems to be that we require sweeping, grand narratives that will embolden us to tackle global-scale environmental challenges and reassure us that we have not lost all control, that our story remains one of progress and upward ascent. Wilson offers us an image of ascent: Icarus flying to the sun, his wax wings melting but his heart beating with wild exultation at his own reckless daring, his brief proximity to the gods. Icarus—a tragic figure—may be more apt than Wilson knows. Perhaps we have now seen how high we can fly. We have encountered our limits. The melting has begun. Maybe now is a good time to return to Earth and to our senses. Here, before it is too late, we can join Rachel Carson in wondering at the miniature universe of a tidepool, or the mystery of a growing seed. We might learn to scale back our ambitions, to cherish what is small and modest, and to tell many stories, in many voices, from many different places. Perhaps we can rediscover our humanity.

Chapter 1

Seeking What Is Good in Wonder

Depending on the company they keep, some wonders are respectable and others disreputable; but none [today] threatens the order of nature and society. Scientists have yet to explain many, perhaps most, wonders, but they subscribe to an ontology guaranteeing that all are in principle explicable. If the first criterion for distinguishing respectable from disreputable marvels is whether they are real, the second is whether there are explanations to reassure us that the apparent exceptions only conform to nature's laws. In practice, the second criterion often decides the first.

—LORRAINE DASTON AND KATHARINE PARK, *WONDERS AND THE ORDER OF NATURE*

WONDER AND ITS COGNATE TERMS

What does it mean to wonder? Wonder is almost routinely exalted as a laudable state, but perhaps not all expressions of it deserve to be celebrated. Wonder seems to exist at the border of sensation and thought, aesthetics and science. It has the power to transfix as well as transport us. It is characterized both as a childlike capacity, closely aligned with sensory and emotional engagement, and as a kind of scientific virtue. Wonder is both the province of the wide-eyed child in the woods and the wild-eyed scientist in the lab. Aristotle considered wonder to be the beginning of philosophy, and René Descartes famously categorized wonder as the first of the passions, an *intellectual* passion that orients us toward understanding the object of wonder. Yet, while wonder is often assumed to hold a privileged place in the production of scientific and philosophical knowledge, it is a deeply ambiguous place as well. In romance languages, wonder's etymological origins show connections to an Indo-European word for "smile," but this is not the case in German and English, where wonder (*Wunder*) may be traceable to *wound*—a tear in the fabric of the ordinary, an "uncanny opening."[1] Wonder, typically expressed as awe, may border on terror or horror in the presence of something that overwhelms the mind with its sheer enormity or power. Wonder in the form of terrifying awe is often associated with encountering something holy or otherworldly, as with God's interrogation of Job from the whirlwind. The ambivalence or outright fear evoked by wonder may be met with a desire to control and domesticate the world, to "systematically insulate it against the intrusion of strangeness."[2] Wonder's terrifying and even painful elements are captured in the more secular category of the sublime. Often distinguished from the beautiful,[3] which connotes something more pleasing than threatening to the mind or the senses, the sublime may be experienced in the presence of nonsupernatural but vast and imposing or powerful phenomena, such as high mountains or a violent, stormy sea.

Yet another distinction emerges between wonder and wonders. The former refers to an experience or response and the latter designates *objects* themselves, such as odd or interesting items, novelties and marvels housed (as they often were in early modern Europe) in curio cabinets. A catalogue of wonders might include a two-headed dog or a lodestone. Historically, the category of wonders has merged the sacred with the secular, including such phenomena as "plants, animals, and minerals; specific events and exotic places; miracles and natural phenomena; the distant and the local; the threatening and the benign."[4] Although contemporary discussions tend to focus more on wonder than wonders, this distinction helps us to appreciate that, in judging wonder's appropriateness or ethical value, we need to attend both to its forms of expression and to its objects.

That wonder and its associated terms can align with such seemingly disparate experiences, ranging from childlike delight to profound destabilization and even pain and death—a "cognitive crucifixion"—suggests its unusual status among our repertoire of responses to the world.[5] Wonder, in its frequent association with scale, may foster a sense of our own smallness or insignificance in relation to its objects, perhaps even a sensed loss of the self. That experience may produce either fear or a more uplifting sense of awe or exhilaration—depending upon how one feels about self-loss! The experience of loss of self, of *letting go* of ego-dominated rationality, is one of the links between wondering responses and experiences often termed religious, as theorists such as William James have noted.[6] In such moments of profound receptivity to the unexpected, we may sense our connection to something that is ontologically or spiritually *more* (as James termed it) than what is given in our daily experience of the world or the world as filtered through familiar categories of knowledge. Loss or decentering of the self, and dispositions that flow from such decentering, can have important ethical value: "openness, availability, epistemological humility in the face of the mystery of being, and the ability to admire and be grateful."[7] On the other hand, as I will argue, wonder that manifests as blunt and irreverent curiosity, or that follows in curiosity's wake as a form of admiration at our knowledge, may have the opposite potential of puffing us up with pride. How can we make sense of the fact that wonder variously engenders or accompanies a salutary sense of smallness and humility, as well as aggrandizes admiration of our own feats?

Wonder is a tapestry rich with meanings, but its very richness makes it easy to pull out particular strands while ignoring others. I want to focus critical attention on a few, very particular meanings of wonder that have often been isolated from their broader context. These include: wonder assumed to be (primarily) a function of ignorance; wonder as the force that drives ongoing discovery and successive puzzle-solving—what I call "serial wonder"; and wonder characterized by admiration or pride at that which is assimilated and known. These strands, which are often intertwined in modern discourse on wonder, actually represent only a small portion of all that wonder has signified, in theology, philosophy, and science, over a span of many centuries. Wonder—properly understood—is not merely an ephemeral response to what is poorly grasped or appears novel; it persists even after ignorance is erased or newness wears off. A strong association of wonder with successive puzzle-solving imputes motives to wonder that more properly belong to curiosity (some of those motives prove problematic, as I will argue). To wonder at the vast store of human knowledge may be understandable, but this orientation effectively strips wonder of much of its ethical potential and admirable dimensions. The stripping away of wonder's virtues also makes wonder the purview of the expert whose task it is to inform the masses where wonder truly resides in the world around us.

The reorientation of wonder as largely a response to *knowledge* will form a focal point of much of the analysis of wonder that follows. In short, much of what passes for wonder in a significant portion of contemporary scientific and environmental discourse (whether the context is celebratory or disdainful of wonder) is scarcely wonder at all. Inappropriate forms of wonder lurk alongside and mingle with more genuine and wholesome varieties. Distinguishing these is not always easy or straightforward. Nevertheless, a good rule of thumb might be this: When expressions of wonder become tinged with celebrations of hubris, or interwoven with triumphalist claims of progress, certainty, or mastery (over nature, or over others, even over ourselves), we can be fairly sure that wonder has somewhere taken a wrong turn. Understanding how and in what ways wonder has been diminished and distorted is the overarching aim of this chapter.

NOVELTY, FAMILIARITY, AND THE PROSPECT OF WONDER'S ENDURANCE

At first glance, it might seem that both novelty and familiarity act to undercut wonder's endurance or resilience—novelty because it gradually wears off, and familiarity because it seems to convey nothing new. But wonder can coexist with either; it is neither—necessarily—dependent on newness nor dispelled by close acquaintance or even intimacy. Wonder as a response to sheer novelty or newness accounts for its common association with children who are more likely than adults to encounter the world with fresh eyes and without the knowledge conditions or engrained habits of mind that can mute our sense of wonder over time. Some theorists maintain that the very nature of wonder necessarily entails that it "decays" and "declines" with age and experience. Wonder participates in an "epistemology of youth," according to Philip Fisher,[8] and a "rapid wearing out of the new is also part of the aesthetics of wonder."[9] However, I am not convinced that this conclusion is warranted (and indeed, there is something fundamentally immature about the demand for constant novelty and titillation in order to sustain a sense of wonder). Prior experiences of wonder, including those in childhood, may serve as a lifelong reference point, a perspective on the world to which we can return again and again. Rachel Carson alludes to a sense of wonder that is sufficiently "indestructible" to last a lifetime, acting as "an unfailing antidote against the boredom and disenchantments of later years, the sterile preoccupation with things that are artificial, the alienation from the sources of our strength."[10]

R. W. Hepburn argues that some instances of wonder "could not be described at all convincingly in terms of response to the surprising and novel." They may arise, for example, from "the linking of present experience with memory-traces of very early experience."[11] As Carson's account also suggests, emotional impressions from early childhood may lend new life, renewed excitement, to sensory experiences in later adulthood that might otherwise affect us little. Indeed, our very awareness of the "wide temporal gap" between this moment and our own remote past may enhance the feeling of wonder, Hepburn notes.[12] This understanding of wonder and enchantment as "renewable" has been central to educational programs for children that aim to instill wonder at (and later, care and responsibility for) the natural world, ranging from the nature study movement of the early twentieth century to modern-day environmental education and ecological literacy programs. Intense sensory and emotional engagement with nature at an early age may have lasting moral impact, even after maturity supplements the child's sense of the magical with a more rational, even scientific, understanding of nature and its processes. Again, Carson's approach to nature education fits this mold. The "emotions and the impressions of the senses are the fertile soil" of early childhood and they prepare the ground for the later acquisition of knowledge.[13] Nature study for children, distinct from training in the *sciences,* has always made sensory and emotional responses central. Given the close, primal link between the senses—particularly the sense of smell—and memory, it seems plausible that wonder has a great deal to do with what Carson calls the remembered delights of childhood.[14] These reflections cast doubt on the pessimistic conclusion that wonder necessarily or completely decays with age.

As this portrait of resilient and recurring wonder suggests, repeated exposure to and knowledge of something, or someone, need not dispel wonder. Familiarity may indeed deepen a wondering appreciation, so long as familiarity is of a sort that disclaims exhaustive, totalizing comprehension of its objects. We may well remain in a state of wonder at that which seems well understood, and we may also experience very little wonder at things that are poorly understood. Even though I cannot say precisely how my toaster works, I do not consider it an object of wonder. The birth process, on the other hand, is rather well understood, but nevertheless remains a process at which we often marvel, and rightly so, for as theorists of wonder have often observed, wonder may have less to do with how or what a thing is than *that* it is. Ontological or existential wonder can foster a mood in which "certainties give way to questions which, so long as wonder remains, can never receive final answers."[15] Hence, while we may be able to explain childbirth in minute detail, we cannot explain why it is "that love should bear fruit in such a strange fashion."[16] Put differently, that which presents itself to us as a mystery is not necessarily unknown or vaguely understood. On the contrary, we can come to know something *as* a mystery. "It is too often assumed that the mysterious is equivalent to the unknown and that, in the light of adequate knowledge, mystery will give way to clarity."[17] Wonder enables us to see things anew in encounters with what we think we "know," but much may depend upon the general attitude that attends the acquisition of knowledge, as I argue in chapter 7.

DEFICIENT KNOWLEDGE: WONDER'S PARTNERSHIP WITH CURIOSITY

An association of feelings of wonder with a deficient state of knowledge has led some thinkers, past and present, to regard wonder with wariness or even disdain. Conflation of wonder's mysterious quality merely with that which is not (yet) understood recurs frequently in science writing. It is a particular hallmark of Richard Dawkins's treatment of scientific wonder, as we will see. When wonder is narrowly defined in terms of deficient knowledge, its presence may evoke a strong sense of dis-ease, even hostility, particularly among those who understand success in science as the progressive eradication of unknowns. On this account, wonder is of value primarily because it can mobilize us to find answers, to *eliminate* the very conditions that gave rise to wonder. But if the sensation of wonder is deemed pleasant and desirable in and of itself, such mobilization may not occur and ignorance will prevail. Thus Francis Bacon referred to wonder as a form of "broken knowledge"—a tendency of the mind to break off its train of thought, to enjoy itself *instead* of knowing."[18] Wonder's capacity to stall the mind, to induce stupefaction, can entail a sudden halt to the process of scientific investigation. Thus, while we may commend and encourage a gaping and gawking form of wonder in children, wonder of this sort might—appropriately—be considered unseemly in adults, and particularly in the world of professional science.

Even when not accompanied by a strong desire to remain in ignorance, wonder has a contemplative or meditative quality that—for better and for worse—can interfere with or distract from mundane and task-oriented activities. Concerns about wonder's potential sloth or lack of utility are bound up with the crucially important distinction between curiosity and wonder. Descartes, as noted above, praised wonder as the first of the passions—the passion that initially energizes the intellect. Yet his celebration was also tinged with suspicion of wonder, a need to liquidate and drain away its potentially dangerous power to disrupt the acquisition of knowledge.[19] Thus, curiosity is sometimes understood as a kind of wake-up call, a jolt to wonder's soporific inclinations: curiosity can narrow and focus the wondering response, encouraging the mind to search for explanation. To the extent that wonder is regarded as something unseemly or unpleasant—or dangerous—curiosity performs a valuable service. Curiosity enters into the wondering process as a helpful heuristic by posing particular (and in principle, answerable) questions.

Contemporary science writing often invokes this dynamic of active, hardworking curiosity and gaping, dreamy wonder. Relatively few scientists write openly nowadays about their experiences of wonder, but such professions of wonder were once fairly common. Those who do so today are often at pains to highlight the uniqueness of scientific forms of wonder from all (or at least most) other kinds; they particularly want to cordon off scientific wonder from forms of wonder that are evoked by, related to, or in any way celebratory of a state of *not* knowing. In order to do so, these thinkers often turn to curiosity as wonder's saving grace. Some scientists maintain that a hallmark of scientific wonder is that, while the nonscientist may spontaneously wonder at any number of phenomena and think "how strange!", the scientifically minded will cultivate wonder to a "more intellectual height" and then devise explanatory hypotheses that can be tested and verified.[20] The claim that all nonscientific forms of wonder are at best only weakly interested in explaining wonder-evoking phenomena is not uncommon, simplistic (and often flattering to the scientist) though it seems. Mark Silverman, a Harvard physicist, argues that the scientist, and the scientist *alone*,[21] "goes beyond 'gapes and stares' employing his experimental and mathematical resources in an effort to understand in some more profound way the significance of his observations."[22] (Note that the scientist's hard work pays off in the form of "*more profound*" insights than the dreamy wonder of the nonscientist can ever produce.) Silverman characterizes curiosity as the laudable dimension of wonder, wonder's "scientific" sidekick, and the driving force of inquiry. Science moves beyond *naïve* wonder—philosophy may do so as well—to a form designed for self-destruction. As Marie George argues, the scientist recognizes that "his wonder will cease upon learning the cause ... it is proper to science and philosophy to break matters down into questions which are resolvable."[23] But as we will see, the story of the relationship between wonder and curiosity is much more complex than these accounts suggest, and it is largely a story about distinguishing—ethically, theologically, and scientifically—appropriate and inappropriate forms or objects of inquiry. This task of discernment remains vital today and it has largely been neglected in the blithe celebrations of scientific wonder that I analyze in later chapters.

As this discussion of the dynamic between wonder and curiosity suggests, wonder becomes something eradicable and self-eliminating: curiosity comes in as a "cure" for wonder, displacing it with new knowledge.[24] Wonder, in this view, is like a ladder we throw down once we have reached understanding. There seems to be little reason to value the state of wonder, *or* the phenomena—including natural entities—that produce it, given that our attraction to such phenomena was rooted in ignorance or muddled thinking. Both the object and the wondering response are merely a means to a more valuable end, the production of clear understanding. To the extent that wonder is seen as rooted in false, misguided, or ignorant perception, the entities that engender our false perception may themselves begin to appear less real, once our wondering response is replaced with clarifying knowledge. Knowledge of the object, in other words, *becomes* the reality.

The claim that curiosity acts as a cure for wonder's vices has deep roots in Western thought.[25] Wonder and curiosity were intimately linked in the minds of seventeenth-century natural philosophers like René Descartes and Francis Bacon, owing to curiosity's "essential role as bait and motivation for intense efforts of attention."[26] This perspective remains alive and well today among some scientists, science writers, and philosophers of science. Over the course of the intertwined history of wonder and curiosity, curiosity has come to be seen as diligent and respectable, while wonder has largely fallen into disrepute as something childish and gaping. By examining some key moments in this history, we can appreciate the way in which we moderns have inherited a greatly diminished version of wonder; moreover, as this history reveals, curiosity has always attracted its own set of vocal and incisive critics, and it is worth keeping them in mind. In recounting some of wonder's fascinating history—a task made more manageable by exhaustive studies of wonder already in existence[27]—I focus special attention on a dubious form of wonder that emerged in the seventeenth and eighteenth centuries, wherein wonder became synonymous with a response to knowledge obtained through scientific investigation. That is, wonder becomes response to the *end product* of inquiry rather than a goad to inquiry. I propose that a contemporary version of this problematic form of wonder—oriented largely toward scientific knowledge and an elite set of knowledge-producers—animates the new cosmology and the worldviews of certain thinkers who are demonstrably foundational to that cosmology.

THE DECLINE AND REORIENTATION OF WONDER

The ascendance of virtuous, industrious curiosity over dull, stupefied wonder is a relatively recent development in the history of science, or what was once termed natural philosophy. In theological circles, by contrast, wonder has sometimes been highly regarded as a fitting response to the divine and to the intricate marvels of the created world. This is not true of the natural philosophy tradition that sought to explicate the basic laws that govern and order the natural world. Among their ranks (and among some natural scientists today) wonder was more likely to be greeted with ambivalence, as an ally of superstition or ignorance of natural causes. In the twelfth century and beyond, wonder came under suspicion by natural philosophers who "marginalized both the passion of wonder and wonders as objects, in favor of a view that emphasized both the regularity of nature and the completeness of the philosopher's knowledge, marred by no unseemly gaps."[28] With increasing professionalization of knowledge and the rise of universities during the scholastic period, wonder increasingly took on this aura of superstition, laziness, or ignorance, a taint it still carries for many today. The pleasure that the philosopher experiences, Roger Bacon (1214?–1294) argued, "arises not from the process of inquiry into the unknown, but rather from the *possession of knowledge already perfect and complete*"—that is, it arises from possession of a solution to or elimination of the "unknown."[29]

Dismissal of wonder as a bedfellow of ignorance contrasts with a venerable old strain, discernible in Christian theology, that saw certain forms of ignorance, and the wonder they generate, as commendable and pious dispositions. Augustine (d. 430) described wonder in these terms as "the proper expression of humility before the omnipotence of God."[30] He considered aimless or restless curiosity, or the pursuit of inessential knowledge, as a function of pride, or lust, something akin to incontinence or concupiscence—a weakness of the flesh, a movement of the sensuous appetite. This earlier understanding of curiosity as sensuous and lustful points to its addictive and potentially insatiable dimensions—qualities evident in what I call "serial wonder." The morally dubious features of curiosity were brought into sharp relief in the early modern period when curiosity was increasingly aligned with greed and avarice rather than lust; that is, curiosity was seen as an unquenchable desire that aims not at *satisfaction* but at the "perpetuation of desire."[31] It is difficult to say with certainty, of course, which forms of knowledge are essential and which are idly sought merely for their own sake. These categories are not static. Augustine's concern about idle curiosity centered largely on the presumptuous *attitude* that accompanied curiosity—the likelihood that such knowledge "puffs us up" with pride verging on self-deification. Philosophers'—in our day, we might say scientists'—presumptive curiosity culminated in a "twofold trespass," Augustine warned: The vainglorious attitude would interfere with an appreciation of the mystery and wonder of the created world (and by extension, of its Creator) that the less knowledgeable masses readily experience. The same attitude also "led [philosophers], and encouraged them to lead others, into error, usurping for themselves the wonder that ordinary Christians should direct not toward other humans, however learned, but rather should reserve for God."[32]

The Augustinian association of curiosity, vanity, and pride, on the one hand, and wonder, humility, and ignorance, on the other, has never faded entirely from Christian thought; the basic spirit of this critique of curiosity was reissued in the sixteenth century by such thinkers as Desiderius Erasmus and Michel de Montaigne, for example. But it has at times fallen out of favor. Augustine's concerns posed difficulties for later thinkers such as Aquinas (d. 1274), who recognized the vicious potential of curiosity but also regarded ignorance as unseemly for natural philosophers concerned with causal knowledge of the world. The task for philosophers like Aquinas was to sort out which forms of inquiry were acceptable and which were not. Problematic curiosity was recognizable in its dilettantish, "half-hearted" quality while true and serious devotion to knowledge—studiousness—was lauded as a virtue. In deploying this distinction Aquinas "simply laid aside the heart of Augustine's argument, replacing it with another set of values, less sympathetic to wonder and more sympathetic to curiosity."[33]

Subsequent centuries witnessed an "intricate minuet of wonder and curiosity" in the Western world.[34] Over the course of the early modern period, curiosity gradually lost some of its taint of lust and pride and took on the mantle of respectability, even a whiff of elitism; wonder, once associated with pious or awe-filled reverence, was now the province of the ignorant masses. So dramatic was the fall of wonder that by the mid-eighteenth century, wonder would be "demoted from premiere philosophical passion to its very opposite, and once-frivolous curiosity took on the virtuous trappings of hard work."[35] And yet, the period from roughly the mid-seventeenth to the mid-eighteenth century saw a brief efflorescence of wonder, as well as a temporary rapprochement between wonder and curiosity. Interestingly, this same period saw the rise of "modern" science, and of the mechanical worldview promulgated by Descartes and Bacon, and often censured by environmentalists, religion scholars, and historians, for its radical disenchantment of the natural world.[36] How is it that this "age of wonder" was simultaneously an age of disenchantment?

One answer to this question leads us to the forms of wonder currently advocated by scientists such as Dawkins as well as some advocates of the new cosmology. But in order to arrive there, we need to look more closely at the terms of the rapprochement that briefly obtained between wonder and curiosity during the rise of modern science.

A REVERSED DYNAMIC: WONDER AT KNOWLEDGE

If wonder has often been regarded with ambivalence, curiosity too has its share of critics. The problem lies not in curiosity's lack of discipline (as associations with restlessness might suggest), for curiosity can bring highly focused concentration. For this reason, it often appears a necessary companion to wonder. During the seventeenth and eighteenth centuries, wonder's marriage with curiosity was, in a sense, one of necessity because, left to its own devices, wonder might be content to dwell wherever it was, to marvel and gawk rather than get to work investigating its objects. The term Descartes used to describe this stunned or stalled mental state was "astonishment" (*l'étonnement*)—an excess of wonder (the roots of this word suggest turning to stone). Too much wonder was pernicious and paralyzing, but too little might not spark the curiosity needed to sustain the spirit of inquiry over a long and sometimes tedious haul. Wonder, therefore, was necessary but not sufficient for science. With this dynamic of curiosity and wonder in place, however, wonder began to appear the less virtuous of the pair. From there, it was but a small step to seeing curiosity, and the knowledge it engenders, as a cure or antidote to wonder, rather than wonder's abiding companion.[37] The marriage of convenience between wonder and curiosity thus turned out not to be a marriage of equals, and by the mid-eighteenth century, the two seemed headed for divorce. Without the prestige and refinement of its erstwhile partner, wonder increasingly became regarded as the "dull, effusive" companion of the vulgar, untutored masses, a disposition far removed from science.[38] (Today, although scientists like Silverman or Dawkins often refer to wonder in science, it is scientific *curiosity*—focused, disciplined investigation inspired by discovery of puzzles—that they actually single out for praise, whatever term they may use.)

Effusive wonder found a somewhat respectable second career in natural theology—distinct now from natural philosophy—during the late seventeenth and early eighteenth centuries. If wonder's vices lay in its tendency to *excess,* then excessive wonder was acceptable (perhaps even virtuous and commendable) so long as it was evoked by *God,* who alone was deemed incomprehensible, worthy of a mind-numbing, gaping form of wonder. Another solution to the problem of "excessive or misplaced wonder" was to permit wonder a more carefully delineated role in natural philosophy as well: here wonder was directed not to God per se but to the comprehended natural order—the "tidy regularity of nature" and the "simplicity and economy of its underlying principles."[39] We see the legacy of this form of wonder in the work of E. O. Wilson and those who seek the tidy, law-like knowledge Wilson promises with consilience. Intimations of the magical or marvelous in nature are antithetical to this type of wonder; then as now, aberrations were deemed less worthy of wonder than were regularity and orderliness. Advocates of this view, such as the French scientist Bernard de Fontenelle (1657–1757), were the Richard Dawkinses of their day, censuring those who turned away from scientific *study* of nature in favor of wonder and admiration at nature *itself* "which one supposes absolutely incomprehensible."[40] False forms of wonder revel in nature without wishing to understand it, Fontenelle believed, for nature "'is never so wondrous . . . as when she is known.'"[41] This attempt to rehabilitate wonder cleanses it of vulgar or mind-numbing excess by reversing its age-old dynamic. That is, it makes wonder not the beginning but the *result* of inquiry, a response to *knowledge obtained* rather than to the puzzling, awesome, or mysterious phenomenon itself. Oddly, it is particularly this form of wonder—wonder at knowledge, and at the discovery of an orderly and comprehensible universe—that makes a strong showing in contemporary science-based mythmaking and the new cosmology.

I say *oddly*, because this interpretation of wonder would seem to have little broad appeal. Wondering at knowledge already obtained stripped wonder of much of its popular allure and failed to elicit great enthusiasm among laypeople (and perhaps even among would-be scientists). Wonder thus continued its downward spiral. "In the end," Daston and Park observe, "wonder proved intractable to such a dramatic reorientation and ceased to be a philosophical passion."[42] From there, wonder gradually reverted to a pedestrian and somewhat silly disposition among common people—the stuff of cartoon superheroes and spongy white bread.[43] Curiosity, on the other hand—in the form of "earnest application" utterly purified of strong pleasure and desire—became the abiding cognitive skill of the natural philosopher, or what we today call the scientist.

It is not very difficult to see why wonder at nature's regularity, predictability, or economy (rather than perceived novelty or marvels), or wonder at knowledge already obtained (rather than mysteries themselves) failed to catch fire, particularly among nonscientists. For only those who have participated in obtaining such knowledge, through investment of long hours spent studying natural objects in tedious and laborious detail, would be rewarded with feelings of wonder at all that they ultimately comprehend. The wondrous aspects of the order revealed by hours of intensive, but dispassionate, study would not necessarily be inviting, or even apparent, to the nonexpert. Moreover, the expert was now in a position to inform the laypeople (or not) of wonders not readily accessible to them in their ordinary experience of the world. The reorientation of wonder as a response to knowledge gained also reaches toward an *internalization* of wonder. As Mary-Jane Rubenstein observes, this redirection of wonder at hard-won knowledge is often "related to a certain will toward mastery, even toward divinity: by *comprehending* the source of the wondrous, the thinking self in effect *becomes* the source of the wondrous."[44] Wonder was now "bestowed on the knowledge won," and by extension, on the one who *knows*, the one who dispenses wondrous knowledge.[45] The role of the scientist may then become, as it has for Dawkins and others, one of explaining to the masses not just why abstruse science is wondrous, but why it is *more* wondrous and awe-inspiring than the delusional or vulgar objects of wonder—religious miracles, tales of the supernatural, fictional stories of children with magical powers, or celebrity reality shows—with which the public seems stubbornly preoccupied. Scientific knowledge is wondrous because it is *real*. The scientist becomes the arbiter of reality.

This reversed dynamic is not just one of many permutations wonder has undergone over the centuries. I believe it has *disproportionately* shaped much of our contemporary thinking about wonder, particularly wonder as a laudatory facet of science. For example, philosopher Jesse Prinz joins with Dawkins in attempting to save wonder from total eradication by reorienting it toward science's ability to unravel mystery. "Scientists," Prinz writes, "are spurred on by wonder. . . . Knowledge does not abolish wonder; indeed, scientific discoveries are often more wondrous than the mysteries they unravel."[46] The power of science to reveal ever greater depths of wonder brings it into close relationship with religion, he believes. Yet, the supposed intimacy of science and religion, allegedly fueled by scientific wonder at discovery, is not obviously occurring in much of the contemporary discourse I examine in this book, and least of all in the new cosmology. Rather, when paired side by side with science, religion is often seen to offer only weak or immature forms of wonder. Nature too, as apprehended by our ordinary senses, may be similarly derided. For "without science, we are stuck with the drab world of appearances."[47] With science, we can wonder at what is real.

In the history of science and theology, thoughtful critics of this reversed dynamic of wonder—wonder at knowledge and explanation rather than mysterious or awe-evoking phenomena—have emerged again and again. They rightly point to its tendency to engender idolatry, vanity, and pride, or self-deification. They worry about wonder that becomes detached from a broader context or horizon of meaning, turning inward toward the self and its catalogued knowledge. We see this warning, for example, in Augustine's portrait of humans who, having become puffed up with pride at their knowledge of creation, turn away from glorification of the Creator. In the seventeenth century, British mechanical philosopher and natural theologian Robert Boyle assailed scientists' desire to usurp God, warning that natural knowledge—whether it generated wonder at nature or at humans themselves—"stole praise and gratitude from God."[48] Closer to our own time, Rachel Carson characterized human pride in our technological and scientific mastery as "idolatry"; she worried that humans, despite their psychological handicaps, were positioning themselves to take over "many of the functions of 'God.'"[49] One need not juxtapose human power and wisdom to the power and wisdom of a *divine* entity in order to discern something problematic in these "puffed up" forms of wonder at human knowledge and achievements (note that Carson puts scare quotes around the word God). Carson, unlike Boyle, did not see wonder at nature as a threat or rival to wonder at God. Yet both Carson and Boyle point to a pious or wholesome form of wonder that is directed outward at something greater than ourselves, wonder strongly shaped by a sense of humility regarding the proper limits of human knowledge and power.

WHAT REMAINS OF WONDER?

Much of the foregoing discussion of wonder, and its relationship and rivalry with curiosity, may give the impression that we have few options: either we can preserve wonder by remaining in an ignorant or stupefied state, or we can pursue knowledge while risking (or celebrating, as the case may be) curiosity's encouragement of pride and hubris. The choice, in other words, seems to be between humble and naive but ignorant wonder, or knowledge tainted by potentially reckless pride and related vices. But other accounts maintain that wonder is not driven out by knowledge; that which evokes wonder is never quite fit back into the ordinary but "breaks open the fabric of the ordinary itself and changes it forever."[50] As our perceptions of the world are fundamentally altered, so too are we. In a phrase often attributed to Oliver Wendell Holmes, "The mind, once expanded to the larger dimensions of new ideas, never returns to its original size." A part of the process that wonder sets in motion can itself be "wonder-preserving."[51] Wonder's capacity for self-preservation rather than self-elimination—even in the presence of scientific understanding—is one of the topics I will pursue further in the following chapters. Wonder of this sort can reinforce an awareness of the *limits* of our knowledge (and vice versa, as advocates of "virtuous ignorance" suggest) without devaluing science.[52] Awareness of these limits, in turn, allows us to see the world with fresh eyes, to remain open to new possibilities, new ways of perceiving the world, because we are not stubbornly invested in current concepts and frameworks. This openness may set the stage for additional encounters with wonder, as well as additional knowledge.

In praising an awareness of the limits of our knowledge, I do not mean that wonder simply *resides* within those unknowns, for this would, once again, entail a banishment of wonder as knowledge is gained and gaps filled in. I am not advocating serial wonder that solves one puzzle and moves eagerly to the next; such a view not only relegates wonder to (temporary) unknowns but also tends to assume that all unknowns will ultimately be overcome. Rather, my claim is that wonder may provide the conditions for novel forms of knowledge to emerge, even as wonder is not exhausted by new knowledge. Confidence in what we know, or think we know, can lead to a freeze-framing of the world around us. Scientific habits of mind—abstraction, isolation, reductionism—may well encourage such freeze-framing. Certainly, celebratory declamations of *all that we now know*—such as those to which I draw attention throughout this work—close off avenues of newfound wonder and knowledge, and discourage the intellectual modesty and prudence needed to engage with complex problems, like environmental problems. Enamored of our own knowledge, we may also forget that scientific concepts provide only a "fragmented view of the world." Failing to recognize this, we "continue to produce myriad unintended effects that inform the ecological, social, and economic problems dominating our times."[53] The modest habits of mind that accompany (genuine) wonder can also encourage deeper reflection on which paths of investigation we ought and ought not to pursue, and why. Indeed, a difference between curiosity and wonder, as I define the latter, is that curiosity is often seen to be deficient in this moral perspective—hence, the frequent critiques of curiosity's vicelike tendency toward greedy appropriation or arrogant and unseemly prying.

Science appropriately has as its object not mysteries but *problems* to be solved; as Gabriel Marcel famously argued, not all mysteries are problems, and vice versa.[54] Taken to its extreme, however, the quest to solve puzzles can become pathological, manifesting as a desire to "seal the ego off against further novelty."[55] When this directed form of curiosity and serial puzzle-solving comes to stand in for wonder as *a whole*—and, I would add, when the knowledge produced by such focused inquiry is understood to comprise full "reality"—a tremendous loss has occurred, with far-reaching implications, ethically, aesthetically, spiritually, and intellectually.

Genuine wonder is the grounding for intellectual virtues and habits of mind. Focusing on the element of mystery commonly associated with wonder helps us to round out a sketch of wonder's ethical potential, that potential having been obscured by our inherited discourse on wonder and curiosity. Mysteries *involve* us in a way that problems do not; this sense of involvement is a key element of wonder. We cannot stand back objectively from a mystery and evaluate it, as we can a problem. Encountering something in wonder may be more like meeting a person, Sam Keen argues, than like analyzing an object. Martin Buber's account of I / Thou encounters (in which we regard the other not as a discrete "it" but as a source of meaningful relationality) is relevant to the experience of wonder. "When Buber speaks of an I-Thou encounter with a tree or Marcel speaks of discovering a presence in a flower, each is indicating a level of experience at which what we normally call an object ceases to be inert and passive."[56] There is often a quality of interchange but not of appropriation. Related to this: we may "take up" an object in curiosity, but an object (or, better, a *presence*) of wonder has the power to take *us* up. The power it exerts allows one to lose oneself in the presence of wonder, or to feel one's smallness vis-à-vis wondrous phenomena. In a telling phrase, Rachel Carson alludes to the sensation (and accompanying ethical insight) of putting oneself "under the influence" of nature.

Wonder's non-appropriative quality and uncoerced relinquishment of control allows recognition of the significance and singularity of what we encounter, even as it takes us up and involves us. Caroline Walker Bynum goes so far as to suggest that "only that which is really different from the knower can trigger wonder."[57] Similarly, Bynum argues, "we wonder at what we cannot in any sense incorporate, or consume, or encompass in our mental categories."[58] We do not, I believe, have to posit the absolute and radical otherness of that at which we wonder to appreciate that wonder involves an encounter with an *external* reality—or many external realities—not merely with the workings of our own minds. Wonder takes us out of ourselves. It is contrary to the solipsistic impulse. This emphasis on otherness, radical or otherwise, might seem paradoxical, or even contradictory, for if we are taken up by wonder, are we not somehow "absorbed" into it? Does not a loss of self, in other words, also bring with it a sense of oneness with something greater or all-encompassing (as in accounts of mystical experiences, where boundaries between self and other dissolve and strong feelings of connection prevail)? How can we encounter a presence that is truly different and other, while denying, as Buber's I / Thou encounter would have it, the separateness and discreteness of the other? The language of oneness or connectedness is appropriate to wonder if it means that we gain a new sense of ourselves as bound up with something that retains some autonomy, that remains at some level unassimilable or unpredictable. If oneness entails homogenization that renders the other—or the world—comprehensible and appropriable, then an important quality of wonder has been muted, if not silenced. Thus, a "comprehensive" story of the universe that integrates all entities together as a cosmic community governed by the same patterns and principles may have a deadening effect on wonder. And even more so, when humanity and its discoveries are given pride of place in the positioning of ourselves vis-à-vis the cosmos. The very task of actively organizing cosmic and human history into a seamless narrative forecloses surprise and novelty. It weakens the wondering perception that we dwell, with awe, fear, delight, sorrow, and ambiguity, in what Loren Eiseley calls an *unexpected* universe.[59] The spirit of wonder sustains the perception of strangeness and is inimical to "investigative thinking that endeavors to assimilate that strangeness."[60] It defies the static ordering of a universal narrative and the quest for security that so often impels such ordering. We risk losing wonder's most laudable dimensions when we seek to grasp the world in its totality, devoid of deep mysteries, uncertainties, and "unseemly gaps."

If wonder is a rich and complex tapestry, which strands do we wish to carry forward into a future seemingly defined by ubiquitous human presence and transformation of the natural world? Which lend themselves to the cultivation of greater reverence for the more-than-human world, and which shift our gaze inward, inviting self-glorification? In practical terms, what difference does it really make, for our own lives and for the lives of other beings with whom we share the planet, how we choose to define and celebrate wonder? To begin thinking through these questions, I turn in the following chapters to two of the world's foremost champions of scientific wonder and enchantment: biologists Richard Dawkins and E. O. Wilson.

Chapter 2

The Book of Nature and the Book of Science

Richard Dawkins on Wonder

There is a hunger out there for wonder, for understanding, and there are people out there who think that the scientific worldview somehow denies, somehow reduces the poetic vision of the universe, which in its petty, paltry way their religion seems to give them. We have something far better to offer.

—RICHARD DAWKINS (SEE NOTES)

What I do blame Dawkins and science for is their lack of curiosity about what this feeling of awe means. They claim the feeling, and claim its popular appeal, without thinking that it needs to be "substantiated statistically," as everything else they consider is required to be. Amazement-before-the-cosmos cannot be tested or proved by observation, and it is not predictive of anything other than itself. In the hands of science, beauty is just a tautology, or a dogma. *The dogma is this: "When presented with the discoveries of science, you will marvel at their beauty. . . you will defer to your betters, those who know, the scientists. If they say the cosmos is beautiful, it's beautiful."*

—CURTIS WHITE, *THE SCIENCE DELUSION*

One of the myths of science may be the wonder that it generates.

—CELIA DEANE-DRUMMOND, "EXPERIENCING WONDER AND SEEKING WISDOM"

In a thoughtful editorial appearing in *Conservation Biology*, a science student named Hanni Muerdter reflects on the vast differences between an unexpectedly wondrous encounter with the natural world and the experience of learning about nature in her biology classes. Out for a walk during one of the first sultry nights of a Midwestern spring, she experienced a revelation: "I realized how long it had been since I had smelled fresh buds and seen the shadow of new leaves dappling the ground. I stopped, awed by the spring night."[1] Like many, she came to the study of biology as a result of childhood encounters with the natural world. Yet, as this spontaneous brush with wonder reminded her, she had not felt such emotions in many years, and certainly not in her biology classes. Though a handful of today's scientists are becoming less reticent about their own experiences of wonder as a motivation for research, the student in question found it puzzling and somewhat troubling that this dynamic between wonder at nature and a career in science was never addressed in any college course she could recall. Not once had her science professors alluded to such motives in their own past or present.

As she began to question science professors about their own feelings of wonder or lack thereof, she also found that while many claimed to find their research stimulating and engrossing, most had long ceased to make the connection between their interest in science and the earlier experiences of wonder that sparked it. As this connection faded, so did any sense that their research was linked to the wider world, or that they had a responsibility to consider the potential impacts of their work or what it might portend for the future, positively or negatively. What emerged repeatedly in these conversations was scientists' abiding belief in the neutrality of their research and an attendant trend toward compartmentalizing their work lives and emotional lives. Compartmentalization allowed them to conceive of their research in isolation from broader realities or concerns, and to maintain a bright and distinct line between personal responses to the world and the intellectual activity of their profession. In the minds of her professors, research was more scientific the greater its distance from personal experience: "to be 'scientific,' research has to exclude any human or emotional connection."[2] Not surprisingly, then, wonder itself is often excluded. While a few insisted that they still felt a kind of wonder at their subject—"the more knowledge I gain about my subject, the more wonder I have for it," one remarked[3]—most seemed motivated by a form of curiosity or excitement purified of the emotional and reverential aspects of wonder they recalled from childhood or youth.

Muerdter goes on to draw a distinction between science approached with "curiosity" (a sense of excitement with one's immediate research questions) and science conducted in an overarching orientation and mood of wonder. On this account, curiosity is a more focused inquiry, whereas wonder opens up larger questions and multiple points of view. Although she characterizes wonder here as an approach "*to* science" (and her piece is titled "The Wonder *of* Science"), she clearly understands reverential wonder to situate science *within* a broader horizon of meaning and value, a horizon that transcends and orients one's immediate research agenda. Letting wonder "re-center ourselves," she argues, would encourage "reverence toward the natural world."[4] In other words, science carried out in an attitude of wonder has something other than (or in addition to) *science itself* as its frame of reference. Wonder detached from proper moral ends or devoid of some means of discernment is subject to distortion. Celia Deane-Drummond similarly argues for "wisdom"—a capacity for insight, holistic thinking, and discernment[5]—as wonder's necessary companion: "if philosophy is simply open to the throes of wonder without wisdom it is in danger of becoming unhinged, especially where wonders are sought for their own sake."[6] Unhinged wonder, we might say, is also a hallmark of consecrated science. Among its dangers Deane-Drummond counts the great potential for self-deception and vices enabled by self-deception, such as arrogance. This pursuit of knowledge without wisdom cannot suggest limits on knowledge itself.

Keeping these preliminary musings on the appropriate moral context and deployment of wonder in mind, I now turn to one of the most prominent champions of scientific wonder in our time, biologist and science popularizer Richard Dawkins. In Dawkins's work, we see the dangers of consecrated science in which celebration of reality comes at the expense of nature and its wonders.

"EVEN RICHARD DAWKINS . . ."

Sustained treatments of Dawkins's views of science and religion typically remark on the fact (apparently startling to some) that Dawkins is capable of quasi-spiritual wonder at the universe. That Dawkins admits to experiencing anything akin to spiritual sensation is often presented as revelatory in itself—a finding worthy of whole articles or even books. Much to Dawkins's disgust, commentaries on his sense of awe and wonder frequently appear in the context of appeals to science and religion to lay down their arms and embrace their shared sensibilities. After all, the argument seems to go, if even Richard Dawkins experiences something approximating spirituality, hope must surely exist for a détente between science and religion. For example, the Templeton Foundation, which funds big questions in science and religion, financed Chris Mooney's journalistic discovery that even neo-atheists like Dawkins experience "spiritual uplift." "Indeed," Mooney writes, "[Dawkins] has written an entire book, *Unweaving the Rainbow,* about the wonder that comes with learning how things really work."[7] In a more scholarly vein, Deane-Drummond observes that "even Richard Dawkins, that *bête noir* of the religious community, admits to wonder through science," though his manner of doing so, she rightly contends, "demonstrates not so much insight but hubris."[8] Dawkins happily concedes the "arrogance problem," even while he confesses to a certain "spiritual uplift" that permeates his secular-scientific fortifications against all things supernatural. Uplift is front and center—it is what science does best, Dawkins insists. It is what science does *better* than religion, to be precise. "Uplift," he writes,

> is where science really comes into its own. All the great religions have a place for awe, for ecstatic transport at the wonder and beauty of creation. And it's exactly this feeling of spine-shivering, breath-catching awe—almost worship—this flooding of the chest with ecstatic wonder, that modern science can provide. And it does so beyond the wildest dreams of saints and mystics. The fact that the supernatural has no place

in our explanations, in our understanding of so much about the universe and life, doesn't diminish the awe. Quite the contrary. The merest glance through a microscope at the brain of an ant or through a telescope at a long-ago galaxy of a billion worlds is enough to render poky and parochial the very psalms of praise.[9]

So, yes, even Richard Dawkins has got wonder.[10] The important question is, wonder at *what,* exactly? We might also ask how it happens that seemingly noble (and even humbling) dispositions of wonder—"ecstatic transport" and "almost worship"—so readily engender unapologetic arrogance and hubris, as clearly they do for Dawkins. The answer to the second question, I argue, follows directly from answers to the first.

WONDER AT WHAT? THE RAINBOW DECONSTRUCTED

In *Unweaving the Rainbow,* Dawkins famously purports to shed light on the human "appetite for wonder." As the title suggests, he chides the Romantic poets who resented Newton for destroying the mystery and poetry of the rainbow by dissecting it into light of different wavelengths. Dawkins's choice of the rainbow as his central motif is more appropriate than he may realize, for the rainbow figures prominently in the history of wonder. In Hesiod's *Theogony,* Thaumas (wonder) is the sea god whose union with Electra produces Iris, the rainbow. "That the rainbow is the 'daughter' of wonder makes it far more than one wonder among many," Philip Fisher writes. The rainbow is wonder's "first and central instance. . . .To understand philosophy we must go to its *arche* wonder, but to think out wonder we must descend genetically (father to daughter) to the rainbow."[11] The rainbow often symbolizes something miraculous: an interpenetration of heaven and Earth, or "the one part of heaven that occurred here on earth."[12] Probably the best-known example of this symbolism in Western mythology is God's choice of the rainbow as a sign to Noah of his promise never again to destroy the world. The rainbow always points to something else—a mixed message of overwhelming fear and relief, a bridge to a world beyond, the pursuit of something tantalizing but seemingly unobtainable. Dawkins has chosen no ordinary symbol with which to demonstrate the power of science to decode nature. In recent history, perhaps only the mushroom cloud rivals the rainbow as symbolic of world destruction and the awesome power of science.

Dawkins argues that the Romantic poets ought to celebrate rather than recoil from Newton's demystification of the rainbow, because the scientific explanation is always more interesting and beautiful than the mystery it "explains away."[13] The language of "explaining away" hints at how Dawkins understands science and wonder to operate. In fact, the deconstruction of the rainbow was the combined effort of Descartes and Newton, and so it may be useful to recall the Cartesian account. Descartes regarded wonder with some suspicion because of its capacity to stall the mind, and because of the "false twins"—akin to what Dawkins calls fake wonder—that are wonder's close associates. For Descartes, astonishment, the state of too much wonder, represents one of wonder's false forms. "The scientific pathos of the liquidation of wonder by explanation runs like a thread through Descartes's work."[14] A similar claim holds for Dawkins. If Descartes's account has wonder as largely self-eliminating, Dawkins sees wonder as persisting—but only by means of making *human powers of explanation,* rather than natural phenomena, the object of wonder. Dawkins has little sympathy for those who believe that "to explain away a good mystery is to be a killjoy, just as some Romantic poets thought about Newton's explaining of the rainbow."[15] Buck up! Dawkins advises: "If you think the rainbow has poetic mystery you should try relativity [theory]."[16] Such remarks suggest an either / or proposition with regard to wonder: you may initially find the rainbow wondrous, but once you understand the scientific explanation, your appreciation necessarily shifts. Thus Dawkins concludes that "science is, or ought to be, the inspiration for great poetry."[17]

To speak of the wonder "of science" is not necessarily to suggest that it is science, *rather than nature,* that appropriately evokes wonder. Scientific knowledge and rational explanation clearly play an important role in enabling wonder; encounters with the unexpected and novel would likely produce fear, rather than pleasurable awe, if we utterly lacked the experience of successfully explaining that which strikes us as wondrous. So we may grant that science, or rationality more generally, contributes to a state of wonder. Yet Dawkins's account clearly sees nature as subordinate to human reason, which usurps nature as the more worthy object of awe. Dawkins makes occasional reference to the idea that when a scientist "solves" a mystery, that solution uncovers deeper mystery. This suggests that mystery always outpaces our current knowledge and that it leads science, and the scientist, onward to the next puzzle (this is one version of what it means to wonder at science and it corresponds to what I labeled, in the previous chapter, serial wonder). The idea that solving one mystery opens up additional mysteries is seen in Dawkins's remark that the rainbow's mystery is replaced with the more worthy "object," namely, relativity theory. What he means is that the solution to the puzzle of the rainbow generated more questions and new theories—about electromagnetism, for example—which in turn produced further theories and insights, leading ultimately to Einstein's brilliant account of special relativity.

Yet it is clear from Dawkins's comments elsewhere that in principle he finds mystery and wonder deeply problematic, even in successive or serial form. Mystery is something to be gotten rid of as soon as possible and, ideally, once and for all. Dawkins is troubled, not attracted, by the category of "deeper mysteries" as he is by the implication that wonder be closely allied with mystery (rather than mystery's dissolution). "Physicists," he tellingly observes, "disagree over whether they are condemned forever to dig for deeper mysteries, or whether physics itself will come to an end in a final 'theory of everything,' a nirvana of knowledge."[18] Note how mystery is presented here as akin to eternal punishment, while the termination of mystery in a final comprehensive theory is the blissful state, the liberation from the samsaric cycle of questions and answers—a kind of eschatology of knowledge.[19]

The lofty status Dawkins confers to science and scientific knowledge is further indicated by his horror that science ever be made into "vulgar fun" for laypersons or even *children*. Science, he stresses, is hard work but "worth the struggle."[20] Wonder is the payoff for intensely earnest but dispassionate studiousness (i.e., curiosity). Popular science demonstrations featuring "whacky personalities and fun explosions" only "store up trouble for the future," he ominously warns.[21] Moreover, "fun sends the wrong signals" and may draw both children and adults to science for "the wrong reasons."[22] The insistence that the day-to-day routine of science is difficult and demanding, and that rewards are hard-won, accords with Dawkins's view that wonder—the reward—comes with solving puzzles and mysteries, not with contemplating them. Science, like the military, does well to recruit "young people dedicated enough to stand the pace"—*not* pleasure-seekers and tourists.[23] Dawkins associates other forms of wonder with mere sloth and dissipation, and in this respect he particularly resembles Francis Bacon, who "seldom let an opportunity pass to reprimand those who pursued the study of nature for pleasure."[24] This *reversed* dynamic of wonder—wonder as reward rather than bait—requires that one be reconciled to a principle of delayed gratification.[25] A general distaste for mystery is also helpful.

This dynamic, as we saw in the previous chapter, made a rather late appearance in the history of science. In the late seventeenth and early eighteenth centuries, this painstaking, arduous form of science partially merged with the tradition of natural theology that sought to glorify God in the details by finding in nature myriad examples of God's intricate design. "Wonder was no longer a goad to curiosity, but to praise, for its ultimate object was in principle not a concrete individual in all its particularity but mind-numbing God in all his perfections."[26] Dawkins's version of science resembles this portrait of painstaking work, followed by hard-won wonder at detailed knowledge. But in natural theology's argument from design, wonder as a payoff for diligent investigation of nature was also, necessarily, wonder at the divine mind behind nature's order and intricacy.

In a sense, then, Dawkins endorses a kind of natural theology without either God or nature as an ultimate object. This leaves only the knowledge and the knower— science and the scientist—as worthy objects. Science, therefore, must never be tainted or debauched. Dabbling in astrology or the paranormal, even if only for entertainment purposes, "debauches the wonder."[27] In order to indicate what is so wrong with programs like *The X-Files*, for example, in which, week after week, rational explanations lose out to paranormal ones, Dawkins suggests this parallel. Imagine a crime show where each week the suspects consist of one black person and one white person; each and every time, the black suspect turns out to have committed the crime. "Unpardonable, of course," Dawkins says. "And my point is that you could not defend it by saying: 'But it's only fiction, only entertainment.'" Dawkins denounces the "populist whoring that defiles the wonder of science."[28] In the same metaphorical vein, he laments that there is a good living to be made by those willing to "prostitute the language—and the wonder—of science."[29] Allusions to defilement and debauchery—and to the *crime* of treating science on a par with pseudoscience—suggest that we are in the presence of something sacred. The scientist's job is to persuade laypersons that even while their cherished sources of wonder (including wondrous *nature*) have been "explained away," something grander, something more mature and satisfying—scientific explanation—awaits them.

NEVER WONDER: DAWKINS ON CHILDREN'S SENSE OF WONDER

> *No little Gradgrind had ever learnt the silly jingle, Twinkle, twinkle, little star; how I wonder what you are! No little Gradgrind had ever known wonder on the subject, each little Gradgrind having at five years old dissected the Great Bear like a Professor Owen, and driven Charles's Wain like a locomotive engine-driver. No little Gradgrind had ever associated a cow in a field with that famous cow with the crumpled horn who tossed the dog who worried the cat who killed the rat who ate the malt, or with that yet more famous cow who swallowed Tom Thumb: it had never heard of those celebrities, and had only been introduced to a cow as a graminivorous ruminating quadruped with several stomachs. . . . When she was half a dozen years younger, Louisa had been overheard to begin a conversation with her brother one day, by saying "Tom, I wonder"—upon which Mr. Gradgrind, who was the person overhearing, stepped forth into the light and said, "Louisa, never wonder!"*
>
> —CHARLES DICKENS, *HARD TIMES*

Dawkins's dedication to ensuring that even children develop demystified and scientifically correct responses to the world around them is one of the peculiar hallmarks of his sense of wonder.[30] He famously penned a letter to his daughter Juliet (aged ten at the time) that explicates "good" and "bad" reasons for believing something, and explains the indispensable role of scientists as "the specialists in discovering what is true about the world and the universe."[31] In *Unweaving the Rainbow,* Dawkins regales us with the story of his efforts to disabuse a young child of her belief in Santa Claus. "I remember once trying gently to amuse a six-year-old child at Christmas time by reckoning up with her how long it would take Father Christmas to go down all the chimneys in the world," Dawkins reports, without the slightest hint of shame. "The obvious possibility that her parents had been telling falsehoods never seemed to cross her mind."[32] Melvin Konner, in a review of Dawkins's book, remarks with wit and precision that "a grown man using statistics as a wedge between a six-year-old and Santa Claus is scarcely the right person to assuage people's fears of science."[33]

In 2011, Dawkins published a book for young readers that explains the true, scientific genesis of many wondrous objects, including the rainbow: *The Magic of Reality: How We Know What's Really True.* This colorfully illustrated volume attempts to address children's big questions, including many that children are likely to encounter in Sunday school: "Why is there night and day?"; "Who were the first man and woman?"; "When did everything begin?"; and even "Why do bad things happen?" *The Magic of Reality* is intended as a myth-busting book, attempting to do for youthful readers what *The God Delusion* endeavors to do for grown-ups laboring under illusions of various sorts. Dawkins juxtaposes myths and fairytales with "lucid scientific explanation" in order to "explode myths and legends about the natural world with science."[34] By myths he means everything from fairytales about the rainbow's origin to Judeo-Christian stories like Noah's ark. A chapter on the sun presents an Aztec myth, an ancient Egyptian myth, and an Aboriginal myth, prior to displacing each and the false wonder they encourage, with an account of the sun's true nature. Dawkins frequently exhorts children to think for themselves, but the book's message is essentially the same as *Unweaving the Rainbow*: what is real in the scientific sense is most deserving of wonder. Science is not one way of experiencing wonder, but the only authentic way. "I want to show you that the real world, as understood scientifically, has a magic of its own," Dawkins explains to young readers, "an inspiring beauty which is all the more magical because it is real and because we can understand how it works. . . . The magic of reality is—quite simply—wonderful. Wonderful, and real. Wonderful *because real.*"[35] By contrast, religious myths "can never offer us a true explanation of what we see in the world."[36] Religion is like a detective too lazy even to bother solving the mystery.

In *Unweaving the Rainbow,* Dawkins argues that science alone can satisfy what he calls our "appetite for wonder." It reveals "strangeness beyond wild imagining" but no spells, wizards, or witches. It allows "mystery but not magic."[37] The line between mystery and magic is not always easy to patrol, even for Dawkins, and his use of the term "magic" in the title of his new book is surprising. Dawkins admits to struggling with the word magic, not wanting to associate the real magic of science with the "the word magic, as in a magic trick," which is cheap and tawdry.[38]

Dawkins's mission to convert the world—adults and children alike—to the bracing tonic of what is really real is applauded by some new cosmologists. We will see that *The Magic of Reality* is touted by Epic enthusiasts as the proper way to guide children through (that is, safely *out* of) the big mysteries of nature and life. Dawkins has long expressed disapproval of most children's stories because of their fantastical aspects; he dismisses C. S. Lewis's *The Lion, the Witch and the Wardrobe* for its reliance on "a magic wardrobe to pass through" and other invocations of a "fake world of wonder."[39] He is a vocal critic of the Harry Potter series for promoting what he considers pernicious and anti-scientific myths (the children's books of his Oxford colleague and fellow atheist Philip Pullman meet with his approval, for reasons that should be obvious to anyone who has read them). Dawkins's critique of what he considers fake wonder makes no allowance for differences between children's and adults' perceptions of the world. The suggestion that children might need or be enriched by forms of wonder that are not fully rational or scientifically grounded is not entertained. Nor is his category of fake wonder limited to the usual suspects such as the marvelous, magical, or miraculous.

In fairness to Dawkins, part of his concern with correcting even children's sense of wonder is that wonder not simply be a function of ignorance, of open-mouthed incomprehension; nor should it be understood as a response to the sort of trickery and sleight of hand involved in a magic show (though his comments also point to a significant concern that *pure* science be respected over and above practical demonstrations and applications).[40] In other words, Dawkins's concerns are neither wholly idiosyncratic nor illegitimate: they are shared by other scientists, past and present, for whom wonder connotes a "check" to our knowledge, a slothful preference for marveling rather than understanding.[41] Mark Silverman, the Harvard physicist I quoted in the previous chapter who delineates two "sides" of wonder, concurs that one type drives scientific investigation and another simply prefers to dwell in the "magical, miraculous, and incomprehensible" rather than seek understanding. Whereas the first type is the "germinal seed" of scientific investigation that, by its very nature, is not content to gape and stare, the second form—which in Silverman's account applies to essentially everyone who is *not* a scientist—"is like a narcotic that destroys curiosity and anesthetizes the intellect into catatonic inactivity."[42] Even (or especially) exposure to the "marvels" of modern physics— quarks, black holes, and other phenomena that appear to lie outside rational explanation—tends to freeze rather than fire the scientific imagination, Silverman warns, because these topics give an impression of science as "an abstruse academic game."[43] Like Dawkins, he wants aspiring science students to understand the difficult, plodding nature of scientific work. Rewards are in the results, in the solving of mysteries, rather than the *contemplation* of seeming marvels. Still, Dawkins's insistence that even children be trained up in strictly scientific forms of wonder and shielded from intimations of the magical is extreme.[44] Particularly troubling is Dawkins's suspicion of the natural world as a legitimate source of wonder, or as worthy of rapt contemplation, in and of itself. His discussion of the relationship between science and poetry provides some insight into the peripheral role he assigns to nature.

SCIENCE AND POETRY

Dawkins's urging of poets to take up science as their subject and source of inspiration recalls Alfred North Whitehead's observation that the rise of modern science gave birth to a sentiment, now widespread among scientists and philosophers, that the human mind is more deserving of wonder than nature itself. In this view (which Whitehead here intends to lampoon),

> Nature gets credit which should in truth be reserved for ourselves: the rose for its scent: the nightingale for his song: and the sun for his radiance. The poets are entirely mistaken. They should address their lyrics to themselves, and should turn them into odes of self-congratulation on the excellency of the human mind. Nature is a dull affair . . . merely the hurrying of material, endlessly, meaninglessly.[45]

Dawkins edited the 2008 *Oxford Book of Modern Science Writing*. His brief introductions to the selections shed additional light on his understanding of the relationship between science and literature, particularly the idea that science generates superior forms of poetry. For example, introducing Loren Eiseley's essay "How Flowers Changed the World" affords Dawkins the opportunity to trot out his favorite reminder that science further enhances rather than diminishes experiences of wonder or aesthetic allure. "All poets know that flowers are beautiful, but not all poets get the important point," Dawkins argues, the point being that the scientist sees "deeper beauty" not readily available to others.[46]

Dawkins's contention that science is "the poetry of reality" is the theme of a musical composition created by John Boswell, a professional composer and science buff. This music video, one in a series called "The Symphony of Science," sets to music the actual words of prominent scientists, such as Dawkins, Carl Sagan, Stephen Hawking, and the atheist blogger and biologist P. Z. Myer. Through the modern miracle of "Auto-Tune" technology, the song's refrain—"There is real poetry in the real world / Science is the poetry of reality"—is "sung" by Dawkins. Other scientists contribute similar lyrics. These include the perception that, e.g., "The quest for truth, in and of itself / Is a story that's filled with insights" or the reminder that "We have through the power of thought / Been able to peer back to a brief moment / After the beginning of the universe." While these lyrics, culled from scientific lectures and texts, make the requisite gestures toward humility and the smallness of humans as revealed by science, the overall tone is exultant. Science is credited with answering our hunger for religion and meaning. Another of Boswell's compositions, titled "A Wave of Reason" (its refrain is also sung by Dawkins), includes this lyrical advice from neo-atheist Sam Harris: "You do not have to delude yourself / With Iron Age Fairy Tales." Planetary scientist Carolyn Porco advises: "The same spiritual fulfillment that people find in religion / Can be found in science / By coming to know, if you will, the mind of God." Sagan chimes in with the following: "Cosmology brings us face to face with the deepest mysteries / With questions that were once treated only / In religion and myth."[47]

I suspect many viewers would find these videos odd and a bit silly, but they represent the displacement of religion by scientific worldviews and, more precisely, the *consecration* of science that Dawkins, and new cosmologists, endorse. The theme that consistently emerges, of science offering something similar but superior to religion, is taken further in Dawkins's own writings on poetry and science. Wonder as a response to *nature* suggests to Dawkins a delusional and muddied picture of reality, a response in need of scientific clarity.

FAKE WONDER AND THE ECLIPSE OF NATURE

Concerned elsewhere with exposing illusions and delusions of all sorts (including, of course, the mass delusion of religious belief),[48] Dawkins devotes *Unweaving the Rainbow* to debunking superstitious and pseudoscientific beliefs such as astrology. Magic, religion, and what Dawkins terms "bad poetry" in science[49] all have in common an "inflation of casual and meaningless resemblances into huge cloudy symbols of a high romance (Keats's phrase)."[50] Dawkins is highly suspicious of virtually all forms of symbolism and representation; needless to say he rejects any whiff of postmodern accounts of science as one way we *represent* the world to ourselves. "All over the world," he complains, "ceremonies are based upon an obsession with things representing other things that they slightly resemble, or resemble in one respect."[51] Among these he counts the lamentable practice of harvesting of rhinoceros horns for aphrodisiac purposes (owing to the horn's phallic resemblance, presumably), as well as religious rituals such as "transubstantiation" (or its counterpart in other cultures). Science, by contrast, proceeds and succeeds by *rejecting* superficial symbolism, by weeding out false and misleading patterns and resemblances that might lead a scientist astray: In science, as in other human activities, "there really are dangers of becoming intoxicated by symbolism, by meaningless resemblances."[52]

The existence of myriad and multiplying fakes—magic, religion, pseudoscience of all sorts—whose currency is also the human "appetite" for wonder gives urgency to Dawkins's task of highlighting the literal truth, purity, and lasting rewards of real science. For magic, ritual, or astrology to hold any charm, the believer has to maintain his belief in what seems contrary to reason. He does not want to learn how the "trick" was done. The same person may not want to know how the rainbow works and may come to resent the scientist for explaining this natural object of beauty and wonder to him. Indeed, nature itself is a source of fake mystery and wonder, alongside magic, religion, and pseudoscience. Admiration of nature, when not placed firmly within a scientific, explanatory framework, when not mediated by scientific knowledge, is, for Dawkins, deeply problematic. Dawkins assumes one must choose between a form of muddle-headed mysticism and scientifically clarified wonder. Analyzing William Blake's lines about seeing "a World in a Grain of Sand / And a Heaven in a Wild Flower," Dawkins recoils from the unscientific quality of Blake's aesthetic and emotional response, and proceeds to correct Blake:

> The stanza can be read as all about science. . . . The impulses to awe, reverence and wonder which led Blake to mysticism . . . are precisely those that lead others of us to science. . . . The mystic is content to bask in the wonder and revel in a mystery that we were not 'meant' to understand. The scientist feels the same wonder but is restless, not content; recognizes the mystery as profound, then adds "But we're working on it."[53]

Dawkins concludes, "we need to reclaim for real science that style of awed wonder that moved mystics like Blake."[54] Reclaim it from what?, we might ask. What is most striking in Dawkins's reading of Blake is the complete neglect of the category *nature*. Dawkins endorses a displacement of "mysticism" (*fake* wonder, as he sees it) with "real science," but nowhere does he recognize Blake's perception of nature as itself worthy of awe or reverence. Like Fontenelle mentioned previously, Dawkins disapproves of admiration of nature that does not culminate in something more scientific. Wonder evoked by such experiences is *fake* wonder, a response to something unreal. The most deserving objects of awe, he goes on to suggest, are the most enduring, yet it is difficult to see how scientific knowledge endures more than the physical realities it studies. Blake's lines might be construed as being "about science" in the sense that science glimpses something vast and seemingly eternal (or something infinitely small)—not only heaven in a wildflower but "Infinity in the palm of your hand / And Eternity in an hour," as Blake puts it. But in order to insist that Blake's lines are at root (or really ought to be) "all about science," Dawkins gives them a certain spin. He interprets the lines about infinity and eternity as being "*about taming space and time*," for example.[55] In other words, Dawkins again subordinates nature to science—to human powers of comprehension and mastery. But one is rather hard-pressed to find in Blake's lines a glorification of humans "taming" nature's forces. On the contrary, the line that soon follows actually decries control and mastery: "A Robin Red breast in a Cage / Puts all Heaven in a Rage." Blake's allusions to infinity and eternity suggest a sense of gratitude and wonder at the opportunity to perceive something almost incomprehensibly vast from the limited standpoint of human experience. Science contributes greatly to that perception, but nature, as Blake might aver, provides the larger horizon of both meaning and mystery. Dawkins's displacement of nature "mysticism" with science and reason is surely what many critics have in mind when they charge him, and the neo-Darwinian, mechanistic worldview generally, with disenchanting nature. And yet Dawkins is clearly enchanted—profoundly so. His enchantment is of the self-congratulatory—and consecrated—sort critiqued by Whitehead in the passage quoted above. It is a form of enchantment with the human mind, and therefore it follows that poetry ought to be addressed to ourselves.

But, we might ask, is it in fact the case that "solving" scientific puzzles, such as the puzzle of the rainbow, is akin to explaining a magic trick? In other words, does it make sense to assert that the rainbow has turned out to be "really" or "only" something else? Descartes seems to have thought so and Dawkins appears to concur. "Unweaving" the rainbow is like discovering that the "Wonderful" Wizard of Oz is *really* a mere mortal with a fancy machine. It is significant that included in Descartes's writings on the rainbow there is a primer of sorts that would allow anyone who understands the principle of the rainbow to create one for his own or others' amusement, using light and a spray of water.[56] This "domesticated" rainbow could then be generated at will, to the amazement of those who do not understand how it is produced. As Fisher notes, "This decline of the rainbow to the point where like a bear in a zoo it can be used for the entertainment of others and the gathering of applause to the magician who stands behind the magic show confirms the extent to which in Descartes's own thinking the path from wonder to thought to explanation is a process that brings the extraordinary into the realm of the banal."[57] Here we approach what Rubenstein calls an "imposed" form of wonder, wonder that *demonstrates* the scientist's knowledge and power. The rainbow as a natural phenomenon and thing of beauty is eclipsed.

Dawkins insists that we shift our experience of wonder to the explanation and, by extension, to the scientist / magician who discovers and manipulates it. The magician, not the rainbow, gathers the applause. This move redirects wonder away from our lived experience of the natural world, and it disparages the wonder felt in natural encounters.

SCIENTIFIC WONDER AS CONSOLATION FOR MEANING LOST

One might ask why Dawkins, as a proud descendant of the Enlightenment, does not follow thinkers from centuries past who claimed that wonder simply *ceases* with scientific explanation, rather than try to preserve wonder at the explanation. Why would a rationalist like Dawkins preserve wonder at all, given its many pitfalls and potential abuses, particularly among the masses? One reason is discernible in Dawkins's express rationale for writing *Unweaving the Rainbow*. The book is Dawkins's attempt to soften the blow of *The Selfish Gene*. He explains that some readers were so unnerved and depressed by his account of nature and human nature in that controversial book that he felt he owed them something in exchange for robbing their lives of meaning. Dawkins recounts letters from readers rendered sleepless and suicidal after encountering the "cold, bleak message" of his book.[58] Readers have demanded to know how, with such a dark view of the world, Dawkins can drag himself out of bed each morning, much less remain so impossibly cheerful and energized. He has come to us with an impassioned defense of a jailed innocent, to show that the villain Science is actually the hero. A similar move occurs in E. O. Wilson's work: having explained the disconcerting "facts" of our (human) nature,[59] Wilson offers to console us with an enchanting vision of the scientific enterprise as a project that redefines humanity's common goals and transcendent purpose.[60] *Unweaving the Rainbow,* like *Consilience,* offers a new and improved form of enchantment in the wake of profound disenchantment. Dawkins wants to introduce readers to "the sense of wonder in science because it is so sad to think what these complainers and naysayers are *missing.*"[61]

But what Dawkins fails to recognize is that science may only be a real and meaningful hero, an abiding object of wonder or profound source of consolation, to those privileged to toil in its hallowed halls. It will not do (as Curtis White points out above) simply to instruct nonscientists to feel wonder at appropriate moments identified in advance by the scientist.[62] This is particularly true of wonder that arises from solutions to problems, or explanations of wonder-provoking phenomena. Gathering additional information about a phenomenon we perceive to be wondrous can, without a doubt, increase our interest and even enrich our awe. I read one day that spiral-shaped galaxies have a steady output of new stars, whereas elliptical galaxies, by virtue of their architecture, somehow lack this regenerative capacity and thus their dying stars are not replaced by new ones. The text I was reading instructed me to respond with wonder. It hailed this special capacity of the Milky Way and other spiral galaxies as "one of the most astonishing features of the creativity of the universe."[63] Looking at deep-space photographs of galaxies one day with my young son, I suddenly recalled this fact about spiral galaxies and shared it with him. We agreed that this was interesting, but I would be hard-pressed to say that this knowledge was more wondrous to me (or to my son) than those haunting, luminous images in the photographs before us. Nor would I concede that my wondrous appreciation of galaxies had been necessarily diminished when I *lacked* that piece of information. And as it happened, sometime later I came across a science article that cast serious doubt on the conventional wisdom that elliptical galaxies are "dying" in comparison to their regenerative spiral cousins.[64] So much the better that my astonishment was not dependent on the "fact" that the universe invests its creative, life-giving powers in spiral galaxies like our own.

There are numerous, everyday examples of the way in which scientific knowledge can enhance our appreciation of an object or experience. But few nonscientists can fully wonder at scientific solutions to difficult and often technical (erstwhile) puzzles. "Matters about which scientists express wonder and excitement often remain mysteries to non-scientists because of the technical language."[65] Even if I possess the sophistication necessary to wonder at a scientific explanation or a solution to a mathematical problem, it seems doubtful that I could return to a *solution* again and again with sustained, wondering appreciation—particularly if the solution is not one in which I, in any way, actually participated. Regarding Dawkins's desire to console us, then: it is a strange form of consolation that would remind us of all that we are *missing*, as Dawkins reminds science's "naysayers." Fellow scientists may admire, and seek to emulate, the discovery of a particularly elegant solution to a problem. But the public can often participate only in a vicarious and diluted form of wonder.

Dawkins seems vaguely aware of the problem. He draws an analogy between enjoying science (without being a scientist) and "enjoying the Mozart concerto without being able to play the clarinet." Appreciation of music is not "synonymous with *playing* it," and by the same token, "couldn't we also teach science as something to read and rejoice in, like learning to listen to music . . . ?"[66] Well, perhaps. But virtually everyone listens to and enjoys some kind of music; music appreciation does not, or it should not, instruct individuals to relinquish their present enjoyment in order to gain appreciation for something difficult but more worthwhile. Moreover, some individuals exhibit enormous musical talent and compose original pieces without ever learning to read music. For the sake of argument, however, let us assume that Dawkins's analogy holds, and that nonscientists can cultivate a form of science appreciation, akin to music appreciation for nonmusicians. The problem is that Dawkins's defense of science goes beyond mere appreciation of science, its methods, or its astonishing discoveries. Philosopher of science Philip Kitcher, who is not unsympathetic to Dawkins's project of enlightening religious believers with science and reason, argues that "contemplation of the cosmos as the sciences have revealed it" is not a sufficient basis for a good life for the vast majority of human beings—and probably not for Dawkins either.[67] Socrates and Aristotle celebrate the examined life, the life of informed contemplation, as Dawkins does; but they also recognized such goods of community, friendship, the cultivation of virtue or aesthetics, as integral to a good life. It is doubtful that even Dawkins's personal satisfactions and sense of worth are derived solely from "passive pleasures of understanding various natural phenomena," Kitcher notes.[68] Even in affluent societies with good education, people do not have access to the form of enlightenment Dawkins presses upon them. As Kitcher notes,

> the vast majority will never be able to recognize themselves as important participants in any impressive joint enterprise that contributes to knowledge and enlightenment. For large numbers of people, daily struggles to cope with threats to their physical wellbeing leave little opportunity for contemplation. Yet some institutions sometimes supply them with satisfying orientations, enabling them to rear their children with devoted love, helping them to create a less harsh and more just world for a few people around them. Some of these institutions are, of course, churches and mosques and synagogues.[69]

One upshot of Kitcher's argument is that in order for science to play this profoundly orienting role in people's lives, it would have to become something more than mere science (and those individuals whose lives it enriched would have to be more than passive recipients of information). Indeed, science would have to be a form of cosmology, a comprehensive, meaning-making framework in and of itself. Why should people give up the meaningful frameworks they have in order to adopt one they cannot fully inhabit or experience?

There is one avenue of wonder that remains open and unobstructed for the nonscientist: Dawkins upholds Alexander Pope's lines in praise of Newton as a paradigm of poetry inspired by science—and by the scientist: "Nature, and Nature's laws lay hid in night: / God said *Let Newton be!* and all was light." Admiration now is directed at the scientist himself, and what Dennis Quinn calls "the virtual deification of the great physicist."[70] For all intents and purposes, the scientist becomes the final object of reverie. Even childhood is not safe from the scientist's imposition of "rational" wonder on the child's sensory and emotional engagement with nature, or his enchanted perception of the world.

THE BOOK OF NATURE AND THE BOOK OF SCIENCE

I began this chapter with an inquiry into the different sensibilities that attend a scientific study of nature, on the one hand, and less mediated, spontaneous experiences of nature, on the other. I want to conclude here by considering a troubling example of the way in which uncritical wonder at science can marginalize, even threaten, the natural world. The problematic marginalization of nature by a brilliant scientist is the subject of an essay by Kenneth Brower.[71] The scientist in question is not Richard Dawkins but the world-famous physicist Freeman Dyson. Many years ago, Brower, who knows the Dyson family intimately, published a book called *The Starship and the Canoe* that dealt with Dyson's vexed relationship with his environmentalist son. In an essay in the *Atlantic*, Brower further speculates about the reasons for Dyson's dislike of environmentalism, and particularly his rather vocal and surprising skepticism regarding the predictions of climate scientists. Dyson is one of the world's most gifted physicists and a lifelong proponent of space travel (he has advocated the use of nuclear bombs as the most efficient way to propel spaceships to other planets). In 2000, he received the Templeton Foundation's Prize for "Progress in Religion." His acceptance speech recited a line from Francis Bacon alluding to a distinction between knowledge in the minds of scientists, on the one hand, and the perception of a mysterious reality beyond the mind, on the other: "God forbid that we should give out a dream of our own imagination for a pattern of the world," he said. Dyson also issued an impassioned plea to look for God in the facts of nature, not in the theories of Plato and Aristotle. I am saying to modern scientists and theologians: don't imagine that our latest ideas about the Big Bang or the human genome have solved the mysteries of the universe or the mysteries of life. Here are Bacon's words again: "The subtlety of nature is greater many times over than the subtlety of the senses and understanding." . . . Science has fulfilled many of Bacon's dreams, but it still does not come close to capturing the full subtlety of nature. To talk about the end of science is just as foolish as to talk about the end of religion.[72]

These are worthy sentiments. But in light of Dyson's commentary elsewhere regarding the absolute power of science and the seemingly negligible status of nature, it is difficult to avoid the impression that Dyson was simply pandering to ideals touted by the Templeton Foundation. In a number of interviews and articles, Dyson has not exactly *denied* the reality of climate change, though he comes perilously close. He believes the Earth is warming primarily in places where warmer weather is a welcome change (such as Greenland), and that change is occurring in ways that make plants "grow better." Dyson blithely contends that, overall, humans have been "kind" to nature and that where we have damaged it, we have generally made amends. In his *Atlantic* piece, Brower draws connections between Dyson's apparent lack of concern for endangered species and ecosystems and his unrestrained enthusiasm for science and technology, particularly biotechnology.

Dyson claims to have been drawn to mathematical calculations for as long as he can remember. That attraction led him to the study of physics, but were he starting out in science today, he says, he might take up biology, given its impressive mathematical and "theoretical" development as a hard discipline, compared to seventy-five years ago. "Now you can do biology pretty well with computers," Dyson notes. "When I was a boy, you had to do wet biology, working with real animals," he recalls.[73] (Wet biology, or wet labs, refers to traditional laboratory preparations using animals or tissue cultures, as opposed to computational or applied mathematical analyses and computer-generated models.) Like Dawkins, Dyson is interested in organisms primarily as "vehicles" for genes, or "gene-machines," and he seems to regard them as machines whose parts can be swapped out, according to the whims of human creativity. In an essay penned for the *New York Review of Books*, Dyson heralds the coming of domestic biotechnology that will put biotech "into the hands of housewives and children," and give us "an explosion of diversity of new living creatures."[74] In this coming era of Open Source biology, "the magic of genes will be available to anyone with the skill and imagination to use it." Designing genomes, he predicts, "will be a personal thing, a new art form as creative as painting or sculpture" that will bring "joy" to its creators, and greater "variety" to our existing lifeforms.[75] In the post-Darwinian future envisioned by Dyson, "species other than our own will no longer exist."[76] Dyson's prediction is not that all other life-forms will vanish, but that species *lines* will be blurred beyond recognition, and ultimately lost, as humans all over the planet give free rein to their creative impulses.[77] Dyson's vision may resonate with many as the dream—or utter nightmare—of the Anthropocene.

It is difficult to see Dyson's vision as anything but a terrifying "endorsement of mass biocide," as Brower observes. Brower entertains various explanations for Dyson's seemingly reckless attitude toward existing life-forms (he considers, but rejects, the onset of senility). Could it be that Dyson's brilliant scientific comprehension—so advanced in the realm of physics that Dyson is virtually in a class by himself—simply does not encompass biological science and the ecological relationships that support all life on Earth? Brower believes that the explanation lies instead in Dyson's profound scientism, his unshakeable faith in a "religion" of science that regards scientific power and progress as unlimited.[78] Dyson's preoccupation with scientific omnipotence and human ingenuity allows no regard for what Brower calls the "authentic" life-forms that struggle to survive in the compromised environment humans have created. His ambition is utterly cosmic in scope: in the words of a colleague, Dyson is "capable of understanding essentially anything he's interested in."[79] Therein lies the problem, for as Brower notes, Dyson's cosmic vision is decidedly *not* terrestrial. "In taking the measure of the universe, Dyson fails only in his appraisal of the small, spherical piece of the cosmos under his feet."[80]

What has this to do with Dawkins? By his own account, Dawkins was similarly drawn to science, and biology in particular, owing not to any interest in nature or "real animals" per se. He readily admits that he was no "boy naturalist," as many prominent biologists (including E. O. Wilson) were in their early days. Rather, he was fascinated with what he calls puzzles or problems. "I only became fired up in my second year of a science degree," Dawkins says of his early attraction to science. ". . . I was never a boy naturalist, to my regret. It was more the intellectual, philosophical questions that interested me."[81] These reflections on his relationship to science occur in a fascinating conversation between Dawkins and the British conservationist and documentary filmmaker David Attenborough. When asked to name the most exciting moment of his career, each gives a strikingly different responses. "One would be when I first dived on a coral reef," Attenborough recalls, "and I was able to move among a world of unrevealed complexity."[82] Dawkins offers his answer: "Something to do with a puzzle being solved," he ventures. "Things fall into place and you see a different way of looking at things which suddenly makes sense."[83] Where Attenborough evokes wonder at complexity and strangeness in a realm almost alien to humans, Dawkins wonders at the way in which everything finally makes good orderly sense; things fall into place, they are not so strange after all. Mysteries are problems, for Dawkins, and solutions more interesting and beautiful than puzzles.

A self-proclaimed naturalist ("I am a naturalist rather than a scientist," he attests), Attenborough finds "simply looking" at a plant or animal "to be just about the most interesting thing there is."[84] If biologists only admired plants and animals, biology would have little to show for itself, of course. Admiration can, and often does, lead to desire for greater knowledge, but knowledge need not displace the actual phenomenon as a worthy object of wondering appreciation. My point is that these two scientists express very different sensibilities about the natural world—how it figures in their work, and the sort of wonder their work generates for them personally. Dawkins's sensibilities are disconcertingly close to Dyson's.

Dawkins almost unconsciously substitutes *nature* with the word *science,* particularly when evaluating the respective merits of religious and scientific forms of wonder and "uplift." In addressing whether science is truly a religion, Dawkins concedes that "science can offer a vision of life and the universe which . . . for humbling poetic inspiration far outclasses any of the mutually contradictory faiths and disappointingly recent traditions of the world's religions."[85] Surely Dawkins does not believe that religion is "disappointingly recent" compared to *science,* though this is what the sentence suggests. Presumably, he means to compare religion's appeal to that of *nature,* which is essentially timeless. Nature is far more ancient than the most ancient religion (or science), and its sheer antiquity provokes wonder. Science gives us the means to apprehend, and confirm, nature's antiquity—it can suggest a "vision of life and the universe," as Dawkins rightly says. But in comparison with nature, science too must be seen as "recent"—and provisional.

Dawkins, who was born in Nairobi, Kenya, and lived in what is now Malawi until the age of eight, is often asked whether the African landscape shaped his choice of biology as a profession. A child of botanists, Dawkins recalls that his parents were able to identify the names of virtually every plant and flower, and that he and his sister were routinely drilled, from an early age, by a cadre of botanically minded relatives. Nature, under his parents' tutelage, was a veritable botanical garden with classifications provided. As for the wilds of Africa, Dawkins admits the impact was negligible: "Africa was lost on me," he says. A self-described "truant from the fresh air and the virtuous outdoors," Dawkins cared little for "watching wild creatures: my original interest in biology came not from the woods and moors but from books."[86] He speculates that like all members of our species he feels some "atavistic affection" for African landscapes—because Africa was home to our early ancestors—but the impact on him personally? "Not a great deal."[87] It is fascinating to see how Dawkins evaluates his own affective response (or lack thereof) to his childhood landscape through the lens of evolutionary theory. He essentially depersonalizes and generalizes it as something encoded by natural selection. The idea that captured Dawkins's imagination and inspired him to study biology, he recalls, was the concept of organisms as "survival machines," which he absorbed during graduate study with his mentor, Nikolaas Tinbergen. The basic insight "[was] that when you study animal behavior, you're looking at the product of a kind of piece of clockwork machinery"—namely, the gene.[88] Dawkins's early contributions as a scientist utilized mathematical models of animal behavior. Wet biology, in other words, was not his fancy.

My point is not to indict Dawkins for failing to appreciate nature and living organisms as a child (or adult), but to call attention to the way in which his devotion to, and awe of, scientific knowledge—like Dyson's—has marginalized nature in fairly consistent ways throughout his life and work. Dawkins's temperament is typical of a certain type of scientist—or person generally—who feels compelled to solve puzzles. Puzzle-solving is key in some areas of science (think of medical science and genetic research, for example), but as Dawkins and Dyson illustrate so well, there is no necessary correlation between such habits of mind and any concern with the well-being of nature. A preoccupation with solving puzzles, or dissolving mysteries, can indeed undermine and interfere with such concern. Dawkins's constant refrain that scientific reality is supremely magical often involves an explicit comparison between science and what we might broadly call religion—cultural myths, folktales, creation stories. However, a closer look at his account of wonder suggests an implicit contrast between science and *nature* as well. Dawkins therefore takes Blake and other poets to task for misplaced, "mystical" wonder at the natural world. The boy who studied books, not nature, advises children in *The Magic of Reality* to follow his own path, to dissect mysteries and dispel appearances. The rainbow, after all, is not a "proper object" but an "illusion."[89]

This radical privileging of scientific reality puts environmental values on shaky ground. It estranges us from what we experience as real, meaningful, and beautiful. Why attach ourselves to this world of illusion? As Hanni Muerdter grasps in her eloquent musings on wonder that open this chapter, *science* is not the same thing as *nature,* and to study the former is not to experience the latter. Nor is the study of the former necessarily conducive to seeking out or cherishing experiences of the latter. The distinction I am invoking here between science and nature was preserved in nature-study movements for children popular a century ago. It was embodied by the naturalist Louis Agassiz (d. 1873) and his well-known injunction to "study nature, not books." Preserving the child's innate sense of the world as magical and mysterious was central to that agenda. Rachel Carson's *The Sense of Wonder* is a perfect distillation of the nature study philosophy of attaching oneself to nature first—in ways that engage the senses, the emotions, and our daily experience—and seeking scientific facts and explanations of nature secondarily.[90]

I believe this distinction is worth preserving and defending, not just for children but for *all* of us for whom the natural world has meaning and value—those for whom nature confronts us as an external *reality.* This distinction between science and nature also hints at differences between the scientist and the naturalist. The term "naturalist" has an almost quaint ring to it today. In his conversation with Dawkins, we see Attenborough claim the title of naturalist for himself. One may be both scientist and naturalist, but being a naturalist suggests, among other things, a more generalist bent, or an ability to move back and forth between the specialist's account and more immediate—*un*mediated by science—experiences of nature.

Naturalist, in fact, is the title E. O. Wilson adopted for his autobiography. "I became determined at an early age to be a scientist so that I might stay close to the natural world," Wilson writes in the opening paragraphs of *Naturalist.*[91] The next chapter focuses in detail on what I consider to be Wilson's lifelong struggle with two competing ambitions and identities: his identity as a naturalist and nature lover, and his identity as a scientist bent on a transcendent quest to complete all knowledge in a grand and final project of consilience. As with Dawkins, Wilson serves as a touchstone for the new mythmakers who seek to reenchant nature, reconnect humans with the wonder of the natural world, and reinscribe the human story within the story of a numinous universe. Yet, Wilson's reverence for science often makes it difficult for him to articulate the environmental values he otherwise professes and aims to promote. By the same token, I argue that the reverential attitude toward scientific knowledge and knowledge-makers, seen in the new cosmology, may erode wondering appreciation and moral commitment to nature and its inhabitants.

Chapter 3

E. O. Wilson's Ionian Enchantment

A Tale of Two Realities

I admit that the confidence of natural scientists often seems overweening. Science offers the boldest metaphysics of the age. It is a thoroughly human construct, driven by the faith that if we dream, press to discover, explain, and dream again, thereby plunging repeatedly into new terrain, the world will somehow come clearer and we will grasp the true strangeness of the universe. And the strangeness will all prove to be connected and make sense. . . . The loom is the same for both enterprises, for science and for the arts, and there is a general explanation of its origin and nature and thence of the human condition.

—E. O. WILSON, *CONSILIENCE*

In a scene from *Dead Poets Society,* students are instructed in a quantitative method by which they may determine whether or not a given poem is truly great. Their charismatic English teacher, played by Robin Williams, asks a student to read from an authoritative text, *Understanding Poetry,* authored by one J. Evans Pritchard. His classmates diligently take notes on the Pritchard method as the student reads aloud: "One, how artfully has the objective of the poem been rendered, and two, how important is that objective. Question one rates the poem's perfection, question two rates its importance. And once these questions have been answered, determining a poem's greatness becomes a relatively simple matter. . . . As your ability to evaluate poems in this matter grows, so will your enjoyment and understanding of poetry." As the class sets to work graphing poems along the two axes of greatness prescribed by Pritchard, their teacher reveals that he has no intention of instructing students in this absurdly bloodless and quantitative method. "We're not laying pipe," he exclaims, "we're talking about poetry!" At his prompting, the students joyfully rip up Prichard's text, and their souls—and the humanities—are saved for another day.

We may chuckle at the uptight and odious J. Evans Pritchard and his ambition to map and measure literary greatness. But to those who have spent time dissecting the claims of consilience devotees, this fictional scene is too close to reality to be laughed off entirely. In this chapter, I turn to one of the world's best-known biologists and purveyors of scientific wonder: Edward O. Wilson. I approach Wilson's work with roughly the same set of questions in mind with which I interrogated Dawkins's celebration of science: namely, what sort of wonder does his work and worldview express? How, if at all, does it orient us toward reverence and care for the natural world? What does Wilson understand to be the ultimate object(s) of wonder, and what ethical implications follow from these investments? To what extent are Wilson's preferred modes of wonder and enchantment available to non-scientists? I also explore in detail how Wilson's arguments for consilience—his vision of unified knowledge among all the branches of learning—have taken hold within the academy and captured the imagination of some prominent advocates of the new cosmology. As I will argue, there are odd and troubling tensions in Wilson's evolutionary cosmology. The environmental themes of his work—his sense of nature's ultimacy and value—sit uneasily with his emphasis on scientific knowledge and the human mind as the most worthy objects of awe. These tensions are reproduced in the work of new cosmologists who heed his call for an Epic of Evolution that will rival, and ultimately displace, existing religions. Wilson provides a case in point of a general weakness of the mythopoeic enterprise, namely that triumphalist science often makes for poor environmentalism.

A CAREER MARKED BY CONTROVERSY

One of the world's leading experts in entomology, Wilson is perhaps best known as the founder of sociobiology. His publication of *Sociobiology* (1975) touched off a firestorm of controversy that has now become part of the Wilson lore, setting the (often hostile) tone for current debates surrounding sociobiology and its offshoot, evolutionary psychology. Though intended primarily as a treatise on ant societies, the book's final chapter wades into controversial territory as Wilson endeavors to draw conclusions about human behavior and society from his study of insects.[1] *On Human Nature* followed in 1978 and garnered a Pulitzer Prize, the first of two Wilson has received thus far. *On Human Nature* spells out in greater detail many of the arguments he sketches in the final chapter of *Sociobiology*. In 1984, Wilson published *Biophilia*, a memoir-like set of essays illustrating his conviction that humans possess an innate affinity for the natural world. *Consilience* (1998) rekindled old controversies and generated some new ones. He contends that disciplinary knowledge has become fragmented and chaotic, and he predicts the emergence of unified knowledge—ranging broadly across the sciences, social sciences, humanities, and arts—that will bridge all disciplinary gaps. A significant portion of Wilson's later-career publications deals more directly with environmental conservation. One of these, *The Creation* (2006), appeals to Christians to join the cause of saving the planet. Wilson has experimented with fiction as well. To the surprise of many readers, he published his first novel, *Anthill*, in 2010, at the age of 80. In 2012, Wilson embarked on a self-described trilogy of works, designed to resolve three ambitious and essential questions about the human "we": Where do we come from? What are we? Where are we going? Wilson's answers to these questions can be found in *The Social Conquest of Earth* (2012), *The Meaning of Human Existence* (2014), and *Half-Earth* (2016), respectively. A recurring theme of the trilogy is that the best thing "we" could do for the planet would be to eliminate religion.[2]

Many of his endeavors clearly aim to provoke, yet Wilson remains the grand old man of ants with a mischievous twinkle in his eye. Like the ants he studies, he is a tireless and undaunted worker. He is also a gifted and wide-ranging reader and writer who exudes charm and wisdom in lectures and interviews—and more than a little arrogance. Above all he is known to be an outspoken advocate for conservation, even proposing that we set aside as much as half of the planet for preservation and rewilding.[3] There is much to ponder and admire in Wilson's account of "biophilia"—the theory that humans possess an evolutionarily engrained love of, and instinctive attachment to, the natural world. The biophilia hypothesis has helped to reanimate environmental education and nature study initiatives for children and young adults.[4] Wilson, like Dawkins, is actively interested in children's science and nature education, but he often takes a different tack. *Anthill*, Wilson's semi-autobiographical novel about a young boy growing up in Alabama who develops a fascination with the natural world, illustrates well Wilson's occasional advocacy of an *experiential* and *sensory* component of children's nature education.

Wilson has also embraced the role of "naturalist" that Dawkins largely eschews. *The Creation* includes a chapter on "How to Raise a Naturalist" and *Naturalist* is the title of Wilson's autobiography as well. Wilson argues that hands-on, unmediated encounters with living organisms in their natural habitats, *not* "systematic knowledge" and rote learning, go into the making of a child naturalist. "A child's mind is prepared for wonder," he writes. "He is like a primitive adult of long ago, discovering the features of his natural environment for the first time."[5] Wilson's portrait of the child as a primitive endowed by evolution with atavistic wonder is also central to the storyline of *Anthill*. The protagonist, Raphael Cody, is a young boy freed of "mechanical toys" and "turned loose" by his parents to wander forests and streams, like his hunter-gatherer forebears. *Anthill*'s narrator, an ecologist and family friend who mentors young "Raff," instructs the boy that the best way to learn about nature is decidedly "*not by reading*" about it in books. An organism's "full reality" is apprehended through firsthand encounters in natural settings. The "real world," the novel suggests, is manifest in nature's "great living library," not in books.[6]

Anthill's overarching message is explicitly environmental. Though trained in science, Raff grows up to be an environmental lawyer (endowed with an encyclopedic knowledge of ants), who wages a moral and legal battle to protect the countryside of his boyhood. Raff chooses not to pursue a career in science, but he never ceases to be a naturalist. Similar themes emerge in Wilson's late career writings and lectures. Drawing on Rachel Carson's ideas about children's relationship to the natural world, Wilson's lectures indict modern parenting practices that insulate children from the real world of nature.

> The worst thing you can do to a child, in my opinion, is take them on a hike through a botanical garden where there are the names of the trees on the side. Rachel Carson once said, so true, take the child to the seashore, turn her loose with a pail, and tell her to go explore the tidepools. Don't tell her the names of any of these things. Let her find them, let her touch them, let her bring them to you . . . . These squeezed-in lives of children who are taken occasionally to a park like that or a zoo to see the labels is all part of what I like to call—I hope I'm not offending anyone—the "soccer mom syndrome."[7]

Wilson here alludes to an argument in Carson's *Sense of Wonder* (1965), where she advises parents to avoid a stultifying "name game," and to engage children's sensory and emotional responses to nature. The idea that children are primitives reborn, innately predisposed to wonder and curiosity about their natural surroundings, finds support in Wilson's biophilia hypothesis. A (less gene-centered) version of this portrait of the child as a born naturalist was integral to the nature study movement for children in the late nineteenth and early twentieth centuries, and Carson was very much a product of that movement. In some ways, Wilson was as well, as the storyline of *Naturalist* illustrates, though his environmental consciousness was awakened much later in life.

All in all, and notwithstanding his penchant for disenchanting language (*encoding, programming, epigenetic rules, algorithms*) there is something very alluring about Wilson's big ideas. There is also no shortage of critics who fault Wilson for shoddy science, lack of philosophical rigor, or superficial understanding of religion.[8] Yet Wilson is seen by many readers, and certainly by the new cosmologists, as uniquely positioned to *lessen* tensions between science and religion. I find this perception of him surprising, given Wilson's stark portrait of science and religion as rivals and his frequent prediction that religion will eventually be defeated by the superior mythology of scientific materialism. Perhaps what attracts admirers is Wilson's call for "consilient" endeavors—a term that carries a falsely *conciliatory* ring—along with his support of mythopoeic science, which may signal the possibility of an aesthetically satisfying worldview that *combines* scientific and religious insights. In other words, many who wish to see constructive engagement of science and religion, or whose sense of religiousness is centered on the natural world, may perceive Wilson's work as more in tune with their values and experiences than it actually is.

The impression of Wilson as occupying or advocating a middle way between science and religion was likely bolstered by the publication of *The Creation*. The book's title, and its dialogue between Wilson and an imagined Baptist minister, suggest an openness to science and religion working together to save the planet. Yet, however much Wilson's ideas about evolution have recently undergone revision (he now supports a form of group selection),[9] his disdain for religion has never wavered. Wilson now seems alarmed and even chastened by the onset of the so-called Anthropocene. But even while he appears to perceive something worrisome about godlike portraits of the human enshrined in some notions of the Anthropocene—a portrait that Wilson himself has often advocated—he remains steadfast in his appraisal of science as salvific and religion as the evil obstacle to reality. For example, *The Meaning of Human Existence* (2014) continues his lifelong condemnation of religion. "The great religions," he writes, "are sources of ceaseless and unnecessary suffering. They are impediments to the grasp of reality needed to solve most social problems in the real world."[10] Despite such commentary, Wilson's popularity has not waned in religion and ecology, and religion and science circles. Indeed, he is often credited as a chief architect and evangelist of the Epic of Evolution. To understand his appeal to seekers of a new cosmology, we must acquaint ourselves with the metaphysical ambitions that have fueled Wilson's career.

EVOLUTIONARY EVANGELISM AND THE DREAM OF CONSILIENCE

Scientists who see that they are in some sense neighbours of religion are sometimes moved, not to an exploration of shared relations and interests, but to the hope of loot and plunder.

—MARY MIDGLEY, *EVOLUTION AS A RELIGION*

The phrase "epic of evolution" appears to have been coined by Wilson in 1978.[11] For many readers, Wilson seems to offer a virtually comprehensive evolutionary cosmology with profound ethical significance and mythic appeal. The Epic of Evolution, which Wilson helped to launch, is heralded as "more than science."

> It is science translated into a story that gives meaning, inspiration and purpose to our lives. . . . As a grand cultural narrative, it is like a myth that informs us of our place and purpose in the cosmos. It tells how the 13.8 billion year-old universe has come to know itself through the consciousness of human beings. For a growing number of people, the Epic of Evolution provides an interpretation of the scientific cosmology that is culturally and personally meaningful. This cosmology gives people reason to celebrate their place and purpose in the evolving universe. It also provides a useful map with which to navigate into the future.[12]

Wilson makes no secret of the way in which his youthful conversion to science filled a void left by his gathering doubts about the Southern Baptist teachings of his childhood: evolution, he came to realize, was "the most important revelation of all!"[13] This experience seems to have left him with a deeply rooted sense of science and religion as necessarily *competing* worldviews. Religious longing permeates Wilson's vision of consilience. Some scholars identify particular parallels between his scientific methodology and worldview and Southern Baptist approaches to religious knowledge in which "truth is discovered rationally by a logical ordering of Biblical texts."[14] Consilience—Wilson's dream of a grand unification of all knowledge—is integral to some versions of the new cosmology because a unified body of knowledge now allegedly makes it possible to tell the story of our universe in an integrated and coherent fashion. The Epic of Evolution can be seen as a narrative product of the unification metaphysics of consilience and its "tormenting desire for unity."[15]

The term consilience originated in the nineteenth century with philosopher and scientist William Whewell (who also coined the word "scientist" in 1834). Whewell defined consilience as a kind of "jumping together" of disparate facts and different bodies of knowledge.[16] Critics object, however, that Wilson's agenda of explaining everything—including various domains of the arts and humanities, as well as religion and ethics—with reference to a few scientific laws and "one class of explanation"[17] is not consilience in Whewell's sense, but crass reductionism. Consilience, in this view, is a scientist's attempt to colonize all other disciplines. In its original meaning, consilience described the convergence of independent lines of evidence, pointing to a similar conclusion. Whewell's vision for consilience, one critic observes, is not Wilson's "one great fundamental truth but a network of total connectivity, which could be travelled in a dizzying array of directions."[18] This dizzying array is precisely what Wilson wants to bring under control. Put differently, Wilson seems not so much to be identifying fruitful areas of coherence among autonomous disciplines as seeking to collapse them all—religion and ethics included—into science. As Stephen Jay Gould observes, "Wilson revives Whewell's word to describe the most powerful putative result of reductionism's triumph: the simplification and gathering together of vast ranges of phenomena by their successive subsumption under laws governing constituent parts, right down to the physics of basic constituents."[19] On the subject of religion and ethics, Wilson's ultimate objective is to displace religion—science's "chief competitor"—with an "alternative mythology" provided solely by scientific materialism.[20] "The mythopoeic drive," he predicts, "can be harnessed to learning and the rational search for human progress if we finally concede that scientific materialism is itself a mythology defined in the noble sense." From there, religion will be thoroughly explained as a "product of the brain's evolution," and its power will cease "forever."[21] More accurately, its power will be transferred to science.

Wilson's account of consilience is replete with allusions to feverish, tantalizing dreams and intoxicating spells; consilience is an all-consuming vision quest, a "Magellanic voyage that eventually encircles the whole of reality."[22] Wilson feels a powerful "Ionian Enchantment"[23] with structures of human knowledge, over and above the natural world that the scientific mind "dissects." Ionian Enchantment consists of a "great enchanting goal of the unification of knowledge"[24] and a "conviction, far deeper than a mere working proposition, that the world is orderly and can be explained by a small number of natural laws."[25] This project has driven much of modern physics, he notes, but "the spell of the Enchantment extends to other fields of science as well, and in the minds of a few it reaches beyond into the social sciences, and still further . . . to touch the humanities."[26] Wilson is aware that some will object to his "unification metaphysics"—particularly philosophers, whom he expects to charge him with "*conflation, simplism, ontological reductionism, scientism,* and other sins made official by the hissing suffix." To all of these charges, Wilson happily pleads "guilty, guilty, guilty."[27] He acknowledges, too, the hubris of his project: there is a "whiff of brimstone in the consilient world view and a seeming touch of Faust."[28] Indeed, Wilson, unlike Dawkins, readily concedes that this comprehensive scientific perspective functions as religion, a "transcendental worldview," and "the light and way" for scientific materialists.

So what, exactly, is consilience? Is it a method? A metaphysics? A dream? It is not always easy to answer with precision, even for Wilson. Passages of *Consilience* seem to call for interdisciplinary exchange among equal partners: "Science is free and the arts are free . . . the two domains, despite the similarities in their creative spirit, have radically different goals and methods."[29] Elsewhere, consilience proffers a *single* method as not only the correct method, but the one that will effect a vertical integration of the disciplines: "Scholars in the humanities should lift the anathema placed on reductionism," Wilson urges.[30] At other times consilience clearly operates as a metaphysics, or something more elusive—something mirage-like, always just beyond the scientist's reach. All scientists, Wilson likes to say, are children of Tantalus, forever frustrated but undaunted in their quest.[31] One formulation of consilience defines its "central idea" as consisting in the belief that "all tangible phenomena, from the birth of stars to the workings of social institutions, are based on material processes that are ultimately reducible, however long and tortuous the sequences, to the laws of physics."[32]

But what does "based on" material processes mean? Evolutionary biologist H. Allen Orr brings against *Consilience* the charge of conflation (to which, of course, Wilson preemptively pleads guilty). Orr discerns two meanings of consilience in Wilson's writing—ontological and epistemic—and argues that Wilson fails, at crucial moments, to distinguish them.[33] For example, it is not clear whether Wilson is pointing out that all entities share a common material substratum (everything in some sense is *made* of atoms) or whether (or additionally) he is claiming that knowledge of, say, atomic or subatomic particles actually explains higher-level entities such as human beings and their behavior. Is he arguing that everything *is* ultimately physics or that physics ultimately explains everything? We could easily assert the former without saying anything particularly interesting or useful. Wilson appears to endorse the latter when he argues that there is "*intrinsically only one class of explanation.*"[34] The key to articulating one class of explanation that includes even sociological phenomena lies in a more complete understanding of the human brain, Wilson believes. All of culture, he argues, is a kind of "communal mind" and "each mind in turn is the product of a genetically structured human brain."[35] Because genes and epigenetic laws shape the brain, evolutionary biology is the key discipline, providing a bridge, or hinge, between the physical sciences, on the one hand, and the social sciences and humanities, on the other. Wilson regards physics as the exemplary science because of its enviable lawlike structure. However, evolutionary biology is the vital link in the consilient chain; moreover, evolution lends itself to a narrative ("epic") structure, and provides rich material for mythmaking. Physics may be the most elegant discipline but evolutionary biology (and offshoots like sociobiology) is where the action is, in terms of consilient unification.

Consilience entails that all enterprises of culture—a huge category—will eventually be explained when we attain complete knowledge of the human brain. Wilson lauds the logical positivists of the early twentieth century who similarly dreamed of grand unification, and he asserts that their program failed owing to their ignorance of how the brain works. For Wilson, "everything that we know and can ever know about existence is created [in our brains]."[36] That knowledge creation takes place in our brains seems hardly revelatory. But Wilson makes the strong claim that we can transform all the disciplines—make them more scientific—by understanding the physiology of the brain and "epigenetic rules" of human cognition. All human activity, he believes, is the product of such epigenetic rules, the "inherited regularities of mental development that compose human nature" and are reinforced by culture.[37]

Epigenetic rules bias cultural evolution in certain directions, though their force is typically rather weak. Examples of epigenetic rules he provides—there are fewer than one would wish—include near-universal, biologically rooted aversion to snakes (mythologized as serpents in many cultures) and incest taboos (often dramatized artistically, as in the myth of Oedipus). The incest example illustrates Wilson's belief that ethical precepts ultimately boil down to scientific facts about the world: widespread condemnation of incest makes good biological sense because the offspring of incestuous pairings are more likely to show genetic abnormalities. Accordingly, evolution has programmed us—our brains—to find this practice repulsive. Other moral laws, Wilson believes, will similarly be shown to have survival value and thus be explicable in terms of evolutionary mechanisms and features of our physical environment.

Wilson has faith that understanding the brain and the rules that govern it might shed light on numerous archetypes of cultural production, allowing us to grasp their evolutionary origin and function. That is, consilient knowledge, including knowledge of the brain itself, will eventually reveal laws at work behind humans' (recurring or enduring) preferences for certain forms of art or literature. "Works of enduring value," he argues, "are those truest to these [evolutionary] origins. It follows that even the greatest works of art might be understood fundamentally with knowledge of the biologically evolved epigenetic rules."[38] Is Wilson claiming that understanding the brain can help resolve debates about the quality, the *aesthetic worth*, of these expressions? Or is he making the more modest, empirical (though perhaps circular)[39] observation that works of art that conform to epigenetic rules are those that tend to endure? The former, bolder assertion seems to follow from Wilson's claim that "quality" in the arts is measured by "the precision of their adherence to human nature. To an overwhelming degree that is what we mean when we speak of the true and beautiful in the arts."[40]

Consilience, as a project that unites and completes all knowledge, is an odd sort of dream in that its realization would signal the end of any fruitful, new lines of inquiry, and thus an end to wonder. As R. W. Hepburn notes, "the situation [for wonder] is like a God-of-the-Gaps theology, increasingly threatened as the gaps in knowledge are filled."[41] Perhaps understandably, Wilson at times seems ambivalent about the realization of his project. He often presents consilience as an arduous but worthwhile endeavor—"a very difficult task"—but something that, like building spaceships or perfecting heart surgery, is undertaken for humanity's good.[42] At times he characterizes consilience as an audacious trespass of mythic proportions—a holy grail, an "Icarian" or "Promethean" project so ambitious that modest success may be the best we can ever hope for. As consilient knowledge advances toward the social sciences and humanities, it encounters its most difficult and most thrilling terrain. "This uncertain conjunction of the disciplines has mythic elements that would have pleased the ancient Greeks: treacherous road, heroic journey, secret instructions that lead us home."[43] At still other times, he claims merely to be documenting an already well-developed trend, and suggesting the form it will logically take in the future. "What I've done is simply point out what the trends are in the increasing [blending] of the scientific disciplines," he remarks in one interview. "We've seen everything that we conventionally call biology and the natural sciences now linked with a webwork of cause-and-effect explanation running from particle physics all the way to ecosystem studies and the brain sciences. . . . Consilience, then, is simply an observation that this is what is happening, and a projection into the future that this will continue. . . . Frankly I'm rather surprised that this idea—or shall we say prophecy or projection—has met so much resistance."[44] These statements are disingenuous, at best. Wilson's lifelong love of controversy, his penchant for portraying himself as an aggrieved but undaunted risk-taker, suggest that anything less than strong resistance to his ideas would disappoint him enormously. The unpopularity of an idea, he believes, is often an indication of its accuracy and importance.[45]

That Wilson's dream is in some sense being enacted is one of the things that concerns me. And it should concern many of us, I believe, particularly because this vision is championed in new cosmology circles, and well beyond. With this in mind, I turn to a discussion of the spread of consilient ideas in the academy at large, in order illustrate what these mythmakers are advocating when they advocate consilience. These developments in the academy, I contend, are of a piece with the modern discourse on scientific wonder I have outlined, particularly as it pertains to the primacy of scientific *reality*. Keep in mind that consilience is not simply a project of uniting the sciences (a daunting enough task, as philosophers of science will attest) but of unifying *all forms and areas of human knowledge and experience* under the banner of science. Let us not disappoint Wilson: resistance to this project is in order.

CONSILIENCE IN THE ACADEMY: CHAOS AND ENVY AMONG THE DISCIPLINES?

Evolutionary thinking is, at present, an aggressively expansive species within the academic world, a kind of emergent Homo sapiens *outcompeting the old-school Neanderthals across a wide swath of intellectual territory. Having colonized the social sciences . . . it has now set its sights on the humanities, the last area of resistance. To subdue it would mean realizing E. O. Wilson's dream of "consilience. . ."*

—WILLIAM DERESIEWICZ, "ADAPTATION: ON LITERARY DARWINISM"

In education the search for consilience is the way to renew the crumbling structure of the liberal arts. During the past thirty years the ideal of the unity of learning, which the Renaissance and Enlightenment bequeathed to us, has been largely abandoned. With rare exceptions American universities and colleges have dissolved their curriculum into a slurry of minor disciplines and specialized courses. . . . Win or lose, true reform will aim at the consilience of science with the social sciences and humanities in scholarship and teaching.

—E. O. WILSON, *CONSILIENCE*

Consilience is not simply (though sometimes it is) an argument for a more creative or lively exchange between the sciences and humanities. Wilson's more controversial claim is that the sciences will ultimately absorb territory currently occupied, and inadequately explained, by the humanities. Wilson oscillates between these possible agendas. The ambiguity of Wilson's claims often works to his advantage, particularly when objections are raised by critics—like myself—who otherwise welcome greater interdisciplinary dialogue. "Consilience is a hazy target seen in a seductive soft focus," Orr observes, "and anyone airing doubts about its stronger claims tends to get greeted by indignant defenses of its weaker aspects ('Surely you don't think economists can ignore the environment?')"[46] Wilson claims that consilience need not be *led* by scientists[47] nor should consilience be understood ("yet") as itself a science. Rather, the quest for consilience should adhere to methods "developed in the natural sciences."[48] Like Dawkins, he suggests that anyone can participate in the grand project, provided certain norms of conduct are observed. For Wilson, the motivation for participating is clear: "The strongest appeal of consilience is in the prospect of intellectual adventure and, given even modest success, the value of understanding the human condition with a higher degree of certainty."[49]

By way of illustrating consilient "interdisciplinarity"—and how intimately it connects with claims about ultimate truth, reality, and wonder—I want to consider two examples of consilient engagement with science. The first comes from philosophy, and the second—a more sustained discussion—is drawn from literary studies.[50] Questions about the proper relationship between the sciences and other disciplines link up in interesting ways with an inquiry into the proper role of wonder in the scientific enterprise, as I hope to show. If the sciences allow us to apprehend and do things with *reality*, and if reality is what ought to command wonder above all else (as some scientists argue), then a proper (re)ordering of the disciplines will usher in not only greater and more accurate knowledge but maximal wonder as well. Peculiar as it may sound, this is the overarching message of Wilson's work, and a similar message is discernible in many who follow his lead.

Scientists who write about wonder often concur on the superiority of scientific forms of wonder to all other varieties. "There is a widespread belief, held to be common sense, that one great virtue of science and mechanistic analysis is that it gets to what is real or to reality itself and that it provides the only concrete descriptions and explanations we can have."[51] Lived experience and the wonder it generates and sustains is regarded as inferior or suspect. Science lifts the veil on these suspect forms and offers us the real thing. If this assessment of reality and wonder holds, then it may also suggest that disciplines that do not grant access to ultimate reality (thus conceived) are rightly subordinate to science. On this account, "those privileging literary, philosophical, or religious manners of understanding are, at best, engaged in abstract imaginings and, at worst, ideological propaganda."[52] The work of philosopher Marie George, discussed briefly in chapter 2, provides a case in point.[53] Her understanding of the relationship between science and other disciplines—notably philosophy—and her arguments about wonder in science closely resemble Wilson's consilient account.

George argues that the sciences and philosophy are both uniquely motivated by self-eradicating wonder, where wonder ceases when solutions to puzzles are located: both "focus their wonder upon questions where at least some evidence is present, for they seek verifiable explanations; and when they discover them, they cease to wonder."[54] But while they share this initial impulse, George claims, science and philosophy part ways when it comes to seeking general (as opposed to particular) explanations, and in the extent to which each seeks measurable results (quantitative answers). George contends that science pursues, and wonders at, more particular and detailed questions than philosophy, though she believes the "best scientists" (whatever that means) tend to set their sights on "the very general questions."[55] Regarding quantitative analysis, she asserts that one cannot really be considered a scientist, and cannot experience true scientific wonder, if one does not respond with wonder to *quantitative* relations. Philosophers, in contrast to scientists, cease to wonder about certain matters when it becomes apparent that they can "only be known in a quantitative way," for "if they were really interested, they would learn the mathematics needed to deal with such matters."[56] This remarkable—and remarkably condescending—characterization of the work of nonscientists is strongly resonant of Wilson's consilience.

Consilience assumes that what can be grasped dimly by one discipline can be better known—known with greater precision and certainty—by science. A similar assumption is evident in George's odd assertion that the philosopher, unlike the scientist, proceeds no further when confronted with the need for quantitative approaches to the problem that interested her. (Neither George nor Wilson seriously entertains the idea that the scientist's tools and methods may be ill suited to the question that interests the philosopher, or the humanist generally.) Scientists are familiar with the claim—sometimes made in jest but often in earnest—that researchers in fields like biology suffer from "physics envy" in their longing for the explicit mathematical models of the physical sciences. Dawkins, for example, invokes with caustic humor what he terms "Dawkins' Law of the Conservation of Difficulty," which illustrates how "obscurantism in an academic subject expands to fill the vacuum of its intrinsic simplicity."[57] Physics, by contrast, is "genuinely difficult" and "profound." Researchers in all "other" fields—not just *nonphysicist* scientists but all other fields—manifest physics envy in their strenuous but transparent efforts to create the appearance of profundity in their disciplines through the addition of meaningless jargon, Dawkins contends, when in fact "their subject is actually rather easy and shallow."[58] Wilson is more diplomatic: "biologists, it has been said, suffer from physics envy."[59] They struggle to "build physicslike models" but are frustrated by their failure to match these with messy realities.[60]

Wilson here limits his diagnosis of physics envy to his own profession, but he elsewhere suggests that all disciplines beyond the hard sciences are inherently fuzzy and in need of scientific clarity. Affirming George's portrait of philosophers as would-be scientists who balk at the math, Wilson assigns consilience the task of "turning as much philosophy as possible into science." Philosophy's purview is "the contemplation of the unknown"—a "shrinking dominion."[61] Wilson portrays philosophy as faint-hearted proto-science, and essentially regards as "filler" anything that science has not yet incorporated. "We are encouraged to view philosophy as a temporary measure, a sort of heuristic scaffolding to be done away with as soon as possible."[62] In his idiosyncratic way, Wilson is actually paying philosophy his highest *compliment* by suggesting its proximity to science, even while close proximity means imminent elimination as the philosopher's territory is ceded.[63]

Science courageously shines a bright light into dark corners, turning unknowns into knowns, while philosophy hesitates in the dimly lit antechamber to genuine science. And in Wilson's view, what is true of philosophy holds even more for *all* other disciplines that lack philosophy's redeeming (but fatal) family resemblance to science.

Allusions to shrinking dominions and crumbling structures of the humanities prompt critics to characterize consilience as harboring a colonizing agenda. While scholars sympathetic to Wilson's project (and Wilson himself) aver that consilience simply points the way to much-needed compatibility between the humanities and explanations in the hard sciences, consilience is far more ambitious than even Wilson generally lets on.[64] Sociological questions, for example, might be informed by behavioral sciences or neuroscience, but it would be prohibitively difficult to explain sociological phenomena in terms of mathematico-physical laws. Even where such laws can be specified for, say, biology or anthropology, the usefulness of constructing these links back to the hard sciences is highly questionable. Resulting explanations would be hopelessly general and uninformative for, as Mary Midgley observes, the more remote the cause, the *less* explanatory force it has. Otherwise, the "big bang would be the only true explanation of everything, and we all ought to be doing astro-physics" in lieu of our present disciplines.[65] While some philosophers embrace the more modest, though still ambitious, project of uniting the sciences, the unity of *all* knowledge is rightly regarded as impractical if not impossible (and to some, undesirable, in any case).[66] Wilson's bold estimation that the unity of science is virtually accomplished—"it has been tested in acid baths of experiment and logic and enjoyed repeated vindication"[67]— is strongly disputed by many scholars. Philosopher of science Philip Kitcher, by no means the staunchest opponent of unity of science movements, argues that in terms of a hierarchy of theories reducible to physics, "the Unity of Science Movement is dead."[68] Wilson does not acknowledge, or is unaware that even among those who consider unity in science achievable, the radical move to include "sociology, psychology, or the humanities is often resisted."[69]

Yet, when consilience encounters resistance of any sort, its advocates often treat resistance as a failure of nerve, or a temporary stumbling block resulting from an as-yet "incomplete scientific ontology."[70] Or perhaps, as religion scholar Edward Slingerland suggests, humanists' wariness of consilience is thinly disguised *ressentiment,* the "envy-driven rigidity that continues to stand in the way of vertical integration."[71] (This ready diagnosis of disciplinary *envy* should sound familiar by now.) Slingerland is co-editor of *Creating Consilience* (2012), a project that represents a "second wave" of consilience.[72] In Slingerland's diagnosis, the humanities know themselves to be a "stagnant lagoon cut off from a great fertile ocean of scientific innovation and progress."[73] He ventures that resentment "is probably intensified by humanists' realization, at some level, that they are all constantly taking advantage of and benefiting from the advances made possible by the natural sciences, as they check into their state-of-the-art university hospitals, fly on airplanes, and type their antiscience rants on slick laptops."[74] This sort of sneering invective is, unfortunately, standard fare in academic debates over the merits of consilience, and it does little to foster good will among would-be collaborators.

For some proselytizers of consilience, virtually any contribution science can make is assumed to be an "advance." Wilson's project attracts a number of supporters in literary theory who are eager to see evolutionary biology (and evolutionary psychology, neuroscience, and related fields) bring order to chaotic, moribund humanities research. *Consilience* is the foundational text for many in this movement.

CONSILIENCE IN DARWINIAN LITERARY CRITICISM

As someone who has lamented the lack of engagement with evolutionary science in my own field, I see nothing especially nefarious in Wilson's assertion that nonscience disciplines have "paid little attention to biology" and might benefit from doing so.[75] Exactly how much and in what ways they stand to benefit are important questions, and different disciplines will have different answers. It seems reasonable that scholars in nonscience disciplines should have some say in how science is relevant to what they deem important and interesting. Evolutionary biology's significance for some fields of study is not obvious, and Wilson's examples of such benefits are not always compelling. Take his biophilia-informed analysis of Milton's botanical imagery in *Paradise Lost*. Milton's portrait of Eden, Wilson concludes, shows a "fine sense of biophilia, the innate pleasure from living abundance and diversity, particularly as manifested by the human impulse to imitate Nature with gardens." Milton summons enduring archetypes "of a kind . . . innate to the human mental process."[76] In other words, Milton succeeds because he draws on natural imagery, and humans are wired by evolution to respond favorably to greenery and botanical displays, particularly flowering plants which were resource signals (indicating the likely presence of food) for our ancestors.

Archetypes discerned in literature or art may well be *compatible* with an evolutionary account without conferring much explanatory or interpretive power, as Wilson's example illustrates. Literature and art, after all, are not animated by a search for universal laws and ubiquitous patterns in human nature. At times, the issue is simply one of scale—"whether the scale of features to which evolutionary approaches allow us to attend is well suited to the scale of the questions we would like to ask about literary objects."[77] Tracing artistic or literary production back to species-wide evolutionary needs and selection pressures is methodologically inadequate to account for the variability and complexity of human artistic expression. Nevertheless, the task of locating archetypes and patterns of human nature in literature has caught on in the wake of Wilson's call for consilient law and order.

Since about the mid-nineties, books have appeared with titles like *Madame Bovary's Ovaries*, *The Literary Animal*, and *On the Origin of Stories*.[78] Frustrated with literary theory's often emphatic disavowal of human nature, Darwinian critics contend that much of academic criticism remains wedded to blank-slate theories and inordinate stress on the local and particular, while neglecting common capacities and species-wide preferences.[79] Biologist have gotten into the game. *The Literary Animal*, for example, is edited by evolutionary biologist David Sloan Wilson and his protégé Jonathan Gottschall—a literary critic known for putting readers in MRI machines and swabbing their saliva for hormone analysis. *The Literary Animal* commences with a triumphalist foreword by E. O. Wilson that applauds these Darwinian critics as an intrepid minority "embattled, even scorned, by tenured constructivists" scrambling to preserve the status quo of "confusion" in literary studies.[80] Wilson reiterates his claim that success in the consilient venture lies in a more complete understanding of the mind. The collection features such luminaries as Ian McEwan, who says complimentary things about Wilson and riffs on the universality of human nature as revealed in both literature and biological science.[81]

Literary Darwinism is easy to caricature, and given the sometimes hostile and patronizing tone of its proponents, the temptation to do so is understandable. Orr humorously observes that applying evolution to literature and art might yield such non-insights as: "most love poems won't be addressed to one's sister (incest avoidance is possibly genetic)" or that "painters won't use pigments that radiate solely in the ultraviolet and infrared (invisible to us)."[82] And how much mileage is gained from observing that *Pride and Prejudice*—the veritable fruitfly of literary Darwinist experiments—is a novel about mate selection? The problem with using evolutionary biology to explain all manner of cultural patterns and productions is not that biological explanations are wrong, necessarily, but that they are too sweeping or trivial to be generative, critics contend.

There is, however, a greater diversity of approaches, in literary Darwinism (or what is called "biocultural critique" or "evocriticism") than these criticisms may suggest.[83] Some Darwinian critics analyze human behaviors that range widely across mate selection, jealousy, altruism, social hierarchy, adultery, maternal love, friendship, the desire for group membership and prestige. Many approach particular works of literature as products of a human mind that evolved in adaptive relationship to its physical environment. They seek, in other words, to construct a sequence of causal links between the mind as a product of natural selection and the particular qualities of a given work. Once scientifically grounded, "literary studies would henceforth involve the gradual accumulation of objectively verifiable knowledge."[84] Given its ubiquity, storytelling likely evolved to solve adaptive problems in our ancestral past. "We like to read and write novels, say, because our very distant ancestors liked to tell stories, and their telling stories provided some sort of advantage for their survival. So their storytelling genes were passed on to their descendants and, like snake-fearing and child-loving genes, are still with us today."[85] Some, like Brian Boyd, believe that arts generally—music, dance, visual arts—might be explained as products of sexual selection, fitness displays aimed at attracting mates (a suggestion once made by Darwin himself). Storytelling and art may be forms of cognitive play. They might help to train and sharpen our minds—instilling empathy, facilitating development of a theory of mind, social learning and cooperation, or enhancing such abilities as pattern recognition. If excellence in the arts confers status to the artist (as seems plausible), then perhaps art is an esteem-seeking activity that draws attention to dominant individuals and increases their (and their progeny's) chances of survival.[86] Some literary Darwinists speculate that evolution designed human brains to have something like story "modules"—neural machinery dedicated to storytelling. Indeed, this emphasis on the human drive to create narrative coherence has particular resonance for Epic of Evolution advocates in the fields of religion and ethics, where evolution provides both the source and subject matter (or plot) of the storyline.

Do these disciplinary liaisons with science put humanities on equal footing? Advocates deny that consilient integration entails that "literary scholars drop their books and become quantum physicists,"[87] and Wilson, we have seen, proclaims the arts and humanities free and autonomous. But we have also seen that philosophy seems imperiled by its consilient relationship with science. Does literature fare any better? Critics of literary Darwinists charge them with pandering to an increasingly utilitarian and scientistic trend in society (and in universities). Rather than a "two-way street" between sciences and humanities, critics discern an "often pedantic tone and the unmistakable, unapologetic imbalance of power, evident each time it boils down to which side holds the knowledge key."[88]

This is not surprising, given that consilience seeks to locate only "one class of explanation" among all forms of knowing. In his analysis of Milton's archetypes, for example, Wilson proceeds from a discussion of how science might facilitate understanding the creative *process* (say, brain imaging of exceptionally gifted artists) to a claim that science can suggest which artistic *products* have greatest value.[89] Should scientific approaches supersede traditional interpretive methods, on the grounds that science provides greater precision and objectivity in evaluating works of art? Joseph Carroll, a pioneer of Darwinian criticism, concedes that "many of the Darwinists do not regard their approach as just one of many potentially fruitful approaches to literature." Rather,

> [t]hey believe that evolutionary research provides a comprehensive, empirically sound, and scientifically progressive framework for the study of literature. Accordingly, they believe that biocultural critique can and should ultimately subsume all other possible approaches to literary study. Most literary Darwinists refer approvingly to sociobiologist Edward O. Wilson's concept of "consilience": the unity of knowledge (1998). Like Wilson, they regard evolutionary biology as the pivotal discipline uniting the physical sciences, the social sciences, and the humanities.[90]

The problem is not that science weighs in on the humanist's subject matter, but that once a scientific account exists, other approaches are demoted or rejected as having nothing "real" to offer.[91]

Yet, literary Darwinism displays many of the weaknesses of its parent discipline, evolutionary psychology, including "armchair speculation, blithe conjecture and bald assertion."[92] Like evolutionary psychology, literary Darwinism is generally past-oriented: it assumes that human behavior can be understood as a response to the Pleistocene environment in which our brains evolved (2.5 million to 12,000 years ago) and attempts to understand how our minds adapted to the environment of a hunter-gatherer past. "Our modern skulls house a stone-age mind," in the famous phrase of evolutionary psychologists.[93] The evolved circuits of the human brain

> were not designed to solve the day-to-day problems of a modern American—they were designed to solve the day-to-day problems of our hunter-gatherer ancestors. These stone age priorities produced a brain far better at solving some problems than others. . . . In many cases, our brains are *better* at solving the kinds of problems our ancestors faced on the African savannahs than they are at solving the more familiar tasks we face in a college classroom or a modern city.[94]

But if this is true, then how competent are our caveman brains at cracking the problem of consilience—uniting all knowledge into a seamless whole? While our ancestors surely lived in accordance with some sort of local cosmology, it is hard to imagine that locating final or all-comprehensive theories, or integrating complex branches of knowledge, was an urgent priority for them, even if (as Wilson believes) it is a pressing and all-consuming quest for humans today. To posit the human brain—an adaptive organ shaped by evolution for particular ends—as an entity capable of the "boundless percipience" required to complete consilience, and to penetrate its *own* mysterious workings, seems "downright unbiological."[95] A more *biological* account might suggest that boundaries we discern between the traditional disciplines mark "natural stress lines between our domains of cognitive competence."[96] Disciplinary boundaries may reflect actual limitations or constraints imposed by our contingent evolutionary path. On occasion, Wilson concedes that comprehensive understanding of nature "comes very hard" to us. "Reality was not constructed to be easily grasped by the human mind. . . . Our species and its ways of thinking are a product of evolution, not the purpose of evolution."[97] The brain is a "machine assembled not to understand itself, but to survive."[98] In light of these and other challenges, the claim that consilience infuses the disciplines with greater scientific rigor and precision looks suspect. But Wilson and his disciples press on.

To see how the foregoing discussion connects with concerns about the constitution of *reality* and *authentic wonder* in the worldview of consilient metaphysics, consider the following claims that emerge from this worldview. One path to moving the humanities "closer" to the sciences is by applying scientific frameworks like reproductive fitness to works of art and literature, or to the study of religion and ethics. A second consists in taking the scientific account of evolution and putting it into narrative or poetic *form*. In the first move, science proffers new and better (more accurate, measurable) insights or methods for "crumbling" disciplines. In the second move, science provides material for new and better (truer, more compelling) *stories*—a new narrative or myth, as with the new cosmology. Wilson and some of his followers believe that consilience accomplishes both of these things and more. It encompasses both method and metaphysics—metaphysics in the sense that consilience reveals and directly responds to humans' need for an overarching cosmology and narrative coherence. Either way, science occupies a privileged position. In the former case, it sets its sights on subsuming other approaches; in the latter, science determines what is most "real" and then packages it in literary, poetic form that meets the requirements of the brain's storytelling "modules."[99] Should scientists with the requisite storytelling talents be in short supply, as they often are, science dictates its truths to the arts and humanities and delegates to them the task of dispensing it with broad poetic appeal, as with the Epic of Evolution. The humanities thus earn their keep by serving science, by embellishing its material with poetry, art, or other forms of creative expression. Wilson explains this preferred arrangement to a rapt and admiring Connie Barlow in an interview recorded in Barlow's *Green Space, Green Time* (1997):

> So what we must have is poetry within the scientific, physical worldview. That means we need the humanities. The humanities could in effect continue to do their thing, but they would have vastly richer material to work with—grander themes—because the real world, the universe—from black holes to the origin of consciousness—offers far more complex and grander themes than does traditional theology.[100]

Curiously, Wilson's assumption appears to be that the humanities have until now derived material from theology—an indication, perhaps, of his limited exposure to both the humanities and theology.[101]

Consilience, as a quest for reality, is also the pursuit of higher forms of wonder, of what is genuinely "grand." This quest places science in a slot that Wilson vaguely assumes to have been occupied by something like "theology." Elsewhere, Wilson insists that transitioning to a new science-based mythology can occur in an open and honest fashion and without dogmatic appeal to authority. We need merely to cultivate greater *engagement* between the sciences and the humanities. Oddly, by way of suggesting what this might look like, he quotes biologist J. B. S. Haldane's arrogant assertion that the sciences are "vastly more stimulating" than, say, the classics. That this is not widely recognized by the public is partly the fault of scientists who fail to put their "more awesome" material into literary form that mimics "the classics."[102] Here again we see an arrangement whereby the sciences deliver superior content in a format resembling what Wilson takes the humanities to consist of (i.e., storytelling). The humanities' chief virtue is their potential to steer a larger audience toward science and its wonders.

How would this partitioning of reality understand what we might quaintly refer to as *nature* (distinct from "black holes" or "consciousness")? How would it articulate an *ethics* of nature? I contend that Wilson and his followers cannot convincingly derive from these assertions about the nature of reality a robust environmentalism that genuinely values nature as a legitimate source of anything real or wondrous. Wilson, for his part, often seems pulled in two directions, caught between celebrating *nature's* ultimacy—direct experience of nature as a reservoir of wonder and profound solace—and exalting a scientific reality that is "far more awesome" than anything else we can know or experience. Put differently, Wilson's project of consilience cannot get him to his ethic of biophilia, or any other environmental ethic worth having.

CONSILIENT WONDER AND REALITY CENSORSHIP

Wilson insists that the current state of fragmented and chaotic knowledge does not reflect reality—though how we can ascertain this is unclear, since reality, as he concedes, is not constructed so as to be grasped by the human brain. Our current disciplinary structures, he believes, are merely an artifact of the haphazard growth of scholarship, a kind of academic sprawl.[103] As with a sprawling metropolis, if we could go back in time and construct the disciplines afresh, knowing what we know now, they would look very different and function more efficiently. Wilson asserts that one class of explanation exists ("intrinsically") *in nature itself.*[104] In competition with disorderly ideas, order "always wins because—simply—that is the way the real world works."[105] The "communal mind" of science "has gained the power to map external reality far beyond the reach of a single mind."[106]

Those promoting the superior charms of scientific wonder often subscribe to some version of what Neil Evernden calls "reality-censorship," wherein human-level perceptions of and encounters with the world are demoted to unreality.[107] We have seen this at work in Dawkins's quest to enlighten children and adults. Consilience advocates engage in it as well, arguing that literature, art, religion, and ethics are all products of our evolutionary history, adaptive solutions to recurrent evolutionary problems. Understanding them as evolutionary products (or by-products) does not diminish their meaning and appeal, the reassuring argument generally goes. But consilience advocates equivocate here. In order to attract nonscientists to their project, they offer ready assurances of the enduring value of "other ways" of approaching and experiencing the world. But in order to claim that an infusion of science necessarily constitutes intellectual *progress,* they default to arguments about science's authentic reality. Commitment to materialism—understanding ourselves and our creations as products of physical laws—will ultimately increase our sense of wonder, even if it seems to diminish wonder and produce disenchantment, in the short term. That is materialism's promissory note, and the idea at the heart of Wilson's Ionian Enchantment. Once consilience is accomplished and we acquire complete understanding of human nature, a "*true* sense of wonder will reinvade the broader culture."[108]

Slingerland's work, mentioned above, provides a good example of this promissory note. He assures religion and the humanities scholars that their disciplines will endure for the foreseeable future, despite the causal links threading them ineluctably back to the sciences. Humanists may continue conducting research in their disciplines on the condition that they understand (but perpetually forget) that they are immersed in an imaginary realm, a kind of false parallel universe. The *Geist* will haunt the *Geisteswissenschaften,* no matter that the sciences (*Naturwissenschaften*) show up the *Geist* as a charming illusion.[109] Slingerland grants that thoroughgoing physicalism has distasteful elements, for it insists that we jettison transcendent notions of ourselves and others as anything other or more than "a very complex physical thing, a product of millions of years of evolution."[110] He concedes that "human-level" perceptions of value and reality seem imperiled when we honestly confront physicalism's implications. These perceptions, however, will continue to *seem* real to us because of a neat trick of natural selection: evolution engineered our brains to accept a (false) reality. In other words, Slingerland contends that humans evolved what Daniel Dennett and others call the intentional stance—an adaptive (in most cases)[111] propensity to project agency and mind onto objects around us. So powerful is the intentional stance that even though we *know* that humans are, in reality, genetic robots, we continue to conduct our lives and order our values *as if* there were something more to the world, and to ourselves and our relationships.

> [H]uman-level reality—reality as seen through the filter of theory of mind—is real for humans . . . so deeply entrenched that no third-person description can ever completely dislodge it. . . . [W]e apparently cannot help at some level seeing a *Geist* in the machine, which means there will always be something importantly different about the *Geisteswissenschaften.*[112]

Human-level reality, manifest in our day-to-day lives and featured centrally in the subject matter of humanities, will not disappear because our persistent commitment to it as real derives from an innate cognitive "module" of evolutionary hardwiring. We are, in Slingerland's enchanting phrase, "robots designed not to believe we are robots." Moreover, our animistic projections onto the world—our perception that the river is *running free,* that the butterfly is *playing* in the wind (Slingerland's examples)—make us feel "really, really good," even if they are mere products of a deceptive but "promiscuous" teleology. And really good feelings are good *for* us: they contribute to evolutionary fitness. He invokes a favorite example among evolutionary psychologists: our hardwiring for kin preference and love of offspring.

> [F]rom the perspective of evolutionary psychology, I can believe that the love that I feel toward my child and my relatives is an emotion installed in me by my genes in accordance with the principles of kin selection. This does not, however, make my experience of the emotion, nor my sense of its normative reality, any less real to me. . . . The gene-level, ultimate causation would not work unless we were thoroughly sincere at the proximate level. The *whole purpose* of the evolution of social emotions is to make sure that these "false" feelings seem inescapably real to us, and this lived reality will never change unless we turn into completely different types of organisms.[113]

So flawlessly executed is evolutionary programming that love of offspring *feels* real to us, though it is actually foisted upon us by our genes' selfish strategy to replicate themselves. Because our genes have safeguarded the sincerity of our feelings, at the human, "proximate" level, all seems well. We might just decide, then, that what we perceive to be real and valuable at that level—whether as academics toiling away in the humanities or as parents bonding with our children—is just as real as anything apprehended by science. But this would be a mistake.[114] Why? Because humans *also* have an "innate empirical prejudice" that causes us to feel differently about our perceptions of the world once science has revealed their true nature. "Once we have explained something—that is, reduced a higher-level phenomenon to lower-level causes—*the explained thing inevitably loses some of its hold on us.*"[115] We cannot shed an innate "preference for lower-level over higher-level explanation." However disconcerting science's revelations, we prefer them to more pleasant but deluded states. What this means for higher-level phenomena like religion (or love) is that we cannot—will not—carry on as if materialism were *not* a direct threat to meaning. "Once we have begun down the physicalist path, we cannot go back to the old certainties." Here Slingerland adds an additional pragmatic inducement that, however counterintuitive scientific reality might seem, it simply "works better": if we want to launch rockets, we had better get straight on the heliocentric reality of our planetary system, even if we continue to speak as though the sun rises and sets in quaint Ptolemaic style.

What evidence exists for this "truth prejudice"—did evolution provide a module? Slingerland's main proof of his claims is drawn from *The Matrix,* a film premised on parallel worlds, one real and one illusory. When it is revealed that life in the Matrix is an illusion (albeit, a very pleasant one, with juicy steaks, excellent wines, and myriad creature comforts), we, the human audience, find it "abhorrent" that anyone would knowingly choose that false existence over the *real* but hardscrabble life beyond. By the same token, religious and other ideals that conflict with truths revealed by physicalism lose their appeal, however much we pine for their erstwhile comforts. Does this argument not also entail that my love for my child—about which I had previously felt such conviction—will diminish upon learning that my feelings are "really" a trick of genetic programming? Having started down the physicalist path, it follows that those feelings "inevitably" lose some of their "hold" on me. This is bad news for my child.

These examples illustrate the harsh disenchantment meted out by science in the *short* term. But a real and fulfilling form of wonder awaits those who persevere. Slingerland invokes the concept of dual consciousness, turning to Buddhist and Christian sources for allusions to the paradox of living simultaneously in two realms, of walking *two paths*.[116] Thus he argues that our false but "promiscuous projection of teleology onto the world assures that we will continue to find the whole materialist universe a rather beautiful place once it is properly understood,"[117] though he has already claimed that experiences "we know to be illusory seem less valuable to us, even if we are assured that they will *seem* real when we get them."[118] This is not dual consciousness, I would argue. It is simply a contradiction.[119] Slingerland himself ultimately spurns the false assurances of human-level reality for the "irresistibly powerful argument" of a bracing but superior physicalism. This path "not only possesses the excellent advantage of being 'demonstrably true,' but also *cannot help but enrich our sense of wonder* at the dependent and tragic human condition, in all its felt beauty and nobility."[120] Physicalism is wonderful and real—or as Dawkins would say, "wonderful *because* real." Those whose sense of wonder is not enriched by the physicalist revelation may return to the world of illusion, if they wish, but the value of that world will now be greatly diminished.

These claims for wonder and reality fit the familiar pattern of consilience-based reality censorship. The status of nature, and human-level experiences thereof, is not a topic Slingerland takes up directly, but the implications seem clear enough. Wilson, on the other hand, certainly *does* take up these topics. Straddling something like the dual consciousness suggested by Slingerland's portrait of experiential, proximate worlds and scientific, *ultimate* worlds, Wilson struggles to articulate nature's value and its connection to what his own metaphysics posits as real and important.

EVOLUTION AS A NEW MYTHOLOGY

To sum up so far: There are two overlapping forms of consilience promoted by Wilson and his followers. One entails applying the tools of science to nonscience disciplines. A second form turns scientific information *itself* into a coherent, wonder-evoking narrative, a literary product. Wilson would like to see both fulfilled: the scientization of the humanities and a mythopoeic harnessing of scientific knowledge. Both moves make Wilson a popular figure for the new cosmologists, but especially the narrative project, which deserves closer scrutiny. To what extent is the resulting narrative of wonder truly indebted to or expressive of nonscience perspectives and values? Put differently, how accessible and appealing is the consilient metaphysics likely to be for nonscientists? And, above all, what ethical orientations on the natural world do Wilson's metaphysics and "alternative mythology" encourage?

Wilson's prophecies regarding the future of consilient knowledge entail a displacement of religion (but not the religious *impulse*) with a scientific mythology, as we have seen. His arguments along these lines occur in *On Human Nature* (1978) and, with greater elaboration, in *Consilience*. In the former work, Wilson assures religious readers that they need not fear the coming "syncretism," as he calls it.[121] He describes his synthetic approach as "a modification of scientific humanism through the recognition that the mental processes of religious belief—consecration of personal and group identity, attention to charismatic leaders, mythopoeism, and others—represent programmed predispositions whose self-sufficient components were incorporated into the neural apparatus of the brain by thousands of generations of genetic evolution."[122] Wilson assures readers that to locate the biological basis for religion is not necessarily to assert that its content is untrue.[123] He is right about that. Yet his own goal is ultimately to decode our evolutionary programming for religious belief in order to *appropriate* and *redirect* that programming for other—safer, nobler, and secular—ends. Wilson believes the mistake humanists make (he means secular humanists) is in not appreciating how powerful, how "ineradicable," religion truly is.

A modified scientific humanism must come to terms with this power, recognizing these programmed predispositions as a valuable "source of energies that can be shifted in new directions when scientific materialism itself is accepted as the more powerful mythology."[124] Wilson asks: "Does a way exist to divert the power of religion into the services of the great new enterprise that lays bare the sources of that power?"[125] In other words, since we cannot eradicate our instincts for myth and religion, why not redirect these innate impulses toward something like consilience that offers an all-encompassing cosmology with purpose and meaning? Cultures organized around such a unifying goal will outlearn and outcompete others, Wilson predicts, and this will happen—is happening, already—with astonishing speed. Scientific materialism *is* the ultimate unifying quest because it is "the only mythology that can manufacture great goals from the sustained pursuit of pure knowledge."[126]

Like Dawkins, Wilson believes science can simultaneously explain and fulfill the human hunger for religion: "Material reality discovered by science already possesses more content and grandeur than all religious cosmologies combined."[127] Wilson, however, recognizes something neglected by Dawkins: human brains did not evolve to worship biology or physics.[128] But we can submit to, and worship, a *story*. (This, he assumes, is what religionists do.) And if "the sacred narrative cannot be in the form of a religious cosmology, it will be taken from the material history of the universe and the human species."[129] Science provides this narrative as the evolutionary epic. "The core of scientific materialism is the evolutionary epic," Wilson explains, and the evolutionary epic "is probably the best myth we will ever have."[130] The religious impulse is engrained in us, but the mythic power of religion can be captured and redirected toward the science that *explains* its power. Effecting this "transfer of spiritual assets" from religion to science is also an imperative of the new cosmology.[131] Wilson articulates the features of the evolutionary epic as follows:

> Scientific materialism . . . presents the human mind with an alternative mythology that until now has always, point for point in zones of conflict, defeated traditional religion. Its narrative form is the epic: the evolution of the universe. . . . The evolutionary epic is mythology in the sense that the laws it adduces here and now are believed but can never be definitely proved to form a cause-and-effect continuum from physics to the social sciences, from this world to all other worlds in the visible universe, and backward through time to the beginning of the universe. Every part of existence is considered to be obedient to physical laws requiring no external control.[132]

Consilience makes a similar case, slightly embellished, and asserted with greater conviction. "Myth" and "epic," now begin to shed their associations with a disposition to *believe* or a lack of definitive proof: "The *true* evolutionary epic, retold as poetry, is as intrinsically ennobling as any religious epic."[133]

During the two-decade interval between *On Human Nature* and *Consilience* Wilson apparently reevaluated the potential of scientific materialism to function as a full-blown cosmology. The earlier work finds him lamenting that science lacks religion's "primal source of power." He hopes that the evolutionary epic will be able to satisfy our "mythopoeic drive"—the book ends with a chapter called "Hope"— but he perceives obstacles.[134] One is that, while scientists will likely locate the biological source of religion's primal power, science nevertheless remains unable to tap it fully. This is partly because "the evolutionary epic denies immortality to the individual," offering no profound assurances comparable to those of religion, but also because "scientists cannot in all honesty serve as priests."[135] With *Consilience*, Wilson's *hope* that the epic might one day achieve universal mythic status has become a conviction that it is doing so now. The aforementioned challenges—the need for a doctrine of immortality, for example—appear to have been vanquished. Science "has brought new revelations of great moral importance . . . *Homo sapiens* is far more than a congeries of tribes and races. We are a single gene pool . . . forever united as a species by heritage and a common future. Such are the conceptions, based on fact, from which *new intimations of immortality* can be drawn and a new mythos evolved."[136] As Wilson considers how the evolutionary epic might be outfitted to supplant the existing stories, he encounters the problem that "every epic needs a hero." Who or what will play the hero role in the epic of evolution?

Wilson's answer: "The mind will do."[137] Science may not grant us *individual* immortality, but it grants genetic or species immortality, *and* it reassures us that humans—our minds—are of utmost significance in evolution's story.[138] Indeed, *Homo sapiens* is a species of unprecedented, paramount importance in Wilson's new cosmology—as with narratives of the Anthropocene.[139] Taken together, *On Human Nature* and *Consilience* present the human mind as both the *adventurer* (the epic hero) and the *adventure* itself (the epic's final, most challenging frontier). Here we encounter Wilson's conviction that as mythopoeic science comes into its own, "a true sense of wonder" will once more be ours.[140]

We should ask: wonder *at what,* exactly? Wilson offers two candidates that ultimately collapse into one: the human mind as an ultimate object of wonder, and, more generally, the scientists who succeed in unraveling its mysteries, thereby completing the consilient project. Revisiting the historical forms of wonder I outlined in chapter 1 will bring these two possibilities, and their perils, into sharper relief.

THE PRESTIGE OF THE SCIENTIST

Recall the way in which "nonscientific" wonder is often assumed to operate differently from scientific wonder in contemporary treatments of the subject: If nonscientists were "really interested, they would learn the mathematics needed to deal with such matters."[141] This argument (however specious) highlights an odd feature of scientific wonder: on the one hand, some scientists insist on the superiority, difficulty, and the *authenticity* of scientific discoveries and scientific wonder, compared to other forms of inquiry. They urge the masses to try the real thing. Yet, they are hamstrung by their own claims about the joy of science, for how can laypersons experience genuine wonder at that which can "only be known" as the scientist knows it—and why should we try?

The public is often drawn to entities or discoveries that fire the imagination. Accordingly, science writing and documentaries tend to showcase the strange and uncanny. Yet, we are told that someone who feels fascination at these discoveries but remains "uninterested in seeing how they are predicted by theories whose consequences are supported by empirical findings is not really interested in science"[142] Consequently, wonder at black holes, time travel, or gluons without a firm grasp of the science and math that undergirds or predicts them is *unscientific* wonder at mere fantastical elements, not unlike wonder at the magical or miraculous. Such wonder—often characterized as the "gaping" or "gawking" sort—may in fact be an "obstacle to arriving at scientific knowledge."[143] This is the form of wonder that stalls the mind, or, as physicist Mark Silverman puts it, wonder that "anesthetizes the intellect into catatonic inactivity."[144] Where advanced mathematics is involved, the layperson may never hope to grasp what the scientist finds wondrous and beautiful. "The simplicity and mathematical elegance of the laws behind the phenomena escape the person who is not able to distinguish a simple and elegant equation from one which is not."[145]

Note that, on these accounts, the bar for scientific "interest" or literacy (and thus proper scientific wonder) is set extraordinarily high. It is virtually *unattainable* by the nonscientist. It follows that the nonscientist has limited options for the "authentic" wondrous appreciation known to the scientist. She can work to master the science and math involved, something few people have the time and talent to do. Or she can accept that, in the absence of such mastery, her wonder is tainted by fakery or cheapness, and resign herself to gaping at what remains, for her, a species of the magical or miraculous, like an image of Jesus appearing inexplicably on a slice of toast. Given scientists' frequent condemnation of such ignorant gaping, we can assume that this option is not something they encourage. An option that remains open to the nonscientist is to wonder at the scientist who understands (and *can* properly wonder at) things beyond the reach of the layperson. In short: if I cannot apprehend and thus show proper wonder at what science reveals about external reality, *and* if it is true that wondering at what I do not fully understand is not "real" wonder, then I can only wonder at one who apprehends that reality, the one in whom understanding resides. These are some of the peculiar implications of a reversed dynamic of wonder "bestowed on the knowledge won rather than the puzzle posed."[146] When wonder is subjected to such radical revision and reorientation, many of wonder's former objects begin to fall away. It increasingly becomes the possession of an elite priesthood.

INTERNALIZED WONDER

But what of Wilson's caveat that scientists cannot "in all honesty" act as priests in our society, even as religious mythology cedes territory to science? Does Wilson really deny scientists this role? He celebrates how far humans have come from murky forms of comprehension embodied in ancient myths or scripture. His preferred example is the story of Job. Much as Dawkins pens a scientific corrective to Blake's mystical awe at the natural world ("we're working on it"), Wilson's rejoinder to God's interrogation of Job essentially rewrites the biblical script.[147] God rebukes Job for his impertinence: "Have you comprehended the vast expanse of the world? / Come, tell me all this, if you know." Wilson's version inserts this confident reply: "And yes, we do know and we have told. Jehovah's challenges have been met and scientists have pressed on to uncover and to solve even *greater* puzzles."[148] Speaking for Job, Wilson brings forth a litany of dazzling scientific feats and breakthroughs, from spaceflight to the mapping of genes. He believes profound wonder is still possible precisely because of humans' new relationship to physical reality, "our" newfound comprehensive knowledge. The mythopoeic task is to transfer the gaping awe once evoked by biblical stories of creation, or wonder at God's comprehensive knowledge, to awe at humans' modern mastery of the universe. But unlike the biblical Job, Wilson's words to God do not represent the *human* experience generally, but merely the experience and ambitions of the scientist—and only a handful of scientists at that. Ironically, there is nothing *universal* in Wilson's version of Job.

Like Dawkins, Wilson "effectively removes deeper questions of meaning and purpose from realms accessible to theologians and philosophers and locates them where only scientists can find them."[149] How, then, can he convince readers that his forms of enchantment remain a project in which they too can find inspiration? Sociologist Howard Kaye charges that "Wilson's scientific religion . . . cannot both 'disenchant the world'—that is, destroy the sense of mystery toward the natural world—and at the same time rekindle the capacity to experience 'a true sense of wonder.'"[150] Yet, this is precisely Wilson's move in offering scientific knowledge and its creators—mythically embellished—as the preferred object. Much as Dawkins in *Unweaving the Rainbow* presents scientific wonder as a comforting balm to readers wounded by *The Selfish Gene,* Wilson offers the Ionian Enchantment of *Consilience* as compensation for the disenchantment engendered by his own sociobiological revelations. In this way, science gives and science takes away.

Indeed, Wilson admits that even *he* was, for a time, despondent over the implications of his research program. He concludes *Sociobiology* on a decidedly gloomy note, suggesting that once science succeeds in explaining humans fully, we may not like what we find. Wilson gives the last word to Camus: "in a universe divested of illusions and lights, man feels an alien, a stranger." In a candid interview with science journalist John Horgan, Wilson provides context for this somber conclusion and describes how he recovered hope. Forays into sociobiology had left him with the disturbing thought that "as we knew more and more about where we came from and why we do what we do, in precise terms, that it would reduce—what's the word I'm looking for—our exalted self-image, and our hope for indefinite growth in the future."[151] He coaxed himself out of depression by focusing attention on the human mind as perhaps the last great frontier, the "immense unmapped area" left to explore. Thus when Wilson characterizes the mind as "hero" in the evolutionary epic, this idea has special, salvific resonance for him. Wilson offers the metaphor of the brain as an "enchanted loom" with a godlike capacity for weaving and reweaving pictures of external reality, "inventing other worlds, creating a miniature universe."[152] As it approaches the final frontier of the mind, science begins "to turn inward, toward ourselves."[153] The epic hero and the epic adventure are now brought together in the most intimate association. They are not united in just *any* human mind, however, but primarily in the mind of the scientist who is privileged to undertake this adventure, to unravel this final mystery. We are left with an epitome of self-absorbed awe: the human standing in awe of itself as the final and most thrilling piece of the cosmic puzzle. Here we see the beginnings of what Mary-Jane Rubenstein calls internalized wonder that presents the knowing self as the agent and object of wonder.[154] Wonder may then become something to be inflicted—an egotistical display imposed upon others and upon a world that has been mastered. This is the sort of idolatry against which Augustine explicitly cautioned.[155] It is this idolatry against which Rachel Carson—who saw scientific and technological mastery of nature as inimical to wonder—also warned.

If the suggestion that Wilson would have us direct a *true sense of wonder* at the scientist and scientific achievement sounds like the hyperbolic antiscience rant of an envy-driven humanities scholar, bear with me a moment longer. In the taxonomy of wonder I sketched out in the first chapter, Wilson's account corresponds, first and foremost, to wonder at a vision of complete and comprehensive knowledge— wonder at final theories. Whereas Dawkins understands science as serial wonder— successful puzzle-solving—and alludes only occasionally to cherished "final" theories that explain everything once and for all, Wilson wonders at the promise of a fully integrated body of knowledge.[156] The difference between these two approaches, some commentators have speculated, may have to do with Wilson's having once been deeply religious. Wilson retains, and assumes others to share, a profound desire for a tidy, synthetic, coherent worldview, an overarching rationale—the secular equivalent of a systematic theology.[157] "When we have unified enough certain knowledge," Wilson earnestly predicts, "we will understand who we are and why we are here."[158] Perhaps this desire for godlike knowledge explains Wilson's apotheosis of the human mind and his need to rewrite the story of Job.

Whatever its source, Wilson's enchantment gives a grossly distorted picture of the universe and our place in it. Drawing on the metaphor of looking through the wrong end of the telescope, Carson suggests that we reverse it, and thereby perceive more accurately our relative insignificance vis-à-vis the long vistas of evolutionary time. Carson felt enormous comfort and wonder at the thought of our smallness in the universe. At times, Wilson expresses a similar sense of profound solace in nature, heightened by our recognition of a force outside ourselves and *beyond* our powers of contrivance. In concluding, then, I consider the question of why that more salutary conception of nature remains undeveloped in Wilson's work (and not infrequently, in the Epic of Evolution generally). My claim is that the loss of nature as something real, valuable, and meaningful is a predictable, and lamentable, outcome of the consilient, mythopoeic project and its forms of reverence.

CONSILIENCE AND THE ECLIPSE OF NATURE

Throughout his long career, Wilson has "worked to invest science in general and evolutionary biology in particular with the attributes of religion and with the zeal of a convert has evangelized on behalf of evolution, biology and science, belief in which will unite humanity and knowledge and save the environment."[159] So what exactly are the links between evolutionary evangelizing and unified knowledge, on the one hand, and protection of the planet's biodiversity, on the other? How does the evolutionary epic engender the "environmental ethic" Wilson abruptly introduces in the closing chapter of *Consilience?* "The problem of collective meaning and purpose," Wilson writes there, "is both urgent and immediate, if for no other reason, it determines the environmental ethic."[160] Yet nature—as something more than an abstract set of principles, a foil for our grand intellectual adventure—is surprisingly absent in Wilson's work, even in passages containing impassioned pleas to save the planet. Wilson's difficulty stems from a deep ambivalence regarding ultimate sources of reality, wonder, and value.

David Takacs comments on Wilson's pursuit of a scientific, ultimate, and objective basis for environmental ethics, an ethic that will "endure because it is 'true' " and because "it is grounded in the real world that Wilson's scientific investigations have revealed to him."[161] In the few places where Wilson seeks to wed his scientific and ethical causes, little clarity emerges. Rather than argue for a clear link between our evolutionary endowments and an environmental ethic, Wilson seems to project biophilic feelings onto the rest of humanity.[162] Yet biophilia, even if widespread, is not sufficient to evoke a broad ethic of conservation such as Wilson would like to see enacted. The strongest claims for the existence of a biophilic response are actually instances of biophobia[163]—recall the allegedly universal fear of snakes that Wilson touts as an epigenetic law of evolution. Other examples of biophobia involve types of environments or landscapes: heights, open water, dark or cramped spaces. These aversive responses are easily triggered and extremely difficult to extinguish; they may well interfere with our ability to extend an ethic broadly toward all life-forms and bioregions. Regarding our positive responses, biophilia claims that these are encoded in us by evolution because they point to some adaptive advantage of a feature of the natural world. We enjoy flowers, for example, because they may signal the presence of food; certain types of landscapes make predator detection or evasion easier. Even if our evolutionary past has sifted and selected our present responses according to their fitness- and survival-enhancing potential, there remain untold numbers of organisms that are largely irrelevant. They neither threaten nor enhance our survival in any significant way. Wilson is optimistic that we can fill in these gaps through additional *information* about the importance of certain (all?) species—perhaps a cure for cancer lurks in the rainforest—or by recognizing the significant "spiritual" role nature has played in our evolutionary development. Yet his arguments generally underscore the spiritual value of *scientific materialism,* not that of nature.

Wilson's *The Diversity of Life, The Future of Life* (both 2002), and *The Creation* (2006) further articulate his belief in humans' innate attraction to nature and living things, and argue that genetic hardwiring provides a sociobiological basis for "protection of biodiversity and wilderness, the ultimate sources of wonder and spirituality."[164] Humans, Wilson argues in *The Diversity of Life,* seek out wilderness

"in search of new life and wonder." Here he even suggests that nature is an enduring source of wonder precisely because its workings are largely independent of us,
"beyond human contrivance"[165] This, of course, is a radically different image of the
human-nature relationship than that celebrated in his dialogue between God and
Job. Here restoration of the natural world—*not* the consilient quest (elsewhere
celebrated as "the greatest of all intellectual challenges" and "ultimate purpose"[166])—offers our species its noblest, most unifying, and uplifting challenge:
"There can be no purpose more enspiriting than to begin the age of restoration,
reweaving the wondrous diversity of life that still surrounds us."[167]

The Creation is Wilson's strongest appeal to religious believers to join the environmental cause, written as an open letter to a Southern Baptist minister whom
Wilson respectfully addresses as "Pastor" throughout. Yet, even here, Wilson's
appeal on behalf of nature becomes unhelpfully entangled in endorsements of his
competing causes: evolutionary apologetics, sociobiological analyses of human
nature, and science's quest for totalizing knowledge. Wilson sets out to convey his
profound sense of nature's value, but winds up celebrating the uniquely gratifying
rewards of science. In attempting to describe the charismatic allure and magnificence of the wolverine, he defaults to trumpeting the thrill of scientific discovery,
the excitement of "paradigm breaking." Like Dawkins who invokes the beauty of
the African landscape merely as evidence of a species-wide, atavistic, evolutionary
response to our ancestral home, Wilson introduces the Japanese maple as proof of
his ideas. "The world's most beautiful tree" is celebrated in *The Creation* not as a
wonder in its own right but as evidence for genetically hardwired (biophilic) reactions to certain types of trees, and thus as testimony *against* the "blank slate" theory
of human nature (though it is difficult to imagine that Wilson's Southern Baptist
interlocutor is heavily invested in blank-slate theories!).[168] Or consider the wonder
that is the humble mouse: "If the DNA helices in one cell of a mouse . . . were placed
end on end and magically enlarged to have the same width as wrapping string, they
would extend for over nine hundred kilometers," Wilson enthuses. "Measured in
bits of pure information, the genome of a cell is comparable to all editions of the
Encylopaedia Britannica published since its inception in 1768." This, ultimately, is
Wilson's argument for a conservation ethic. An organism's "ethical value" is "substantiated by close examination of its biology."[169]

Wilson recognizes and wants to defend another kind of value, which he calls
"stewardship," but this value interests him primarily because "it appears to arise
from emotions programmed in the very genes of human social behavior."[170] The
stewardship impulse, in other words, is simply exhibit A (or B, or C) for his cherished hypotheses. These are interesting facts, to be sure, but they are the musings
of the laboratory scientist, more likely to garner a "gee whiz" response than to
engender love of nature. Wilson's conviction, apparently shared by many new
cosmologists, is that the sheer accumulation and recitation of information about

the natural world will prompt the necessary wonder, and thus care and concern. "I believe," Wilson writes, "that as the scientific study of human nature and living Nature grows, these two creative forces of the human self-image will coalesce. The central ethic will shift, and we will come full circle to cherish all of life—not just our own."[171] Put differently, his key argument for valuing nature is that vast stores of "scientific information" or "biological wealth" are being lost, through extinction, before they can be "mapped" and "counted."[172]

Yet, the knowledge that species are nearing extinction, and that they have impressive biological machinery (which they share with us), does not entail that we are duty-bound to save them, as Wilson seems to believe. He cannot establish the straightforward connection between biological facts and ethical directives that his work assumes. The quest to *catalogue* global biodiversity will take on a kind of religious significance, he believes, leading to the "transcendent and only dimly foreseeable complexity of future biology." In this transcendent realm of future biology we will find a *"new theater of spiritual energy."*[173] As Wilson draws an implicit comparison between the great spiritual potential of future science, vis-à-vis the fading glory of traditional religions, his plea for nature and nonhuman life becomes strangely muted.[174] The result is that *The Creation* often reads less as an appeal to save the natural world than as "an evangelical tract for Wilson's greater cause of consilience."[175]

My point is not simply that Wilson's arguments for engaging and protecting nature are anthropocentric, though they usually are. More troubling is that Wilson's total immersion in the values and culture of science leaves him *unable* to articulate what is compellingly or uniquely valuable about nature. The problem here, as Evernden aptly puts it, is that "the values detected by the environmentalist in the natural world are among the features missing from the official maps of reality."[176] Wilson confuses the map for the territory; only the map seems to him fully *real*. He fails to grasp that the unity of science is not the same thing as the unity of life. We are not—most of us—moved automatically to profound appreciation of the latter by admiring the brilliant tidiness of the former. The evolutionary cosmology of consilience is ill suited to become an earthly cosmology in which environmental values can take root and flourish.[177]

Wilson was a latecomer to environmentalism. Though it is clear from autobiographical sources that nature provided peace and stability during some troubled childhood years, he first became engaged in environmental issues in 1979—at about age 50—when he encountered reports of rainforest destruction (and attendant losses of biological *information*). Since the 1990s, Wilson has come to be seen as nature's ardent defender, a kindred spirit of Rachel Carson. Wilson penned the afterword to the fortieth anniversary edition of *Silent Spring* (2002) and in public lectures and interviews he often invokes her, as we have seen. Yet Wilson and Carson defend very different accounts of what constitutes ultimate reality. The notable exception is Wilson's novel *Anthill* in which he celebrates young Raff's preference for the "reality" (and "mystery") of nature, over textbooks, taxonomies, and science classrooms. Raff's teacher instructs him in the proper method of nature education as follows:

> To learn a frog in a full and lasting manner, you must find one where it lives in nature, watch it, listen to it if it is calling . . . . The concept of frog will be with you forever if you follow this kind of education. You can pick up additional information from science and literature and myth, and all those things you have at school, but you will be wiser for being rooted in the full reality of frog. You will care about frog, too, like nobody else.[178]

Wilson's allusion here to full reality ("nature is the real world"[179]) and to the indispensable, unshakable—and even moral—foundation provided by sensory encounters in nature is strongly resonant of Carson's philosophy. Wilson here casts science in a supporting role as "additional information" akin to "literature and myth." It is almost startling to encounter a passage like this in Wilson's writing, after immersing oneself in his generally triumphalist oeuvre. Does Wilson believe that celebrating the wondrous reality of nature is suitable only for children?—or, perhaps, only in works of fiction? He seems unable to resolve the tension between his commitment to transcendent science and his appeal to nature as ultimate reality.

In *The Diversity of Life,* Wilson characterizes Earth as "the mystery we were chosen to solve."[180] His portrait of humans as solvers of puzzles and mysteries makes it difficult for him to defend the legitimacy and value of experiences in nature not driven by these impulses. Wilson invokes myths about hubris, not as a warning, but as elaborate *justifications* for unprecedented scientific trespass—Icarus and Prometheus, the very symbols of transgression, are the scientist's inspirational figures. But humans are not the heroes of the evolutionary story. The problem is not that an evolutionary worldview cannot nurture environmental values, for Carson's worldview was thoroughly Darwinian, as is Aldo Leopold's, and that of many other environmental thinkers who endeavor to dislodge humans from the center of the universe. Indeed, it takes a certain amount of special pleading to tell the evolutionary tale in a way that presents humans as the most awe-inspiring point of reference. But Wilson succeeds in doing it.

And so do the new cosmologists. The problem, then, is that these appeals to the Epic of Evolution and similar cosmic narratives make humans and the scientific quest so central that nature appears as something like a *rival* to science in an ongoing contest to determine what is ultimately wondrous. Why, as scholars, as environmentalists, or as human beings, should we accept this imposition of science as the final arbiter and purveyor of meaning? Why embrace this peculiar bargain that asks us to surrender values we already cherish in exchange for dubious values that, in their most potent, scientific manifestations, remain largely inaccessible to most of us?

In a well-known passage from one of Darwin's letters, he relates an experience of drifting off to sleep in the soft grass and waking to "a chorus of birds" singing all around. "And it was as pleasant and rural a scene as I ever saw," Darwin writes, "and I did not care one penny how any of the beasts and birds had been formed."[181] Darwin's words suggest a division between the world as given by science and the phenomenal world of sense and experience—of sleep and wakefulness, mellifluous birdsong and soft grass. Darwin's scientific habits of mind, his preoccupation with understanding the genesis of these organisms, made it difficult simply to enjoy them, except in such moments of drowsy forgetfulness. Explaining how birds were made was beside the point in the moment of joyous reverie Darwin describes. As R. W. Hepburn notes, "it is not the genesis of the phenomenon that elicits the wonder" in such moments "but the phenomenon itself, colour, sound, or combination of the impressions."[182] Can the relationship between these two realms—science and sense perception or information and experience—be understood as dialectical rather than rivalrous? How we might properly value science and even see it as a lens onto wonder, without losing sight of nature's reality, is a question we will continue to pursue as we track the encroachment of suspect forms of wonder on environmental and spiritual values.

Chapter 4

Evolutionary Enchantment and Denatured Religious Naturalism

A religion, old or new, that stressed the magnificence of the Universe as revealed by modern science might be able to draw forth reserves of reverence and awe hardly tapped by the conventional faiths. Sooner or later, such a religion will emerge.

—CARL SAGAN, *PALE BLUE DOT*

In chapters 4–6, I turn to the variety of ways in which scientific accounts of the natural world are being consecrated and reenchanted to serve as a new global myth. Recall that these narratives go by a variety of names, including the Epic of Evolution, the New Story, the Universe Story, the Great Story, and Big History.

> Whatever the name the core idea is the same: there is emerging today a coherent story, based on modern, scientific information that tells the history of our Universe, from its very beginnings to today. That story can help each one of us understand our place in a larger Universe. The evolutionary epic links modern accounts of the origins of the Universe, the Earth, life, and human societies into a single story about origins, so it can play in modern society a role similar to that of traditional creation stories in all earlier societies.[1]

These narratives aim to reshape the spiritual, aesthetic, and moral sensibilities of a potentially global audience. Immersion in this new cosmology, it is hoped, will engender greater commitment to protecting nonhuman life and safeguarding the unfolding of natural and cosmological processes. And yet, the products of such mythmaking often ring surprisingly hollow where nature and its purported value and sacredness are concerned.

The present chapter focuses on two proponents of nontheistic religious naturalism: religion scholar Loyal Rue and cell biologist Ursula Goodenough. Rue and Goodenough's narrative endeavors, and their philosophy of educational reform, affirm Wilson's call for an alternative science-based mythology and they share a commitment to a form of religious naturalism[2] that is indebted to the consilient paradigm in very specific ways. Both apply evolutionary frameworks to traditional religions, evaluating their adaptability and "fitness," and both diagnose these traditions as dysfunctional in the modern context. The evolutionary epic, they believe, affronts the plausibility of traditional faiths and exposes their nonadaptive character, their inability to evolve and change in response to science or global issues. Consequently, they forecast bleak prospects for these traditions. Individually and jointly, Rue and Goodenough also take up the cause of reforming education in accordance with a consilient curriculum that places the Epic of Evolution at its very center. They (correctly) discern affinities between Wilson's quest for certain, totalizing knowledge and the new cosmology's broad dissemination of an integrated, revelatory scientific story that aims to reorient all our beliefs and values. It is not enough that the new story be universal and true, of course. It must also attract a critical mass of adherents who feel its superior power and allure, and assent to its truth and grandeur.

In previous chapters, I argued that proponents of the new cosmology often reproduce the internal tensions in the value frameworks of thinkers like Wilson and Dawkins. To be sure, Goodenough and Rue esteem nature and appear genuinely concerned with planetary well-being. Goodenough's book-length work, *The Sacred Depths of Nature*, calls upon feelings of reverence for nature and intimations of "mystery" and "humility."[3] Rue piously affirms similar sentiments: "I take nature to heart and affirm the mystery and sanctity of creation."[4] Yet, many who craft a new religion from scientific materials are invested in competing agendas: evangelizing and proselytizing science, on the one hand, and cultivating wonder, reverence, and ethical concern for the more-than-human world, on the other. The new mythmakers *as a whole* often succeed in promoting the first agenda, at the expense of the second. Along the way, they instrumentalize wonder as valuable for its potential to enhance the prestige of science vis-à-vis religion. The hubristic certainty that inflects the new cosmology has much to do with this pitting of science against religion as the latter's superior rival. In defining their worldview against the traditional faiths, these mythmakers have further disconnected it from the natural world as a locus of value, meaning, and wonder. As I will argue over the course of the next few chapters, those invested in celebrating the superiority of scientific wonder, and the eventual victory of science over religion, do not always make the best advocates for *nature*.[5]

THE QUEST FOR A NEW STORY

It may be helpful to trace a brief history of the new cosmology and how it arrived at its present assumptions, ambitions, and values. A particular group that has long held the project of mythopoeic science in high regard is the Institute on Religion in an Age of Science (IRAS). IRAS publishes the science and religion journal *Zygon* and convenes conferences that have featured Universe Story advocates Brian Swimme and Mary Evelyn Tucker, former *Zygon* editor Philip Hefner, and philosopher of science Michael Ruse, a frequent contributor to *Zygon*. Ursula Goodenough is also actively involved in this group, having served as IRAS president, as is Loyal Rue. Discussions of the meaning of myth and the need for a new story have filled the pages of *Zygon* for well over a decade. However, the roots of the new cosmology pre-date *Zygon*'s earnest promotion of the Epic and its values. Thomas Berry, powerfully influenced by Teilhard de Chardin, issued one of the earliest calls for a New Story in a 1978 article in *Teilhard Studies* where he characterized the traditional religions as dysfunctional cosmologies out of touch with modern science and the environmental crisis.[6] (Berry and Teilhard's influence on Universe Story enthusiasts remains strong, as we will see in the next chapter.) Interestingly, Berry's call for a New Story and Wilson's celebration of the "epic" dimensions of evolutionary science both emerged in 1978. Hence, *Zygon*'s endorsement of the evolutionary epic affirmed a broader enthusiasm for "Epic Science" already underway in the late 1970s and 1980s. More about epic science in a moment.

Among religion scholars, Rue was one of the first to throw down the gauntlet. In 1993, he convened a special session at a meeting of the American Association for the Advancement of Science called "Scientific Resources for a Global Religious Myth." Among those responding to Rue's call for "science-based mythmaking" were Eric Chaisson and Brian Swimme.[7] In a 1994 piece in *Zygon* provocatively called "Redefining *Myth* and *Religion*: Introduction to a Conversation,"[8] Rue argued that the emergence of a global culture calls for a global story: "we must articulate a common story, a narrative of origins, nature, and destiny that can give us a shared orientation in nature and in history."[9] This short piece sketches an argument that Rue develops in subsequent monographs like *Religion Is Not about God* and *Everybody's Story*, namely that the traditional religions cannot meet the challenge of our "global problematique," owing to their provincial rather than universal appeal, and their failure to establish coherence with science. In June 1996, the evolutionary epic was the topic of a week-long meeting of the Institute on Religion in an Age of Science. This event, co-chaired by Rue and Goodenough, featured Tucker, Hefner, and John Grim, among others. The following year, a conference titled "The Epic of Evolution" convened at the Field Museum of Natural History in Chicago, sponsored by the Templeton Foundation and the American Association for the Advancement of Science (Program of Dialogue on Science, Ethics, and Religion).[10] The conference attracted some 450 attendees and featured papers by Goodenough, Rue, Tucker, Swimme, Berry, Hefner, and theologian John Haught.[11] During September 1998, Wilson appeared in scholarly panels on cosmology and ecology at the Religions of the World and Ecology conference series, hosted by the Center for the Study of World Religions at Harvard Divinity School, and organized by Tucker and Grim. In the wake of these events, Connie Barlow and others founded the Epic of Evolution Society with E. O. Wilson and Goodenough as charter members, and with support from environmental ethicists including J. Baird Callicott.

As these trends were developing, Callicott published *Earth Insights* (1994). The book boldly proposes a globally acceptable evolutionary-ecological worldview that can serve as a universal environmental ethic, a Rosetta stone for translating the environmental insights of the myriad religious traditions.[12] Callicott presents a "global sampler" of multicultural religious perspectives, and evaluates their insights (often positively) from the standpoint of the evolutionary-ecological worldview.[13] Religion plays a supporting role, contributing symbols, myths, metaphors, and narratives to the science-based worldview, as in the new cosmology. The evolutionary-ecological worldview, in other words, is not just one among many but provides a standard against which the tenability of other worldviews is measured.

Callicott's approach is suggestive of mythopoeic science, though he has never articulated his ethic in mythic *form,* so far as I know, and he does not engage in the proselytizing activities of new cosmologists. He defends a middle ground between the omnicompetence and hegemony of grand scientific narratives and what he considers the damning nihilism and ambiguity of deconstructive postmodern critiques.[14] Callicott proposes a "reconstructive postmodernism" that values cultural and biological diversity (and the necessary link between the two). However, while wary of arrogant claims of positivist science, Callicott sometimes portrays science and religion as oriented to the same end or aspiring to the same *explanatory slot,* as do the new cosmologists. Creationist or literalist interpretations of religion sometimes stand in for religion as a whole in his assessments of the relative merits of science and religion.[15] The impulse to present science as a worldview that can function much like religion is itself, I would argue, a holdover from the positivistic modernism that Callicott abjures, and it conjures elements of epic science, as discussed below. Still, Callicott's reconstructive postmodernism engages in deeper and more sustained reflection on the nature of science—its value as well as provisionality—than the new cosmology. Despite early ties to the movement, and his current enthusiasm for the "religionization of science,"[16] Callicott insists that the Epic of Evolution is "not exactly my project."[17] On the whole, I agree with his self-assessment.[18] However, his work deserves mention here, and occasionally in subsequent chapters, as suggestive of a broader turn (or return), in the late twentieth century, to global science as a new candidate religion.

In the mid-1990s, Barlow, a science writer, began chronicling these movements and their common devotion to what she terms the "way of science."[19] An *Epic of Evolution Journal* was published from 1998–2000.[20] Another major conference devoted to the Epic was held in Hawaii in January 2008, and conference proceedings were published in a 2009 volume, *The Epic of Evolution: Science's Story and*

Humanity's Response, with contributions by Swimme, Rue, and Goodenough, David Christian, and many other "famed pioneers in the development of the epic of evolution."[21]

In a 1997 editorial in *Zygon,* Hefner took note of this rapidly developing trend and affirmed *Zygon*'s commitment to keeping it near the journal's "front burner." "Scientists and philosophers of science who write in a popular vein, in the style of Sagan, Loyal Rue, Ursula Goodenough, Richard Dawkins, and Daniel Dennett," he noted, "seem to be making the claim that E. O. Wilson articulated some years ago when he wrote that the evolutionary epic is the best myth our minds will ever entertain."[22] As Hefner's invocation of these figures suggests, calls for extending the evolutionary paradigm far beyond the realm of biology were pivotal for some of the new mythmakers. Wilson's felicitous phrase, the "epic of evolution," has iconic status in numerous texts and internet sources promoting the new cosmology. What Wilson's evolutionary epic has in common with the Harvard conferences (and the resulting multivolume treatment of religion and ecology), Berry's call for a New Story, and *Zygon*'s endorsement of mythopoesis is the assumption that stories—cosmologies—fundamentally determine how we live our lives. We must have a story, Wilson argues, "to tell about where we came from, and why we are here."[23] Tucker and Grim concur in their programmatic foreword to the Harvard series: religions have long provided "basic interpretive stories of who we are, what nature is, where we have come from, and where we are going," but their dysfunctionality can no longer be ignored. They echo Berry's call for a "new cosmology" that treats "evolution as a new story of the universe, namely, as a vast cosmological perspective that will resituate human meaning and direction in the context of four and a half billion years of earth history."[24]

THE RETURN OF "EPIC SCIENCE"

The Epic of Evolution / Universe Story and associated conferences and publications are paradigmatic of a broader genre—epic science—that gained prominence in the 1970s but has much deeper roots in Victorian science, notably in the work of such grand synthesizers as Herbert Spencer.[25] Historian Bernard Lightman argues that the "evolutionary epic became one of the most important narrative formats in the second half of the nineteenth century" and has remained a "versatile genre" for science popularizers ever since.[26] Today, as in Victorian times, these movements exhibit a "shared belief among the converted that by finally replacing older mythologies, the new scientific epic will provide an overarching background for human self-understanding, moral reflection, and personal and social communication," according to physicist-turned-philosopher Martin Eger.[27] Wilson's work is a case in point, with its sweeping, confident narrative of progress and its adulation of science and scientists.[28]

Historian Ian Hesketh has chronicled the recent "recurrence" of the evolution-ary epic, a genre that he, like Eger, traces to nineteenth-century philosophers and naturalists.[29] Hesketh's list of modern seekers of a unifying, epic story includes "Edward Wilson, Brian Swimme and Thomas Berry, Connie Barlow, Russ Genet, Ursula Goodenough, Loyal Rue, and most recently Mary Evelyn Tucker, to name just a few of the key authors who, taken together, form a subgenre of popular sci-ence writers invested in the evolutionary epic."[30] All evolutionary epics, he notes, involve "non-Darwinian theories of evolution, which are necessarily progressive, teleological, and ultimately can be directed by an all-knowing subject."[31] He sug-gests that the recurrence of this "grand anthropocentric tale"[32] illustrates our deep-seated desire "to believe that we are not only the ultimate purpose of creation but that in gaining such knowledge we can thus take over the processes of nature and guide them to our favor."[33] However much this storyline appears to be an historical relic, it seems to reappear "whenever human history is written into the larger his-tory of the cosmos."[34]

Other common features of the epic genre identified by these thinkers include an extension of the evolutionary paradigm as far as possible, an emphasis on the unifica-tion of the sciences, and an agenda of reconciling science "with a specifically human reality."[35] Epic science revolves around a single story of evolution, but evolution is here "explicated in greater detail than ever before, deepened, unified, extended far beyond biology—'universal' or 'cosmic' evolution."[36] Eger notes the genre's "flagrant excitement" about all that science can offer to an understanding of our daily lives, and even "unabashed *calls for a new morality* or a new 'vision' of the world."[37] Big histories and evolutionary epics read like works of "revelation," Hesketh concurs.[38] Typically it is claimed that the extension of evolution in these directions is close to being realized, "that we are living in a time of 'the last frontier,' of the crucial unifica-tion of the scientific worldview, of the dissolution (at least in principle) of the final mysteries."[39] For many, a chief insight of the new epic is that the universe attains the fullness of self-awareness in humans who "act as an animated conduit for the Uni-verse's self-reflection."[40] All these features of epic science apply to the new cosmology, with its commitment to unified, integrated knowledge dispensed in mythic form for a broader public.[41] The new cosmology, and particularly the Universe Story, cele-brates the modern human species and its unprecedented scientific knowledge as rep-resentative of the universe becoming conscious of itself.

Epic science often seeks to reshape society's moral values and aesthetic prefer-ences in accordance with values inhering in (or believed to inhere in) science. In much the same way, some of its advocates see the decline of traditional religions as welcome and inevitable, owing in part to their lack of empirical credentials. Reli-gion's decline will make way for a science-infused cosmology that prescribes *how things are* and *which things matter* in terms that foster global unity. A good exam-ple is Loyal Rue's efforts to construct "everybody's story," to which we now turn.

EVERYBODY'S STORY

This vision of secular, global unity is captured well in John Lennon's popular song, "Imagine," interpreted by many as an atheist anthem celebrating a world devoid of religious and national identities, and the bloody strife that attends these stubborn allegiances.[42] It is fitting that a radio interview with Loyal Rue commences with the familiar opening piano chords of "Imagine," subtly inviting fellow humanist "dreamers" to embrace the Epic's vision of a world living as one, without the distractions and divisiveness of religion.[43] For some seekers, Rue's provision of a new science-based myth may have the same welcoming, rational appeal as Lennon's portrait of earthbound priorities and global peace and solidarity. But there is a dark side to Rue's quest for unity and rational assent to scientific wisdom. His work assumes an apocalyptic scenario in the near-term future, and offers a common myth as our best chance of survival. Rue's narrative appears deeply and earnestly invested in complex, multivalent concepts such as *myth, meaning, purpose, wonder, awe,* and *gratitude,* but he approaches his subject matter—as Wilson advises— with a commitment to a confident brand of materialism, a tidy, consilient account of human nature and the physical world. The resulting story, which Rue grandly calls "everybody's story," is offered as a viable and alluring alternative to the existing traditions and their dangerously outmoded value frameworks.

How alluring is it? In the work of the new cosmologists, the superior wonder that awaits converts to the new story is often baldly asserted, as though it too were an empirically demonstrable fact of the universe. How one might go about measuring and comparing the "grandeur" of competing cosmologies, individually or as a whole, is not obvious, of course. Rue's work exhibits these tendencies. But, as we will see, what Rue offers with one hand, he takes away with the other. He *instructs* us to react with wonder and gratitude at the astonishing, creative universe revealed in the cosmic epic, even as he contends that the universe is dead and devoid of meaning and that "nihilism" is the more reasonable stance. As I will argue, one possible key to deciphering Rue's seemingly schizophrenic stance lies in his fascination with the evolutionary uses of guile and deceit.[44] Like many devoted students of evolutionary psychology, Rue understands deception as a key dynamic and central strategy of adaptation and survival. Hence, his ostensible celebration of nature's wonder and value is an artful, strategic ploy: In a move reminiscent of Edward Slingerland, discussed in the previous chapter, Rue hopes to convince the untutored, story-seeking masses to adopt a robust "biocentric" or "ecomoral" framework that he himself believes to be illusory. His understanding of mythmaking is beholden to an evolutionary account of myths as adaptive strategies. Deploying a kind of reverse engineering, he begins with the moral beliefs and dispositions he assumes humans need to survive. He then works backward, crafting a "religion" that remains true to science (as he understands it), while triggering the requisite ecofriendly, adaptive behaviors. In this sense, Rue is perhaps Wilson's most apt pupil: He not only retools science to serve as an alternative mythology, but also deploys evolutionary logic in order to deconstruct and explain—and thereby appropriate *for* science—the power of myth.

As we delve beneath the surface of Rue's story, intimations of meaning, wonder, sacredness, and affective attachment evaporate before our eyes (they are mere projections of our biological nature), leaving behind their evolutionary antecedents— the "real" stuff of genes, memes, and brain modules. That Rue stages his mythopoeic performance as an act of legerdemain suggests the emptiness of his expressions of wonder and environmental values. Ultimately, though it requires a few steps to see how he arrives there, Rue presents an aggrandizing vision of humans as central to the story's plot. Wonder is pressed into service as fostering devotion to the *story* of cosmic evolution.

OF MYTHS AND MEMES

Rue follows Wilson in treating sacred myths as competing with one another to spread their core ideas and gain adherents. *Everybody's Story* (2000) includes a foreword by Wilson. *Religion Is Not about God* (2005) carries a blurb from Wilson, praising the book as an "important step toward the naturalistic, hence truly general theory of religion" and a persuasive blend of the science of "human nature" with a "positive view" of religion's place in culture.[45] While Rue borrows from Dawkins's concept of memes—the cultural analogue to genes as a unit of selection—he agrees with Wilson that religion will not disappear so much as its primary functions will be ultimately (and legitimately) usurped and fulfilled by science. Though Wilson's foreword to *Everybody's Story* concludes with a somewhat tepid endorsement—"I find his argument persuasive"—it effectively sets the stage for Rue's vision of rival religious stories engaged in fierce Darwinian struggle. "To have credibility, the religious epic must be thought superior to the stories of competing tribes," Wilson writes. Competing epics generate divisiveness among their adherents. What is needed is a universal, unifying story, Wilson argues, composed "from the best empirical knowledge that science and history can provide of the real human story. Spirituality is beneficent to the extent that it is based on verifiable truth."[46] Rue affirms these sentiments in noting that religious pluralism has democratic appeal— it is a nice *idea*—but in practice, diversity engenders social instability. Rue considers humans' increasing awareness of religious plurality to be a major force eroding the plausibility and competitive edge of each tradition. The Epic thus has "astringent implications" for existing faiths, for it "affronts the intellectual plausibility and the moral relevance of traditional religious worldviews."[47]

Rue characterizes our current societal predicament as one of "amythia": we lack a serviceable myth that is globally relevant and evidence based. In this view (which echoes Berry's earlier pronouncements, but with a distinctive biological twist), our environmental crisis is, at root, a crisis of *storylessness*. For Rue, amythia engenders numerous societal ills, ranging from environmental crises, to rampant consumerism, to widespread use of antidepressants. A new science-based myth may catch on as a successful meme, Rue hopes, for it has the power to bind humanity into a global culture with a "shared perception of how things are and which things matter."[48] In *The Selfish Gene* (1976) Dawkins first proposed memes as units of cultural inheritance that function analogously to genes in natural selection. "Just as genes propagate themselves in the gene pool by leaping from body to body via sperms or eggs, so memes propagate themselves in the meme pool by leaping from brain to brain via a process which, in the broad sense, can be called imitation."[49] How do we know whether or not the Epic is a successful meme? Story traditions act as the agents that "select out" unacceptable memes in cultural evolution, Rue contends. He suggests that the elimination of existing, unacceptable myths is a natural, impersonal process. "The cultural narrative that integrates ideas about how things are and which things matter will be the ultimate standard against which any new memes are judged," Rue argues. "If a new idea is pronounced unfit by the custodians of the narrative tradition then measures will be taken to discourage it."[50] Exactly who these custodians are and what measures of "discouragement" they are empowered to use Rue does not say. A good guess is that they are the scientists under whose "critical and watchful eye" mythmaking proceeds.[51]

Whether or not a myth is competitive depends on how well it aligns with external (scientific) reality and with the evolutionary features of our own brains, as Rue sees it. Myths provide "memes for the ultimate realities and values that are reflected in our goal hierarchies."[52] They tell us "how the world is made up, how it works, what its point is, what the possibilities are," as well as "how humans fit into the picture, what our point is, what in the world is good for us, and how we should seek to fulfill our lives."[53] Religious traditions, he believes, are fundamentally mythic traditions that strive, through narrative, to integrate facts and values. Their central function is to *manage human nature*, conferring a sense of personal wholeness or integrity, as well as social coherence (stable, reliable social networks). Just as organisms (or, rather, their genes) persist by means of mechanisms enabling survival and replication, so too religions "develop a variety of enabling strategies, or *ancillary strategies*, designed to assure that the narrative core will continue to be replicated indefinitely in the minds of individuals."[54] All religious traditions, Rue maintains, have root metaphors that function to link facts to values or cosmology to morality. When the fusion of fact and value begins to break apart, a religious tradition is approaching its expiration date. Ancillary strategies of various sorts (e.g., ritual or intellectual strategies) can extend their shelf-life, helping them appear relevant and plausible. But only for so long. This fate has befallen the world religions: "the specter of nonrealism already haunts the great religions of the world and will continue to do so."[55]

The haunting specter of *nonrealism* gains its power from humans' increasing awareness of religious pluralism and from progress in science and technology. "We are forever beyond the multiple stories of this mountain or that valley, of this or that tribe or nation or god." The view of the Earth from space, Rue believes, has taught us one thing with certainty: "*there is only one story.*" This is a narrative that must be told "at some distant remove, where the earth can be seen whole."[56] Like Wilson, Rue (ostensibly) rejects postmodern disavowals of metanarratives and universals in human nature or culture. He gives a brief nod to the view that scientific knowledge, including knowledge of human nature, is provisional: "recent work in the philosophy of science," he concedes, "has severely compromised the view that scientific knowledge is completely objective or undistorted by bias."[57] But he lays far greater emphasis on the self-correcting nature of the scientific method: Scientists "have this thing about the truth."[58] He lands on the idea of science as—like religion—a narrative enterprise. Far from weakening the authority of science in society, this narrative shift illustrates that science is uniquely qualified to tell everybody's story. Science not only provides the necessary resources for crafting such a story but "to a certain extent the narrative of modern science *is* everybody's story."[59] This argument echoes Rue's own 1994 essay, "Redefining Myth and Religion," which concludes with the following challenge: "I am simply asking whether science, *as science,* has the resources relevant to the expression of a new myth."[60] Rue answers his own question in the affirmative.

Rue's strong affirmation of biological human nature also comes into play here: cultural programming, however powerful, cannot overthrow "the universal layers of organization ordained by the genes."[61] Genetics and neuroscience suggest that a story like the Epic is a particularly good fit with our nature and, especially, with our brain's "story modules."[62] That is, our brains are set up to integrate information about *how things are* with *which things matter.* The Epic of Evolution facilitates this integration more seamlessly and persuasively than any existing story. So while the Epic is admittedly one meme in a sea of memes, it is specially tailored to the structure of our Stone-Age brains. Our brains are *predisposed* to such a story. Meanwhile, the traditional faiths remain "unsatisfying in their accounts of how things are" and "inadequate in their judgments about which things matter."[63]

A competitive, gene- and meme-centered vision of evolution inflects Rue's brand of storytelling and grounds his expectation that everybody's story will outcompete the established traditions. In contrast to heartening metaphors of creativity, relationality, attraction, and bonding that characterize the Universe Story, Rue's cosmic narrative stresses the aggressive, contentious nature of the unfolding universe as though cosmic "evolution" were a bloody battle or zero-sum game.[64] The first living systems "diversified aggressively."[65] Molecules in the early Earth "competed for the attention of unbound atoms," creating "big winners in this chemical free-for-all."[66] The fundamentally competitive quality of the cosmos encompasses the process of mythopoesis itself. There can be only one "big winner" in this competition, and losers who stubbornly remain on the playing field may be subject to harassment and intimidation. This account of myths as competing for the top slot accords with Rue's general suspicion of religious pluralism. These elements come into sharper relief as we further explore his debt to consilience.

HOW THINGS ARE

Rue fully subscribes to what he terms consilient scientific materialism.[67] Theoretical breakthroughs across the disciplines "have gradually revealed what Edward O. Wilson has called 'consilience,'" making it now possible "to construct a coherent narrative of the emergent properties of matter, life, and consciousness."[68] Like other enthusiasts of materialism, Rue characterizes consilience as the "ultimate prize of inquiry," promising that apparent existential losses entailed in a thorough naturalization of religion will be fully offset by "an acquired sense for the mystery and sanctity of nature itself."[69] Rue here lays stress on nature's sanctity, but it turns out that nature's value is at best peripheral and instrumental, as we will see.

For Rue, the Epic gains universality and power to unite from the unity of knowledge itself. Consilience suggests that in *reality* there is not a multiplicity of stories in the universe, but just one. Consilient naturalism goes beyond garden-variety scientific materialism to advance an even bolder claim "about the unity of science."[70] Rue believes the disciplines are beginning to converge, becoming less specialized and increasingly integrated to form a complete and compelling epic (the current, and highly artificial, state of academic sprawl notwithstanding). "What has made this integration possible is the evolutionary paradigm."[71] This integration suggests that education at all levels should reflect a new core curriculum "focused on the evolution of matter, life and consciousness-culture."[72] Even children's science education will take the form of narrative instruction because "the brain is a narrative spinning modular system."[73] "Consilience among scientific disciplines," he argues, "now makes it possible to construct a coherent narrative."[74] Rue's wording might suggest that unity extends primarily to the sciences, but in fact he shares Wilson's faith that *all* areas of knowledge and experience will be subsumed under categories of science or what he calls "natural facts."

Rue's educational agenda would establish a few "faculties" in lieu of our current (as he sees it) haphazard and redundant collection of disciplines. These units would correspond to four kinds of natural facts found in the universe: physical, biological, psychological, and cultural/symbolic. He laments that the last category of cultural and symbolic facts is currently tended by an "unruly hoard" of disciplines in desperate need of scientific streamlining. This ragtag collection includes sociology, anthropology, political science, economics, history, linguistics, mathematics, philosophy, and "the various 'critical' disciplines focused on literature, the arts, and religion."[75] In Rue's account, a physical fact would be a statement about relationships between bonded subatomic particles, while a biological fact might describe how information is transmitted in genes. Psychological facts have to do with information encoded in "neural assemblies."[76] What, then, is a "cultural fact" and how does it fit within the broader category of *natural* facts? Here Rue falls back on the concept of memes: "In socio-symbolic-cultural systems," Rue argues, "information is preserved in *memes*, Richard Dawkins's term for the unit of symbolic variation, transmission, and selection. A cultural tradition is the sum total of its memes."[77] Cultural facts are "naturalized," and thus made part of the repertoire of natural science, by means of an *analogy* to a biological unit of information—the gene—that *does* have physical properties. This dubious move borrows from Dawkins's playbook in *The Selfish Gene.* An analogy is not an argument, of course, and Rue's claims for unity seem rather forced. He simply asserts that culture can be broken down into gene-like units of selection, in order to proclaim a unity of all knowledge—and thus a complete and seamlessly integrated story of who we are, physically, psychologically, culturally. "My confidence in the potential of everybody's story to stimulate a new wisdom tradition is based, in part, on a belief that we will continue to make progress in science," Rue explains. As science progresses, "the features of everybody's story will become more complete and more compelling."[78]

WHICH THINGS MATTER

Turning his attention to "which things matter," Rue develops some original lines of argumentation about what is of value to human and nonhuman well-being. What matters ultimately is something Rue terms "viability." Viability eludes simple definition but a fair rendering would be that, for all living things, what ultimately matters is living. "There is always a set of particular conditions valued by organisms of the species, when pursued effectively, deliver the ultimate good—that is, life."[79] Viability—striving to live—means little in the absence of a life *worth* living, at least for members of our species. Few people would agree to be placed on life-support for the remainder of their life, even if it meant their lives were greatly extended. Proximate values come into play here. Humans have innate motivational systems that drive our curiosity, our desire for pleasure, and our sociality; satisfying these systems creates a sense of a life worth living. What matters proximately, then, are values cited previously: personal wholeness and social coherence. Personal wholeness is achieved, within an individual, by harmonizing our need for intelligibility, pleasure, and emotional fulfillment.[80] These needs are basic to all humans but how we decide to harmonize them varies considerably. Social existence requires that the variety of ways we integrate them be kept under control: "There may be many authentic ways to become a whole person, but encouraging a diversity of these ways is hardly the way to create a coherent society," Rue warns. Social coherence thus entails "reducing diversity . . . by getting the wholeness process as close to a single formula as possible."[81] The Epic offers such a formula.

Achieving balance between values of personal wholeness and social coherence is one of our key lines of defense against threats to our survival or viability. This balancing act takes place, of course, within the broader context of natural systems and thus we have an implicit commitment to "safeguarding" the integrity of natural systems that make our life, and our values, possible.[82] All humans have a vested interest in "sustaining indefinitely a level of biodiversity conducive to the pursuit of personal wholeness and social cohesion."[83] Taken together, what matters proximately are three interrelated goals: achieving and maintaining biospheric integrity, personal wholeness, and social coherence. The "wild card" in all of this is self-esteem, a motivator central to personal wholeness. Our current crisis stems from the fact that self-esteem is often enhanced by behaviors destructive to the environment—"three car garages and lavish vacations."[84] We desperately need to find ways of linking self-esteem and social approval to sound environmental behaviors. "We should scorn opulence and waste while rewarding those who reduce, reuse, and recycle."[85]

Rue's point about our problematic sources of self-esteem is well taken, and his arguments linking personal and societal needs to natural systems are a reasonable defense of the idea that humans need to create enduring, stable interactions with one another and with the natural world (his distaste for diversity notwithstanding). As expressed, however, his argument does not suggest that nature has particular value in its own right, much less that it is "sacred" or worthy of reverence, as his religious naturalism often asserts. We will see that, as his arguments undercut a sense of nature's sacredness, they simultaneously elevate the status of humans. Rue's exaltation of human consciousness, or what he calls "the neural self," treats nature as little more than an inanimate backdrop.

THE WONDER OF THE NEURAL SELF

So far I have presented a largely descriptive account of Rue's work. I now want to draw out what is troubling about the values central to his mythmaking endeavor. These come to the fore when Rue explores the Epic's ability to arouse emotional and moral dispositions such as awe, gratitude, or admiration. Rue's account of the neural self is key here, for, in a complicated and peculiar sense, it is this entity that is celebrated as both the *object* and the *seat* of human storytelling. Other living beings—nonhuman creatures living today, as well as those that preceded our arrival on the evolutionary scene—fade into insignificance as Rue clarifies what is valuable and "thankworthy" in the evolutionary epic. Drawing heavily on arguments of neuroscientist Antonio Damasio, Rue offers "the truth" that the self is an emergent reality, something halfway between Cartesian / realist notions of the self (or soul) and Buddhist assertions that the self has no reality.[86] The emergence of the neural self is bound up with the brain's language and storytelling "modules," its construction of narrative events going on within the body and outside the body. In response to these two narratives, the brain constructs a third metanarrative of its own, as well. From this metanarrative "there arises the reality of self, *a unique subjective perspective* that corresponds to a sense of being alive in an object-filled world."[87] In complex, language-using organisms such as ourselves, narratives take on an intersubjective quality, Rue argues. "The articulate story traditions of a culture interact deeply with the narrative streams constructed by individuals," and thus the neural self comes into being "as a convolution of individual and social construction."[88] Nonhuman organisms are *not* similarly endowed with our complex intersubjectivity and cannot be said to have a neural self.[89]

Recognition of the extreme odds *against* human conscious existence emerging from cosmic processes is in part what provokes gratitude and wonder, including wonder at the neural self. While some of the new cosmologists highlight an inherent teleology and inevitability to cosmic unfolding, Rue stresses improbability and contingency as evocative of a grateful response.[90] "That such an ad hoc and haphazard process has created the most complex and intricate designs in the universe is the most stunning and ingratiating fact one can behold . . . this fact alone compels the humility and gratitude of every person alive."[91] True to the evolutionary paradigm, Rue maintains that responses like gratitude are reinforced by biologically encoded reciprocal altruism—"an emotional response that evolved to regulate reciprocal behavior."[92] Feeling gratitude for the unlikely event of our being here inclines us to "pay it forward."

Rue's discussion of the impulse to respond reciprocally, owing to the gratitude we feel, raises important questions regarding where (to whom or what) we direct the moral and emotional responses triggered by the Epic. Theists who embrace the Epic have no difficulty here, Rue notes, since they have an entity—or at least an image or concept of such an entity—toward whom to direct their affective responses. For nontheists, simply knowing the 14-billion-year-old universe story means loving it. "And to love it is to serve it."[93] The task, then, is to tell our common story in a way that evokes love, wonder, gratitude, and so on. Rue encounters a complication here, in asserting that we love that which we know. What we *know* is the story. Surely our loving, reverential, or grateful response, our *service,* is not owed to the story itself, that is, to the concatenation of facts and the (often long-past and remote) events told in story form. Or is it? Can the story itself serve as a proper object of veneration? Wilson, we have seen, believes it can, insisting that humans learn to worship the evolutionary epic.[94]

Rue struggles to articulate how "social emotions" can be directed toward the Epic, which, he concedes, manifests as an abstract temporal framework and "arrow of time."[95] Something more, it seems, is needed beyond "the unvarnished truth, goodness, and beauty of the epic of evolution" itself.[96] Perhaps the story needs imagery to focus the emotions and direct the will.[97] Rue casts about for a worthy object of love and gratitude for the nontheist—an "imagined target," a secular counterpart to a divine entity. He argues that there are suggestive precedents in the faith traditions for "redirection" of gratitude, as when Jesus tells his followers that loving him means feeding his *sheep*. The same sort of redirection is appropriate for "our story" as well. "If the ultimate value is the continuation of life, then it makes perfect sense to repay our gratitude for the evolutionary past by endowing the future."[98] Put differently (and somewhat counterintuitively), we are in the position of "thanking the future" for the gift of "the evolutionary past."[99] Surrounding ourselves with images and symbols of our natural history, much as medieval Europeans were surrounded by Christian images, will "arouse gratitude *for the epic of evolution* and transform this deficit into a commitment to future generations."[100] These images of natural history "have not yet arrived," but Rue is confident that they will come "if the story gets out there."[101]

It is an odd and impoverished form of religious naturalism that struggles so perceptibly to identify something of value in the universe toward which to direct affective and awe-filled responses. Rue seems unduly preoccupied with reverence for the scientific *story*. This misplaced reverence leads him to suggest that images and symbols of the natural world act as devotional aids to the story. Shouldn't we instead understand the story as a means of facilitating and reinforcing commitment to the natural world and its creatures? Why wait for the arrival of *images* and *symbols* of natural history to inspire us, when the "real" living characters in the evolutionary epic exist all around us? Rue's peculiar conflation of the scientific narrative with its presumed objects results in privileging the narrative and its symbols over and above the living world. A one-dimensional interpretation of religions as coherence-inducing *texts* and *narratives* undergirds Rue's endeavor, as does an "evolutionary" understanding of myths in competition to produce a winner.

To be fair, he does suggest at one point that we direct affective responses to *future generations* of humans, a "cult of our descendants," if you will. "If thanksgiving requires a face, then let it be the face of future generations."[102] This is a commendable, if difficult goal (a good deal of literature on the ethics of climate change attempts to grapple with this problem of obligations to future generations, for example.)[103] But how do the faces of *non*humans figure into his value framework? Rue highlights the continuation of life and "viability" as what matters ultimately, but there is a peculiar absence at the heart of his ostensibly nature-reverencing naturalism. "The story of cosmic evolution reveals to us the common origins, nature, and destiny shared by all human beings,"[104] he notes, yet his quest for a global story and culture neglects the larger point about the shared kinship and fate of *all life*.

If nature sometimes figures as backdrop to Rue's Epic, humans are foregrounded and held aloft. Ultimately, the human neural self emerges as the most "thankworthy" entity in the universe. "If I could save but one thing it would be [the neural self]," Rue confesses.[105] The Epic of Evolution "humbles us before the magnitude and complexity of creation," and yet contemplation of the neural self is less conducive to humility than its opposite, as Rue acknowledges: "There may be an element of species arrogance embedded in the attempt to exalt the power and glory of human conscious existence," he concedes. "If there is, I hasten to confess it, for I believe that the human neural self is the most thankworthy reality in the universe."[106] Because human conscious existence is the "most highly contingent reality we know," it is the thing to "cherish." Gratitude for the "splendors of consciousness" entails that we preserve systems that allowed it to evolve and persist: "If we want to save the neural self," Rue admonishes, "then we will fiercely safeguard the integrity of the natural and social systems by which it comes to be."[107] Much as images of the natural world (or its history) merely facilitate reverence for the story, the natural world is valued as the necessary condition for the continuation of a more truly inspiring entity, human consciousness.

RELIGIOUS NATURALISM — WITHOUT NATURE?

If Wilson seems slightly underwhelmed in his endorsement of *Everybody's Story,* the problem may lie with Rue's generally uninspired narration of the Epic. Rue has moments of eloquence, to be sure: "A mere slip of the genetic tongue could bring down a majestic elephant," he observes.[108] Echoing Carl Sagan, Rue evokes humans' essential "star-born" nature. "We are geological formations," in Rue's suggestive phrase. This is the language of metaphor and myth, the "poetic" translation of science. Often, however, Rue simply demands that the reader respond with gratitude and awe to the evolutionary epic: "I am at the point of suggesting it is appropriate that we feel grateful for matter."[109] As anyone who has raised a child can attest, people seldom feel gratitude simply because they are instructed that they should, in light of certain facts about their existence. Rue flatly asserts that the Epic of Evolution has "potential to arouse and direct the emotional regulators of behavior."[110] Part of the problem lies in Rue's fixation with religions as mythic projects that (when properly designed by the custodians of memes) effectively "trigger" appropriate feelings and behaviors. Religious myths work by "manipulating our brains so that we might think, feel, and act in ways that are good for us, both individually and collectively."[111] It is as though Rue believes religions to function as calculated and calibrated efforts of mythmakers to trigger responses from an audience, as a scientist might induce a lab rat to press a lever.

Habituated to the logic of evolutionary strategies, Rue's approach is reminiscent of Wilson's flat-footed insistence that biophilic responses will automatically be prompted through sheer dint of information about DNA helices and genomes. For all his interest in the wonder-provoking nature of contingency, Rue understands his task as narrating what is confidently known, namely, "the least contingent and the most accurate cosmology available to us."[112] But where is the mystery in that? Where in these narratives are the questions that confound us—the "aporiai, blocked passages, difficulties, obscurities, obstacles to understanding"—that are the stuff of poetry and storytelling?[113]

POST-APOCALYPTIC SPIRITUALITY AND RUE'S BIOCENTRIC LIE

Rue's commitment to myths as survival strategies is also reflected in his assumption that religious naturalism will emerge in a post-apocalyptic (in his phrase, post-holocaust) world, with society's realization that humans need nature to survive. "A post-holocaust mythic vision would seek to integrate this [evolutionary] cosmology with an eco-centric morality, the imperative to sustain human life on the planet by addressing needs for personal wholeness and social coherence within the limits of natural systems."[114] Myths are borne of crises and sustained by fear. Mythmaking erupts when a society must quickly "wise up," when it is pushed to the edge. "Radical changes become possible only when the ancillary mechanisms lose their effectiveness and the prevailing wisdom of a culture begins to look implausible and irrelevant."[115] Under extreme evolutionary pressure, alternative stories emerge. Not surprisingly, this apocalyptic perspective leaves little room for positive feelings of wonder and affinity with nature. The natural environment confronts us first and foremost as "everybody's problem."

Rue concludes *Religion Is Not about God* on a note of what he calls irony, but cynicism seems more apt. Just as religion is not really about God, he writes, religious naturalism is not really about nature. Both are ultimately "about" optimizing human reproductive fitness and regulating human behavior. "Religious naturalists may affirm the sacredness of nature and practice eco-centric piety sincerely, yet deep down they must know that religion is no more about Nature than it is about God."[116] Rue's *By the Grace of Guile* (1994) expounds on deception's central role in human interactions and evolutionary history. He explains that the book grew out of his long-standing interest in distinguishing appearance and reality. *Reality* for Rue (as with Slingerland) consists in the wonder-evoking revelation that our most deeply held values are elaborate forms of genetically wired deception and self-deception. Rue advances a case for myths as forms of deception that have enabled human survival. Near the opening of *By the Grace of Guile*, he professes with a certain bravado his allegiance to the "monstrous truth" of nihilism and the futility of searching for any universal truths.

> The universe is blind and aimless, it has no value in and of itself, it is unenchanted by forces or qualities or characteristics that might objectively endorse any particular human orientation toward it. The universe is dead and void of meaning. Its significance is not demonstrably one thing or another. The universe *just* is.[117]

The nihilist view is true, he believes, but also fundamentally maladaptive. Rue reiterates these ideas in *Religion Is Not about God*, arguing that in the holocaust aftermath, nihilism—and supernaturalism—will finally be understood as "potentially, as well as historically, maladaptive."[118] Therefore, new myths are necessary in order to keep anomie, despair, and societal chaos at bay. In an interesting departure from the truth claims made on behalf of the new myth—claims made elsewhere by Rue himself—he here declares their truth to be "irrelevant." Traditional religions have functioned as *noble lies*, intended to cover over actual meaninglessness, but their persuasive power is rapidly declining. We need a *new noble lie* that will "re-enchant the universe by getting us to perceive, *in spite of ourselves*, that its significance is objective."[119] We have seen this move before among champions of evolutionary (dis)enchantment, as with Slingerland's insistence that genes dupe us into feeling love for offspring. We are deceived into embracing values that science has actually discredited, simply because embracing them is maximally adaptive.

In this spirit, Rue proposes what he acknowledges to be a *false* myth of "biocentrism," constructed around an equally false notion of *anima mundi*—the Earth as a sacred, living entity. The biocentric lie consists in the idea that "we are bound together with all other species in a planetary symbiosis wherein each unit of life is organized in the service of viability."[120] The main criterion for judging the value of the biocentric myth, he argues, is its conformity to the "new naturalism"—physical reality as described by up-to-date science. From here, Rue's argument becomes disturbing as he proceeds to draw parallels between this false biocentric myth and Plato's noble lie in *The Republic*. In Rue's blueprint of society, some members—the "best-trained minds"—will know the noble lie *as* a lie, while others—a majority not so well trained—will be kept in the dark. Biocentrism is "a noble lie, one that washes down with a minimum of deception and offers up a maximum of adaptive change. And if it is well and artfully told, it will reenchant the earth and save us from the truth."[121]

These cynical revelations may well come as a shock to readers who have taken Rue advocacy of nature's sanctity and worth at face value. Note the shift in language from *By the Grace of Guile*, where he depicts a universe that is dead, blind, aimless, and devoid of "enchanted forces," to his account in *Everybody's Story* of matter as "busy, creative, surprising, and melodic . . . order-seeking, system-building, self-organizing, well-informed, excited stuff." "Matter," he rejoices, "is just as grand as it can be."[122] A subsequent monograph, *Nature Is Enough* (2011), finds Rue pondering why the vibrant "intellectual / spiritual / moral" vision of naturalism "hasn't blossomed into a full-fledged religious tradition."[123] It is difficult to reconcile Rue's emphatic postmodern disavowal of universal truth in *By the Grace of Guile* with his enthusiasm in later works for consilient unity of science and universal truths of human nature. "I am so persuaded by the postmodern critique of foundationalism," he writes in *By the Grace of Guile*, "that I am compelled to embrace its nihilism in a way that postmodernists are generally reluctant to do: Here, I'll even say it: *Nihilism is true*."[124] This confession places Rue in an awkward position vis-à-vis his scientific and ideological guides, Wilson and Dawkins, especially given Wilson's foreword to *Everybody's Story*. Wilson, remember, understands consilience as a resumption of the Enlightenment project; he explicitly pits consilience against all forms of postmodernism as their "ultimate polar antithesis."[125] Which version of Rue are we to believe? Is he merely striving for "irony"? A reasonable explanation is that *Everybody's Story* and *Nature Is Enough* represent Rue's own effort to construct a *noble lie*, an attempt to persuade others to embrace a myth about the inherent moral and spiritual significance of the natural world that Rue himself holds to be false, but highly adaptive. Little wonder, then, that his narration of the Epic fails to convey nature's value.

BIOLOGICAL AND CULTURAL DIVERSITY

I have dwelled at length on Rue's work in order to indicate its bankrupt expressions of wonder and "ecomorality," but we should also attend to his claims regarding the Epic's "astringent" implications for religious tolerance. Observers and practitioners of new forms of religious naturalism or green spirituality hold out hope that these movements may inspire a united, worldwide response to pressing environmental concerns. Bron Taylor gives the name "dark green religion" (DGR) to a spectrum of religions grounded in evolutionary worldviews and a profound sense of ecological affinity. Other elements, such as prophetic and apocalyptic dimensions, and recourse to "extralegal" forms of environmental protection, may be present in these religions as well. Taylor is well aware that certain perils inhere in dark green worldviews, but he offers the following defense:

> The traits typical of dark green religion—such as a stress on ecological interdependence, an affective connection to the earth as home and to nonhuman organisms as kin, and the overturning of anthropocentric hubris—are unlikely to promote either suppression of others or lead to cultural homogenization .... This is in no small measure *because both biological and cultural diversity are highly valued as the fruits of evolution.*[126]

These potential perils are thus "miniscule compared to the risks of an anemic response to what are potentially catastrophic environmental dangers."[127]

Rue's worldview fits with several features of DGR, such as its grounding in evolutionary science, and its apocalyptic and prophetic dimensions. Rue's epic, like DGR, offers potential for "advancing global solidarity" and for "harnessing the emotional effectors of kin selection and reciprocal altruism to serve the integrity of natural and social systems."[128] Evolutionary cosmology, Rue writes, reveals to us the common origin, nature, and destiny shared by all human beings. It documents our essential kinship as no other story can do . . . [It] shows us in the deepest possible sense that we are all sisters and brothers—fashioned from the same stellar dust, energized by the same star, nourished by the same planet, endowed with the same genetic code, and threatened by the same evils.[129]

Rue sometimes identifies biospheric diversity as a (proximate) value, though he stops well short of positing intrinsic value for all life, emphasizing *human* solidarity and kinship where one might expect him to celebrate a broader affinity with life. By no means does Rue's emphasis on diversity in *biological* systems translate into an affirmation of cultural diversity, as Taylor hopes. It is odd that Rue sees religious diversity as primarily a destabilizing force in society, given the strong parallels he affirms between biological systems (e.g., genes) and the generation of cultural and symbolic "facts" such as memes. In short, Taylor's contention that green religions grounded in evolutionary perspectives will likely embrace *cultural* manifestations of diversity is not borne out by Rue, who disparages the world religions as potentially unleashing a "hemorrhage of diversity."[130]

Whether an oppressive or repressive social regime would accompany the cultural homogenization Rue desires (should it emerge) is an open question. But homogenization seems unlikely to foster tolerance for dissenting views, especially if, as Rue predicts, supernaturalism and adherence to the old faith traditions come to be seen in post-holocaust society as "maladaptive" worldviews *responsible* for the conditions of the environmental collapse. ("After all," Rue says of the traditional faiths, "the crisis developed under their watch."[131] Survivors will understand that "the established religious traditions failed to prevent the most horrific event in human history."[132]) That Rue's naturalism puts insufficient stress on values Taylor identifies—nonanthropocentrism and a "deep sense of the value of biological *and* cultural diversity"—is further cause for concern. Rue might object that he is not advocating the universal naturalism described in his books, but merely *predicting* its emergence in the chastened, post-holocaust world.[133] That defense is hard to take seriously in light of his call for a new biocentric myth and science-based religion in *Zygon* and elsewhere. *Everybody's Story*, it seems, is Rue's articulation of a new noble lie.

URSULA GOODENOUGH'S RELIGIOUS NATURALISM

One of Rue's supporters and collaborators on a consilience-based evolutionary epic is Ursula Goodenough. A cell biologist and author of a widely used genetics textbook, Goodenough came to wider attention with *The Sacred Depths of Nature* (1998), a scientist's personal and spiritual reflection on nature and natural processes. Like Rue, she regards the Epic as the one narrative capable of fostering the values needed to cope with our current global challenges, and she shares Rue's conviction that consilience sets a radical new agenda for university education. Goodenough also takes up Rue's challenge of mythopoesis—or what she terms religiopoiesis: "the crafting of religion" based on scientific materials.[134] Indeed, she credits Rue with "explain[ing] to me most of what I understand about theology and philosophy."[135] Rue's influence is discernible in her basic division of reality into "how things are" and "which things matter." *How things are* is recounted with reference to the Epic of Evolution.[136] The category of things that "matter" is composed of Goodenough's religious-like reflections on that story. *The Sacred Depths of Nature* is thus set up as a series of biological explanations of various phenomena, a "walk through the Epic of Evolution," followed by "religious" responses. As we will see, a *religious* or *spiritual* response is, for Goodenough, more or less synonymous with subjective feelings and emotional reactions.

RELIGIOPOIESIS AND SCIENTIFIC WONDER

The biologist daughter of a Methodist minister and religion scholar, Goodenough encountered a range of religious ideas growing up, but never settled into any tradition. Though shaped by insights from Rue and Wilson, her form of religious naturalism appears more genuinely open to the presence of cosmic mystery—"big questions" that are, and will likely remain, unknowable. In a series of blogs sponsored by National Public Radio, Goodenough confesses that she began her journey toward religious naturalism in a state of depression and terror over the "apparent meaninglessness and indifference" of the enormous cosmos. Gradually she came to embrace a "covenant" with mystery that allowed her to suspend questions of ultimacy. "The idea, as well as the challenge, is to become comfortable with not-knowing, comfortable with having no answer to the question of why there is anything at all rather than nothing."[137] If covenant implies a kind of "deal" or "exchange," then the benefits, for Goodenough, include freedom from the crushing imperative of having to figure everything out. "I wiggle my toes in the relief that comes from no longer needing to join this quest."[138]

Goodenough's reconciliation to mystery, as already hinted, distinguishes her somewhat from scientific mythmakers of a more positivist bent. Dawkins, in fact, takes Goodenough and her project of religiopoiesis to task for deploying religious-sounding metaphors to convey what are actually (in Dawkins's view) secular-scientific expressions of wonder and uplift. "If we are allowed to relabel scientific awe as a religious impulse," he notes, "the case goes through on the nod. You have *redefined* science as religion, so it's hardly surprising if they turn out to 'converge.'"[139] No fan of convergence or harmony between science and religion, Dawkins contends that his own "'atheistic' views are identical to Goodenough's 'religious' ones. One of us is misusing the English language," he concludes, "and I don't think it's me."[140] Dawkins is onto something here, though not quite in the way he believes:

he correctly understands Goodenough's wonder as a response to *science* and as stemming from an attempt to refashion science as a religion. But it is not quite the case that he and Goodenough share a sense of mystery. She would agree with Dawkins that the workings of life "are not mysterious at all"—sperm and egg, cell division, genes switching on and off, brain development, etc., are well within human understanding. But a distinct feeling of "cosmic Mystery" remains, quite apart from these inquiries into how things work.[141]

Goodenough's awe in the face of cosmic mystery has been described by others as ontological wonder—the mystery of *"being* itself" or wonder at why there is something rather than nothing.[142] Wonder at *what* something is or how it works (a more mundane expression of curiosity) is distinguished here from wonder *that* a thing is. The latter sometimes involves the apprehension of contingency, because *that* a thing came to be at all is part of the wonder.[143] In contrast to Dawkins's quest for a "nirvana" of final knowledge and his dread of ever-deeper mysteries, Goodenough stresses the *emancipatory* quality of acknowledging that some mysteries are not problems to be solved. Yet Goodenough is clearly more at ease in the "sacred depths" of genes and cells—where evolutionary processes are well understood and the mysteries few—than in the disorienting depths of cosmic unknowns. Her covenant with mystery seems more like an uneasy truce than a willing embrace, in light of her commitment to articulating and disseminating a coherent, consilient, integrated story of evolution. More on that shortly.

Turning her attention to existing religious myths and the need for a shared scientific story, Goodenough makes short work of the world religions. "I set about analyzing religious systems," she explains, "using the paradigm most familiar to me, the paradigm of biological evolution."[144] She imposes a simplistic typology on all the major religions and finds them wanting in terms of their cognitive appeal and environmental potential. Here, differences between her worldview and Dawkins's become harder to discern, for she ends up defending a rarefied form of wonder that is, as she concedes, inaccessible or unappealing to the scientifically uninitiated.

Before examining the details of her classification of religions, it is worth noting that Goodenough's rather ambitious undertaking of classifying all of the world's religions ("My goal was to develop a taxonomy of religious systems that would allow me to understand what they attempt to achieve") does not cite a single scholarly source on religion, theories of religion, or any other relevant discipline or study.[145] Other than a passing reference to Camille Paglia, her *only* sources are the *OED* (for definitions of "cults" and "faith") and Rue's essay in the same issue of *Zygon* (Rue, in that essay, cites no one).[146] The assumption that scientists can and should dive into disciplinary waters of religious studies or the humanities—with no particular training or preparatory study—is evident in Goodenough's approach to religiopoiesis generally, and it is an unfortunate feature of many consilient endeavors.

Goodenough essentially agrees with Rue that existing "myths" (the traditional faiths) do not provide the unified and unifying story we need, and like him she envisions religions as competing evolutionary strategies. Religions exhibiting the most compelling myths or appealing *rewards,* such as promise of an afterlife, tend to be high in evolutionary fitness or what Goodenough calls "reproductive success."[147] She arrives at a schema consisting of three categories: ancestor cults, sky cults, and earth cults. The category of ancestor cults includes virtually "all religious systems" insofar as they create continuity with the past by means of art, ritual, and belief, and regard the dead as "actively engaged in bestowing benefits or harm."[148] Sky cults, which may also function as ancestor cults, ask questions about ultimate origins and destiny, and often display belief in a supernatural creator who is actively involved in the day-to-day lives of believers. Together, the first two categories encompass the main established traditions: "The major present-day religious institutions are sky cults with myths that feature active, judging gods."[149]

Earth cults, her third category, are often characterized by nature-centered rituals like rain dances or seasonal celebrations, but offer little in the way of otherworldly rewards such as afterlife or immortality. Lacking the "reward" component of otherworldly forms of liberation, belief in afterlife, reincarnation, or immortality, they do not compete successfully with ancestor or sky cults "in the evolutionary lottery."[150] Ancestor and sky cults, on the other hand, offer appealing rewards but cannot serve as viable options in today's world because they "leave global matters largely unaddressed."[151] A scientific worldview has nothing to contribute to these types of religions—*all* of the major world traditions, according to her classification scheme—because they are essentially closed systems, providing answers to questions about why we are here and where we are going on their own unscientific terms. "After hundreds of years of effort, in thousands of books written by thousands of theologians and physicists, the science/sky-cult dialogue remains a standoff."[152] Moreover, these traditions tell stories that are too particular to be expanded into a global myth. Because they evolved to fill a particular niche, they cannot tell *everybody's* story, and that makes them deeply problematic. Any attempt to reform the world religions to the point that they could offer a global orientation and universal appeal "would be the equivalent of trying to transform one species into another."[153] Science can gain no point of entry here, no foothold.

Still, Goodenough holds out modest hope for the rehabilitation of earth cults. The sciences of the earth—"biology, geology, anthropology, and psychology [*sic*]"—are potentially of interest to earth cults that embrace nature spirituality and are oriented to earthly concerns. But earth cults present other difficulties as candidates for a global myth. Goodenough notes the mystical appeal of "New Age" earth cults (earth goddess traditions or contemporary appropriations of Native American traditions, as well as Earth Day rituals or celebrations), but dismisses their forms of mysticism as insufficiently embedded within cognitive reality. Indeed,

New Age and earth cult adherents, she believes, are often overtly *hostile* to science. Like other religions, earth cults fail to yield to "contemporary understandings of How Things Are derived via scientific inquiry"; consequently, they produce "all-too-familiar conflicts about which accounts are 'true.'"[154] There are simply too many deficiencies in the existing traditions, even the earth-centered varieties. "Therefore," Goodenough concludes, "if we want an earth cult grounded in a scientific cosmology, we're going to have to invent one."[155] Enter the Epic of Evolution.

A SCIENTIZED EARTH CULT

What values animate the scientized, cognitively satisfying cult Goodenough hopes to establish? Or, in the mythmaker's language, what does her new religion say about *how things are* and *which things matter?* Goodenough (like Wilson) often frames her call for a new mythology in terms of what science can do for religion, but it is more accurate to say that science is being retooled to serve as a religion, the existing traditions having been rejected as inadequate. To see this, we need to look more closely at what is entailed in embedding a new earth cult within scientific reality, and what counts as knowledge of that reality.

Goodenough offers the seemingly modest proposal that scientific knowledge is *one* path to discovering, and wondering at, nature's power and beauty.

> [T]he beauty of molecular and cellular organization is a powerful complement to the beauty of rainfall and redwoods and owls. Life is beautiful all the way down. . . . [T]he biological world yields an increasing sense of sacredness the better it is known. The more we know about life, the more we can care about it. . . . We can therefore say that the more we know about life, the deeper becomes our affection for it.[156]

Here she alludes to a scientific perception of beauty and awe (say, that of cells and molecules) that *complements* beauty and awe directly experienced when one encounters majestic trees or wild creatures, without the aid of "deeper" scientific understanding. Is the molecular and cellular perspective *necessary* for a full appreciation of what is truly wondrous about the natural world? In other words, is appreciation of redwoods and owls otherwise deficient? Sometimes she asserts that perception of nature's sacredness is increased "the better it is known" (that is, as a scientist knows it). At other times, she presents this perception of nature's beauty or sacredness as apprehended through the lens of science as a mere personal preference. "*For me*," she writes, "a religion works only if it offers the opportunity for mystical experience, but it needs . . . to be embedded in my cognitive reality."[157] Yet her project of religiopoiesis is no mere expression of personal preference but an astonishingly broad indictment of all religions, including earth cults, as disconnected from scientific reality. In those religions, she concedes, "the earth is evoked as power, energy, magic, fertility, a source of transformation. . . .

symbolic use of fire, air, and water, and rituals focus on lunar and seasonal cycles."
But they fall short because "none of this is oriented within the present-day scientific worldview." It therefore becomes necessary to "invent" a science-based global cult that can be adopted by all. Thus, in answer to the question of whether grounding in scientific reality is an "essential" feature of an earth cult, Goodenough answers with "a most emphatic yes."[158]

Goodenough recognizes that nature-oriented religions have emerged in cultures that knew (or know) nothing of "genes or molecules or plate tectonics," but she nevertheless maintains that science ought to function in such religions as something like a main text or canon, like the Bible or Koran. "The earth sciences could be such a text . . . a basis preferable to the authority of custom." She urges scientists to share with others their sense of the "mythic potential" of cells and molecules.[159] "Awe" made possible by science will turn to "affection" for nature.[160] "The more we know about life, the more we can care about it." As an example, she offers sociobiological claims about kin selection that present a "calculus" of genetic relatedness. This calculus, she ventures, explains why we care more for organisms with whom we share genes. And since we share genes with all life, sociobiology actually *enables* a broad concern for the whole Earth: "Our cognitive understanding of evolution now allows us to take this concept much further: to the extent that the genes are shared throughout all of life, this gives us a lot more to care about."[161] It is precisely this link between *is* and *ought* that Wilson tries, and largely fails, to forge between sociobiology or consilient unity, on the one hand, and environmental ethics on the other. Goodenough similarly holds that a cognitive understanding of evolution directly "enrich[es] the mythos of an earth cult."[162] But does it? What is to prevent this "calculus" from justifying a position of caring very little or not at all for organisms far removed from us on the genetic spectrum? This calculus could simply *reinforce*, rather than correct, our existing biases.

We have seen that, in Goodenough's account, religious belief is, ideally, met with "rewards" that enhance its reproductive success.[163] She recognizes that the cognitively embedded and accurate earth cult she endorses will likely encounter difficulties with the "reward component," for it cannot easily compete with appealing rewards like afterlife or reincarnation offered by major world traditions. Her proposed solutions to this problem redirect attention to the wonder of science. One "way out" is to suggest that the greatest rewards of science may yet be forthcoming, and may come in forms we cannot yet understand or imagine.[164] In other words, she proposes that science may *yet* produce wonders to rival—possibly outcompete—the rewards of the existing faiths. Another proposal favored by Goodenough (and familiar to readers of this book) is that "the awe and wonder generated by *understanding of scientific cosmology* is itself its own inherent reward."[165] Goodenough concedes that this argument will not "carry much freight in our times since most persons find the scientific cosmology difficult and alienating" and, as

nonscientists, have little or no direct access to the forms of wonder scientists celebrate. Nevertheless, she believes that poetic and metaphorical renderings of the
story can "convey meaning and motivation" even for the untutored.[166] Religiopoiesis will allow laypersons to experience the scientist's awe in a vicarious way. The
scientist's task, she claims, is to "pull back the curtain," revealing wonders not seen
by the uninitiated.[167] She hopes other scientists will join in her scientized "earth-
cult evangelis[m]."[168]

It strikes me that Goodenough's solution to the problem of insufficient rewards
for her scientific religion does not mention meaningful connection and intimate
rapport with the natural world itself, as a possible source of "inherent" motivation,
meaning, or reward. She seems to have forgotten a primary goal of inventing this
cosmology in the first place. In a move reminiscent of Dawkins, she proffers the
more difficult forms of awe afforded by scientific understanding as intrinsically more
rewarding than a vaguely "mystical" response available through other channels.

A fixation with religions as texts, stories, and narratives is part of what drives
this neglect of nature. Goodenough believes that the authoritative "text" of science
ought to displace the authority of local custom and belief, or traditional environmental knowledge not grounded in contemporary scientific reality. Does Goodenough really believe that a culture with minimal regard for nonhuman life will
awaken to biospheric, interspecies consciousness, owing to a lesson in biology—
perhaps swapping out Genesis for genetics? Or that a culture with enormous
regard for the natural world is deficient because it lacks an exhaustive understanding of biology and the "mythic potential" of "cells and molecules?"[169] It may well be
that, to certain scientifically trained individuals, nature appears sacred "all the way
down" to the molecular level. But it does not follow that mastery of molecular biology is a prerequisite for experiencing the wonder and sacredness of nature. Perhaps Goodenough has immersed herself too long in genetics textbooks.

ONE STORY OR MANY?

When charged with endeavoring to replace the traditional faiths with a scientized
global cult, new cosmologists (with the possible exception of Rue, who makes
plain his distaste for pluralism and diversity) proclaim deep respect for the inherited traditions. Goodenough's "planetary epic" makes no claim "to supplant existing traditions," she insists, "but would seek to coexist with them, informing our
global concerns while we continue to orient our daily lives in our cultural and
religious contexts."[170] Near the conclusion of *The Sacred Depths of Nature* she professes "love" for the "traditional religions," noting that "once we have our feelings
about Nature in place, then I believe that we can also find important ways to call
ourselves Jews, or Muslims, or Taoists, or Hopi, or Hindus, or Christians, or Bud-
dhists."[171] In other work, she reiterates these benign intentions: "I am in no way

suggesting that this new tradition would compete with, let alone 'bury,' the existing traditions. Rather it would coexist with them, informing and guiding our global concerns while fully respecting, indeed celebrating and often appropriating, the many deep truths to be found in traditional texts and practice."[172] How do we align these calls for "coexistence" of traditional faiths alongside the Epic with Goodenough's argument that the major traditions—ancestor cults and sky cults—are impervious to earthbound or scientifically informed concerns (recall that, together, these two categories comprise nearly all of the established faiths). Goodenough's proposal that the world religions be "informed" or "guided" by a new scientific myth is puzzling, given her assertion that older traditions *cannot* incorporate scientific materials: "To my mind, the worldview provided by science cannot make any contribution to these orientations, nor should it attempt to do so."[173] Indeed, as we have seen, she likens the prospect of these religions transforming themselves to instances of one species evolving wholesale into another—an evolutionary impossibility.

Talk of respecting, cherishing, treasuring, celebrating diversity—"not only geodiversity and biodiversity but also mythic diversity"[174]—is common among the new mythmakers. These disclaimers are issued even as the new cosmologists trace culpability for the environmental crisis to these traditions, and indict their particularity and diversity as a root cause of their obsolescence and dysfunctionality. Goodenough's project of religiopoiesis leaves the reader wondering on what bases, exactly, these traditions are to be cherished and respected by New Story converts. On the grounds that (as Goodenough believes) their narratives are "untrue," and their worldviews narrow? Perhaps on the grounds that their texts and customs lack "authority"? Or that they spurn ecomorality and are "hostile" to science? That their forms of mysticism clash with "cognitive" orientations? In short, what are the "many deep truths" Goodenough discerns in the existing faiths? Her public speaking venues often include liberal religious congregations where she discusses with church members the possibility of weaving their own traditions, and their "God beliefs,"[175] into the evolutionary epic. As she concedes in an interview conducted by Epic evangelists Michael Dowd and Connie Barlow, combining traditional beliefs and stories with the Epic *can* be done, but "it's a lot more work. It's much easier if one just takes this [Epic] as their story and responds to it religiously, because there aren't any other projects that one is attending to at the same time."[176] Goodenough's interlocutors concur. Having long reflected on the "one or two story" dilemma, Dowd (a former Christian minister) recommends adopting the Epic as one's *only* story, because doing so "doesn't require the mental effort of trying to figure out how they mix."[177] Yet it is hard to imagine that those holding *God beliefs* and other "many deep truths" will assent to the simple expediency of responding "religiously" to a scientific narrative instead. (Imagine exchanging a central tenet like "God loves you" for the idea that "the cosmos worked really long and hard to create you and you should be really appreciative."[178]) This candid discussion among some of the foremost proselytizers of the Epic—Goodenough, Rue, Barlow—suggests that even they are skeptical that retaining the established traditions and their alleged truths alongside the new myth is a workable and worthwhile undertaking.[179]

The conviction that all should adopt—or submit to the imposition of—the "one story" option is perhaps best illustrated by Rue and Goodenough's joint call for reforming college education, the subject to which we now turn. With this discussion, we also gain a clearer idea of what it means to respond "religiously," as Goodenough understands it.

CONSILIENT EDUCATIONAL REFORM

Excitement about transforming university education in light of a new cosmic story has roots in Thomas Berry's rationale for "universe education," and E. O. Wilson's call to shore up the presumed crumbling structure of the disciplines by applying consilience. New Story enthusiasts call for humans to forge greater intimacy and rapport with the universe. But what can rapport with the entire universe possibly mean, in practical terms? As Berry sees it, our universities are far too fixated on our "existing cultural forms," and the disciplines have therefore failed to reconceive themselves in light of current scientific cosmology. Our present situation demands that "the university find its primary concern in a functional cosmology."[180] Berry's vision treats the universe as the "emergent reality" that grounds all else.

> Education at all levels would be understood as knowing the universe story and the human role in the story. The basic course in any college or university would be the story of the universe. . . . Our greatest single need is to accept this story of the universe as we now know this as our sacred story. It could be considered as the most magnificent of all creation stories.[181]

Like Wilson, Berry contends that the sciences are converging on a new synthesis and unified understanding of reality.[182] Once complete, this integration empowers science as the basis for a metareligious vision. The new vision constitutes the "greatest religious, moral, and spiritual event . . . the supreme humanistic and spiritual as well as the supreme scientific event."[183]

New cosmologists see the transformation of university education as the direct application of the new myth. Dominican University in California, for example, requires students to take a two-semester "first year experience" course on Big History. The course weaves human knowledge into a master narrative and a modern, scientific creation story. It regularly features lectures by Brian Swimme and readings are drawn from a textbook coauthored by big historians David Christian and Cynthia Brown.[184] Eric Chaisson has taught a similar undergraduate course on

"Cosmic Evolution" at both Tufts and Harvard. At Northern Arizona University, Russell Merle Genet, an astronomer and Epic enthusiast, teaches a grand tour of "physical, natural, social, and cultural sciences."[185]

These courses represent consilience in action, whether they invoke the term or not—and many do. They endeavor to yoke the sciences to the humanities in a grand narrative project that is ostensibly multicultural, and interdisciplinary (though note Genet's emphasis on the *science* of cultural and social studies). "If scientists were to agree that the epic's evolutionary contents are correct, and humanists were to concur that it is presented in a thoughtful, artistic manner, sensitive to the values and nuances of the various cultures represented by the students," Genet argues, "how could anyone ask for more?"[186]

But how nuanced and culturally sensitive are these course materials? It is impossible to know, in many cases, whether and how these courses encourage critical reflection among students or allow them to dissent from the "one story" solution. It would also be interesting to know whether these materials spark student concern and engagement with *environmental* issues. My impression, drawn from a perusal of available course materials, and an analysis of the rhetoric promoting such courses, is that these curricular interventions function largely as a vehicle for conversion to the Epic and its attendant esteem of science.

Goodenough, who for several years taught an undergraduate course at Washington University in St. Louis called "The Epic of Evolution," is a case in point. Assignments ask students to respond to course material (primarily science) in a "narrative form," through use of storytelling, poetry, prose, or drawings. The course moves from Big Bang cosmology to the emergence of sentient life on Earth, engaging themes of "complexity, scale, energy and entropy applied to the Big Bang, origin of matter, formation of the Earth, geological history, origin of life, how life works, and how life evolves." It also endeavors to explore "the implications of the epic for philosophy, religion, global polity, and environmental ethics." Texts include Goodenough's *The Sacred Depths of Nature* and Loyal Rue's *Everybody's Story,* as well as readings from physicist Steven Weinberg and ethologist Frans de Waal.[187]

Rue and Goodenough's commitment to teaching the Epic at the college level is inspired by "Wilson's bold vision" of a consilient curriculum.[188] A co-authored essay spells out their rationale for such a course, echoing several claims integral to the "epic science" genre. It is argued, for example, that recent breakthroughs in science make it possible to extend the evolutionary paradigm broadly, in novel directions; doing so will produce a fresh, coherent vision of nature and ourselves that has the potential to transform our lives and culture. "We may now speak of the unity of knowledge in a way that has never before been possible," Rue and Goodenough claim. "Inherent in this story is a rich and satisfying account of who we are, where we have come from, and how we might become fulfilled," they confidently assert.[189] The *Kulturkampf* over core curriculum (the Western canon vs. multiculturalism; conservatives vs. liberals) has grown increasingly tedious and irrelevant, they contend. Rue and Goodenough argue that these debates emerged before the watershed publication of *Consilience*. In that less enlightened time, before science emerged as the authority on "human nature," it was popularly believed that the *humanities* spoke authoritatively about humanity's greatest stories. "Understanding humanity was then the exclusive province of the humanities," Rue and Goodenough note. "But this is no longer true, as Wilson's *Consilience* makes abundantly clear. Indeed, it is so far from being true that one might insist (as we do) that any story of human nature not firmly grounded in the sciences does not merit the attention of youthful minds."[190]

Consilience presents an opportunity, Rue and Goodenough continue, for us all "to rethink the issues at stake in the on-going debate over the American college curriculum."[191] As we continue to debate which stories young people in our culture should be learning, the evolutionary epic emerges as the one narrative encompassing everything that matters. "The sciences and the humanities now tell a consilient story about the systematic development of matter, life, and consciousness," they argue.[192] "Debates over the core curriculum should be focused on how best to tell this story to the next generation"—not *whether* the story should be told as a grand, unifying narrative. Rue and Goodenough go on to argue that a core curriculum is "all about coming to terms with human nature," or what they term "human reality."[193] They propose a liberal arts curriculum distributed across (or rather, *united* by) three consilient domains: physical, biological, and cultural evolution, or, as they also frame it, "natural systems, social systems, and *creative potential*," the latter referring broadly to the arts and humanities. "One world calls for one story," they conclude. "The Epic of Evolution is it."[194]

What does the master narrative portend for the future of academic disciplines? With these three major categories of the evolutionary paradigm in mind—natural, social, cultural / creative—disciplines like religious studies appear to fit the category of "cultural evolution" or "creative potential." This might mean studying religion as an evolutionary phenomenon, an approach clearly endorsed by Rue and Goodenough. It might also mean (as they suggest) that "literature, art, music, dance, theater, religious and philosophical reflection, and athletics" are disciplines falling within the "adventure of transcendence." Participating in this adventure means "learning to express ourselves in the *forms* of transcendence."[195] Put differently, within the three consilient domains, religious studies represents the domain that instructs students in self-transcendent expression—a claim that may conjure up visions of students and teachers chanting together in some incense-infused chamber. Unfortunately, this image is not altogether dispelled by a perusal of Goodenough's course materials, which stipulate that students are to craft creative responses (art, poetry) to scientific material presented in lecture. Students can choose to "write a story as you would tell it to a parent or a younger sibling. You might choose to include your own feelings about the material from e.g. a philosophical or religious perspective. You might write it in prose or poetry, or include some fantasy or art."[196] Students, in other words, are asked to participate in a form of religiopoiesis, as Goodenough understands the term—responding "religiously" (that is to say, *feelingly*) to scientific materials.

Are students and professors in the "creative" and "transcendent" disciplines also empowered to problematize neat categories and settled concepts of human nature and comprehensive "reality" assumed by the evolutionary paradigm? To what extent may students question—perhaps even reject—this pre-packaged account of who they (*all*) really are, and how they can best find fulfillment? Where, other than to their own "feelings," do students turn for sources that enable philosophical and religious reflection demanded by the course assignments? Essentially no reading materials from philosophy, religion, or ethics appear on the syllabus. This aligns with Goodenough's claim that lack of "philosophical training" is no obstacle to scientists participating in religiopoiesis.[197] The instructors' role is merely to give the "straight" science and allow students to interpret meanings on their own, Goodenough explains.[198] Perhaps so, but this modest agenda undercuts virtually everything that has been claimed on behalf of the Epic's richness of meaning and superlative, universal truths. Exam questions, drawn predominantly from scientific material, seem to allow little room for probing presumed "facts," and sometimes the meanings of the purported facts are given in advance. Indeed, some questions are not really questions at all. To wit: "We live on just the right kind of planet in just the right solar system in just the right place in just the right galaxy for humans to have had the opportunity to evolve. List and describe five of these 'just right' factors."[199] One item offers up a favorite old chestnut of evolutionary psychology: "Explain why, in animals, it's in the male's best interest to compete and strut his stuff while it's in the female's best interest to be choosy."[200] These "questions" are, of course, already charged with particular social and political meanings.

My observations are based on material gleaned from just one course; clearly the details of an entire college curriculum have yet to be fleshed out. Dominican University, with its year-long Big History courses, appears to be moving in that direction. Still, these examples allow us to glimpse how nonscience disciplines and courses might participate in the ambitious project of overhauling education along the lines of *Consilience.* The expectation that students respond "religiously" or "philosophically" to the Epic—with little or no instruction in how to engage or critique material from these disciplinary perspectives—seems to me consistent with Goodenough's casual approach to constructing, *de novo,* a taxonomy of world religions, without apparent recourse to scholarly work, past or present. It resonates with her suggestion that churchgoers learn to respond "religiously" to a scientific narrative, rather than grapple with vexing questions of textual interpretation and belief, history and community, ritual and liturgy, authority and tradition, ethical practice and values, or any other of the numerous, complex dimensions of religion. For Goodenough, religion is a *story*. A scientifically derived religion is a *true* story. And a religious response to that story is something vaguely subjective or creative. Religion is not necessarily something worthy of study as a discipline, but it has value as a *feeling*. If those feelings enhance the prestige of science and solidify allegiance to it, so much the better.[201]

Religiopoiesis is presented as a collective, nonhierarchical, democratic endeavor. "No one person is setting himself or herself up as the guru. . . . we're all responding from our own perspectives, offering rather than professing."[202] But it is difficult to avoid the impression that one is free only to *resonate* with the scientific story. These courses introduce students to a grand narrative whose meanings are already given and whose options for student self-understanding are pre-scripted. This approach may well reinforce a sense of passivity or powerlessness in students. Berry, for example, characterizes education as a kind of "cultural coding," akin to genetic coding; the New Story, he believes, offers a superior form of coding. Analogies with evolutionary and genetic mechanisms may discourage students from understanding themselves as active agents who are both culpable (in part) for our current environmental problems and able to change their behavior.[203] Meanwhile, the text of *Consilience* is invoked by Rue and Goodenough much as a fundamentalist might reference the Bible, as self-evident proof that we are now in possession of the greatest story ever told, one that clears away all doubts about human nature and destiny. But how exactly has *Consilience* made it "abundantly clear" that all foregoing debates—about what it means to be human, or how we experience fulfillment, or about the essential qualities of liberal arts education—can now be shelved? As Wilson freely admits, consilience is a statement of conviction, primarily prophetic in tone and content, and "driven by the faith that if we dream, press to discover, explain, and dream again, thereby plunging repeatedly into new terrain, the world will somehow become clearer."[204] Consilience is the tantalizing vision of a *single* biologist—albeit one with megalomaniacal tendencies. It is proof of nothing, except that scientists, like all humans, are susceptible to blind faith and the distortions of judgment introduced by ideology.

Science, in and of itself, is not a sufficient *source* of environmental values, or of moral motivation generally. It does not give us grounds for caring. Above all, science remains a dubious object of wonder and reverence, even when gilded with the accoutrements of myth and poetry and celebrated for its production of charismatic, enlightened figures. Like many human endeavors, it offers a powerful but imperfect tool, subject to the limitations and biases of its practitioners.

But rather than reject the new cosmology wholesale—as some of its advocates have spurned traditional faiths—we should attend to a broader spectrum of its claims and adherents. The next two chapters take up the sprawling mythmaking enterprise inspired by Thomas Berry's work and the findings of Big Bang cosmology, notably the Universe Story projects promoted by Mary Evelyn Tucker, John Grim, and Brian Swimme. In chapter 6, Richard Dawkins's reductionist biology and his portrait of science as *poetic reality* again make a strong showing among Berry's ardent disciples, Connie Barlow and Michael Dowd. These evolutionary evangelists blend elements of Berry and Teilhard de Chardin's cosmological vision with an enthusiastic endorsement of Dawkins as the prophet of a new religion of reality.

Chapter 5

Anthropic and Anthropocene Narratives of the New Cosmology

The modern scientific vision of the vast universe does have enormous grandeur. Contemplation of it certainly can enlarge our mental horizons, distract us from mean preoccupations, raise our aspirations, remind us of wider possibilities. This is a real benefit, for which we should be grateful. The trouble about it is that, once we have this new vision, there are many different interpretations that we can put on it, many different dramas that arise, many directions in which it can lead us. It is quite hard to distinguish among those directions and to map them in a way that lets us navigate reasonably among them.

—MARY MIDGLEY, *SCIENCE AND POETRY*

Many people feel a new sympathy with the natural world on this planet. But the gargantuan cosmos beyond remains remote. We might understand at some intellectual level that those tiny points of light in the night sky are similar to our sun, made of the same atoms as our bodies, and that the cavern of outer space extends from our galaxy of stars to other galaxies of stars, to distances that would take light rays millions and billions of years to traverse. We might understand these discoveries in intellectual terms, but they are baffling abstractions, even disturbing . . . . Science has vastly expanded the scale of our cosmos, but our emotional reality is still limited by what we can touch with our bodies in the time span of our lives.

—ALAN LIGHTMAN, *THE ACCIDENTAL UNIVERSE*

Despite all the stars and galaxies that form a backdrop, cosmic evolution is a story that places life and humanity on center stage—and that's not an anthropocentric sentiment as much as an honest statement about human curiosity and inventiveness.

—ERIC CHAISSON, *COSMIC EVOLUTION*

What is the relevance of cosmology for ethics? Do the stories we tell about our place in the vast universe impact our deepest values and daily practices? Does cosmic wonder inspire greater care and concern for the natural world? These questions have emerged in various forms throughout this book. In this chapter I turn to Universe Story movements for whom questions about cosmology—and their answers—are especially central. Like other grand narratives, the Universe Story heeds the call for a functional "New Story" that properly orients human culture to scientific realities. Its enthusiasts have gone further than most in crafting and widely publicizing both a book-length narrative and feature-length documentary film of the cosmic "journey" from the Big Bang to the present. By tapping into a sense of wonder and excitement about our role in the great cosmic adventure, Universe Story proponents believe they can ignite passionate concern for our planet and its diverse life-forms.

I do not deny that these narratives evoke a certain sense of wonder, though exactly what kind of wonder it is and where it might lead us will be a significant focus of this chapter. Nor do I dispute that science can provide an appropriate window on the wonders of the universe. Without this window, many—though certainly not all—of nature's wonders would simply be unknown or unavailable to us. As always, my concern is rather with the particular modes of wonder and enchantment celebrated in these narratives and the uncritical reverence they foster for scientific knowledge and knowledge-makers.

More specifically, the cosmic stories whose merits I assess in this chapter display the following features. First, a marked centrality of humans and human consciousness in cosmic unfolding. Second, a commitment to cosmic processes as expressive of particular—highly anthropic and teleological—modes of purposeful intentionality, or directionality. Third, a conviction that the new cosmology, revealed by modern science, is a necessary and functional corrective or superior alternative to previous religious traditions and their stories. And fourth, a peculiar sense of anticipation and optimism regarding a dawning geological era in which humans will intervene in and even direct planetary and cosmic unfolding. These features stand out alongside others I have previously flagged as indicative of the "epic science" genre, its claims for a comprehensive story, and its proselytizing impulse. The emphasis on scientific *reality* is more subtle here than in some iterations of the new cosmology as a religion of reality (notably Dowd and Barlow's), but it is there nevertheless, in the form of repeated insistence that all other varieties of knowledge and of human experience and expression be grounded in current knowledge of the cosmos. Far less subtle is the foregrounding of humans and human consciousness as the standard-bearers of cosmic significance and creativity. Insofar as these narratives are proffered as functional and more appropriate storylines for the modern world and its urgent crises—crises both of meaning and of ecology—I argue that these projects miss their mark.

These overtly anthropic stories encourage expressions of wonder that are power-less to critique or correct environmentally destructive attitudes and patterns of behavior.

Central to my analysis is the much-discussed concept of the Anthropocene. I interpret the Universe Story as articulated by Mary Evelyn Tucker, Brian Swimme, and Thomas Berry as a particular type of "good Anthropocene" narrative. Scien-tists and other scholars propose that our planet is entering a new geological epoch signaled by the unprecedented rise to dominance of one species: our own. Large-scale, human-caused transformation of our planet, notably climate change, is a kind of shorthand for the Anthropocene. Dramatic alterations of the planet seem to entail an equally dramatic scaling up of the human as something akin to a geological force.[1] Humans—not as individuals or even communities, but as a global and cosmic *species*—now collectively enact a form of spatiotemporal agency, a force powerful enough to induce radical biospheric changes previously associ-ated with dinosaur-decimating asteroids or tectonic processes. Our new role in nature, if that is what it is, also seems to suggest more forcefully than ever that the fate of the planet lies in human hands. How should we respond to this enormous responsibility?

Scholars continue to debate whether the Anthropocene transition ought to generate fear and grief, or optimism and excitement, and whether this term for a new epoch, in all its human-centeredness, should be embraced at all. The environ-mental humanities, and the study of religion in particular, have much to contrib-ute to this important discussion. Perhaps our cosmic storytellers are right to sense the epic dimensions or mythic proportions of this moment in human evolution. Yet a transition of this magnitude requires that we think *more carefully than ever* about the metaphors and stories we create and propagate. In this context, I am concerned that Universe Story narratives and their attendant forms of hubristic wonder lend support to—and at times appear indistinguishable from—visions of the Anthropocene that are environmentally disastrous and morally bankrupt.

Universe stories featured in this chapter and the next share two key thinkers as their source and inspiration: Jesuit priest and paleontologist Pierre Teilhard de Chardin[2] and cultural historian Thomas Berry. Teilhard and Berry, together with some of their ardent supporters—Mary Evelyn Tucker, Brian Swimme, Michael Dowd, and Connie Barlow, among others—exemplify a mode of Conscious Evolu-tion that sees the "creative edge of evolution" as unfolding "through ever-more integrated realms of mind and consciousness."[3] For these spiritual futurists "the evolutionary process has become a cocreative act, and its continuation depends on our awakening to the unique cosmic role and responsibility that comes with the gift of self-awareness."[4] The same foundational thinkers, Berry and (especially) Teilhard, are also inspiring current theorizing about the Anthropocene and its brave and suspect new forms of environmentalism.

THE UNIVERSE STORY

Thomas Berry, a former Passionist priest, was strongly influenced by Teilhard de Chardin, as well as Eastern philosophy and religion, Native American religions, and the science of cosmology. Berry famously characterized himself as a "geologian," that is, an historian of the Earth and Earth processes, with a deep developmental sense of time. Teilhard and Berry's insight, shared widely by Universe Story proponents, is that the cosmos is not just a place, but a dynamic, unfolding story—a cosmogenesis characterized by increasing complexity, consciousness, and cephalization (development of the central nervous system toward large-brained humans). One of Berry's key contributions was to recast the somewhat abstruse cosmic philosophy of Teilhard as a story accessible and applicable to all. In doing so, Berry sought to make the cosmic story directly relevant to the environmental crisis and the dangers of runaway technology—issues to which Teilhard seemed largely oblivious. While Teilhard sought a mystical synthesis of science and religion for its own sake, Berry was interested in how this synthesis could powerfully evoke positive human change and an "ecological praxis."[5]

For both Teilhard and Berry, the universe as a whole exhibits a psychic-physical character, but in humans, consciousness has developed into complex forms of self-consciousness or reflective thought.[6] This development is understood to be an inherent feature and tendency of the cosmos to evolve toward increasing cephalization. Anthropomorphic intentionality of the cosmos—belief in the universe's subjective interiority, its purposiveness and deep desires—is woven through the Universe Story. These cosmic attributes are not merely added as poetic flair designed to engage readers. Rather, they reflect what these storytellers understand to be the empirical, observable *reality* of the universe. "With our empirical observations expanded by modern science, we are now realizing that our universe is a single immense energy event that began as a tiny speck that has unfolded over time to become galaxies and stars, palms and pelicans, the music of Bach, and each of us alive today."[7] The insight that our universe is a "story" is treated as a "great discovery of contemporary science."[8] Above all, storytellers influenced by Teilhard embrace a deeply anthropic universe with astounding capacities for enabling life, particularly life-forms such as *ourselves*. Indeed, our arrival on the cosmic scene is presented as an inevitable outcome of cosmic patterns. Awakening to these cosmological patterns and processes, we are told, will inspire in humanity a renewed sense of purpose and meaning.

Writing in *Teilhard Studies* in 1978, Berry, as we have seen, argued for a functional cosmology that more accurately reflects both the broader cosmological context, as revealed by modern science, and humans' special role in cosmic unfolding. Modern humans exist in a "chasm" between the stories of the past, represented by the great faith traditions, and a new story for the future drawn from current scientific cosmology. "It's all a question of story," Berry famously wrote. "We are in trouble just now because we do not have a good story."[9] The traditional narratives, especially the Christian story, are dysfunctional in the modern context, for they are "no longer the Story of the Earth" but rather "sectarian" stories greatly limited by "redemption rhetoric."[10] "A new creation story has evolved in the secular scientific community, the equivalent in modern times to the creation stories of antiquity . . . . It seems destined to become the universal story taught to every child who receives formal education in the modern form anywhere in the world."[11] Berry foresaw the dawning of a new mythic age, and with it a new paradigm of the human.

Although our modern crises are dire, Berry and his followers express an abiding trust that the same "guiding process" that awakened life in the universe and steered it through numerous obstacles and challenges is now awakening humans to a new consciousness, a clearer understanding of our place and purpose. "Sensitized to this guidance," Berry argues, "we can have confidence in the future that awaits the human venture."[12] In a similar spirit, Swimme and Tucker's *Journey of the Universe* concludes with vague but confident assurances that this new story will provide direction, that wonder will guide us. "This sense of wonder," Tucker affirms, "is one of our most valuable guides on this journey into our future as full human beings."[13] Therefore, we should ask: Wonder at what, exactly? How is wonder articulated and celebrated in this narrative? And where, if anywhere, does it seem likely to guide us? The Universe Story often appears vague on these points, but its deep Teilhardian roots suggest some answers.

PIERRE TEILHARD DE CHARDIN'S NOOSPHERE AND COSMIC TELEOLOGY

Teilhard de Chardin's mystical philosophy is one of the bonds uniting Berry, Tucker, Grim, and Swimme. Tucker and Grim first met Berry (and each other) in 1975 at the Riverdale Center for Religious Research, situated on the Hudson River north of New York City. There, under Berry's tutelage, they commenced a wide-ranging study of world religions and deepened their understanding of Teilhard's philosophy.[14] The three formed an unusually close and enduring connection. Berry presided over Tucker and Grim's wedding a few years later and would become their lifelong mentor until his death in 2009. Another key moment in Berry's life and work came in 1982 when he met Brian Swimme. Currently at the California Institute of Integral Studies in San Francisco, and author of several works on the significance of cosmology for ecology, Swimme originally embarked on a more traditional academic path, teaching physics and mathematics at the university level. By his own account, he quickly became disenchanted with exposing students to the major developments in modern cosmology as if they were merely disconnected or neutral facts, with no larger meaning for human destiny. Eventually Swimme left mainstream academia and sought the guidance of Berry, who encouraged him in a deeper study of Teilhard, among other thinkers.[15] Thus began an intense collaboration between Swimme and Berry, resulting in a scientifically informed and updated version of the "New Story," published as *The Universe Story* in 1992. Swimme subsequently teamed up with Tucker to launch *Journey of the Universe,* a multimedia project that narrates the 14-billion-year story of cosmic unfolding.

As with Grim and Tucker's mentorship under Berry, Swimme's studies with him were shaped by Teilhard's philosophical and spiritual interpretation of evolutionary processes. Swimme—who now routinely refers to himself as an evolutionary philosopher—names Teilhard as the first thinker to convey the profound significance of a "new story of evolution," an appraisal frequently echoed by Tucker.[16] Swimme explains: "the central idea of Teilhard is his law of 'complexification-consciousness'. . . . He sees that the whole process is about complexifying and deepening intelligence or subjectivity . . . a movement further into the depths of consciousness, or interiority."[17] Swimme also cites the significance of Teilhard's understanding of the Earth system as composed of developmental layers or envelopes—the lithosphere (the surface layer of rock), the atmosphere, the hydrosphere, and the biosphere. In our present stage of Earth development, Teilhard's philosophy asserts, a radically new and transformative sphere is emerging with enormous relevance for the future well-being of life on Earth. Teilhard calls this the "noosphere," i.e., the mindsphere or sphere of intellect.[18] The noosphere emerges as an additional thinking layer of the Earth system, created though human thought and artifacts (as through technology).

Teilhard's noosphere merits more than passing mention here because it marks an important link between cosmogenesis and current Anthropocene discourse. Like some versions of the Anthropocene, noospheric and Ecozoic concepts developed by Swimme and Berry entail a form of prescriptive geology, a normative account of a coming geological era. For Teilhard, the noosphere represented "an ultimate and inevitable sphere" of a universal, evolutionary process in which intelligent life takes on a wholly new form of existence, thus "plac[ing] humans in a superior position vis-à-vis the natural environment."[19] Swimme also cites with approval Teilhard's related idea of "hominization," that is, "the way in which human thought transforms previously existing practices and functions of the earth."[20] The noosphere superposes on the biosphere as an agent of planetary transformation that results in greater hominization. Human decision-making, akin to natural selection's transformation of the biosphere, has hominized the natural selection process of the planet as a whole, as Swimme sees it. Put more simply, the noosphere is reshaping the biosphere—to such an extent that our species will ultimately direct the course of evolutionary unfolding. This pivotal moment in cosmic evolution when humans assume a directorial role is greeted with great anticipation by Teilhard and many of his followers, whether Universe Story advocates, science and religion enthusiasts, futurologists, or transhumanists.[21] The noosphere marks "the evolutionary convergence of mind through technology" and the eventual fusion of all of humanity into a global super-mind.[22] Teilhard was fascinated by emerging computer technology and many credit him with presaging the development of the internet in his prediction of a planetary mind.

Along with Teilhard, the Russian biochemist Vladimir Vernadsky (1863–1945) made important contributions to the noosphere idea (the two collaborated on the idea in Paris in the 1920s).[23] Although there are differences between Vernadsky's and Teilhard's noosphere concepts—Teilhard's noosphere is mystical and transmundane, while Vernadsky's remains more earthbound and materialist—conflation of their respective concepts is common and is "especially apparent in works by Teilhard's ardent supporters" such as Berry.[24] This conflation is important because Vernadsky's noosphere explicitly entails not only human transformation of the environment but also an idea strongly resonant of Universe Story narratives that "human knowledge offers the potential for longer-term sustainable management or even improvement . . . [and] the notion of some form of *planetary management.*"[25] In other words, Teilhard's supporters in the lineage of Berry appear to blend aspects of Vernadsky's and Teilhard's noosphere, in such a way that the mindsphere remains within the evolving material world, rather than shearing off as a spiritual layer that hovers above the material realm. Teilhard's mystical noosphere conception and Vernadsky's materialist one are both products of "evolutionary thinking in which civilized Man emerges as a geological force *incrementally* over deep time."[26]

The evolutionary unfolding that both thinkers embrace is generally Lamarckian "in the sense that the noösphere develops progressively as a higher stage of the [human-]directed evolving biosphere."[27] As human knowledge of the cosmos increases, the noosphere incorporates additional facts, including knowledge gained regarding the general direction of the cosmos itself. The mindsphere becomes a microcosm of the macrocosm—both a "mirror" of the cosmos and its "directive agency."[28] As Teilhard puts it, the human "holds [evolution] in its hands, responsible for its past to its future."[29] In this sense, we are not the center of the universe but "something much more wonderful—the arrow pointing the way to the final unification of the world."[30] Because of his unique capacity for thought, "man has been the leading shoot of the tree of life," Teilhard argues. "That being so, the hopes for the future of the noosphere (that is to say, of biogenesis, which in the end is the same as cosmogenesis) are concentrated exclusively upon him as such."[31] This idea finds expression in the Universe Story as humans fulfilling the role of heart, mind, or consciousness of the cosmos. As we will see, a cosmic stage of noospheric transformation is recast as the "Ecozoic" in Swimme and Berry's work:

a dawning geological era and higher stage of cosmic evolution marked by a new mode of human involvement in the Earth system.

Teilhard remains a hugely important figure to Universe Story enthusiasts. Teilhardian-Vernadskian ideas of noospheric transformation, hominization, and anthropic cosmic unfolding percolate through various iterations of the new cosmology. Swimme and (especially) Berry, Tucker and Grim have assumed active leadership roles in the American Teilhard Association, a decades-old organization whose mission is to explore and propagate Teilhard's "vision of the human as part of a dynamic unfolding universe."[32] The association seeks to create "a future worthy of the human community as a high expression and mode of fulfillment of the earth's evolutionary process."[33] Since launching *Journey of the Universe* (book and film) in 2011, Tucker has frequently commented on the project's Teilhardian roots. A regular contributor to *Teilhard Studies,* she echoes Swimme's affirmation that "it is Teilhard who has given us some of the first metaphors to describe our role as the consciousness of the earth itself," and she embraces evolution as a goal-oriented process marked by increasing complexification and overriding purpose.[34]

While evolution on a small scale may not unambiguously reveal pattern and purpose, this is not the case at the macro-level of long-term evolution or cosmic unfolding, Tucker believes. "To accept change and mutation at many points in the microphase by no means negates the sense that evolution has a direction in its macrophase," she argues. "When we step back from the particular to the general sweep of evolution we cannot but be impressed with the sense that self-organizing processes are leading to greater complexification."[35] *Journey* affirms these "self-organizing dynamics" and "innate ordering processes" as key findings of modern science.[36] These findings suggest that the emergence of humans is no mere *chance* occurrence in evolution; recognizing this, in turn, suggests our species' responsibility "for guiding this evolutionary process in a sympathetic awareness of its profound connection to ourselves."[37] The purposeful universe of Teilhard's account is "so widely drawn as to be a dramatic challenge to all traditional spiritualities."[38] Indeed, *Journey*'s creators regularly assert that this view of the universe "changes everything."[39] Teilhard's perspective gives us a new "zest for life" and—significantly—it inspires what Tucker calls a "will to participate in evolution."[40] For Berry too, humans' complexity and capacity for conscious reflection distinguishes us from other creatures, and "gives humans a special role in the evolutionary process."[41]

These ideas all bear the strong imprint of Teilhard. But the recent rise of rampant technology and the global environmental crises means that our role in cosmogenesis has taken on a particular urgency and meaning, for humans will now determine which life-forms continue and which die out. "We have become co-creators as we have become conscious of our role in this extraordinary, irreversible developmental sequence of the emergence of life forms."[42]

Humans as the supreme consciousness of the universe is an idea with additional roots in the progressive evolutionary thought of Julian Huxley, who popularized Teilhard's ideas for Anglo-American audiences. (We will see that Huxley is also a significant figure for Epic enthusiasts Dowd and Barlow.) Huxley's humanism and his predictions regarding the fate of our species resonate with Swimme and Tucker's evolutionary philosophy. "Whether he likes it or not," Huxley famously pronounced, "[man] is responsible for the whole further evolution of our planet."[43] Huxley's phrasing might suggest some degree of ambivalence or wariness regarding humans' geological role. Swimme displays these words prominently and without any apparent wariness, on the website for his Center for the Story of the Universe, whose ambitious mission is to redirect the course of human society by creating a community that "transcends individual, human, and geo-political boundaries."[44]

A crucial point to note is this: however lamentable our modern crises, our species' emergence in the Ecozoic as evolutionary driver is *not itself* an unintended or troubling outcome of cosmic processes for these thinkers. Rather, that role is essentially foreordained in cosmogenesis. The move from cosmos to cosmogenesis is a shift from the universe as mere process to cosmic unfolding as discernible, irreversible *progress*—the universe as "a sequence of meaningful irreversible events best understood as narrative."[45] The danger of grand narratives lies in their power to normalize events that are not, in fact, inevitable or irreversible. In doing so, they make it difficult to challenge or critique particular outcomes or discern alternative paths. So it is with the Ecozoic. Berry himself set out to temper Teilhard's overly optimistic, human-centered assessment of technological progress as a benign outgrowth of human creativity, and the power of science to enhance human life. His *Universe Story* co-authored with Swimme warns of an alluring but dangerous "mystique" of technology, juxtaposing a possible "Technozoic"[46] future with the more holistic, healing vision represented by the "Ecozoic."[47] The Ecozoic is seen to counter the entrancement of the Technozoic by resacralizing the Earth and facilitating the transition to a "mutually enhancing human presence upon the Earth."[48] Yet, the Ecozoic not only entails but welcomes pervasive human influence and intervention at all levels. This welcoming attitude reflects a Teilhardian investment in humanity's unique mode of conscious self-awareness. The nature of our unique consciousness becomes clearer when Berry introduces the anthropic principle, as discussed in more detail below.

Though shorn of Technozoic entrancement with certain forms of unbridled technology, the Ecozoic retains a powerful entrancement with the human, and with progressive evolution of the human intellect and science. The new cosmology positions humans "in the driver's seat of geological evolution, directing the course of Earth history out of the Cenozoic period" and into a new geological era whose features we will determine.[49] It is not surprising, then, that both Berry and Teilhard emerge as inspirational figures for some of today's Anthropocene dreamers.

FROM COSMOGENESIS TO UNIVERSE EDUCATION:
GLOBAL UNITY AND SPECIES CONSCIOUSNESS

A foregrounding of humans qua *species* and a fixation with an emerging *global* consciousness characterize Teilhard's cosmogenesis and Berry, Swimme, and Tucker's Universe Story. These preoccupations drive their commitment to disseminate the story worldwide, and, as we will see, they are also characteristic of Anthropocene narratives gaining popularity in environmental discourse.[50] Teilhardian cosmogenesis as a process of increasing cephalization skews the storyline in both anthropocentric and universalist directions. Noospheric unfolding posits gradual evolution toward cultural convergence—the human species as a "single inter-thinking group based on a single self-developing framework of thought (or noosystem)."[51] Deeply invested in the idea of an evolving, worldwide noetic convergence, Teilhard tended to marginalize the value of cultural diversity. Huxley explains that because Teilhard was "so deeply concerned with establishing a global unification of human awareness as a necessary prerequisite for any real future progress of mankind, and perhaps also because he was by nature and inclination more interested in rational and scientific thought than in the arts, he did not discuss the evolutionary value of cultural variety in any detail."[52] Echoes of Teilhard's privileging of universal science and a global cultural convergence, over and above cultural and religious diversity, can be discerned in the educational mission of the new cosmology.

Berry, as we know, strongly endorses what he calls *universe education* oriented around the cosmic story.[53] The "entire college project can be seen as that of enabling the student to understand the immense story of the universe and the role of the student in creating the next phase of the story."[54] He envisions a unified curriculum in which "the evolutionary universe should be the primary referent in every field of academic concern as well as in every human concern."[55] While wary of the analytical reductionism of E. O. Wilson's consilience, Berry nevertheless shares Wilson's lament that we lack a "unifying paradigm" to confer order and coherence to education and to the disciplines. Also like Wilson, he proposes that the emerging, unified body of knowledge will breathe new life into humanities disciplines. "The deeply felt antipathies between the sciences and the humanities could be eliminated. The amazing new discovery by science of the story of the universe would be recognized as a supreme humanistic achievement and as providing a basis for the further expansion of all the traditional humanistic cultures."[56] A unified course of study would mirror an emerging species unity, or what Berry terms the "reinvention of the human" at the "species level."[57] Berry suggests that anthropocentrism is worsened by our *failure* to think of ourselves as a species.[58]

Berry urges critical reflection on this process of reinvention, to avoid succumbing to an inordinately romantic attachment to nature, yet he sometimes lapses into less-than-critical assessments of *science* as revelation. "In the Epic of Evolution," he writes, "science becomes a path to wisdom."[59] The universe revealed by science is for Berry a self-evident, shared reality whose meaning is legible to all. The scientific endeavor, he writes, is "truly the Yoga of the West"—a devotional practice that puts us in right relationship with reality.[60] He proposes immersing students in values that are indicated by "reality itself," values found in the "self-emergent processes of the universe."[61] The interpretive context of this course of study, Berry naively asserts, "is bound in only a minimal way to any prior cultural context."[62] The traditional stories around which cultures have organized themselves cannot provide this universal context and sense of identity.

> For the first time the peoples of the entire world, insofar as they are educated in a modern context, are being educated within this origin story. It provides the setting in which children everywhere . . . are given their world and their own personal identity in space and time. While the traditional origin and journey stories are also needed in the educational process, none of them can provide the encompassing context for education such as is available in this new story, which is the mythic aspect of our modern account of the world.[63]

Tucker, Grim, and Swimme have revitalized and greatly extended the reach of Berry's pedagogical ambitions. While it coheres with Berry's mission of universe education, *Journey of the Universe* seems to follow Teilhard's example more than Berry's, in articulating a mystical-scientific narrative of the cosmos over and above an *ecological praxis*. To be sure, Tucker elsewhere invests enormous energy in mining the "green" resources of world religions, but connections between *Journey*'s cosmic vision and environmental values are often difficult to discern. At times, the narrative's overarching themes appear inimical to such concerns, as I will argue. Nonetheless, *Journey* is an ambitious endeavor that includes a documentary film, a companion book and website, a curricular accompaniment to the film, and a DVD series of interviews with scientists and environmentalists. Since the release of the film and book, Tucker has held numerous worldwide screenings and discussions of *Journey*, promoting it as a catalyst for environmental concern and action, as well as a much-needed cosmological context for the mutual flourishing of humans and the planet. Tucker has also teamed up with biologist and Epic enthusiast Ursula Goodenough and others to introduce *Journey of the Universe* as "an organizing framework for high school teaching and learning."[64] Like Berry and Wilson, *Journey*'s enthusiasts claim that their project confers needed coherence and integration to the disciplines—combining "astronomy, geology, biology, ecology, and biodiversity with humanistic insights concerning the nature of the universe."[65]

The prospect of galvanizing a new vision of global ethics, universal science, and even unity among the disciplines may sound appealing, particularly in a world that seems increasingly afflicted by religious and cultural conflict and held hostage to climate denial and obstructionism, or political inertia. Dreams of a global humanity united in its commitment to a new mode of human-Earth relations is central to current Anthropocene discourse as well. But these universalizing moves have a significant shadow side, critics contend. I turn now to some of these critiques, adding to them my own particular concerns with the Universe Story's evocation of wonder and its potential—and actual—impact on how we understand our relationship to the more-than-human world.

FROM COSMOGENESIS TO ANTHROPOCENE

A (surprisingly) small number of commentators express misgivings about the missionary zeal with which the Universe Story is proclaimed to religious and secular communities around the globe, and its proponents' claims for the unique power, relevance, or veracity of their story vis-à-vis other traditions. I share many of these concerns.[66] Some note, for example—and I agree—that the Universe Story often positions itself to supersede and displace other traditions. As with Rue and Goodenough's presentation of the evolutionary epic, a manifesto-like quality pervades Universe Story narratives, suggesting a definitive or final aspect, as if the story were immune to or above critique. "There is the implication that the variety of criticisms to which the great storytellers of the past have been subjected are somehow irrelevant to the universe story, a text without a context, the story of life itself."[67] Berry and Swimme, both strongly influenced by Catholicism, construct a cosmology that appears "consistent with the way in which hegemonic discourses are constructed in the Roman Catholic intellectual tradition . . . codified and disseminated as a definitive teaching."[68] The story reads less as an "invitation" than a "manifesto."[69] Similarly, critics point to the "omnicompetent" mode with which the Universe Story presents its insights. While our cosmic storytellers are not always consistent on this point, "it seems clear that the universe story is meant to replace the specific stories of different religions." At the very least, "this larger story is taken to provide an overarching framework for interpreting them."[70]

Those invested in mythopoeic projects might object that the new cosmology underscores its own genesis as a transparently human creation, not Truth with a capital T. Environmental ethicist J. Baird Callicott, who, I noted previously, also defends a universal science-based worldview in *Earth Insights* and elsewhere, is a case in point. "To advertise your story as a story, to call it a 'myth,' an 'epic,' or a 'grand narrative,'" he argues, "is to disavow any intention to make a claim of truth or to deny the possibility of cogently organizing experience some other way."[71] Yet it is precisely by laying claim to truth and reality that these narratives often advertise their superiority. The Universe Story is championed as a text without context, as though the cosmos were directly and unambiguously transmitting its truths through human consciousness. To wit: "It is not that we think on the universe,"

Berry maintains. "The Universe, rather, thinks *itself* in and through us."[72] The authoritative tone threatens to constrict our world to what Neil Evernden calls "one habitual brand of reality."[73]

Yet, narratives that are meaningful and deeply resonant with a given community, and those most likely to inspire transformation, are "not simply handed down from philosophers or theologians"—or cosmologists—"on high and then adopted uncritically by the moral community that receives them."[74] Moreover, a narrative with an omnicompetent plot device requires other stories, other genres, to correct, interrupt, or problematize its trajectory, if it is not to collapse into a "triumphant metanarrative."[75] We have seen that these storytellers often take pains to assure us of the continuing relevance and importance of older stories. But these disclaimers are undermined by emphasis elsewhere on the narrative's unique authority or functionality,[76] as when Berry and Swimme defend the Universe Story as "the only way of providing, in our times, what the mythic stories of the universe provided for tribal peoples and for the earlier classical civilizations in their times."[77] Their collaborative work concludes that "there is eventually only one story, the story of the universe."[78] At most, the world religions—in light of their former significance—deserve a dignified death and / or decent burial, Swimme appears to suggest: "The stories of the past we regard as important, and we pay a lot of respect to them but we *know* that they don't actually give us a careful, accurate depiction of the universe. . . . We've surpassed that level of knowledge that we had at that time. . . . We need a new story."[79]

The narrative's omnicompetence might seem especially at odds with the metaphor of *journeying* that has surfaced in recent iterations of the Universe Story. A journey may connote something meandering or nomadic—an openness to surprise and discovery rather than rote narration of what has already been discovered and catalogued. Whitney Bauman points out that journeying signals, or ought to, a sense of *un*knowing.[80] *Journey of the Universe,* however, is not a tale of unknowns and uncertainties. When pressed into service as a universal story, "journeying" may devolve into anthropocentric or teleological visions of the universe, as I believe it does in *Journey of the Universe.* While journeying sounds "at least in part inimical to singularity and its epistemological cousin certainty," Bauman cautions narrators of the Universe Story to "avoid singularity in its telling. Such singularity may play into the power play of assuming that one needs a single journey, a single reality, and a single truth in order to justify agency, responsibility, morality, and ethics." This sort of singularity, he notes, has often bred "violent certainties."[81] Bauman suggests envisioning our planet and the vast cosmos beyond as a multitude of evolving worlds, multiple paths, and multiple knowledges, perhaps even multiverses. Multiplicity entails that a story of the universe "precisely cannot become a universal story."[82]

Other lines of critique question the narrative's ethical value. While proponents insist on the "eminently practical" rather than abstract nature of Teilhardian cosmology, some commentators discern in the story of the universe no particular norma-tive guidance.[83] Willis Jenkins astutely observes that an evolving cosmos actually *underdetermines* ethics, offering little guidance on pressing moral issues like climate change or geoengineering. "If all possibilities of action can write themselves into a story of nature, then that cosmology has little normative purchase for practical eth-ics."[84] It is a truism, he notes, "that everything that exists is a product of the processes preceding it"; hence it is difficult to see how looking to those processes might "reform specific exercises of power" that have put the planet at risk.[85] Similarly worrisome, one critic worries, is that the Universe Story "can be slotted potentially into virtually any context, whether it be that of radical environmentalists, white liberal Christians, or neoconservative capitalists . . . . The new cosmologists have perhaps left their story vulnerable to a panoply of appropriations."[86] To claim that these stories offer little moral guidance and fail to challenge destructive practices is to point to nothing less than the project's failure. After all, the story is so comprehensive, its meaning so compelling, we are told, that it "changes everything."[87]

The narrative's presentation of a homogenized human species also leaves it open to critique from the standpoint of social and environmental justice. Eleva-tion of the species category and the call to cultivate species-level unified con-sciousness may easily obscure differential responsibilities for the environmental crisis. The species category is not sufficiently responsive, for example, to differen-tial claims for justice among the planetary rich and poor.[88] As we will see, this is an increasingly common complaint against Anthropocene narratives as well.

As damaging as these criticisms may be, I propose that a more serious set of charges can be lodged. I contend that these narratives may actually *encourage* a will to secure and perpetuate human dominion over the planet. They celebrate a naive and potentially dangerous trust in humans' ability to manage and direct the course of planetary evolution. Humans understood as the fulfillment of cosmic creativity and complexification lends legitimacy to imperatives to intervene in and control evolutionary unfolding. Our cosmic role, as identified in these narratives, naturalizes large-scale planetary management, underwriting what Tucker calls our will to participate in evolutionary unfolding. Thus, I argue (in contrast to some critics) that these stories *do* offer some direction and guidance, and that they seem likely to guide us in precisely the wrong direction, toward intensified "hominiza-tion" of the planet in its supposed new geological stage. Recall the claim that humans mirror and direct cosmic unfolding, that our species manifests the *arrow* of evolution. In this respect, these stories—particularly more recent iterations of the Universe Story—exhibit parallels with some of the most ethically problematic strains of Anthropocene discourse to have emerged in recent years.

To begin to see this point, we need only return to a central question that inter-rogates these projects on their own terms. So let us ask again: Where is wonder guiding us? What *kind* of wonder and ethical sensibilities might we derive from this story? Does this story, on the whole, provide an appropriate and functional narrative for our times, as proponents routinely claim? In answering these questions, I pay particular attention to *Journey of the Universe* as the narrative that alleges to be scientifically up-to-date, while remaining faithful to its Teilhardian roots.

WONDER AT AN ANTHROPIC UNIVERSE

The very concept of the Anthropocene crystallizes human dominion, corralling the already-pliable-in-that-direction human mind into viewing our master identity as manifestly destined, quasi-natural, and sort of awesome.

—EILEEN CRIST, "ON THE POVERTY OF OUR NOMENCLATURE"

Proponents of the Universe Story typically embrace some form of the anthropic principle, asserting that the universe appears finely tuned for the evolution of life-forms like ourselves.[89] *Journey* portrays a universe that is "just right" for human emergence. For example, had the universe expanded more slowly—"even one millionth of a percent slower"—it would have collapsed. Had expansion happened more quickly "it would have simply diffused into dust, with no structures to bring forth life."[90] Remarking on the identity of humans with the overarching emergent order of the universe, Berry notes that "this identity is expressed by physicists in terms of the anthropic principle."[91] He endorses the related view that "the human is that being in whom the universe comes to itself in a special mode of conscious reflection," adding that conscious reflection of this sort was "implicit in the universe from the beginning."[92] In this spirit, *Journey* cites Freeman Dyson's claim that the universe seems to have *known* we humans were coming. Dyson, recall, is the physicist whose religious reverence for science leads him to dismiss climate concerns and to promote Open-Source biology to suit humans' creative whims. Is it coincidence that he also promotes a purposeful universe in which the generation of sentient and complexly conscious humans is the implicit cosmic tendency?[93] In a universe "shot-through with a cosmic order necessary for our very existence," as Swimme recognizes, "it becomes possible to imagine that we are here for something higher, something nobler" than our mundane preoccupations would suggest.[94]

The anthropic principle has intimate ties with Teilhardian cosmology. Teilhard subscribed to a strong version of the anthropic principle in his conception of the Omega Point, a predestined and final state of material complexity and unified consciousness that for him had eschatological and Christological dimensions. John D. Barrow and Frank J. Tipler's signal work, *The Anthropic Cosmological Principle*, draws heavily from Teilhard. The strong anthropic principle sees the universe as compelled to bring life into being, and as Swimme's commentary suggests, may support a sense of human significance for the universe. Belief in the strong version is often seen as a departure from scientific method and theorizing, a covert means of resuscitating an ancient, unscientific, and even intelligent design-like belief that the universe is made for us.[95] Alan Lightman, quoted at the opening of this chapter, is one of many physicists who remain skeptical of anthropism. An essayist, novelist, and humanitarian (he is the only physicist at MIT ever to hold a joint appointment in the humanities), Lightman argues that current cosmological science points to an "accidental universe," one that is "uncalculable [*sic*] by science."[96]

Journey's eager embrace of anthropism appears ad hoc, less a product of its commitment to cutting-edge science than a transparent effort to imbue Teilhard's mystical cosmic vision—which dates from the mid-twentieth century—with scientific veracity. The same species of anthropism that keeps humans at the heart of these narratives gives rise to exaggerated claims for the significance, truth, or comprehensiveness of the story, even as the confident tone of the narrative actually erodes the sense of cosmic mystery that the story purports to inspire. Humans' unique ability to pierce the cosmic veil gives us access to a story that is "telling us." Stated differently, our great significance to the universe and our unique ability to comprehend and narrate it are two sides of the same coin. Marilynne Robinson's reflections on science and the humanities contain a similar insight: "The notion that the universe is constructed, or we are evolved, so that reality must finally answer in every case to the questions we bring to it, is entirely as anthropocentric as the notion that the universe was designed to make us possible," she notes. "Indeed, the affinity between the two ideas should be acknowledged."[97] These twin articles of faith also propel the banishment of mystery (understood in this context as merely that which science has not *yet* captured), and they are complicit in the general devaluation of the "terrain of the humanities."[98]

For Universe Story enthusiasts, humans' "discovery" of the story, like our ancestors' discovery of fire (an analogy favored by Swimme), marks a pivotal moment in evolution that gives rise to a whole new form of human being.[99] A narrative distillation of cosmic unfolding is understood to be "the single greatest achievement of the entire scientific venture from Copernicus to the present."[100] In other words, both science and the universe find fulfillment in humans' ability to know and tell the new story. "It is the story become conscious of itself in human intelligence."[101] Our species' creative participation in evolutionary unfolding is a reflection and intensification of the universe's own creative, intentional impulses. *Journey*'s narrative is replete with metaphors of cosmic creativity and passion, and universal impulses toward relationships, bonding, and community.[102] "To commune may be one of the deepest tendencies in the universe."[103] Earth and sun are portrayed as a bonded pair—lovers locked in an enduring embrace. Earth is also intimate with its enduring partner and collaborator, the atmosphere. The cosmos at large is depicted as an intentional life-form. The universe has always "moved toward creating relationships," *Journey* tells us. "In our observable universe, various forms of bonding are inescapable."[104] All of life unfolds in accordance with such principles: Chemicals self-organize into complex relationships, and over time, mere rock transforms itself into "monarch butterflies, blue herons, and the exalted music of Mozart."[105] Cosmic energy is charged with awareness and intentionality, and matter is self-organizing and cooperative. Agency and discernment are assumed even in the prebiotic conditions of the early cosmos and in rudimentary forms of cellular life. Following Teilhard's philosophy, these qualities find their greatest expression in human consciousness.

With the emergence of humans, *Journey* tells us, the universe "reached a new fever pitch," spawning a creature of "white-hot awareness" and "blazing imaginations."[106] Our cleverness, manifest particularly in the advent of symbolic consciousness—language, mathematics—may prove a liability, however, for as we have learned to map, measure, and manipulate nature, we have transformed it into resources to be utilized recklessly. Cultural evolution has now run roughshod over natural selection, *Journey* explains, such that we are "leaving behind the Holocene period of the past ten thousand years and entering the Anthropocene, an era shaped primarily not by natural systems but by humans."[107] In Teilhardian language, the noosphere is transfiguring the biosphere.

How should we feel about this transition? The same mood of expectant cosmogenesis that surrounds discussions of the Ecozoic phase and the noosphere also attends *Journey*'s sequencing of cosmic events, despite occasional acknowledgments of the severity of the planetary crisis. *Journey*, as I have noted, ends with a celebration of wonder as the key to finding our purpose and way forward. Wonder is "one of our most valuable guides on this ongoing journey into our future as full human beings. Wonder is a gateway through which the universe floods in and takes up residence within us."[108] Embracing wonder, we understand that we are born of the stars, an idea "intuited" in the myths of our ancestors and now affirmed by modern science. "By following this wonder we have discovered the ongoing story of the universe, a story that we tell, but a story that is also telling us."[109] *Journey* stresses our species' childlike proclivity for play and curiosity—we are uniquely able to "become astounded with almost anything in the universe"[110]—but stops well short of acknowledging the destructive turn these proclivities may take unless tempered and restrained by other values. Could it be that our childlike penchant for wonder and curiosity is driving the current crises? If so, how will these same qualities show the way forward?

WHERE WONDER MAY LEAD

The narrative provides few *direct* answers to these questions. *Journey* explains that wonder led humans to discover the story of the universe in the first place—a story "that is also telling us."[111] So what guidance does this story impose on humans' ability to wonder at "almost anything"? We have learned that "our human destiny is to become the heart of the universe that embraces the whole of the Earth community."[112] We are here "to drink so deeply of the powers of the universe we become the human form of the universe."[113] Although we may feel small amidst its vastness, humans are nevertheless "beings in whom the universe shivers in wonder at itself."[114] We alone are beings capable of "discovering" this ongoing story. Deep acceptance of our position as the *heart and mind of the universe* may enable us to align all of human culture with "the grain of cosmic evolution," we are told.[115] What, then, does the pattern of this grain reveal? Looking to *Journey*'s account of cosmogenesis, and its narrators' express commitment to Teilhardian "consciousness complexification" as the cosmic direction, we can—again—safely conclude that the grain of cosmic evolution is deeply anthropic. That is, the discernible pattern of the universe culminates in the emergence of *human* consciousness. Back to our question then: Where is wonder leading us? Hints at an answer, though somewhat convoluted and circular, direct us back to ourselves as both subject and object of cosmic wonder. In a nutshell, *Journey* tells us this: wonder has led us to discover a scientific story. That story affirms that the overarching purpose of the universe is apprehended in its intention to birth creatures like ourselves. Aligning ourselves *with* the cosmic grain, then, means attuning our existence to the universe's patterning and purpose, which, in turn, consist in its production of uniquely complex, conscious creatures. Creatures like us. Creatures who discovered this scientific story in the first place.

As Ian Hesketh notes, cosmic storytellers assume there is "something intuitive about wanting to see the organic and inorganic worlds as one, as if we are tapping into some infinite being at the origin of all things *that is in fact ourselves*."[116] The narrative's principal theme seems one of solipsism rather than wonder; or more accurately, *Journey*'s mode of wonder *is* a kind of solipsism. It remains unclear how a robustly other-oriented ethic of the "whole earth community" springs from these anthropic insights.[117] To be sure, the narrative stresses cosmic interconnectedness and relationality, which might suggest a mood of solidarity with the whole spectrum of life.[118] Even if we grant *Journey* its principle of interconnectedness, however, the problem remains that, in the context of its own progressive logic, this principle suggests that other creatures have value insofar as they participate in (or adumbrate) the culminating consciousness and complexity of the human. Following Teilhard, the presence of valuable traits in other life-forms, such as incipient mind or what *Journey* calls discernment, is inferred by a backward extrapolation from the human sphere to the biological realm, and from the biological realm to the inorganic.[119]

Journey's cosmic unfolding resembles the "escalator" model of cosmic evolution often critiqued by philosopher Mary Midgley.[120] Midgley questions the "cosmic optimism" that imputes to evolution a "steady, linear upward movement, a single inexorable process of improvement."[121] While cosmic optimism might seem harmless—less destructive, certainly, than ruthlessly competitive, survival-of-the-fittest myths of evolution—it nevertheless "gives an unwarranted sense of security, and can easily distract us from the need for other changes."[122] Moreover, Midgley notes, an anthropocentric and sapience-centered narrative "distorts both evolutionary theory and our attitude to the natural world."[123] *Journey*'s cosmic escalator, as one reader notes, carries humans "to the top of the animal world and on to greater glories. By seeing all of creation as tending toward self-reflective consciousness, Swimme and Tucker give all creation a human head to head for."[124]

Keep in mind that this narrative purports to "evoke in humans awe, wonder, and *humility* . . . [A]s a *functional cosmology*, it can encourage the 'great work' of ecological restoration and environmental education so needed in our times."[125] Yet *Journey*'s "new" story offers nothing like the "comprehensive reevaluation of human-earth relations" that its creators believe is needed to challenge the "largely anthropocentric" tone of the inherited faith traditions and their stories.[126] In short, *Journey*'s planned hierarchical order, its resemblance to a Great Chain of Being, feels disappointingly familiar.

THE GEOLOGICAL TURN AND THE NATURALIZING NARRATIVE

In many ways, universe stories exhibit standard features of Anthropocene narratives that aspire to tell us who "we" as humanity are, how we got here, and where we are headed in the near and long-term future.[127] First proposed by the atmospheric chemist Paul Crutzen and geobiologist Eugene Stoermer in 2000, the Anthropocene is the proposed name for our current geological epoch, an age dominated and—some would say—guided by the human species. These narratives often evince a "geological turn" in their dissolution of the long-standing boundary between human and natural or geological history.[128] A prominent Anthropocene storyline is what Christophe Bonneuil identifies as the *naturalizing narrative*. Its key features include: narrative foregrounding of the (collective or aggregate) human "species"; claims for a recent or emerging "environmental consciousness" that is superseding a past dark age of "unconscious" impacts on the planet; and a celebration of scientists and scientific knowledge as "shepherds" of humankind and the planet—a mode of celebration that effectively downplays environmental knowledge, experience, or solution-making efforts of average citizens, laypersons, and previous generations.[129] Our entrance into a new geological era in which humans influence every aspect of the Earth system is naturalized, and depoliticized, as a cosmic imperative; a necessary development set in motion by our ancestors' first discovery of fire or a logical outgrowth of our essential human "nature" as tool users and knowledge-makers. Techno-scientific prowess that brought us to this perilous but exciting point in cosmic history will also—if aligned with new consciousness of our place in deep geological time—point out the bright path to planetary salvation. Science, in the naturalizing narrative, is naively seen as the *deus ex machina,* a force that was somehow "not part of the cultural-political-economical nexus" that *created* the crises.[130] Or if science was once complicit in that process, the assumption is that we have *now* arrived at a more enlightened, purified mode and vision of science.

The centrality and authority of science are often bound up, in this narrative form, with the human-as-species concept. E. O. Wilson's commentary on our species is influential in this context[131] and provides a case in point. In terms that recall consilience, Wilson presents the task of defining who "we" are as a species as far too difficult and daunting to be left to (mere) humanities scholars, who routinely fail to explain "why we possess our special nature" and "have not accounted for a full understanding of our species' existence."[132] Explaining our *special nature,* for Wilson, means defining our essential biological nature, a project rightly spurned by many humanists (and posthumanists). The naturalizing narrative's dream of species unification defers principally to a narrow scientific verdict on who "we" are. Wilson asserts, paradoxically, that having transformed and consumed so much of our planet's resources, our species is "smart enough and now, one hopes, well informed enough to achieve self-understanding as a unified species." We would be "wise to look on ourselves as a species."[133] This storyline simply doubles down on faith in scientific progress—the conviction that we are now, at last, "smart enough"—as our best way forward.

My contention is that universe stories show troubling affinities with the main contours of this naturalizing narrative and its "Age of Man" environmentalism. As we will see, there is another, related Anthropocene narrative—the "post-natural"—with which the new cosmology also has some resonance. These similarities are suggested by the overlap between the new cosmology and its founding figures—Teilhard, Berry—on the one hand, and the emergence of what some are heralding (or deriding) as the "good Anthropocene," on the other.

First to the naturalizing narrative. An incipient Anthropocene concept[134] is articulated in Berry's conception of the Ecozoic, and in Teilhard's noosphere idea, giving greater meaning to Berry as a "geologian" inspired by deep time perspectives. (Crutzen himself names Teilhard as an earlier source of the Anthropocene idea.)[135] The Universe Story proposes a fourth geological era, the Ecozoic, giving a nod to "the scientific tradition that divides the Phanerozoic eon into the Paleozoic, Mesozoic, and Cenozoic eras."[136] The Ecozoic will be marked by new "creativity" and "mutually enhancing human-Earth relations." In this promising era, "*the entire complex of life systems* of the planet will be influenced by the human in a comprehensive manner. . . . Almost every phase of the Ecozoic will involve the human."[137]

"The human" that figures prominently in the Ecozoic is the human-as-species, akin to what Bonneuil calls the "undifferentiated" Anthropocene "we." This unified human has deep roots in Teilhard's noosphere and its call for an emerging planetization of man.[138] Keen interest in unity and global consciousness is also central to current Anthropocene discourse. Global, species consciousness may be necessary to respond to challenges like climate change, according to prominent commentators on the Anthropocene like Chakrabarty, and the idea is greeted enthusiastically by some scientists (Wilson included). As with concerns cited earlier about the Universe Story, a number of scholars offer trenchant critiques of the way in which this unified vision masks severe inequalities and obscures differential responsibilities in an era of global climate change. Seen in this light, a vision of unified humanity is not a *solution* to our global environmental crisis, as Universe Story narratives suggest; it is, rather, a driving factor of that crisis. An "undifferentiated 'we, the human species'" narrative conceals the fact that negative impacts on the planet are in actuality "the result of technical, cultural and economic choices made (unevenly) by *specific* social groups, organisations, and institutions."[139] In much the same way, the Universe Story's entreaties that we become universe people glosses over social justice issues and the real-world disparities between global "winners and losers."[140] Humans are not simply conveyers of a common cosmic story but political actors engaged in choices about power, oppression, and freedom. These disparities will only be worsened by climate change—and, quite possibly, by efforts to *mitigate* climate change through geoengineering strategies and other technological fixes deployed by the wealthiest and most powerful nations.[141]

THE ECOZOIC AND / AS THE ANTHROPOCENE

Universe Story enthusiasts align the Ecozoic with the Anthropocene in various ways, while also suggesting that the Ecozoic signals a transition on an even *grander* geological and cosmic scale. Berry's commentary on the Ecozoic posits humans as shutting down not only the Holocene *epoch* but the whole Cenozoic *era* altogether.[142] Tucker suggests the Ecozoic as a particular incarnation of the Anthropocene—or, perhaps, the Anthropocene as the opening act of a much longer Ecozoic era. Although the Ecozoic was Berry's way of "marking the end of a geological era in which thousands of species were disappearing," he did not counsel despair, anticipating instead a new "emerging period in which humans would recover their creative orientation to the world."[143] The Ecozoic entails an all-pervasive human presence on Earth that enhances both nature and society.[144] Berry, in Tucker's interpretation, understood his life's work to "assist in the transition" from the Cenozoic era to the Ecozoic era. "Many geologists," she adds, "are naming this new period the Anthropocene because of the effect of humans on Earth's ecosystems."[145] Note the peculiar elision here of the Ecozoic with the Anthropocene. Tucker characterizes the Ecozoic as a period of *positive* human-directed enhancement and flourishing: it is a *welcome* transition (as it is for Berry and Swimme also). Yet the Anthropocene is marked by unprecedented human impacts—very *negative* impacts—on planetary systems: climate change, rising seas, extreme weather, social and political upheaval. Should we also, then, welcome the Anthropocene?

Like proposals for a good Anthropocene, the Ecozoic is not a *critique* of or *retreat from* the idea of our species as overseers of the whole Earth system. Put differently, the idea that the human shapes every aspect of the Earth system is not itself up for debate. Rather, these storytellers assume that better management will follow from additional scientific knowledge and a new consciousness of our place in the cosmos. The Ecozoic appears to be a *good Anthropocene* by another name.

Boosters of the Ecozoic or a good Anthropocene might respond that it is simply a *fact* that humans are shaping every aspect of the planet. Given this state of affairs, we can proceed to transform the planet wisely or recklessly. In light of the available options—essentially, the choice between a good Anthropocene and a bad one—what right-minded person would choose a bad Anthropocene? As long as we are managing, why not aspire to be *wise* managers? Moreover, doesn't the linguistic emphasis on "eco" rather than "Anthropos" suggest the Ecozoic's more generous embrace of *all* life and a less Promethean human? Yes and no. The celebratory mood of the Ecozoic suggests that this transition to a human-run planet is, in Eileen Crist's apt phrase, "still a Hallelujah."[146] It remains a vision of the future "backed by enthrallment with narratives of human ascent," even if *not* grounded (as the Ecozoic is not) in a vision of all life as dead matter or mere resources.[147] That the Ecozoic is the exclamation point to a story of progressive, purposeful cosmogenesis makes it even more troubling than garden-variety Anthropocene boosterism. Why? Because the coming geological era is treated as a natural unfolding, an event written into the *very fabric* of the universe. The universe, after all, is thinking itself in and through us. In this way, the narrative forecloses certain possibilities, including the possibility that humans—or at least those most responsible for the crisis—could break away from this trajectory and choose to manifest our "humanness" in other ways.

Like some modes of Anthropocene discourse, the Ecozoic—less in name than in its expectant mood and rhetoric—screens us from the truth that human domination of the planet is "an *unexamined* choice" that is, in Crist's words, "within both our power and our nature to rescind."[148] Perhaps a first step toward sober self-examination is to stop and grieve—truly grieve—for all that we have lost, are losing, and will lose. At the same time, we must also recognize that much Anthropocene—and Ecozoic—rhetoric overstates the degree to which humans reshape the planet. The language of "responsibility," seen in the frequent claim that humans are responsible for the future unfolding of Earth and its evolution, is highly misleading. As Ned Hettinger points out, "we are not responsible for the existence of sunlight, gravity, or water; nor for the photosynthetic capacity of plants, the biological processes of predation, or the chemical bonds between molecules; nor, more generally, for the diversity of life on the planet or its spectacular geology!"[149] These appeals to "responsibility" overlook nature's own "responsibility" for these processes and the values we perceive in them—beauty, biodiversity, resilience. That humans can damage these processes does not entail that we are the godlike entity that brought them into existence. "Age of Man" environmentalism too easily embraces "an arrogant overvaluation of humans' role and authority."[150]

SCIENCE AS ITS OWN CURE?

To be sure, universe stories sometimes lament that we are leaving behind the Holocene period and moving into "the Anthropocene, an era shaped primarily not by natural systems but by humans."[151] And yet, these narratives perpetuate faith that better knowledge conditions (especially as secured via the new scientific story) will safeguard our interventions—our will to participate in evolution—from intellectual or moral errors that tainted human intervention in a less enlightened time. Where previously we created accidental, unintentional harms—say, climate change—we now intervene in ways that produce only mutually beneficial outcomes for humans and nature. Unintended consequences will themselves be a thing of the past, the storyline suggests. Even Berry, despite obvious concerns about the allure of the Technozoic, occasionally lapses into rhetoric that praises science as a cure for its own ills and excesses. "If our science has gone through its difficulties, it has cured itself out of its own resources."[152] *Journey* is also quick to point out that any harms, large or small, perpetrated against nature through humanity's exercise of science and technology were purely unintentional and accidental. Yes, ice caps are melting, species disappearing, and coral reefs dying, but "we thought we were making a better and more prosperous world . . . . The paradox of *unintended consequences* is now becoming evident."[153] "Though certainly *unintended*," they repeat, "one of the consequences of the modern form of humanity is the termination of the Cenozoic era" signaled by "current mass extinction."[154] "From its inception," they further assure us, "modern science was committed to discovering knowledge and using it to make a better world."[155]

This unduly sanguine appraisal of the benign intentions of *all* of modern science and technology recalls Wilson's portrait of humans as now "smart enough" to manage nature properly. It leads our storytellers to ponder how humanity's uniformly good intentions went so badly awry. Interestingly, *Journey* diagnoses the problem as stemming from our previously "inadequate understanding of *matter itself.*"[156] The narrative then proceeds with a simplified history in which the "deterministic" and "materialistic" science of Galileo, Newton, and Descartes, and the attendant assumption of "passive" matter, is now superseded by new scientific concepts of "creative emergence" and the "self-organizing dynamism" of the cosmos.[157] This new understanding of matter—the cosmos not as a machine but as a vital, purpose-driven, life-giving entity—reveals a universe that "brings forth" its creations when the time is right. In language resonant of Ecclesiastes, *Journey* praises the wisdom manifest in cosmic unfolding: there was a time for hydrogen atoms and a time for galaxies; a time "when the Earth became ignited with life." Armed with a new consciousness that will effectively reverse humans' past unconscious and unintentional harms, and with guarantees of the universe's inherent wisdom, humans can confidently remake the world. Now is the most exciting time of all, *Journey* tells us, for "we live in that time when Earth itself begins its adventure of conscious self-awareness."[158]

In describing our present geological moment, Swimme elsewhere announces, in similarly excited tones, the end of the Cenozoic. Though marked by mass extinctions worse than any Earth has witnessed in 65 million years, our moment is one of enormous "creativity." "End times" such as these bring creative inspiration, Swimme insists, "a new way of being human" and even "a new planet." The human is now engaged in unprecedented creative powers "at the level of *planetary* creativity."[159]

The sense of excitement and adventure seems out of place, even deeply inappropriate, coming as it does among numerous citations of environmental collapse: mass extinction, dying oceans, and catastrophic climate change. This rhetoric makes the Ecozoic difficult to distinguish from "good Anthropocene" boosterism. Clive Hamilton calls attention to the dangers of applauding a transition to a geological epoch (or era) in which humans assume the evolutionary reins. He worries that in recent expressions of Anthropocene optimism, "we are witnessing a contemporary recovery of the idea of a second creation"—an idea he attributes to Francis Bacon—and a "reframing of the Anthropocene as an event to be celebrated rather than lamented and feared." The Anthropocene becomes, perversely, "an opportunity for humans to realise their full potential," much as the Ecozoic marks the fulfillment of cosmic destiny.[160] Good Anthropocene visions tend to treat planetary crises as an exhilarating challenge that can be met with human ingenuity, smarter technology, or adaptive strategies of various sorts. Some believe, as the new cosmologists do, that an emerging global or species-level consciousness will allow us to fulfill what appears—from the standpoint of naturalizing narratives—a preordained role. The hard core of these Anthropocene boosters call for a moratorium on traditional conservation practices, such as the establishment of nature preserves or designated wilderness areas or eradication of invasives. In their minds, nature does not exist anymore (if ever it did), and antiquated conservation must give way to pragmatic, high-tech, human-centered approaches.[161]

To sum up: The stories we tell in the Anthropocene are performative. "They preclude or promote some kinds of collective action rather than others."[162] The problem with universe stories, then, is not so much the lack of normative purchase. Rather, they *too easily* normalize and justify an environmentally destructive status quo and encourage more of the same—more and better knowledge, intensified creativity and "participation" in the cosmic process. Expressed through science and technology, human creativity is an outgrowth of the creativity of the universe itself, and integral to its telos. In this way, *Journey* suggests that we can keep intact, even celebrate, a progressive, linear, optimistic, teleological portrait of both science and cosmogenesis, provided we merely jettison its supposed materialist, mechanistic, Cartesian underpinnings. We need only swap out passive, inert matter for matter personified and imbued with incipient consciousness and purposive behavior (qualities we happen to admire in ourselves). The remainder of the progressive storyline remains largely untouched and unchallenged. The "new" epic story, then, largely reproduces the "grand narrative of modernity, that of Man moving from environmental obliviousness to environmental consciousness, of Man equaling Nature's power, of Man repairing Nature."[163]

Like the cosmic optimism critiqued by Midgley, the Ecozoic may encourage an unwarranted sense of confidence that the Anthropocene idea—if it has any value at all—ought to disrupt.[164] Confidence that managing the planet is merely a matter of acting with intentionality, proper motives, and improved knowledge conditions readily conforms to an increasingly common Anthropocene trope. According to this view, "we have not given enough thought to the side effects of our technological progress, so to save the situation we need better scientific understanding and technological know-how."[165] Rather than interrogate the progressive, human-centered storyline, the narrative simply raises "to a higher level the characteristic of humans that makes us distinctive as a species"—our perfectibility, our intellectual capacities.[166] Instead of signaling a need for greater restraint and humility, a scaling back of impacts and ambitions, the Anthropocene is read, bizarrely, as "an invitation to assume total control."[167]

Yet if *Journey* took its own claims for an *animate* cosmos to heart, serious doubt would be cast on humans' unique and powerful role as the primary cosmic agents. For example, the new cosmologists—notably Berry and Swimme—invoke the Gaia concept implicitly and explicitly (*Journey's* portrait of a dynamic, self-organizing universe suggests the influence of this idea; Swimme and Berry engage directly with the concept and its implications).[168] Yet, as Bruno Latour and others believe, embracing Gaia suggests not that humans play a decisive or directorial role in evolutionary unfolding but that the planet is populated by innumerable agents. Granting agency and vibrancy to matter ought to decenter humans and instill caution and humility regarding our interventions into complex, tangled webs of living stuff. To take the planet's all-pervasive agentialism seriously is to understand that we are not and never have been in the evolutionary driver's seat.[169] Indeed, the fact that we now inhabit a planet that may no longer support human life as we know it seems as clear a demonstration as we could possibly have of humans' lack of directive agency over planetary processes.

The Universe Story gestures at times in the direction of agency distributed among human and nonhuman life, and inhering even in rudimentary cells and primitive matter. In place of matter as dead and inert, it celebrates a newly discovered "deep truth about matter" as dynamic, vibrant stuff.[170] One might expect this vision of an animate universe to entail a new appraisal of the startling potency and vitality of matter, vis-à-vis human power and importance, as suggested by theorists of New Materialism.[171] But new cosmologists seem oddly reluctant to take seriously the animate universe they narrate into being. Often the nonhuman universe figures as little more than background for the more compelling human drama. Perhaps if they embraced an animate universe, they would more clearly perceive the folly of assuming that humans can foresee and manage the many consequences of our actions and interventions in nature's unfolding; that we can leave behind unintended consequences of past (bad, mechanical) scientific and technological interventions and move forward with the confidence inspired by the bright new science of a dynamic cosmos. A cosmos that is truly alive does not sit still and take direction as humans impose their strategies for planetary management, because "the intentions of 'man' will inevitably become conditioned by those of the matter he attempts to steer."[172] Ultimately, the narrative retreats from a vision of potent, multifarious, alien agencies. In doing so, the Universe Story turns away from *wonder* to embrace a more orderly assimilation and tidy organization of the cosmos.

AGE-OF-MAN ENVIRONMENTALISM

Is it really possible to connect the dots between cosmogenesis in a Teilhardian vein and the blind excesses of the good Anthropocene? As noted previously, Paul Crutzen, in tracing the evolution of the Anthropocene concept, identifies Teilhard as an early source. Andrew Revkin who suggested a similar word—*Anthrocene* ("a geological age of our own making")—as early as 1992, also places himself in the lineage of Teilhard and Berry.[173] Revkin is a Senior Fellow for Environmental Understanding at Pace University and *New York Times* blogger who pitches the good Anthropocene to the general public. He is also a member of the Anthropocene Working Group, tasked with deliberating about the formal adoption of the term Anthropocene for our current epoch. In regular blogs and elsewhere, Revkin peddles an upbeat techno-optimism while simultaneously chiding the old-fashioned piety of environmentalists as mired in a perpetual dynamic of "woe is me, shame on you." He frequently spars with critics like Clive Hamilton over the merits of a good Anthropocene as an environmental ideal. Revkin characterizes the Anthropocene mood as one of celebration rather than *mourning*. Specifically he likens the sensation of the coming epoch to the excitement of finding oneself "in the first car on the first run of a new roller coaster that hasn't been examined fully by engineers."[174] New models of environmental thought and action are warranted, Revkin believes, by the recognition that "Earth is increasingly what humans choose to make it."[175]

Revkin meanwhile heartily endorses scientists like Peter Kareiva, a theoretical biologist and Chief Scientist at the Nature Conservancy who, like other so-called "new conservationists," argues for replacing nature preservation with "pragmatic," human-centered management strategies aimed at safeguarding ecosystem services over and above wild nature, and management of "working landscapes" instead of wilderness tracts.[176] Thinkers lionized by Revkin endorse a "trickle down" theory of mutual enhancement for human and natural systems, arguing that when people's incomes and prosperity increase, so will their affection for wildlife and nature.[177] New conservationist rhetoric, at its most extreme, is often peppered with punchy, irreverent, ad hominem attacks on beloved environmentalists. Edward Abbey, who delighted in the harsh beauty and isolation of desert lands, is mocked as a hypocrite for celebrating wilderness solitude while privately confessing to loneliness. Thoreau is ridiculed as a "townie," dependent upon relatives to feed and clothe him while pretending to rough it in the wild. Rachel Carson is condescendingly portrayed as issuing "plaintive" but misguided pleas to respect nature's fragility. These heroes of the "old" guard are charged with fueling technophobia and misanthropy, spawning narratives of eco-tragedy and apocalypse. New conservationists are optimistic about smarter technology and techno-fixes and believe nature to be tough and resilient.

Like the new cosmologists, the new conservationists see themselves as purveyors of a more functional and inspirational new myth. A case in point is the "Ecomodernist Manifesto," published in 2015 by an ensemble cast of scholars and entrepreneurs affiliated with the Breakthrough Institute.[178] The manifesto scoffs at the idea of ecological limits, offering the quintessential fantasy of futurists that humans can "decouple" from nature. Inspired by the emancipating vision of the Anthropocene, their provocative treatise promises to meet future challenges with intensified agriculture and urbanization; nuclear energy; genetically modified food sources; climate engineering; and other amazing technological feats. As with the new environmentalists generally, they endorse a radically human-centered vision that regards nature-centered conservation as a "dysfunctional, antihuman anachronism."[179] Armed with perfected knowledge and ever-new technologies, they anticipate a *great* Anthropocene, a new "dream" to replace the nightmare vision of traditional environmentalism.[180] Above all, they believe the future belongs to those who embrace humans' expanding domination of the planet and managerial control. With the arrival of the Anthropocene, humans become "de facto planetary managers."[181]

While critics decry the breathless hubris and the quick embrace of techno-fixes that attend these visions, Revkin praises their "provocative and refreshing" departure from environmentalists' typically mournful or alarmist refrains.[182] In promoting his breezy "that was then, this is now" environmentalism, Revkin invokes the wisdom of his personal heroes. Specifically, he credits the philosophies of Teilhard de Chardin, Thomas Berry, and Vladimir Vernadsky as shaping his optimistic take on the Age of the Human.[183] Revkin notes that his reading of Vernadsky's early intimations of the Anthropocene concept prepared him to accept Teilhard's noosphere concept. Having discovered Teilhard, Revkin also grasped how his cosmic philosophy intersected with thinkers like Berry he had long admired. Revkin gives his own spin to Teilhard's "noosphere," referring to it as the "knowosphere"—an intentional echo of the idea of the planetary mind. He understands our modern, high-tech knowosphere, symbolized by global networks of information and technology sharing, as key to our collective salvation. Above all, he believes in refraining from "judgmental" environmental discourse. Sharing knowledge in a nonjudgmental way—via the knowosphere—is our ticket to a bright and well-run future. Properly understood, Revkin argues, the Anthropocene epoch has "a nice feel to it," more a "celebration" than a lament. The coming Anthropocene epoch, he insists, "is 'the great work', as Thomas Berry put it."[184] Berry's Ecozoic evokes for Revkin the exciting project of "taking full ownership" of the Anthropocene. In a blog post written immediately after Berry's death, Revkin deploys a stream of mixed metaphors honoring Berry as a visionary "Pied Piper" for humanity who used "awe . . . as a kind of rocket fuel for powering a new way of life."[185] In the same spirit, Revkin provides a "testimonial" for *Journey of the Universe,* praising *Journey*'s upbeat storyline and refreshing disavowal of woe-is-me / shame-on-you finger wagging. A mood of nonjudgmental optimism—what Revkin elsewhere calls "anthropophilia"—is necessary for paving a "path to a good Anthropocene."[186]

Are hierophants like Revkin wrong to discern in Teilhard, Berry, and the projects their work has spawned, intimations of a good Anthropocene and a feel-good knowospheric future? Is it really possible to trace excited technophilia and runaway ecomodernism back to these thinkers? Not exactly. It is clear from *The Universe Story* that, in comparison to Teilhard, Swimme and Berry eschew techno-optimism and environmental fixes. They offer the Ecozoic as a wholesome alternative to Technozoic enchantment, and as Berry's admirers frequently note, he meant to temper Teilhard's enthusiasm for technology and his human-centered flights of fancy. In a biographical sketch of Berry, Tucker presents the two in a contrasting light:

> Berry has also critiqued Teilhard's overly optimistic view of progress and his apparent lack of concern for the devastating effect that industrial processes were having on fragile ecosystems. He has pointed out that Teilhard was heir to a western mode of thinking which saw the human as capable of controlling the natural world, usually through science and technology. Teilhard's challenge to "build the Earth" reflects some of the unrestrained optimism of humans whose faith in science and technology had no bounds. This overly anthropocentric and blindly optimistic view is something Berry has frequently critiqued.[187]

Tucker's appraisal makes one wonder why she regularly credits Teilhard as the inspiration for *Journey,* for the flaws she identifies are not peripheral to his work.

More to the point: rather than see Teilhard's unrestrained optimism for controlling nature as a logical outgrowth of his anthropic and progressive cosmogenesis, Tucker cites Berry's claim that a pernicious "western mode of thinking" crept into his work. Yet is easy enough to see how uncritical enthusiasm for human techno-scientific prowess springs directly from Teilhard's central belief in progressive cosmogenesis and noospheric transformation of the planet—ideas whose provenance, incidentally, are largely Russian. (As with Teilhard's thought, the Russian "Cosmism" that inspired the noosphere has also spurred transhumanist and techno-futurist aspirations.)

It is not difficult to understand how a techno-enthusiast Anthropocene booster like Revkin finds inspiration and affirmation in *both* Teilhard and Berry. For while it is indeed true that Berry's managerial agenda for the planet does not similarly idolize technology, he remained captivated by the noosphere's transformative power. For example, Berry's *Dream of the Earth* celebrates five major components of the Earth system as identified by modern science. He labels these the geosphere, hydrosphere, atmosphere, biosphere, and noosphere, adding that "we need to reflect especially on the mindsphere [or noosphere]—the latest of these five powers that constitute the earth functioning."[188] The other four spheres, he argues, once displayed "exuberant creativity," but their functioning has *now* "given over to the mindsphere the major share of directing the course of earth development."[189] Earth gives its blessing to human directorship, Berry suggests, *entrusting* us to take over its once instinctive functioning. "The earth that directed itself instinctively in its former phases seems now to be entering a phase of conscious decision through its human expression," Berry continues. "This is the *ultimate daring venture for the earth, this confiding its destiny to human decision, the bestowal upon the human community of the power of life and death over its basic life systems.*" In light of our radical transformation of these planetary processes, Berry continues, "we must wonder at ourselves and what we are doing and what is happening to the larger destinies of the earth, even perhaps of the universe."[190]

Yes, but wonder at what, exactly? And to what end? To be sure, Berry stops well short of techno-domination, yet his vision here is at odds with humans as a mere "subset of the earth, not dominant controllers."[191] Ecomodernists like Revkin are not wrong to discern in such prophesies a mood closer to celebration than woe and lamentation. When the Earth dreams, it dreams of us.

CONCLUSION

Parallels between the Ecozoic / noosphere and the (good) Anthropocene ought to give us pause. The new cosmology is easily co-opted as an ideal companion myth for Anthropocene boosters. The appeal of a hopeful message is clear, but these narratives propagate wishful thinking that is woefully out of sync with the nature of the crisis that confronts us. All of this matters because, as Michael Soulé argues, "the naïve and unscientific new environmentalism, if implemented, would accelerate extinction and would be a disaster for civilization, hastening ecological collapse globally while pulling the trigger on thousands of beautiful kinds of plants and animals."[192] Ecozoic, noospheric, and good Anthropocene narratives evoke an anticipatory vision of human-Earth relationship, wherein humans emerge as a geological force gradually over deep time. The developmental, deep time framework of cosmic unfolding may indeed have a "deflationary" effect[193] that misconstrues the severity of the Anthropocene, treating it as the culmination of creative processes set in motion by the Big Bang.[194] The narrative's steady drumbeat of progress and complexification—from the Big Bang to human tool use, to symbolic consciousness and our exciting moment of Anthropocene transformation—tells a story that encourages "serious underestimation and mischaracterization of the kind of human response necessary to slow its onset and ameliorate its impacts."[195]

In the next chapter, as we turn to the work of evolutionary evangelists Michael Dowd and Connie Barlow, we will not be leaving Teilhard de Chardin and Thomas Berry far behind. Dowd and Barlow's mythopoeic science and evolutionary evangelism, presented as a new religion of reality, brings Teilhard and Berry's ideas into close contact with the science-reverencing worldview of a scientist now quite familiar to readers of this book: Richard Dawkins.

Chapter 6

Genesis 2.0

The Epic of Evolution as Religion of Reality

The late Catholic "geologian" Thomas Berry inspired many (myself included) to learn the Universe story, the Earth story, and the patterns of human cultural evolution on a global scale. Together these stories constitute the epic of evolution—what academia now calls the interdisciplinary study of Big History. Thomas encouraged us to go beyond learning the story and to develop our own ways of bringing this Great Story to others. . . . Big History goes by many names. Harvard biologist Edward O. Wilson referred to it as "the epic of evolution." Thomas Berry and Brian Swimme celebrated the evolutionary journey in a 1992 book titled The Universe Story. *The academic discipline of Big History began in the late 1980s when historian David Christian taught a survey course of this title to college students in Australia. . . . Big History (by whatever name) is the new Genesis.*

—MICHAEL DOWD, "EVIDENTIAL MYSTICISM AND THE FUTURE OF THE EARTH"

There is something very cheap about magic in the supernatural sense, like turning a frog into a prince with a magic wand. Reality has a grander, poetic magic of its own.

—RICHARD DAWKINS (SEE NOTES)

If it's real, we believe in it.

—MARC PERKEL, FOUNDER, THE CHURCH OF REALITY

In 2002, a conservative Christian pastor named Michael Dowd and his wife, a successful freelance science writer named Connie Barlow, quit their jobs, sold their possessions, and purchased a van that they decorated with emblems of a Jesus fish kissing a Darwin fish. Since that time, Dowd and Barlow have lived as itinerant preachers whose "good news" is not the word of God, but the wonder of evolution and the sacred story of science. The kissing fish represent the "marriage of science and religion for personal and planetary wellbeing."[1] In homage to Thomas Berry, the license plate on their iconic van reads "Ecozoic."

Dowd and Barlow are two of the most prominent advocates of a sacralized Epic of Evolution—if prominence may be gauged by media attention and strong internet presence. Barlow, whose works include *Green Space, Green Time* (1997) and *Ghosts of Evolution* (2000), has been part of the new cosmology since its inception. Together she and Dowd spread the gospel of evolution and host "evolutionary revivals" for thousands of groups throughout North America.[2] Their audiences include children and adults, in both secular and religious venues (ranging widely across the liberal Christian denominations, but with particular focus on Unitarian Universalist congregations). Dowd and Barlow also offer online seminars on "evolutionizing your life" that draw heavily, if selectively, on science to "decode human behavior, eliminate self-judgment, and create a big-hearted life of purpose and joyful integrity."[3] These seminars promise participants that they will feel "as if the Universe has put its stamp of approval on your life, and you will know the thrill of living in right relationship to reality and in alignment with your highest values."[4] Their emphasis on the necessity of achieving proper alignment with scientific reality is a hallmark of their evangelism.

Like Universe Story narratives examined in the previous chapter, Dowd and Barlow's version of the Epic is invested in the progressive nature of evolutionary unfolding. Their narration of the Epic draws on thinkers we have previously encountered. As Dowd writes:

> The Evolutionary spirituality movement has been evolving and producing its sacred texts for decades, and indeed much longer. From the early explorations of Julian Huxley and Teilhard de Chardin to the work of Epic of Evolution pioneers—Thomas Berry, Brian Swimme, Miriam MacGillis, Mary Evelyn Tucker, and Eric Chaisson—to leading evolutionists such as Edward O. Wilson, David Sloan Wilson, and Ursula Goodenough to popularizers of evolutionary psychology and evolutionary brain science such as Robert Wright.[5]

The list goes on to include many other theologians and scientists. Dowd and Barlow are especially indebted to Loyal Rue's partitioning of reality into *"How things are* (that is, *What is real?*) and *Which things matter* (that is, *What is important?*)."[6] In a move that distinguishes their project from the Universe Story, Dowd and Barlow also induct the new atheists into their pantheon of heroes. Indeed, one of the most interesting features of their evolutionary ministry is the merger it effects between a religious thinker beloved by many—Thomas Berry—and a great antagonist of religion, Richard Dawkins. Their work suggests, for example, that Dawkins's promotion of reality and purified scientific wonder is entirely of a piece with Berry's call for a new, functional story.

At first glance, it might seem counterintuitive that a convergence is occurring between Berry and his disciples and the devotees of the world's most celebrated, or reviled, atheist. That is precisely what makes these evolutionary evangelists worth watching. When someone like Dowd—well versed in science and religion—draws inspiration from and pays tribute to Berry and Dawkins in almost equal measure, I suspect he is not merely confused (or impossibly eclectic) in his choice of mentors. These evangelists have identified genuine elective affinities between seemingly disparate worldviews. The seeds sown by Berry's call for a new story, and nurtured by enthusiasts like Brian Swimme, Ursula Goodenough, and Loyal Rue, as well as evolutionary preachers like Dowd and Barlow, have borne fruit as a scientistic "religion" of reality that exalts Dawkins and other scientists as prophets. The intensity of reverence felt by Dowd and (especially) Barlow for scientists and the scientific enterprise might surprise even avid enthusiasts of the Universe Story. A strong proselytizing impulse also fuels these projects, as with the Universe Story. But, as we will see, the educational mission extends more broadly to include children as a key target audience.

Dowd's biography entails a rather dramatic conversion narrative. Much like E. O. Wilson, he converted from Bible-based Christianity to "a knowledge-based, evolutionary form of religion."[7] Science, which Dowd heralds as a form of "public revelation," came to fulfill many of the functions of religion in his life, providing answers to personal and existential questions that had long troubled him. Dowd describes himself as a former "born again believer" who became a "born again knower" upon hearing the scientific account of the universe told as a sacred epic.[8] Berry's work was central to this conversion and Dowd frequently cites him as his main mentor. In the wake of his "new story" epiphany, his life's work became oriented to "the service of a religiously inspiring understanding of evolution, such that others, too, might experience our common creation story as gospel and be inspired to love and serve accordingly."[9] Serve what, exactly? Dowd sometimes refers to himself as a Christian, sometimes as a religious naturalist, and sometimes as a "post-theist" or "new theist." "New Theists are *not* believers," he explains, "we're evidentialists."[10] Barlow, who came to the Epic with no particular religious commitments, describes herself as an atheist or "creathiest."[11] Because Dowd and Barlow work closely together, I examine their ideas in tandem;[12] but I will also examine Barlow's claims separately and in depth, owing to the especially strong connection her work attempts to forge between embracing the Epic and espousing environmental values.

Dowd's *Thank God for Evolution* (2007) encourages people to see the meaning of their lives within the context of the sacred narrative of evolution. He is influenced by and frequently quotes Berry and Teilhard, while leaning heavily on evolutionary psychology and gene-centered biology. Dowd's evolutionary worldview is rather a grab-bag of diverse and sometimes competing evolutionary arguments and concepts, combining insights from evolutionary theorists known to have engaged in heated disputes over the details of evolutionary processes, such as Richard Dawkins and Simon Conway Morris, for example, or E. O. Wilson and Stephen Jay Gould. He is untroubled by the suggestion of some evolutionary biologists that the emergence of religion is explicable in terms of an evolutionary misfiring or exaptation[13] (Gould's term) of some other (or previously) serviceable trait in our evolution. Dowd counts among his favorite evolutionary psychologists Steven Pinker and David Sloan Wilson, from whom he draws, respectively, his views about humans' unchosen animal nature and the development of cooperative social arrangements in evolution. Dowd and Barlow write especially glowing reviews of Dawkins's work. Both seem to regard Dawkins's *The Greatest Show on Earth* (2009) as a sort of companion book to *Thank God for Evolution* and, as noted in chapter 2, they strongly support Dawkins's efforts to lure children away from fantasy, fairy tale, and religious mythology, toward the superior magic of reality. Barlow is especially invested in crafting evolutionary "parables" and ritual enactments of the evolutionary epic for children, frequently in religious educational settings.

PURPOSEFUL PATTERNING AND ELUSIVE WONDER

Like other new cosmologists, Dowd and Barlow maintain that science has arrived at knowledge comprehensive enough for us to tell a coherent story with clear and profound meaning for humans. Our species has an inborn "mythopoeic drive" and science offers rich materials from which to fashion meaning.[14] All that is needed is an infusion of poetry, myth, song, or other phenomenological or experiential embellishments. "Science unquestionably provides the foundation," Dowd writes. "For this tale to be experienced as holy, however, it must don the accoutrements of myth. Barebones science must be embellished with metaphor and enriched by poetry, painting, song, and ceremony."[15] Changes in science, and thus to the story, are to be welcomed, not feared. "Whenever a new discovery is made and broadly verified in the sciences," Dowd argues, "our understanding of the Great Story of the Universe changes," and in this sense there is little danger of becoming a "Great Story Fundamentalist."[16] By way of illustrating the Epic's openness to revision, Dowd and Barlow make light-hearted use of Pluto's official demotion (in 2006) from a true planet to a dwarf planet. The story of Pluto's "identity crisis" is fashioned into an evolutionary parable for children.[17] Yet, despite the story's alleged openness to mystery and its adaptability to a variety of religious or cultural perspectives, cosmological and evolutionary history are perceived as directional, imbued with purpose or progressing toward a goal. This aspect of the narrative appears nonnegotiable, for the unmistakable "arrow of evolution"[18] makes it possible for cosmic and planetary unfolding to coalesce into a big picture. Regardless of what happens in the universe, Dowd joins Teilhard and his followers in asserting that the universe can be "deeply trusted" to move in "the same five-fold direction: the direction of greater diversity, greater complexity, greater awareness, greater speed of change, *and* greater intimacy with itself."[19] This cosmic optimism—to borrow Midgley's phrase again—also finds support in Berry's claim that "sensitized to such guidance from the very structure and functioning of the Universe, we can have confidence in the future that awaits the human venture."[20] Dowd lists several other features of the universe and its narrative that commend the Epic of Evolution as a guide for all of humanity. He insists, however, that the story is not a new religion *competing* with existing ones but, rather, a "metareligious" or "metamythical" perspective that can be "absorbed independently by each faith and worldview."[21]

Their attraction to directional modes of evolution leads Dowd and Barlow to embrace an interpretation of evolution as rife with "convergences," as famously promulgated by paleontologist Simon Conway Morris. Evolution is here understood to converge on the same "solutions" to evolutionary problems again and again in independent lineages. Evolutionary strategies such as wings, echolocation (sonar), or the evolution of sight recur in species not closely related to one another. Conway Morris, in contrast to Gould, makes the (now familiar) argument that the evolution of humans, or something basically like us, was inevitable.[22] Dowd and Barlow celebrate what they see as a renaissance of convergence studies in evolution, all allegedly pointing to patterning and directionality in evolutionary history. As Barlow notes, convergent evolution provides "good material for mythmaking" because it suggests purposefulness evolutionary unfolding—even inevitability—rather than random meandering.[23] Our planet seems actually "determined" to generate and repeat certain evolutionary breakthroughs, Barlow ventures.[24]

Whether convergence or contingency is the dominant mode is not a settled issue in biology, and in some sense it is not an "issue" at all. A scientist's perspective may have much to do with his or her area of specialty (convergence is important in comparative anatomy, for example, but less so in paleobiology). Barlow regards convergence—not altogether accurately—as a neglected area of research now undergoing rapid efflorescence, in a manner significant for the mythopoeic enterprise. In any event, the extent to which Dowd and Barlow's rendering of the Epic depends on directionality and patterning casts doubt on the revisability of the Epic. In other words, their enthusiasm does not extend equally to all modes of evolution, but to those with strong mythic appeal. Their evolutionary epic seems committed to a convergent—and relatively fixed rather than improvisational—understanding of life's narrative.[25] This preference may explain their attraction to Big History, which seeks common themes and patterns over the broadest possible sweep of history.[26]

When it comes to defining *human* nature, Dowd also defends a rather settled account of who we are and why we behave as we do. He eagerly embraces evolutionary psychology's potential to explain human failings that some religions would attribute to sin or Satan—drug, food, and sex addictions, infidelity, impulses to cruelty—as well as gender differences and other inherited tendencies "deeply rooted in our reptilian brain."[27] The Epic, for Dowd, is a means to personal salvation. He gives cute names to human instincts: "Lizard Legacy" for our "reptilian" impulses, "Furry Li'l Mammal" for our more evolved social instincts. These labels seem ready-made for young audiences gripped by powerful hormones.[28] "Evolutionary psychology," he argues, "gives us a way of understanding our true nature. It makes it easier for us to live."[29] Dowd's evolutionary sermons preach that personal failures and moral lapses are "not your fault" but stem from "inherited proclivities that served the survival and reproductive interests of our human and pre-human ancestors."[30] For Dowd, evolution's assumed directionality clearly provides a normative guide to how we should live. When asked, for example, why an account of instincts, as supplied by evolutionary psychology, should inspire us to *change* our behavior for the better (however "better" might be defined from a scientific standpoint) rather than simply acquiescing to the instinctive pull of evolutionary forces, Dowd falls back on evolution's directional groping toward increasingly cooperative and benign social arrangements. "When we look at the pre-human world, then at human cultural evolution, we see greater spheres of cooperation, of complexity and interdependence at an ever-wider scale . . . the people for whom we have cooperation and compassion keeps expanding."[31]

Whatever we make of these evolutionary diagnoses of human failings, Dowd's commitment to patterning and directionality undermines claims about the open-ended, provisional nature of the Epic. Ultimately, Dowd offers no substantive response to the question of how to avoid turning what is at best a current consensus of science into a static teaching. But revisions to certain parts of the scientific storyline could have enormous impact on the meaning derived from it. Barlow (though equally enamored of convergent evolution) is more circumspect about the proposition that certain values are *discovered* or *revealed* in scientific accounts of the physical world. Desired values can, however, be made to emerge from the available data, provided the story is told in the right way.

EMBRACING REALITY

Dowd and Barlow promote a life of "ecological integrity" as one of the positive transformations produced by better alignment with reality. Environmental concerns make an appearance in Dowd's oft-repeated, TED-talk-ready summation of his "Factual Faith," and both Dowd and Barlow make regular reference to the crisis of climate change. Factual Faith, as Dowd defines it, consists of the following ideas: Reality is synonymous with god (or god is reality personified); scientific evidence is scripture; Big History is the common creation story; ecology is the new theology;

integrity is the spiritual path; and a just and healthy future is the overriding mission.[32] What we moderns call reality or nature, Dowd contends, the ancients referred to as God or gods. Dowd's sermons on reality often cite Berry's influence. "Connie and I," he testifies, "would never have met and neither of us would be evangelizing evolution if it weren't for Thomas."[33] As noted above, he characteristically borrows freely from new atheist thinkers as well. A key area of overlap between Berry and Dawkins, which Dowd rightly recognizes, is the emphasis each places on science as having *revelatory* significance. Faith in these ongoing revelations inspires trust and confidence in the future, and in the cosmos generally.

Dowd's lectures and essays also refer frequently to Big History and its chief proponent, David Christian. With an approving nod to Rue, Dowd offers up Big History as the cure for the widespread cultural malaise of amythia. The focus of Big History, he writes, is on "finding the patterns—the patterns that not only make sense of the whole shebang but that launch a frontal assault on the plague of amythia."[34] A world immersed in global trade and communication needs "a global story that can quench the fires of global conflict ignited by unilateral allegiances to ancient, competing mythic stories interpreted literally."[35] Here Dowd appears confused about whether our global problem is a lack of believable myths—as the term amythia would suggest—or whether our crisis stems from too much belief in too many myths. Either way, he asserts that a new big picture of reality is "an inspiring way forward through the thorny and tangled bank of the science-and-religion debate."[36]

This "way forward" entails supplanting religion with consecrated science. Science, he writes, is "now how we seek truth about the nature of reality, of which we are an inseparable part." Dowd further contends that "those who speak on behalf of reality are the true prophets of our age, whether they be religious, nonreligious, or even anti-religious."[37] In this context, he depicts Dawkins, as well as Sam Harris and Christopher Hitchens, as much-needed "prophets of reality."[38] Our culture is on the brink of an "Evidential Reformation," in which religions are beginning to "honor and celebrate evidence as divine guidance, and big history as our common creation story."[39] When the blessed day arrives, we will have the new atheists to thank. Dowd's contention here, for which he once again draws support from Rue, is that religion is not "about God" but about having a right relationship to "Reality," as given by science.[40] Facts, he likes to say, are the language in which God speaks to us. Neo-atheist critics of religion are therefore "well-positioned to see what's real and what's important today."[41]

RITUALIZING THE EPIC

To be compelling, the divine language of facts needs the accoutrements of religion. To foster a more tangible connection with reality, Dowd and Barlow preside over a variety of evolutionary rituals, in religious and secular settings. These include a

Cosmic Communion that invokes Carl Sagan; the recitation of evolutionary parables and songs; ritual use of Great Story beads that mimic rosary beads; and a candlelit Cosmic Walk symbolizing the unfolding universe.[42] In Cosmic Communion rituals performed in liberal churches or spiritual retreat centers, participants are "anointed with 'stardust' (glitter) to signify, as Carl Sagan pointed out in the 1980s, that we are quite literally 'made of stardust.' "[43] Participants may string together Beads of the Cosmic Rosary intended to represent key moments in evolution. The shape and color of beads are suggestive of cosmic events like supernovae, or signify the evolution of particular life-forms such as dinosaurs, birds, or flowers. Beads can be personalized, much like a charm bracelet.

For the Cosmic Walk, a rope is placed on the ground in a spiral shape, symbolizing 14 billion years of cosmic unfolding, while candlelit stations around the spiral signal cosmic and evolutionary events: the Big Bang, the death of dinosaurs, and the emergence of early humans.[44] Markers near the end of the Cosmic Walk represent major discoveries by twentieth-century scientists, including the discovery of the expanding universe—the very discovery that "revealed" the storied structure of our cosmos. In this way, the ritual becomes self-reflexive, visually evoking the central insight—celebrated by new cosmologists of all stripes—that humans are the universe become conscious of itself. Human knowledge of the universe is itself ritualized as an event of cosmic proportions and significance, a key turning point in cosmogenesis.

Dowd and Barlow aspire to attract audiences large enough to rival modern mega-churches. Barlow describes her vision of "evolutionary revivals" that preach the message of evolutionary psychology and brain science, particularly to young people.

> I see my preacher husband (Michael Dowd) . . . being able to let loose his Pentecostal, celebratory energy for praising evolution. In addition to our new, wholesome, inspiring, and healing evolutionary cosmology, we can also offer help and support with the troubles and challenges in people's everyday lives. Michael and I have been working for more than a year on some cool stuff in evolutionary psychology and evolutionary brain science, that helps us understand WHY we have these challenges, helps us accept our "inherited proclivities", our "unchosen nature" (Michael's phrases) . . . . We have found that teens and young people especially tune into this part of our programs, as these are their new and frightening struggles. With the help of local liberal churches (talk about re-energizing mainline congregations!), we could pour a lot of energy into an amazing event that would be the template for doing more and better "Evolutionary Revivals" all around the country—which would be a new form of participatory concert for college kids, too![45]

Dowd and Barlow turn to Dawkins for help in ritualizing their religion of reality, with children's conversion particularly in mind. One ritual draws on Dawkins's narrative of evolutionary history in his book *The Ancestor's Tale*. Dawkins

conceived of the book in a way that makes it an obvious choice for Epic proponents. He intends it as a scientific version of an epic journey, akin to Chaucer's
Canterbury Tales or Bunyan's *Pilgrim's Progress.* He even permits himself to draw
parallels between this project and a religious quest—albeit, not without a certain
amount of discomfort. ("Pilgrimages? Join forces with pilgrims?" Dawkins asks.
"Yes, why not. Pilgrimage is an apt way to think about our journey to the past . . .
an epic pilgrimage from the present to the past.")[46] As with Chaucer's tale,
Dawkins's journeyers each have stories to tell: the Gorilla's Tale, the Seal's Tale, the
Fruit Fly's Tale, and even the Cauliflower's Tale.[47]

Dowd and Barlow distill these ideas into whimsical rituals that allow partici-
pants to "greet their concestors" (common ancestors). "Child-friendly" versions of
"The River of Life" are rich in visual imagery and accompanied by rhyming songs.
Lyrics describe "ant-eaters, tree sloths and ground sloths of long ago / All South
American, 'cept Armadill-e-oh," or "lettuce and lima beans / All feed on solar
beams." The song's refrain underscores the core message: "these are our relatives."[48]
Dowd and Barlow have also designed a Dawkins-inspired "Ancestors Meditation"
that invites participants to think themselves back into evolutionary time where
they rendezvous with ancestors both recent and remote, as a way of connecting
with "this long, awesome story of evolution." The message is that "we are the universe, turning to look in awe at what we come from, and what we have become."[49]

Why so much interest in children and young people? The goal of connecting
children to the web of life is commendable (though time spent in nature, rather
than indoor recitation and enactment of evolutionary highlights, would seem a
more direct path to forging such connection). An additional and often overriding
agenda is apparent in the need to "inoculate" children against religious ideas, to
"get them while they're young."[50] In this way children will "always want to feel
themselves as part of the grand evolutionary process—no matter what they may
hear later from anti-evolution friends or adults."[51] The goal of shielding children
from the encroachment of religion goes beyond fortifying them against fundamentalist or creationist beliefs. It also means disabusing them of any and all
childlike beliefs or fanciful notions that are not demonstrably of scientific
provenance. Barlow, for example, teaches children an enlightened version of
"Twinkle, Twinkle, Little Star" in a way that would make Dickens's philistine
schoolmaster Gradgrind supremely proud. The song's signature expression of
childlike awe, "How I wonder what you are" is updated by Barlow as *Now I know
just what you are.*[52]

Dowd and Barlow's promotional video for Dawkins's children's book, *The Magic
of Reality,* opens with the pair avidly affirming Dawkins's commitment to scientific
reality as more wondrous than traditional myths and stories: "the truth is more
magical . . . than any myth or made-up mystery or miracle," in Dawkins's words.[53]
Dawkins's message, they recognize, has "really broad implications for society along

EPIC OF EVOLUTION AS RELIGION OF REALITY

the lines that we've been promoting for ten years." Dowd interjects his analysis that much of world's suffering results from people being "out of touch with reality," and characterizes Dawkins's work as an audacious step toward eradicating widespread delusion. The video also references Rue's notion that the Epic tells us what is "real" and what is "important." Barlow expresses her long-standing admiration for Dawkins, adding that she considers *The Ancestor's Tale*, rather than *The Magic of Reality*, to be his first real "contribution to children," owing to its potential as an evolutionary ritual for young children.[54]

One segment of the video finds Dowd and Barlow reading aloud from sections of the book that meet their strongest approval. An example is Dawkins's distinction between "supernatural" magic (a category that includes religious myths and miracles, Grimm's fairy tales, and the Harry Potter series, among other pernicious sources of fake magic) and the *real* "poetic magic" offered by science. Dowd and Barlow affirm that supernatural magic encourages only false explanations of the world that interfere with attaining a true grasp of reality. "To say that something happened supernaturally is not just to say 'We don't understand it' but to say 'We will never understand it, so don't even try.'"[55]

Dowd and Barlow are undeterred by Dawkins' distaste for presenting scientific reality in mythic or religious form (recall his critique of Goodenough's faux religiosity).[56] That Dawkins does not take the additional step of mythologizing scientific reality for children is no reason *they* cannot, they insist. They estimate that *The Magic of Reality* is suitable for children of approximately fifth-grade level, but urge viewers to introduce the book to children as early as possible, before they "are old enough to understand." The video concludes with Boswell's music video "The Poetry of Reality," mentioned in chapter 2, in which Dawkins "sings" the lines "There is real poetry in the real world / Science is the poetry of reality."[57]

Dowd has opined elsewhere that today's children are demanding *reality*, not stale old myths and fairy tales, and that they spurn stories not up to their evidentiary standards.[58]

> Now kids expect the real deal: magnificent BBC, National Geographic, Discovery Channel, and History Channel productions that enflesh T. rex and trilobites, and that spectacularly feature (and animate!) the fresh news delivered by Earth's orbiting population of space telescopes. . . . Ancient stories that contradict the new stories beloved of modern children (the stories of black holes and fossil behemoths) will be met with insistent protests, "But that's not true!"[59]

One wonders why so many children have in recent years demanded so much Harry Potter and similar magical tales. These realists are doing their part to contain this social menace.[60]

In typical fashion, Dowd and Barlow often deny that the evolutionary epic competes with existing myths and stories. The Great Story embraces all comers.

Yet Dawkins's endgame is to demonstrate the inferiority of other stories—and indeed the impoverished nature of all experiences of the physical world not grounded firmly in science. To side with Dawkins's central claims in *The Magic of Reality* is to embrace a vision of science and religion as competing explanations of the world, and to reject other stories as nothing more or less than dangerous holdovers from a primitive past. Drawing on biological metaphors, Dowd sometimes likens certain features of our inherited religious traditions to a life-threatening illness or a dangerous vestigial organ. As global religions evolve from "flat-earth understandings" to "evolutionary understandings of those same doctrines," a few stubborn pockets of resistance—evolutionary throwbacks—will likely remain. "The sickness might originate and fester in just a tiny subset of the body, but with little warning it may burst in ways devastating to the whole in the same way as the rudimentary appendix of the human intestine can provoke life-threatening sepsis."[61] Flat-earth religion must evolve to rely on data as its scripture: "Evolutionary religion's alternative to reliance on ancient scriptures is empirical data. In a way, the data are our scriptures—and to these we submit."[62]

Further evidence of Dowd's consecration of science is seen in his support of a peculiar initiative called the Church of Reality.[63] His numerous websites and blogs provide readers with links to sources that he sees as cohering with the basic teachings of the Epic or Big History. Among these is the Church of Reality, which aims to "evangelize reality" in accordance with the credo, "If it's real, we believe in it."[64] The Church of Reality promotes scientific reality as a full-blown religion, complete with tax-exempt status. (Founder Marc Perkel boasts of his success in trademarking both the phrase "Church of Reality" and "Reality" generally.)[65] The website exalts the scientific method as the "Sacred Method," and dubs the future of evolution as the "Sacred Direction." The Church of Reality draws inspiration from the new cosmology and Big History. "Big History represents the creation story of the Church of Reality," Perkel notes, "which is based on our factual understanding of the history of the universe." Church teachings are categorized under the rubric of "The Magic of Reality," a phrase with obvious Dawkinsian resonance, intended to capture the potential of science and technology to fulfill humans' need for "wonderment and amazement." For his own part, Perkel promotes TED talks by Dowd and hails him as his "favorite reality evangelist."[66]

Unabashed reverence for scientists as heroic, even godlike, figures is even more pronounced in Barlow's activities. Alongside Dawkins, she identifies E. O. Wilson and Julian Huxley as beloved mentors. Like Wilson, Barlow struggles to root her "green" values within the evolutionary cosmology she passionately embraces and urges others to adopt. Although she contends that the proper cosmology will lead to the desired environmental values, the assumed dynamic between science and values is flimsier than she and her fellow Epic supporters like to acknowledge.

SCIENCE AS SURROGATE RELIGION: CONNIE
BARLOW'S "WAY OF SCIENCE"

Barlow's *Green Space, Green Time* explores the promise of a new science-based religion. Drawing on taped interviews and spontaneous conversations with numerous scientists and academics, the book chronicles the birth of the Epic movement as a new, comprehensive cosmology, or what Barlow dubs "the way of science." Knowledge of evolutionary wonders, she argues, "has been made available for human delight only by way of science."[67] The book's immediate circle of interlocutors includes Mary Evelyn Tucker, John Grim, Brian Swimme, Ursula Goodenough, and Loyal Rue. Detailed conversations and interviews with each are transcribed in the text. Barlow also interviews E. O. Wilson and various other lesser-known scientists. While not an actual conversation partner in the book, Dawkins exerts a strong influence on Barlow's interpretation of biological and cultural evolution, as does Julian Huxley, one of the twentieth century's most aggressive champions of progressive evolution. Barlow lavishes particular praise on Rue, Swimme, and Wilson for initiating a "new mythopoeic enterprise." Our environmental crisis, and our general crisis of amythia, "demands a mythopoeic solution on a global scale," she writes. "That solution is commonly held to be some version of what Rue and Wilson call the 'evolutionary epic' and what Swimme calls 'the universe story.'"[68] Barlow also expresses her profound debt to Berry's New Story and expounds on the affinities between Berry's project and those of Huxley and Wilson. For Wilson, she explains, "humankind is *life* become conscious of itself. For Huxley, humankind is *evolution* become conscious of itself. But for Berry, humankind is *the universe* become conscious of itself." This identity of the human with the universe implies that humans' "gift" to the universe is to be its "knowers and celebrants."[69] Barlow embraces Berry and Wilson's proposals for enlivening and renewing the humanities through a comprehensive scientific story: "Humans are to tell the Universe Story—what Berry also calls the New Story—in imaginative and empowering ways. Humans are to sing the Universe Story, dance the Universe Story, stage the Universe Story."[70] Like Wilson, Barlow believes that this division of labor, whereby the arts and humanities perform and celebrate scientific reality, accords to nonscience disciplines "a place of peerless honor."[71]

Together with Tucker, Swimme, Rue, Goodenough, and others, Barlow discusses the need for a new myth and the features of the Epic that commend it as the ideal candidate. As these conversations proceed, the discussants encounter a few criticisms of the movement as well. Many portions of the book are confessional in tone, as Barlow and other Epic enthusiasts grope their way toward this new religion, often exchanging personal histories of how they came to feel its power. In the course of such sharing, many of them acknowledge that their "green values" were preexisting and were instilled, in many cases, by formative experiences in the natural world. What they seek is a deeper worldview or religion—a cosmology—in which those values can take root. Rue, for example, describes a prior sense of having a "moral imperative just floating loose . . . . I was in search of a cosmology. I eventually found it in learning more about biology and physics." Now, with the Evolutionary Epic in place, his moral commitment "goes down like a taproot," anchored in the cosmos.[72] Barlow concurs that environmentalism was for her a long-standing commitment that later found "mooring" in the evolutionary epic.[73] That prior environmental commitments led so many in this group to seek a compatible scientific cosmology—and not the other way around—is surprising, given how much emphasis new cosmologists place on the primacy of cosmology for *creating or enabling* a sense of connection with the natural world. Why do Epic proponents present their sweeping narrative as a necessary path to green values when they themselves arrived at those values by other means and other forms of experience? This question is never explored.

Barlow celebrates the "surprise from sociobiology," namely, the discovery that religious impulses are deeply rooted in our biology, and she shares Rue's attraction to biological explanations for cultural phenomena, as suggested by the meme concept. The actual content of religious belief or ritual is filled in by whatever memes happen to circulate and become predominant in our culture, she argues. "Memes are what give substance to our inchoate capacities for religious feelings."[74] Barlow's aim in spreading the Epic is to circulate *greener* memes that will "enhance our bond with other species and with Earth itself."[75] Here Wilson's ideas also come into play, as Barlow invokes the concept of biophilia to suggest that memes may be helpfully biased by evolution in favor of environmental or "nature-philic" memes that could foster protection of biodiversity.

HEROIC SCIENCE

Barlow acknowledges, more or less, that the "green" values she espouses do not simply fall out of an evolutionary history of Earth or the universe as presented by science. But science can be extended into the realm of meaning even if it cannot dictate a particular set of values. "Values to which I am predisposed," Barlow argues, "can be made to emerge from the underlying cosmology."[76] Rather than scrutinize the claim that green values must be rooted in an evidence-based cosmology, Barlow finds ways of reinterpreting science so that the science seems to point to the values she desires.

Because evolutionary biologists often spar publicly over the particular details of the evolutionary process, such as the unit of selection, rates of evolution, or interactions between genes and the environment, these differences allow for some range of interpretation regarding the meanings one might discern in, or assign to, the process. "Choose your authority [that is, a particular scientist] . . . and thereby choose your answer," advises Barlow. "Choose your answer and thereby choose your worldview."[77] This approach might seem reasonable enough (deference to authority notwithstanding), but it is difficult to see how the "worldview" arrived at via this formula can be given the official stamp of "reality," as Dowd and Barlow's ministry insists.

As Barlow's phrasing suggests, authority and expert knowledge play a key role in her advocacy of the Epic, in ways that go beyond checking in with science to ensure fidelity to current developments. Of course, deference to authority is not unusual among the new cosmologists—discussions of Berry and his work, for example, frequently take a hagiographic turn—but Barlow goes further. A general preoccupation with leading figures ("heroes" as Barlow calls them) reflects the imprint of Joseph Campbell's claims for the centrality of a hero figure and the prominence of the epic journey in mythic narratives across the globe. (Every epic needs a hero, as Wilson points out.) This idea also gains support from Wilson's claims about the function of religion and myth in humans' evolutionary psychology and our feelings of awe for charismatic leaders. Wilson credits Campbell with inspiring his portrait of scientists' search for consilience as a mythic quest,[78] and he stresses that religious or quasi-religious institutions have played as important a role as the myths themselves in galvanizing adherents. Group identity, the need for charismatic leaders, and a penchant for mythopoeism all "represent programmed predispositions whose self-sufficient components were incorporated into the neural apparatus of the brain by thousands of generations of genetic evolution."[79] Submission to a superior or charismatic being is an ingrained evolutionary survival strategy, in other words. Epic proponents, particularly those influenced by sociobiological or memetic evolution, take this into account in constructing a religion that can outcompete the existing traditions.

While Wilson at times hedges on whether or not scientists can function as priests in our society, Barlow is explicit in her endorsement of scientists as new religious leaders. Chief among her deceased heroes is Julian Huxley, who, we have seen, played an instrumental role in bringing Teilhard's *The Phenomenon of Man* to the English-speaking world. Barlow carries on imaginary conversations with Huxley in *Green Space, Green Time* ("Marvelous term, *evolutionary epic!*" is Huxley's encouraging remark to Barlow in one such imagined exchange. "Is that your creation?" he inquires. "No," replies Barlow, "that's Ed Wilson's term. We're all using it now.")[80] Huxley belonged to the well-known family of scientists and philosophers that included Aldous Huxley as well as Thomas Henry Huxley (Darwin's contemporary and one of his most ardent and pugnacious defenders). Julian Huxley, a prominent player in the modern synthesis of biology, sought to extend evolution into many areas of life. He was an early pioneer of the "epic science" genre, which explains his attraction to Teilhard. Huxley is known for promulgating a "positivist philosophy

in which science is the only source of knowledge," and evolution "the new foundation of morality, replacing the transcendental source of values invoked by religion."[81] Like Teilhard, Vladimir Vernadsky, and Berry, he believed that humans
would evolve to manage the planet's evolutionary process and guide its future
course.[82]

Barlow feels a powerful, emotional connection to Huxley's evolutionary worldview. Describing his enduring influence on her life, she often sounds like someone
in the grip of a schoolgirl crush. When she first encounters criticism of the Epic
movement, during one of the many conversations she records in *Green Space,
Green Time*, her response is to search Huxley's texts for reassurance. Having
located, with the help of more imaginary conversations, a passage in Huxley that
seems to put the criticism to rest, she is reminded of why she "fell in love with this
guy" whom she credits with changing her life, and who reassures her in moments
of doubt: "I am with you!"[83]

A potential criticism of the Epic that sends Barlow back to Huxley for reassurance has to do with the danger of hanging one's "star"—one's understanding of the
world, interpretation of the past, hope for the future—upon provisional science. If
the science turns out to be incorrect, the storyline may be imperiled. Still troubled
by this criticism, Barlow seeks to supplement Huxley's beyond-the-grave guidance
in the matter by soliciting advice from like-minded colleagues. Some suggest that
provisional religion based on provisional science has great advantages, even virtues, compared to traditional, dogmatic religion. Because science does not stand
still, the story itself remains dynamic, and one simply has to have "faith"—as Barlow puts it—that meaning is there in the story no matter how much the facts
change. And because of the way science works, with old paradigms typically hanging on until new ones gain strength to cast them out, those who practice the way
of science are never left for long "without a god," Barlow observes. "There's a new
god, ready-made, just waiting to be acknowledged" in the nascent scientific paradigm.[84] Dubious insight in hand, Barlow proceeds to draw additional parallels
between witnessing breakthroughs in science and experiencing the birth of a religion. "It's like thinking about having been able to live in the time of Jesus," she
comments to a colleague. Pursuing this thought further, she concludes that

> we are living in the time of Jesus, from the way-of-science standpoint. Somebody you
> or I know might well be the equivalent of Jesus, in that they may utterly change the
> world of science and therefore all the personal varieties of religious feelings drawn
> out of science. A hundred years from now, somebody we know might be considered
> as Darwin is now.[85]

The "equivalence" Barlow discerns between a divine figure like Jesus and a scientist
engaged in trailblazing research goes well beyond appreciation for science and its
power to improve or enrich our lives. When religions are built around such deep

reverence for science, those feelings naturally extend to scientists as religious leaders, the purveyors of new, public revelation. Epic proponents' investment in an evolutionary psychology framework that affirms humans' ineradicable need for charismatic leaders blinds them to the dangers of such reverence. Focusing on the mythic appeal of science and scientists also assigns a peripheral place to nature itself, as I have argued, even though valuing nature is an express (if often secondary) goal for these seekers. Barlow appreciates that scientific knowledge cannot fully replace experiences in nature—"knowledge about the carbon cycle is no substitute for a stroll in the woods."[86] But she fails to consider that a spiritual orientation grounded in experiences of nature, rather than expert knowledge *about* it, is far less likely to be a casualty of changing times and shifting evidence. In *Green Space, Green Time*, one of Barlow's science colleagues outlines a position in opposition to hers, arguing that while science provides gratification akin to solving a puzzle or deciphering a complex machine, science is not a source of enduring "inspiration" or grounds for caring for nature.[87] Another scientist colleague similarly expresses skepticism about Barlow's project of mythologized science as a source of green values, citing his lifelong attraction to birds and plants as the wellspring of his environmentalism. "I became a biologist because I love nature," he explains to her. "I do not love nature because I became a biologist."[88] As a devotee of the way of science, Barlow seems perplexed by such demurrals, especially when voiced by scientists.

Determined to create a science-based religion that is functional on all fronts, Barlow worries about how to respond to the suggestion that science may not supply all the inspiration or normative direction we need. What to do, for example, when ritual celebrations of aspects of the Epic become ingrained in certain communities, and then the science *shifts,* rendering both the facts, and rituals based on those facts, essentially obsolete? What if people are reluctant to give up the now out-of-date ritual? Barlow searches for ways to lend greater stability and enduring meaning to the story. Tyler Volk, a biologist and Epic proponent, suggests the following solution: built into Epic rituals themselves should be a celebration not just of the key ideas or events in cosmology (say, the Big Bang or star formation) but "celebration of the fascinating ways we came to those ideas and how we keep moving nearer and nearer the truth."[89] We have seen this insight ritually enacted in the Cosmic Communion described above, where humans' discovery of the storied nature of the universe is itself a cosmic milestone. Volk and Barlow refer to this subplot as "the story of the changing story"—that is, the story of how scientists discover the Epic. (Martin Eger comments on precisely this move in his analysis of epic science, referring to the subplot of scientific discovery as the "minor epic.")[90] Barlow characterizes this blend of big and little epics as "an equal celebration of the universe and celebration of the human mind discovering how to know the universe."[91] Volk concurs that if evolutionary psychology dictates that humans need an "immortal story" then the "most immortal" part of the grand narrative is not the facts themselves, which may change, but rather the "current semi-immortal way of finding out those facts: It's a celebration of the scientific process . . . and how we keep moving nearer and nearer the truth."[92] So, in other words, one way of coping with shifting data and meanings that attend an evolving epic is to focus on humans' steady march toward scientific truth. Moreover, Volk suggests, an inspiring sense of "immortality" and thus stable meaning infuses humans' epic quest. Note how this move coheres with Wilson's proposal of the human mind as Epic hero, and with his own attempt to locate a collective immortality for our *species* in a progressive scientific myth.

Clearly, Barlow and her colleagues engage in a great deal of special pleading in order to present the "way of science" as both a strong competitor with existing religions and a good fit with evolutionary psychology. The hubristic elements of this story are evident in the recourse to the minor epic—the story of the story—which effectively allows an "immortal" theme of progress to slip back into a story billed as provisional and open-ended. Barlow struggles mightily against the provisional nature of the Epic, much as she struggles against the suggestion that attaining the "right" cosmology may not be the only or most enduring foundation for loving nature. The more determined she is to construct a functional religion from scientific materials, the more detached her quest becomes from nature as a locus of value. Despite her efforts to skew the Epic in "green" directions, it remains unclear how the values to which Barlow and others are "predisposed" will emerge from a cosmology that revolves around reverence for knowledge and the humans who uncover it. It is far more plausible that a message of unlimited human progress, unbridled ambition, and achievement—with all the negative valuation of the natural world such a message typically entails—will prevail.

THE MORAL OF THE NEW STORY

Questions about what is or ought to be the main message of the new cosmology have plagued the movement since its inception. A perusal of these debates indicates that the new cosmologists are unclear about their own goals or (less charitably) not altogether honest in articulating them to others. In a discussion forum published in the *Epic of Evolution Journal* in 1998, proponents of the Epic debated how to understand words like myth, narrative, and epic, as well as the need for the Epic to be oriented around mythic heroes.[93] Some participants in the discussion doubted that the story of the universe had successfully achieved the status of myth, and many wondered whether it makes sense to treat history or science as mythmaking material. Can a narrative that is literally true become a myth, some wondered? And if so, how will we know when that has happened? One participant queried whether there is enough "personal drama for people to relate to in a story that otherwise resembles an updated, quasi-spiritualized remake of Carl Sagan's *Cosmos.*"[94]

Some wondered whether any myth has ever been so deliberately and consciously constructed as the Epic of Evolution. "When that happens," one participant warned, "the result always seems shallow—obviously cooked up to seem mythic."[95] An important question also surfaced regarding what or who constitutes the *hero* in the Epic. Few participants in this discussion recalled Wilson's original designation of the human mind as the Epic hero in *On Human Nature* (1978). Others proposed evolution itself as the hero of the story; or the child as the hero, since children symbolize the future and hope of our planet. Yet another ventured that each human being constitutes an epic hero in the story. Barlow, who organized the discussion, proposed that ancient life-forms—living fossils such as the ginkgo tree whose antiquity makes it one of the great elders in our evolutionary story—be revered as heroes.[96] The conversation turned to the problem of mixing scientific terms such as "proton," or the names of chemical elements, with metaphors of the sun's "generosity" or the universe's "flaring forth" in the Big Bang. Barlow opined that the awkwardness of scientific terms will fade with time as more and more children are "imprinted" with the Epic at an early age.[97] "If the first place children hear the word proton is in the context of an Epic ritual they participate in every year, then by the time they encounter that word in their school textbooks it will sound like their religion to them—and only secondarily like science."[98] Concerns were also raised about whether an Epic centered on a hero—particularly a human hero—is incongruent with the story's emphasis on interdependence and co-creation. Some voiced misgivings that heroic consciousness might encourage destructive forms of individualism and capitalism that have compromised planetary health, as well as the scientific mentality that "colonized the domains of art and spirituality in its insistence that the scientific method is the only true measure of all knowledge."[99]

These discussions and disagreements are very important, and they anticipate some of my own concerns. These issues seem never to have been resolved, but only muted as the new cosmology has gained popularity. Do these storytellers mean to exalt the human or underscore our humble insignificance? Is the story past or future oriented? Can scientific facts sufficiently convey a sense of something sacred? As with Wilson's dual focus on evolutionary evangelism and environmental conservation, Dowd and Barlow oscillate between different agendas of spreading the story in order (ostensibly) to foster greater connection to nature and spreading the story in order to win more converts to evolution as the most awe-inspiring reality. These agendas get blurred and confused insofar as Epic proponents are convinced that wonder and concern for nature are necessarily dependent on adopting evolution as a sacred worldview. They even come into conflict. For example, debates have emerged among Epic enthusiasts regarding whether it is wise or necessary to solicit converts among individuals or communities that *already have* a sense of ecological connectedness and green values but whose ethics are not fundamentally grounded in the Epic story. "If someone (no matter what their spiritual path or lack of path) is acting in their life in such a way that the planet's species and ecosystems can evolve and flourish," one participant asks, then does it matter that the Epic is not their "cup of tea?"[100] Barlow's response indicates that she sees the Epic as unnecessary for such individuals or cultures. So long as one's "worldview promotes a deep commitment to ecological values, that is all that really matters."[101] Her own "ministry," she adds, targets those *already* oriented toward science that is, "science minded" and "secular environmentalists" who do not think of themselves as religious, but can find spiritual fulfillment in science.[102] Her goal, she claims, is to persuade those individuals to perceive the sacred dimensions of what they *already* know.

This answer is inadequate, and raises many other questions. It does not explain why Epic proponents, notably Barlow, devote considerable time and resources to exposing *children* to the scientific narrative—the younger the better. Is it appropriate to impose scientific "reality" on children who may not have yet formed attachments to nature in other ways, whether those ways are deeply spiritual or merely sensory and emotional? What does this imposition of reality suggest to children about the trustworthiness of their own impressions of the natural world and its wonder, value, or reality? And why does a secular environmentalist of any age need the Epic at all, if he or she already has a "deep commitment to ecological values"? The debate about whether or not conversion to the Epic is necessary—for children or adults—seems to assume that a deep commitment to nature remains inadequate so long as that commitment is not embedded within an even more profound devotion to science. In short, the new cosmologists assume their deep need to ground environmental values in a totalizing scientific narrative is shared by all. This conviction feeds the proselytizing impulse. But surely it ought to be the other way around. Scientific knowledge ought to be in the service of a profound commitment to life; and wonder at science should be appropriately delimited and oriented within a larger framework of valuing and caring for nature. It is this view that Barlow's scientist colleague expresses when he proclaims that his love of nature led him to biology, and not vice versa. Scientific wonder and wonder for nature need not be rivals. The new cosmologists create this rivalry by pitting mythopoeic science against religion, and our lived experience of the world against a superior reality gained through scientific knowledge.

TELLING A BETTER STORY?

Before concluding, I want to offer a few observations about the new cosmology as a whole and its commitment to the narrative form, a theme picked up again in the final chapter. I have noted already the mixed messages of these narratives (humility or hubris, mystery or certainty). These are brought into sharper relief by an apparent mismatch between narrative content and format. Narratologist Paul A. Harris identifies a central and seemingly unintended paradox in these cosmic stories. The choice of the epic genre and the mode of linear narration conflict with the content and pedagogical goals. As typically told, the tale commences with the beginning of the universe, and ends with the emergence of humans. As Harris points out, the epic form, wherever it appears, normally involves a fixed history: epics aim to *preserve* events in the distant past that have particular and profound meaning for a given society. Typically, an epic "has no interest in the future; its sole function is mnemonic."[103] The historical, fixed nature of the evolutionary epic is particularly emphasized in Big History projects, admired by Dowd. Big History is possible because of what David Christian calls a chronometric revolution that allowed historians to assign "absolute dates" to past events like the extinction of the dinosaurs 65 million years ago. Thus, Christian understands creation stories and myths to function as *maps of the past,* and sees the Epic as the first creation story to meld human history with the history of the Earth and universe, as a "single account of the past."[104] Yet, because it is based on science, the Epic of Evolution cannot simply be a fixed history or finished product, though it is often narrated as such. It necessarily changes and *evolves* along with fluctuations in what is deemed accepted scientific knowledge.[105] From the standpoint of narratology, an "evolutionary epic" is therefore "an oxymoron"—at once a fixed epic and evolving science.[106] Moreover, epic seems the wrong genre for a story that is meant to orient us to the future, to what comes *next.*

The metaphor of journeying fares somewhat better in this respect, but *Journey of the Universe* retains the story's linearity, commencing with the Big Bang, describing certain well-established events, and culminating in humans as the consciousness of the universe. To deemphasize the perception of humans as the apex, Harris proposes avoiding linear narration and fashioning the story in a more labyrinthine, present/past/present form, "starting the Evolutionary Epic with our present, moving back through the past, and then returning to the present with an eye to the future."[107] Telling the story as a movement back through time would entail that familiar human events and scales gradually give way to increasingly "less intuitively accessible" events and scales, such as the geological, evolutionary, and cosmological. A backward-looking epic will ultimately arrive at "the mystical *aporia*" of cosmic origins, allowing the reader or audience to contemplate the "ever-elusive question of beginnings," the ultimate mystery of our universe.[108] Following this encounter with mystery, we journey back to the present with greater awareness of the vastness of the universe and all that we do *not* know.[109] I would argue that a narrative of this sort might more convincingly support an ethic of humility and prudence, a salutary sense of our own limits or finitude, while also shifting focus away from humans and toward a broader enchantment with the mystery that interpenetrates all life.

Without jettisoning the basic linearity of the storyline, the cosmic narrative might be told in other ways that similarly open it up to mystery or surprise. Noting the fixed and frozen quality of the grand epic narrative, Celia Deane-Drummond advocates the idea of *drama* or *theodrama*, in place of epic, arguing that the epic form tends to become "deterministic and creates the wrong impression of being objective." As she correctly notes, "Evolution as incorporating some sort of *necessity* is also a typical reading of evolutionary history" in the epic genre.[110] Drama, as she defines it, confers greater agency to the players and is suggestive of a more improvisational and contingent storyline with "unexpected twists and turns."[111] When drama expands to include all of evolutionary history it allows for "viewing other evolved creatures *as more than* simply the stage for human action."[112]

Dowd and Barlow's ritualized version of Dawkins's *Ancestor's Tale* gestures in some of these directions, offering a pilgrimage *back* through time where we meet up with animal ancestors, and ultimately arrive at a mysterious beginning point in evolution. Why is the Epic or Universe Story not told this way more often? I would argue that the paradox Harris identifies goes beyond narrative *form,* right to the heart of the story's moral message. Harris briefly notes the narrative's "admixture of hubris and humility," but it deserves greater scrutiny for its direct relevance to the *forms* of wonder the story inculcates. It is not merely that different iterations allow for different emphases; rather, these tensions are apparent throughout. For Wilson and some of his followers, hubris seems the dominant note: the consilient account on which the story is based is a celebration of human intelligence and epic daring, an illustration of our quasi-omniscience. For storytellers under his influence, such as Rue, the history of human knowledge overlays and merges with the story of the universe, as if to suggest that the even the universe is a product of our expanding, and increasingly unified, knowledge. Rue depicts the unfolding story of the universe in terms of the sciences developed to understand it, as though the journey through it amounts to a cosmic tour of answered questions. In the earliest chapters of the story, when the universe was an expanding cloud of gas, "physics was the only science that would have made sense." The story continues with the birth and death of stars, and exploding supernovae emptying their contents. At this point, he notes, chemistry begins to "make sense." As life on our planet evolved and diversified, "increasingly complex neural systems enabled the capacity for learned behavior. Psychology," Rue notes, "would now begin to make sense."[113] This is a story told via a hierarchy of scientific disciplines, as if a human spectator is looking on, godlike, conferring sense and order. As a whole, the universe "makes sense."

Other storytellers, of course, express an intention to evoke humility and wonder—not wonder merely at humans' special status or accumulated knowledge, but at the universe that is grander than anything we can know or aspire to on a human scale. But to lead the audience to the aporetic moment suggested by Harris—a profession of *not knowing*—would undercut the Epic's central boast that the comprehensive story can now be told because of stunning scientific successes and the cosmic triumph of human consciousness. Some narrations of the Epic place particular emphasis on human breakthroughs as pivotal moments in the narrative: the advent of stone tool-making is characterized as a "Little Bang," a creative explosion that put humans on "a novel evolutionary journey that has never been traveled by any other species in the history of life on Earth."[114] Similarly, for Barlow and her cohort "the story of the changing story"—the ongoing epic of scientific discovery—presents a competing storyline to that of the universe, thereby restoring to the human intellect its rightful place in the "immortal story" of science."[115] A few enthusiasts even devote their careers to explaining how humans really are the center of the universe in a variety of empirical ways: "the ancient human instinct to experience ourselves as central reflects something real about the universe—something independent of our viewpoint," they argue. "We are made of the rarest material, and our size scale is at the center of all possible sizes."[116] Meanwhile, Swimme and Tucker believe the narrative's enormous power to lie in its capacity to *dismantle* our assumption of superiority, to "decenter" humans once and for all.[117] However, the *epic* genre (which Swimme and Tucker both invoke) is not similarly decentralized: an epic is a vehicle for its hero who is arguably its most important element, and who embodies the values of a particular society or civilization. In this sense, both the scale and the focal point of an epic are in tension with the notion of a vast, expanding universe. For while it might be argued that the fate of Earth, or at least human civilization, depends in part on the success of the epic hero—a frequent Anthropocene trope seen in the Epic—the same cannot possibly be said about the fate of the *universe as a whole*.[118]

The oddly mixed message would seem to be that our "monumental accomplishment" of discovering the Epic allows us to assume a *more* humble place within the universe that we moderns alone have comprehended.[119] This confused message, I propose, is partly a function of the Epic's inability to decide whether it is tale of mystery or of mysteries clarified. I have argued throughout that it is primarily the latter. Perhaps if the new cosmologists took a labyrinthine image and metaphor to heart, the hubristic thrust might be offset, suggesting the story as an invitation to lose oneself in humble contemplation of what is infinitely vast, complex, and beyond mastery. I am not convinced, however, that this is the story the new cosmologists, on the whole, feel especially moved to tell. For it does not advance the largely anthropic and knowledge-based wonder that (wittingly or otherwise) characterizes their mission, and it would entail contradicting beloved figures like Wilson, Huxley, or Teilhard.

Reflecting on narrative ambitions of the Universe Story, nature writer Scott Russell Sanders urges the wisdom of recalling our limitations, of inviting mystery and uncertainty into our stories. Sanders quotes Borges's remark that "one should work into a story the idea of not being sure of all things, because that's the way reality is." Anyone who claims to comprehend our vast universe is "either a lunatic or a liar," Sanders writes.

> Why there is a universe, why we are here, why there is life or consciousness at all, where if anywhere the whole show is headed—these are questions for which we have no final answers. . . . In the beginning, we say, at the end of time, we say, but we are only guessing. . . . The elegant infinite details of the world's unfolding, the sheer existence of hand or tree or star, are more marvelous than anything we can say about them . . . . In scriptures we speak of God's thoughts as if we could read them; but we read only by the dim light of a tricky brain on a young planet near a middling star.[120]

Sanders concludes that if we must have cosmic narratives, we must also understand them as imperfect human creations "filled with guesswork." Perhaps, he suggests, meaning is what we find *within* mystery, not in in its hoped-for banishment. The new cosmologists are, at best, deeply ambivalent about these sentiments.

What, then, finally commends the Universe Story and the Epic of Evolution to us as a global story, a new creation myth for our times? However much the hubristic, uncritical, and omnicompetent elements of the new cosmology (in all its forms) might be mitigated by recasting it in ways I have suggested, to my mind there remains no truly compelling reason why the story ought to be adopted as our new myth. In and of itself, it is neither true (in the strict and narrow sense often claimed), nor obviously superior (in terms of its aesthetics or ethics) to stories and value frameworks it aims to supplant. Of course, anyone who wishes to adopt this narrative as their creation story and orienting worldview should be free to do so, just as anyone may freely pledge allegiance to the Church of Reality. My point is that I see no compelling reason that anyone—much less everyone—*ought* to do so.

Chapter 7

Making Sense of Wonder

The senses reveal a world that is ambiguous and open ended, and by looking more closely, or by listening more carefully, we will always discover new things. But if you don't trust the intelligence of your senses, then what is it that you are going to trust? You will have to place all your trust in the so-called experts to tell you what is really going on behind the scenes. It is rather like the situation of a church, or a temple, that tells you, "Well, the real Truth is not here but is in that heavenly dimension hidden beyond the stars, and only our high priests have access to that unseen realm."

—DAVID ABRAM (SEE NOTES)

Scientists, perhaps more than most, recognize that the universe was not made for human beings and so neither perfect knowledge nor absolute safety are achievable. Science is therefore fundamentally not about security but about doubt, not about knowing, but about asking, not about certainty, but about skepticism. Scientific stories are written not to be believed but to be understood, made use of as appropriate, and revised.

—PAUL GROBSTEIN, "REVISITING SCIENCE IN CULTURE"

Where can wonder find purchase in modern scientific and environmental discourse? In this chapter I turn to some proposals for a rehabilitated sense of wonder, keeping in mind, as always, wonder's proper relationship both to science and the natural world. To better appreciate the options for wonder that remain open to us, let us recap some of the key claims of the preceding chapters.

I have argued that forms of consecrated science promoted by public icons like Richard Dawkins and E. O. Wilson, and showcased in mythic narratives of the new cosmology, encourage celebrations of wonder and reverence for *science* over and above nature, and wonder at humans over and above the more-than-human world. Consecrated science directs our wondering gaze to all that has already been explained. It also expresses ephemeral and fleeting wonder at mysteries that turn up, successively, in the wake of those just solved. Wonder may be directed at the sheer accumulation of knowledge: knowledge acquired in its cohesive totality, as with consilience, or knowledge produced in particular, paradigmatic cases of puzzle-solving, as with Dawkins's invocation of the rainbow as the archetype of nature demystified. Dawkins proclaims the "poetic quality" and spiritual "uplift" of science and urges poets to take science as their subject matter, while Wilson offers the evolutionary epic as the basis for an alternative mythology. The new cosmologists often turn to these thinkers for inspiration or validation of their projects or for specific materials with which to construct modern myths. We have seen that some varieties of mythopoeic science understand the evolutionary paradigm or consilient unity of knowledge as suggesting the coalescence of a single, true story. Others locate narrative coherence in Big Bang cosmology and the alleged story-like structure of the cosmos as a whole. From these efforts to consecrate science, the human species emerges as a symbol of planetary unity and cosmic consciousness and a supreme object of wonder. The unifying impulse of the new cosmology and its feel-good appeals to unity and harmony may mask its less egalitarian aspects, as I have argued, while wonder at humans erodes a humble sense of reverent care and moral restraint in our interactions with the more-than-human world.

A hubristic celebration of the human mind is pronounced in Epic of Evolution myths inspired by consilient positivism, but an incipient apotheosis of the human is evident in Universe Story movements as well. Mythic appropriations of science, I maintain, embody aspirations to omniscience and are presented in a spirit of omnicompetence, with the human as a virtually all-knowing narrator of a cosmos that finds its fulfillment in our species' evolutionary ascent. Mythic narratives like *Journey of the Universe* lay claim to wonder at the *mystery* of the universe, and at the smallness of humans within its vast reaches, but the story's progressive plot and triumphalist tone suggest a different message. At best, narrative tensions in the story between certainty and mystery or hubris and humility remain unacknowledged and unresolved. At worst, these narratives ratify our role as godlike planetary managers, effectively naturalizing and depoliticizing the Anthropocene proposition that humans occupy the geological driver's seat. These narratives also give pride of place to the story *of* the story, that is, the story of how humans discovered the way things "really" are. A godlike image of humans is bolstered by the turn to mythic tropes of forbidden knowledge, hubristic trespass, or the revelation of divine secrets, symbolized by Icarus, Prometheus, or Tantalus. These myths are deployed not as cautionary tales of disastrous overreach, as one might expect, but as justification and enticement for bold transgression and the pursuit of unlimited knowledge. Taken together, these movements embody a response to the unknown or unknowable that ranges from ambivalence to irritation to fear and hostility. Within the confines of consecrated science, there remains little room for wonder, except as a dubious expression of admiration—often issued in tones of self-satisfied hauteur—for all that humans can discover and cogently narrate.

I have further argued that a fleeting form of serial wonder frequently accompanies the portrait of science that inspires the new myths. On this account, each mystery solved churns up a *new* source of bafflement in its wake. Wonder here is less an orientation on the world or an enduring disposition than a delimited *reaction* to something new or surprising. Perhaps the process of discovering new mysteries will cycle on indefinitely; or perhaps, as Wilson and Dawkins hope, a built-in terminus to questioning will finally be reached. Either way, serial wonder expresses intolerance for mystery and the unknown. As I have argued, this association of wonder with temporary ignorance transforms wonder into something like a "'God-of-the-Gaps' theology," wherein wonder is like the deity whose plausibility is "increasingly threatened as gaps in knowledge are filled."[1] Whether or not one assumes that the generation of mysteries will finally run its course, the *hope* that it will do so is telling. Hope for *deliverance* from questioning and wondering often inflects grand theories of everything, cosmic mythmaking, and the consilient unification of all knowledge. This flight from uncertainty or ambiguity betrays a need to coddle the ego, to seal it off from whatever threatens. Insofar as mystery has value, it is relished only as something to be liquidated—successively or finally. Wonder becomes a "temporary irritant," a condition in need of a cure.[2]

This is not to say that something inherently sinister lurks in the enjoyment of puzzle-solving; readers of mysteries and puzzle enthusiasts, among others, are familiar with these innocuous pleasures. But when the impulse to unlock mysteries and solve puzzles occurs in the *absence* of an ethical framework that demands critical reflection on our scientific objectives (Which projects ought to be undertaken and why? Are some lines of inquiry off-limits? What goods do we aim to promote?), it becomes apparent that this impulse is far from morally neutral. I will return to this claim later.

Gabriel Marcel's protestation that mysteries are not *problems* is apposite here. In scientific investigation, mysteries are often regarded as problems in which science takes an interest for the sake of solving them. When mystery becomes synonymous with what is presently unknown, or with ignorance, it appears slightly shameful—something to be done away with. Wonder at a succession of mysteries arising in the wake of puzzles solved is in fact more akin to, or dependent upon, a motive of curiosity than wonder. Unlike curiosity, genuine wonder "does not vanish when the cause of a surprising phenomenon is discovered, nor does it relentlessly seek out new marvels to calculate, comprehend, or possess."[3] Curiosity and puzzlement are characterized by a transient state of shock or surprise at the emergence of something novel—outside the explanatory framework—and a need to assimilate what appears novel back into an orderly world. Often, the knowledge produced in this restless pursuit "is seen as a kind of possession, a tick on the tourist's place-list."[4] Were one to dwell in wonder, one might miss the next exciting mystery that awaits, just as the tourist continually rouses herself to visit the next site on her itinerary. For this reason, Bacon famously derides wonder as "broken knowledge" that severs the train of thought.

Suggestive as it is, the tourist metaphor for wonder might imply that scientific curiosity flits about idly or pursues things at random. This is not necessarily the case. Scientific investigation entails a heuristic narrowing of its subject, and this narrowing process entails that certain elements of the problem be isolated or abstracted from some larger context. The processes deployed in scientific investigation—*isolating, abstracting, simplifying, objectifying*—have a proper role to play and are not in themselves suspect or unethical. These terms signal practices of disciplined engagement that enable interrogation of some concrete, delimited phenomenon. Only when knowledge gained through such practices is invested with claims to ultimate meaning or superior and totalizing reality does science overstep its bounds. Thus scientific knowledge threatens to dismantle mystery and wonder when "used hostilely to reduce the dimensions of meaning in an object to those that can be manipulated and controlled."[5] When we are told that proper attunement to *reality* means aligning ourselves, first and foremost, with the particular findings disclosed by such (necessarily) limited methods, we should raise skeptical questions. I believe it is one of the perennial tasks of the humanities to raise such questions and keep them alive. The humanities do not exist merely to translate the reality "revealed" by science into celebratory poems, stories, songs— or seductive new religious myths—that venerate science and its practitioners.

But back to mystery. Within the culture of science, wonder that dwells in mystery rather than seeking its eradication might understandably be viewed as unseemly or even vicious, as scientists ranging from Descartes to Dawkins have warned. "We do not wish to be found in the posture of foolish wonder—wonder that is purely a function of our ignorance," Hepburn concurs.[6] But neither do we—many of us— wish to banish wonder and mystery from our lives. So what options remain? So long as wonder is associated with an ephemeral reaction to something temporarily unassimilated—a failure to grasp, an illusory perception—there may indeed be little reason to celebrate it. And yet, when viewed within the context of ethics, particularly environmental ethics, dwelling in wonder has distinctly virtuous dimensions. This is because wonder shows affinities with a cluster of welcome dispositions that include compassion, generosity, vulnerability, openness, empathy and respect for otherness, and—most significantly—humility. How, then, are we to understand wonder as something other than a fleeting reaction, an obstacle to knowledge, or self-congratulatory, hubristic awe at human discovery? Can wonder be reclaimed from common associations with mere ignorance, momentary surprise, or—as seen prominently in the new cosmology—the cataloguing of all that is known?

COMPATIBILISM OF WONDER AND SCIENCE

I want to begin to answer these questions by sketching a "compatibilist" account of wonder, where a wondering response endures in the presence of scientific interrogation without making knowledge into an idol of sorts. Compatibilist wonder often engages us at the level of the *senses*. Were the world simply like a puppet show where one peeks behind the curtain to ascertain the cause of the puppets' motion, it might be foolish to continue marveling at the spectacle as though it were miraculous.[7] But we do not inhabit such a simple universe, nor is knowledge of *causes* always what we seek when we desire to understand something or when we find it difficult to grasp. For example, many of our sensory impressions cannot simply be reduced to their causes. A case in point might be Dawkins's (or Newton's) scientifically clarified and deconstructed rainbow. The rainbow is not merely an "illusion" whose sole claim to reality lies in the physical laws that explain its genesis. Wonder at the natural world is, at least in part, a visual and sensory experience. Why should it be destroyed by a causal account that does not itself directly participate in or affect what the senses perceive? In the case of the rainbow—and other cases come to mind, such as the pulsating aurora borealis or an oddly enormous, rusty-orange harvest moon—that which is causally explicable may nevertheless remain "phenomenally irreducible."[8] "It is not the genesis of the phenomenon that elicits the wonder, but the *phenomenon itself*, colour, sound, or combination of impressions. There is no 'going behind' it," as Hepburn notes.[9] The explanation is not the experience.

Another expression of (not unscientific) wonderment is often seen in the work of good nature writers who combine their writerly gifts with scientific insight and careful observation. Their words call our attention to contrasts between our own impressions and the disparate meanings we attach to them. We may wonder, for example, at an organism's sheer will to live and persevere against the backdrop of nature's seeming indifference. Hepburn alludes to wonder at the "persistence of 'fragile' living beings on the thin habitable zone of the earth's surface, surrounded by enormous airless spaces."[10] Loren Eiseley expresses similar wonder in marveling at the ability of Earth's "stolid realm of rock and soil and mineral" to diversify itself into myriad animate life-forms in all their "beauty, terror, and uncertainty."[11] Or consider writer and poet Annie Dillard's poignant narration of a childhood memory involving the life and probable death of a Polyphemus moth. Dillard recalls seeing the large moth emerge from its cocoon in a glass jar too small for it to spread its wings. The newborn moth, its wings permanently hardened into useless, golden clumps, was released to the outdoors by her schoolteacher. Dillard captures the insect's doomed yet jubilant aspect as it crawled down the driveway and headed into town. This "big walking moth," she writes,

> could not travel more than a few more yards before a bird or a cat began to eat it, or a car ran over it. Nevertheless, it was crawling with what seemed wonderful vigor, as if, I thought at the time, it was still excited from being born. I watched it go till the bell rang and I had to go in. I have told this story before, and may yet tell it again, to lay the moth's ghost, for I still see it crawl down the broad black driveway, and I still see its golden wing clumps heave.[12]

Readers are drawn to this story again and again—I know that I am, anyway—because it seems to contain some hidden meaning or truth about life. Dillard does not *instruct* us in its meaning, but we sense something powerful and haunting in the experience of this newborn, death-bound creature, and we are left to ponder it in wonder. In the work of these writers, wonder arises in part from an inability to assimilate what we apprehend; yet failure at assimilation is not a failure of *knowledge*. Confronted with Eiseley's or Dillard's expression of wonder, a scientifically minded person might respond that there is nothing surprising or unexpected in what the wonderer wonders at. To Eiseley he might point out that our planet meets the conditions necessary for life, and that potentially destructive or countervailing forces do not, typically, overwhelm or undermine those conditions. Evolution, he might say to Dillard, equips organisms like the Polyphemus moth with instincts for struggle and survival. "What else would you expect?" the scientist might blithely retort. Nevertheless, as Hepburn puts it, there remains "the contrast for perception and imagination between living beings and their cosmic environment, between their sensitivity, sentience, internal complexity, vulnerability and the indifferent and mindless regions around them. This contrast, and the wonder it can evoke, survive the acceptance of a causal account."[13] Again, this account of natural processes does not much enter into the experience of wonder; but neither does wonder in these instances entail a rejection or denial of the causal account.

Note that in wondering at natural processes that generate beauty, terror, or diversity, Eiseley is not interrogating the causal account, nor questioning the adequacy of an evolutionary framework to explain such diversity ("I am an evolutionist," he asserts). Wonder here is less an orientation to *what* something is or *how* it came about than *that* the thing is. It entails not a question of how A emerged from B, but instead a "quasi-aesthetic appreciative response to the phenomenal contrast between A and B."[14] At times the contrasts that engender puzzlement and reflection may be those of scale, as when we contemplate the existence of a micro-world of cells or molecules alongside deep-space images captured by the Hubble telescope. For those *not* driven by temperament or training to locate or impose total unity, order, and coherence, wonder may be a response to living in a universe that exhibits an incommensurable play of scales and a perplexing array of possible meanings.

In a related vein, wonder may be prompted by the sheer contingency of the world—wonder at the fact that things happened as they did when they might have unfolded quite differently.[15] Often, as we see with Eiseley and Dillard, there is a certain poignancy or sense of the tragic (though also joy and beauty) in life's contingent unfolding. Wonder is not always a positive or affirming experience, but may be deeply unsettling. We might say that science enables us to perceive contingency at work—to know and appreciate it as a facet of natural selection or cosmic processes, for example—but contingency itself is often what holds our wondering attention. A sense of absolute contingency might arise from contemplating the universe as a whole, for we can arrive at no reason for its being rather than not being. Hepburn and others refer to this as "existential" or "ontological" wonder.[16] Wonder here is not threatened by "the network of causal relationships" among its constituent parts; moreover, as Hepburn notes, the totality of the universe "is itself ungraspable in experience," and thus existential wonder remains secure.[17] As I have argued, wonder is not secure—though much else is—in anthropic narratives of the universe that force the cosmos into predictable patterns and purposes.

These examples help to establish wonder's compatibility with scientific understanding or interrogation. We may experience wonder in the face of contingency or contrasting impressions, in the presence of a brilliant rainbow, or an anomalously large moon, or when witnessing the birth, or likely death, of a small and fragile organism in a vast and indifferent world. The questions that fill our minds in such moments are not questions we put to science, though science often has a role in prompting them.

It seems to me, however, that we want to press this inquiry further, for part of what we want to know is what *inclines*—or *disinclines*—a person to feel wonder in such situations? I alluded above to temperament and training. Why does one person respond to a particular encounter with wonder, while another gives a dismissive shrug or—as with Dawkins—merely treats the encounter as yet another opportunity to rehearse the causal scientific account? Might there be a preexisting reservoir of wonder, so to speak, on which these particular experiences can draw? Can one habitually orient oneself toward the world in ways that lend durability and constancy to wonder, or make experiences of wonder more *likely* to occur? Can we cultivate a general—and not unscientific—predisposition to wonder? Sam Keen argues that there are certain "open" and "creative" types of scientific thinkers for whom all the "abstractions and explanations which arise out of the desire to understand and control the world do not prevent a return to the object in a spirit of wonder."[18] What, aside from the vagaries of individual temperament, enables certain thinkers to return in wonder even to "familiar" or "explained" objects again and again?

I propose that wonder's investment in the world as a phenomenally sensuous *experience* is indispensable. In supporting this claim, I call on the testimony of nature writers and interdisciplinary thinkers whose celebration of wonder and tempered enthusiasm for science provide a welcome contrast to the wonder discourse I have critiqued. It is not my intention to offer a systematic or definitive account of wonder, or cosmic counter-narrative to which all should assent, but rather to present some of wonder's essential ingredients, enabling attitudes, and nurturing contexts. Reflecting on wonder-enabling and wonder-preserving attitudes and practices leads us to some refreshingly modest proposals regarding what science is, how it works, and what it reasonably aspires to do. These include proposals advanced by scientists who find the current public presentation of, and contemporary discourse about, science to be largely uninspiring, misleading, and, in some instances, environmentally irresponsible (as do I). In what follows, I argue for an enduring form of wonder that dwells in mysteries without turning away from science.

CREATIVE SCIENCE AND NATURE WONDER

If, as I believe, Keen's "open" and "creative" scientist is one who does not turn to science as the arbiter of all meaning, then Rachel Carson and Loren Eiseley fit Keen's portrait well. Carson's life and work in particular suggest the possibility of a stable form of wonder that coincides with *apprehension* (not *mis*apprehension, not *false* perception) of a given phenomenon or truth, but that nevertheless preserves an abiding appreciation of mystery. Science may be fully valued without being transformed into an object of reverence in its own right or something to be valued for the divine glow it casts on human knowledge-makers. One key to understanding this sense of wonder lies in grasping the somewhat elusive claim that reality *is* mystery; the two are not in conflict. Apprehension of life's mysterious essence is imperiled by a lack of sensory engagement, for only through such direct and affective connection to nature do we form an attachment that is—potentially—both ethical and enduring. On this account, desiring to understand the natural world is emphatically not a pursuit of certainty and security, not a celebration of all that we know. Released from the quest for security, we begin to appreciate wonder's family resemblance to other (praiseworthy) dispositions: humility, caution, empathy, as well as what we might provocatively call "virtuous ignorance."[19]

My first witness is Rachel Carson, whose insights about wonder, science, and nature remain vital today. Carson is best known for *Silent Spring* (1962), which alerted the public to the environmental and health impacts of chemical pesticides and, by most accounts, launched the environmental movement. But Carson was an established nature writer well before the publication of that book.[20] Trained as a marine biologist, Carson worked for what is now the Fish and Wildlife Service for many years until she gained enough commercial success as an author to devote herself to writing full-time.[21] Carson's early works were devoted to the sea and sea life. Her first book, *Under the Sea-Wind* (1941), was greeted with critical acclaim but due to wartime preoccupations, sales were somewhat disappointing. Ten years elapsed before Carson published her second and hugely successful book, *The Sea Around Us,* a beautifully crafted scientific exploration of the ocean and its role in our planet's natural history. *The Edge of the Sea,* a study of shore life, appeared a few years later in 1955. Carson began work on *Silent Spring* in the late 1950s and experienced frequent disruptions and delays in the form of health problems and various crises in her extended family. In 1960, Carson was diagnosed with breast cancer and during the next four years, she underwent an array of conventional and experimental treatments and suffered numerous health complications. Carson died of metastasized cancer in 1964, less than two years after the publication of *Silent Spring* and at the age of only 56. A final book that had begun as a magazine essay in 1956, *The Sense of Wonder,* was published posthumously in 1965.

Carson might initially seem an unlikely counterpoint to mythopoeic science. Her work might even appear to track the same agenda as the narratives we have examined. She is, after all, frequently hailed as a scientist with the rare talents and vision of a poet, and one who calls on us to rethink our place in nature. She is routinely praised for her translation of abstruse scientific information into lyrical prose. "Carson's fresh voice—both objective and lyrical at once—could give the processes of nature spiritual meaning without sacrificing the scientific accuracy of the biological facts or behaviors," as one commentator puts it.[22] The haunting "Fable for Tomorrow" that famously opens *Silent Spring,* wherein Carson portrays an imaginary American town that is frighteningly transfigured by an unseen chemical menace, is often touted as a model of scientific (and other) truths couched in a kind of timeless narrative. Not unlike narratives of the new cosmology, Carson's narrative of our planet's history in *The Sea Around Us* suggests an alternative, scientific version of Genesis, with allusions to shadowy beginnings and a primordial formless void. Carson begins *The Sea Around Us* with a quote from Genesis, and her prose mimics the style and cadence of scripture, though the story she tells is pieced together from contemporary science.[23] Moreover, one might argue, Carson's message is that by aligning ourselves with "reality" we cultivate a caring and intimate relationship to the natural world. Carson—seemingly like the new cosmologists—appeals to us to curb destructive impulses by attending to the wondrous *realities* of our world: "the more clearly we can focus our attention on the wonders and realities of the universe about us," she advises, "the less taste we shall have for destruction" of one another and of the planet.[24]

It is certainly true that Carson was a skilled translator of science, and that she believed that greater exposure to the realities of the universe could have a salutary effect. But we will need to look more closely at her understanding of the relationship of science to nature and ethics, and especially the way she defines *realities.* Science molded into religious-like myths that train our sense of wonder upon the heroic nature of the scientific enterprise would have alarmed Carson, who sought to expose the perils of scientific arrogance and overreach and the threat it poses to the nonhuman world. This is a sensibility she shares with Loren Eiseley, whose testimony I also invoke. Both Carson and Eiseley present a balanced but trenchant critique of science, a critique "rooted in ethical engagement with nature, the rejection of anthropocentric values, and a healthy suspicion of blind faith in scientific and technological progress."[25] Both voiced an alternative "to the discourse and practices of 'Big Science.'"[26]

Eiseley was born the same year as Carson (1907), though he outlived her by some thirteen years. During the course of Carson's writing career, they became friends and supporters of one another's work. Eiseley was one of Carson's loyal defenders when controversy erupted over *Silent Spring* (1962), praising the book as a "devastating, heavily documented, relentless attack upon human carelessness, greed, and irresponsibility."[27] For her own part, Carson was deeply affected by Eiseley's writing, particularly *The Immense Journey* (1957) and *Firmament of Time* (1960). Carson and Eiseley recognized in one another a similar sensibility. "I have read more of Eiseley's *Firmament of Time*," Carson wrote to her close friend Dorothy Freeman in 1961, "and do find myself in agreement with so much he says—and so appreciative of the way he says it."[28] They approach their subject as naturalists, first and foremost, rather than scientists: for both, that is, the narrative voice emanates from, and gives priority to, firsthand experience and observation of nature rather than the "abstract musings of a theoretical scientist."[29] As we will see, this approach reflected Carson's deep conviction that acquaintance with the biological world should come "through nature—in fields and forests and on the shore," and only "secondarily" through the "laboratory aspects" of the subject matter.[30]

Carson and Eiseley also shared, and eloquently expressed in writing, a keen sense of the *limitations* of science. This is seen in Carson's explicit critiques of inordinately positivist and progressivist appraisals of science and technology (notably, in *Silent Spring*), but also in the subtle but consistent way in which her work highlights scientific uncertainty and the vast unknowns. These writers remind us that science is an imperfect, all-too-human activity, not a sacred or revelatory enterprise. They share a similar sense of what does and does not constitute reality, and the way in which scientific lenses, when habitually applied, produce a narrowed and distorted vision of the world around us. Though deeply engaged with the science of their time, neither writer was much invested in presenting scientists as heroic trailblazers.[31] Eiseley urges a wider study of the history of science in order to appreciate the *flawed* process of discovery, and thereby instill a "humbling and contrite wisdom which comes from a long knowledge of human folly in a field supposedly devoid of it."[32]

Eiseley's fellow scientists sometimes chided him—or worse—for wasting time composing personal, "mystical" essays when he could be furthering anthropological research. Some warned him that he was a "freak" among scientists and that many scholars would not look kindly upon his spiritual and ethical musings. "You don't stay in the hole where God supposedly put you," observed one friend. "You keep sticking your head out and looking around. In a university that's inadvisable."[33] Eiseley, in turn, had little patience for what he deemed narrow, conformist, or absolutist tendencies of his "scientifically inclined colleagues" who too often "confused the achievements of their disciplines with certitude on a cosmic scale."[34] He voiced a critique that might today be extended to enthusiasts of the new cosmology: "to those who have substituted authoritarian science for authoritarian religion, individual thought is worthless unless it is the symbol for a reality which can be seen, tasted, felt, or thought about by everyone else."[35] Eiseley engages the reader "not in the denigration of science, but, rather, in a farther stretch of the imagination" where "predictability ceases and the unimaginable begins." In these remote realms we encounter the "heretical suspicion" that perhaps "our own little planetary fragment of the cosmos has all along concealed a mocking refusal to comply totally with human expectations of order and secure prediction."[36]

Like Carson, who worried about humanity's retreat into a "perilously artificial world" of its own creation,[37] Eiseley saw science as potentially removing humanity "ever farther from its sense of responsibility to the natural world ... in order to create an artificial world to satisfy its own insatiable appetites."[38] While his writing plays on the motif of a *journey* through natural history, Eiseley's *Immense Journey* is no totalizing narrative but "a series of many interlocking journeys"—one might say, a composite of *little* stories[39]—that pronounces no overarching meaning or transcendent truth.[40] "Do not look for purpose," Eiseley warns.[41] He offers his journey through deep time not as "an account of discovery so much as a confession of ignorance and of the final illumination that sometimes comes to a man when he is no longer careful of his pride."[42] Readers who accompany him on the journey are forewarned that "the essays in this book have not been brought together as a guide." Eiseley's petite narratives are merely "the prowlings of one mind."[43] His reluctance to seek transcendent truth and purpose in nature, or to act as our authoritative cosmic guide, stems from his abiding distaste for hubristic science and—especially—his rejection of teleological frameworks for evolutionary processes. In stark contrast to *Journey of the Universe*, Eiseley's work makes it clear that viewing the evolutionary past as foregrounding a human drama is an enormous, egotistical mistake.[44] The human-told version of evolutionary unfolding is "perhaps too simplistic for belief," he warns.[45] The *Immense Journey* likens "man's optimistic pronouncements about his role and destiny" in the universe to the "little shrilling chorus" of frogs singing into the night air.[46] At such moments, Eiseley expresses a dark-hued, brooding loneliness, a sense of the haunting ambiguities of the universe around us. Yet, as with Carson—though she is generally not one to brood—mystery and ambiguity create a space for a peculiar kind of solace and a persistent mood of wonder. "Eiseley concluded his life without any pretension that he understood what the explanation for life was, yet he never wavered regarding his intuition that it was a miracle and worthy of reverent care."[47]

I wish to champion the humbling and ambiguous wonder that certain "creative" scientists like Carson and Eiseley are able to cultivate, even in the midst of scientific study. But Eiseley is important for other reasons as well: as it happens, he was a significant influence on the life and work of Thomas Berry, and he remains an inspiration to many engaged in the mythopoeic enterprise. In particular, Eiseley's influence can be discerned in Berry's conception of the New Story as a narrative of deep, developmental time.[48] Indeed, the motif of "journey" in Tucker and Swimme's *Journey of the Universe* is an homage to Eiseley.[49] *Journey*'s creators offer the project "in the spirit of Loren Eiseley, the American anthropologist and nature writer, whose books and voice are a major influence on *Journey of the Universe*."[50] Tucker praises Eiseley's religious sense of awe at the universe. She highlights passages of his work that illustrate a human urge to connect with something larger that ourselves, an impulse "to identify with the all and to affirm in spite of all."[51] Similarly, Connie Barlow has composed a tribute to Eiseley, and she understands him to have laid the groundwork for her own brand of religious naturalism and the Epic of Evolution in particular.[52]

My claim, however, is that Eiseley's signature warnings about the *limitations* of science, and his critique of scientists' tendency to distill their findings into a monistic, authoritative reality, go unheeded in these projects that claim him as inspiration. Notably absent from consecrated science are Eiseley's persistent warnings against distortions introduced by purposeful, human-centered interpolations of cosmic and evolutionary processes. Among Eiseley's chief targets, as his biographers make clear, are teleology, hierarchy, determinacy, and progress as wishful, anthropic impositions on the natural world.[53]

Differences between these two approaches to science-inspired storytelling— the creative, compatibilist view of wonder, on the one hand, and heroic, mythopoeic science on the other—owe much to the way in which the former celebrates and prioritizes nature and direct experience over scientific information. Carson and Eiseley, for example, condemn the excesses of science from the standpoint of a *prior* and overriding commitment to nature's value and significance. Scientific practice "must be rooted both in a personal engagement with nature and an ethical attitude toward the environment."[54] Prior ethical and affective relationship with nature gives shape to a moral framework from which to *evaluate* prospective scientific projects. Put differently, wonder at nature provides the (antecedent) basis for having knowledge that is rightly ordered and moderate in its aims. The new cosmologists, by contrast, attempt to derive *from science* an environmental ethic and "ecocentric" value framework *for nature*. On their account, ecocentric values are rooted in and justified by science.

In this context, Eiseley's essay "Science and the Sense of the Holy" is worth quoting at length because it speaks to today's impoverished discourse of wonder, and the "reality censorship" that currently inflects scientific mythmaking. Eiseley profiles two distinct types of scientifically inclined thinkers:

> One is the educated man who still has a controlled sense of wonder before the universal mystery, whether it hides in a snail's eye or within the light that impinges on that delicate organ. The second kind of observer is the extreme reductionist who is

so busy stripping things apart that the tremendous mystery has been reduced to a trifle, to intangibles not worth troubling one's head about. The world of the secondary qualities—color, sound, thought—is reduced to illusion. The *only* true reality becomes the chill void of ever-streaming particles.[55]

In his devotion to this distorted sense of "true" reality, the scientist may come to embrace treatment of other creatures that borders on sadism, Eiseley worries, for he will know nothing of the "*mysterium* which guards man's moral nature."[56] While Eiseley's specific charges of reductionism do not apply across the board to proponents of the new cosmology, the valorization of a singular true reality, best apprehended by the expert, is much in evidence. Eiseley would have thought it strange indeed to align this worldview, and the "true" reality it venerates, with a project of ecospiritual transformation, as the new cosmologists suggest. For we have seen the first view "plead for endangered species and reject the despoliation of the earth," he writes, while the second "has left us lingering in the shadow of atomic disaster."[57] Here Eiseley points to two incompatible forms of wonder, one symbolized by concern for imperiled wild nature, the other by the absolute power and destruction of the atom bomb.[58] His portrait of the two types of scientist suggests that mythmakers like Barlow who draw equally from Eiseley on the one hand, and from Dawkins or Wilson on the other, in justifying their "reality-based" religion, have a muddled sense of the values these writers actually defend.[59] Eiseley clearly positioned himself as an apologist for the "universal mystery" that science does not strip away in its sometimes too-fervent desire to articulate a unified reality.

So too did Carson. Frequently, Carson dispenses with scientific modes of organizing reality—and suggests that readers do the same—in seeking a *true* understanding of nature and its inhabitants. For Carson, this could entail simply observing creatures in their natural habitats, in circumstances where we normally do not encounter them or do not bother to look closely. It might involve trying to imagine the whole life history and experience of a single organism: where it travels, what it eats, what sort of creatures prey upon it, how it perceives and navigates its surroundings through sense of smell or sound, or through the fluid world of water. "To understand the life of the shore, it is not enough to pick up an empty shell and say 'This is a murex' or 'That is an angel wing.' True understanding demands intuitive comprehension of the whole life of the creature that once inhabited this empty shell."[60] To gain "intuitive" understanding, Carson recommended creeping into a garden at night with a flashlight in hand, delving beneath the shore rocks at low tide, or gazing at length into the tiny universe of a tide pool. Seen in its proper perspective, science sheds light on the eternal mysteries and realities of the natural world; indeed it may enable us to *know* mysteries. But fuller understanding comes from standing on the shore and sensing "the surge of life beating always at its shores—blindly, inexorably pressing for a foothold."[61]

ARTICULATIONS OF IGNORANCE AND MYSTERY
IN CARSON'S WORK

Carson's love of mystery is but one expression of her heightened awareness, and, in many cases, positive valuation of uncertainty and ambiguity. She consistently turned away from systems of belief, religious or scientific, that laid claim to absolute certainty and security. In confronting her own imminent death, she expressed deep acceptance of the unknown and a profound openness to what, if anything, lay beyond, as "an acceptable substitute for the old-fashioned 'certainties' as to heaven and what it must be like," she wrote. "I know that we do not really 'know' and I'm content that it should be so."[62]

Carson's abiding sense of all that we do *not* know sets a distinctly positive tone for her sea writing. Marine worlds provided an ideal illustration of a favorite theme: humankind's smallness and, in some sense, irrelevance as seen from the standpoint of natural history. Carson was convinced for much of her life that however humans might transform the landscape, the sea was virtually inviolable.[63] "The ocean is too big and vast and its forces are too mighty to be much affected by human activity."[64] The supreme otherness—the *non-humanness*—of the sea was part of its attraction, not because Carson held misanthropic or unduly pessimistic views of humanity, but because she believed that the sea would forever resist and elude our attempts to understand it, to assimilate its meaning. Above all, the sea was for Carson "a place of mystery."[65] It might be more accurate to say that her sense of the ocean's enduring otherness and inviolability constituted a hope rather than a dogmatic conviction. Humans' increasingly destructive impact on natural and marine environments would eventually test this cherished idea, ultimately moving Carson to an explicit affirmation of humility and wonder, and a condemnation of hubristic science in *Silent Spring*.

Reality, on this account, is overlaid with and inseparable from mystery: "The mysteries of living things, and the birth and death of continents and seas, are among the great realities," Carson writes.[66] Passages of *The Sea Around Us* reiterate a theme that runs through all her sea books. "Even with all our modern instruments for probing and sampling the deep ocean, no one now can say that we shall ever resolve the last, the ultimate mysteries of the sea."[67] What does Carson mean by ultimate mysteries? Like other scientists and science writers, she finds excitement in the prospect of new discoveries, relishing the idea that mysteries, even when "solved," leave us at the threshold of another—"perhaps a deeper"—mystery. But Carson casts doubt on the last, final mysteries ever being dispelled by science, adding that "I cherish a very unscientific hope that they will not."[68] The *meaning* of the ocean is something about which science can make no definitive pronouncements, after all. In characterizing her hope as "unscientific" Carson has in mind a particular version of the scientific enterprise that discourages or even censures the desire to wonder at mystery. In this, she expresses the very *opposite* sentiment of someone like Dawkins who fears that scientists may be "condemned forever to dig for deeper mysteries."[69] She aligns herself with the "wondering" type of scientist whom Eiseley commends.

A good example is Carson's invitation to readers in the opening pages of *The Sea Around Us*. A story's opening lines must be carefully crafted, as any writer knows. This holds especially true of a narrative that commences with the dim and remote beginnings of our planet—a creation story. David Abram writes of Navajo elders who, prior to narrating their creation story, recite an incantation that expresses their profound deference to the sentient cosmos: "I am ashamed before the earth; I am ashamed before the heavens."[70] In a similarly humble spirit, Carson's opening words convey reverence and caution. Readers sense that we are entering a realm where angels fear to tread. Carson's Genesis-like narrative of the sea's origins repeatedly plays on the absence of human eyewitnesses, and thus the lack of certainty regarding when and how our planet acquired its ocean. Carson stresses the lack of humans in this story, not merely as a reminder that nature's forces have long cycled on without us, but to drive home the incomplete and imperfect nature of knowledge: "Beginnings are apt to be shadowy," she cautions. "No one was there to see it"; there are no "eyewitness accounts"; "no man was there to witness this cosmic birth."[71] The story she tells is conjectural and relies heavily upon our powers of imagination. Constructed from what she calls "hints" and "pieces" of information, her story contains "whole chapters the details of which we can only imagine."[72] The modest tone is sustained through much of the narrative that follows. Writing about the primeval sea, Carson speculates in some detail about the processes by which the first living cells may have come into existence. "But at present," she hastens to add, "no one is wise enough to be sure."[73]

Compare these passages to the opening paragraphs of *Journey of the Universe*, where readers are immediately apprised of the unprecedented, comprehensive nature of present scientific knowledge, and its power to transform our most fundamental values and beliefs:

> This book is an invitation to a journey into grandeur . . . that no previous generation could have fully imagined. We are the first generation to learn the comprehensive scientific dimensions of the universe story. . . . The great discovery of contemporary science is that the universe is not simply a place, but a story . . . . This story has the power to awaken us more deeply to who we are. . . . And this changes everything. . . . [A] new integrating story has emerged. This immense journey evokes wonder from scientists and nonscientists alike. And it challenges some religious traditions to rethink or expand their worldviews. . . . [T]his is such a comprehensive story that it challenges our understanding of who we are and what our role might be in the universe. . . . The discovery that the universe has expanded and is still expanding is one of the greatest of human history.[74]

These are grandiose claims, even when judged by humility standards less stringent than those set by Eiseley or Carson. They strike a particularly incongruous note when we consider that the subject matter of this text is not merely the origin, history, and nature of the cosmos (a daunting enough topic), but also the universe's *meaning and purpose*—its verdict on "who we are"—for everyone. As an opening gambit, moreover, it seems ill advised to inform readers in blunt and patronizing fashion of the unparalleled profundity of the story the reader holds in her hands (should the reader not be trusted to judge for herself?), and its capacity to sweep aside commitments or values to which the reader might naively subscribe. This is a story told from on high, by those in possession of wisdom.[75] In this respect, *Journey* adheres to the conventions of epic science. Such writing "typically begins with a very excited scientific sage wanting to share his exploration of a wonderful subject that will inevitably overturn some previously common misperception," Ian Hesketh observes. "Such books seek something closer to revelation than to enlightenment."[76]

Carson, by contrast, cultivates a modest tone out of genuine reverence for the sentient cosmos, as well as an abiding respect for her *readers,* whom she assumes to have intelligence and sound ethical impulses.[77] We will see Carson adopt a similarly cautious approach to knowledge and uncertainty in *Silent Spring,* though her treatment there of all that is *unknown* takes on a darker hue. There too she invests, or reinvests, authority in the public sphere and in the average citizen who is empowered to *question* the presumed wisdom and knowledge of the specialist or the authoritarian. Our new mythmakers effectively reverse this arrangement: accurate knowledge and proper ethical orientation reside within the story, while the reader is seen to be largely unenlightened and quite likely mistaken about her "role in the universe" (whatever that can mean). In this respect, *Journey* conforms not only to the conventions of epic science. It also adheres, as we have seen, to narrative conventions of Anthropocene storytelling that regard previous generations of humans, and perhaps current generations of nonexperts, as benighted.

Like Eiseley, Carson is drawn to meaning that *eludes* us, that invites us to return again to the source of mystery. A close association of mystery with the unveiling of essential, elemental realities is equally pronounced in *The Edge of the Sea.* There Carson writes of a certain "elusiveness" of meaning that "haunts us, that sends us again and again into the natural world where the key to the riddle is hidden."[78] She recalls a night-time excursion where, flashlight in hand, her discovery of a single ghost crab has the force of a revelation: "I have seen hundreds of ghost crabs in other settings," she writes, "but suddenly I was filled with the odd sensation that for the first time I knew the creature in its own world—that I understood, as never before, the essence of its being."[79] Here, perception of mystery is not dispelled by familiarity; wonder in this instance is no mere reaction to something *novel* but comes with seeing something familiar with fresh eyes—with sudden "visionary intensity."[80] The wondering response is not bound up with ignorance, nor dispelled by subsequent knowledge. For in claiming knowledge of the creature's "essence" Carson is not suggesting that the "riddle" has been solved. She is not saying "Now I know just what you are." Rather, its essence is mystery—that is the revelation. The ghost crab symbolizes the mystery of *life itself,* the will of creatures to struggle and survive, to create their own worlds, in the midst of processes that often thwart their designs. As with Dillard's tale of the crippled moth, Carson apprehends in this small, strange creature some deep truth about the "delicate, destructible, yet incredibly vital force that somehow holds its place amid the harsh realities of the inorganic world."[81] It is precisely this apprehension of elusiveness of meaning, of reality as mystery, that consecrated science lacks.

Carson's conviction that humans were a small and insignificant part of the universe, like her cherished belief in nature's eternal mystery, was a source of comfort, not fear. I argue that a certain "Jobian" perspective inflects Carson's writing. A sense of humanity's insignificance within the universe recalls the Biblical tale of Job and its theme of decentralizing humans and their preoccupations and vanities, while encouraging wonder at natural processes that are fully comprehended only by God.[82] Many of Carson's readers resonated strongly with these themes. "I am overwhelmed with a sense of the vastness of the sea," one wrote to her, "and properly humble about our goings-on."[83] Much as our Anthropocene age calls into question long-standing assumptions about the human-nature relationship, Carson's belief that humans were too insignificant to alter nature on a large or permanent scale would be tested by rapid developments in science and technology during the 1950s and '60s. Among those was the launch of Sputnik in 1957. Sputnik, and the unprecedented technological conquest of Earth and space it symbolized, challenged Carson's Jobian vision of humans, nature, and God. Carson describes her reaction in a remarkable letter to Dorothy Freeman in which she recalls her profound comfort in believing that nature's forces are beyond humans' "tampering reach" and expresses alarm that idolatrous tendencies may triumph over humility and wonder.

> It was comforting to suppose that . . . however the physical environment might mold Life, that Life could never assume the power to change drastically—or even destroy— the physical world. . . . I still feel there is a case to be made for my old belief that as man approaches the "new heaven and the new earth"—or the space-age universe, if you will, he must do so with humility rather than arrogance. . . . Of course, in pre-Sputnik days, it was easy to dismiss so much as science-fiction fantasies. Now the most farfetched schemes seem entirely possible of achievement. And man seems actually likely to take into his hands—ill-prepared as he is psychologically—many of the functions of "God."[84]

Passages such as these allow us to appreciate the continuing relevance of Carson's work. Here she anticipates something like our Anthropocene moment with its human-centered modes of enchantment and elevation of humans as the "God species."

Silent Spring would reassert her "old" belief that humility remains integral to our moral compass. Wonder in and of itself, detached from proper moral ends and wholesome sensibilities, cannot act as a trustworthy guide, precisely because Sputnik—or DDT, atomic weapons, genetically engineered organisms, or any number of exciting new gadgets—might also be, and often are, hailed as objects of awe and wonder. Carson set out to expose DDT, and other chemicals hailed as miracles of modern science, as dangerous and highly suspect objects of wonder. *Silent Spring* castigates the folly of wondering at human creations—at the latest "bright new toy"—particularly when these are deployed against the web of life and give a "giddy sense of power over nature to those who wield them."[85] Wonder must be tethered to something other than, something *greater* than, the scientific enterprise and its insistent, internal logic of discovery, innovation, and control. Only then can wonder subvert, rather than embolden, hubristic fantasies of certainty and omnicompetence, as Carson and Eiseley understood.

Today, as we contemplate scientific and technological transformations of ourselves and our planet, from gene-editing and de-extinction to full-scale climate engineering, it is imperative that we scrutinize our mode of wondering, and that we ask where wonder is leading us. Of these transformative projects Ben Minteer aptly observes that "the sense of wonder and respect once directed at nature has become instead a regard for our own technological prowess." We should remain on guard against exchanging appreciation for "the sublime qualities of wild nature for a celebration of our own technological ingenuity, power, and control."[86] The narratives of the new cosmology and mythopoeic science are ill equipped to subvert dreams of human centrality and control.

Perhaps nowhere does the contrast between Carson and modern consecrated science emerge more starkly than in the writing of E. O. Wilson.[87] Recall Wilson's gleefully arrogant rebuttal to God in his retelling of the story of Job. God demands: "Have you comprehended the vast expanse of the world? / Come, tell me all this, if you know." Speaking for Job, Wilson confidently replies, "And yes, we *do* know and we have told."

> Jehovah's challenges have been met and scientists have pressed on to uncover and to solve even greater puzzles. The physical basis of life is known; we understand approximately how and when it started on earth. New species have been created in the laboratory and evolution has been traced at the molecular level. Genes can be spliced from one kind of organism into another. Molecular biologists have most of the knowledge needed to create elementary forms of life. Our machines, settled on Mars, have transmitted panoramic views and the results of chemical soil analysis.[88]

Wilson's faith in human omniscience, evident in this aggrandizing litany of scientific and technological wonders, leads him to assume that *more* knowledge, and the increasing confidence and control it confers, will unerringly steer us toward proper care for the Earth.[89] Wilson's updated tale of Job presents, in miniature, the sort of exultant "new story" he believes humans must rally around: a new scripture with humanity usurping the role of God. What moral guidance can be gleaned from this alternative mythology and its scaled-up vision of the human? Nothing is off-limits; indeed the riskier, the more "forbidden" the knowledge, the greater the excitement: "Let us see how high we can fly."[90] It is precisely this breathtaking hubris that true wonder must challenge, for such rhetoric heeds no caution and brooks no restraint.

While Wilson exults in our species' progressive mastery of life and the universe, Carson decries the sinister attractions of what some now call the Age of Humans, and what Carson, in a biblical turn of phrase, calls the new heaven and the new earth.

> Mankind has gone very far into an artificial world of his own creation. He has sought to insulate himself, in his cities of steel and concrete, from the realities of earth and water and the growing seed. Intoxicated with a sense of his own power, he seems to be going farther and farther into more experiments for the destruction of himself and his world.[91]

The further we retreat into this world, the more detached we become from the realities of the universe that would decenter and humble us. Carson's *reality*, then, is one in which human intoxication with power is revealed to be a dangerous delusion, unsupported by acquaintance with the wider universe. "Wonder and humility are wholesome emotions, and they do not exist side by side with a lust for destruction."[92] Carson's indictment of arrogance was strongly shaped by a lifelong sense of "Calvinistic responsibility and civic obligation,"[93] and a distinctly Calvinist association of sin with glorification of the self.[94] A lapsed Presbyterian in adulthood, she retained her conviction that knowledge must be tethered to a strong sense of piety. To lose this humble sense of our place in the universe was to lose our humanness.

As Carson's concerns about the eclipse of humility, humanity, and wonder intensified, her treatment of the *unknown* took on a new twist. *Silent Spring*, unlike her previous works, makes science central, in terms of explicating the precise chemical makeup and potential environmental impacts of pesticides, and in its overriding agenda of problematizing the moral *attitudes* that attend techno-scientific "progress." The book is a departure from Carson's typical approach in its explicit focus on the "unpalatable facts" deliberately obscured by certain scientists, technicians, and government authorities. "I myself never thought the ugly facts would dominate, and I hope they don't," Carson said of *Silent Spring*. "The beauty of the living world I was trying to save has always been uppermost in my mind."[95] *Silent Spring* is, above all, a social commentary issued with all the force and conviction of Carson's lifelong suspicion of humans assuming an idolatrous role vis-à-vis God or the planet, and of experts assuming an authoritarian stance vis-à-vis the public.[96] As a "biologist, crusader, Jeremiah, preacher," and "secular daughter of Presbyterianism," Carson "awakened the conscience of a nation and called it to repentance."[97] She did so through an incisive critique of a pernicious enchantment that is, at root, wonder at ourselves. Carson maintained that a "large share of what's wrong with the world is man's towering arrogance—in a universe that surely ought to impose humility and reverence."[98] *Silent Spring* warns of the human propensity to become "intoxicated" with power—frequently symbolized, in Carson's prose, by the man with a chemical spray-gun in his hand.

IGNORANCE AND ARROGANCE: THE SINISTER UNKNOWNS OF *SILENT SPRING*

Carson never abandoned the positive valuation of mystery that defines her sea writing, but she grew increasingly concerned about dangerous forms of willful ignorance that accompany, and even enable, scientific hubris. *Silent Spring* deploys a consistent rhetoric of uncertainty, not as an obstructionist or filibustering tactic— as climate change skeptics might invoke uncertainty today—but as a platform for engaging public participation in science.[99] The book is replete with examples of all that is poorly understood: how chemicals react with one another, where they go when they pass into underground streams, how long they stay in the environment, what forms of havoc are wreaked in the hidden ecology of bodies. Carson embeds cautionary phrases throughout the text—"no one knows," "we know too little," "scientists do not agree"—as well as numerous articulations of potential for harm. She used scientific uncertainty (uncertainty about what *is*) to galvanize political and ethical certainty about what needed to be done (certainty about *ought*). "Carson's text invited readers to critique science on the levels of both knowledge production (we should know what is in our water), and civic action amid risk (there should not be toxic chemicals in our water)."[100] Injecting uncertainty and troubling unknowns into the debate about chemicals and the environment "engaged and motivated the public."[101] *Silent Spring* ties together an argument for citizens' right to know about environmental and health risks with an endorsement of the precautionary principle. Uncertainty here has a galvanizing rather than paralyzing effect, underscoring the need for decisive ethical action to reduce unnecessary risks. "The choice, after all, is ours to make," Carson reminds us.[102] In this way, "the writer's ethos changes from an authoritarian voice ('Let me tell you what is') to a more collaborative one ('Let me tell you what we don't know and what might happen')."[103] Carson's text effectively models the civic, democratic, and modest discourse that she believes is critical to public engagement with environmental and scientific matters. She is a hero to many, but she acquired that status by lambasting the scientist's heroic posture. Carson condemned authoritarianism in industry, science, and government, and reminded the public that power lies with *them*.

Who has decided—who has the *right* to decide—for the countless legions of people who were not consulted that the supreme value is a world without insects, even though it be also a sterile world ungraced by the curving wing of a bird in flight? The decision is that of the authoritarian temporarily entrusted with power.[104]

We have seen this collaborative, nonauthoritarian tone in Carson's writing before. Where *Silent Spring* takes a different tack is in suggesting a sinister aspect to what is unknown. These unknowns are dangerous because they are both perpetuated and obscured by an obstinate attitude of certainty. In this sense, Carson critiques what some have called "imposed" or "purposeful" ignorance (in contrast to "humble ignorance" often accompanied by a wondering attitude). Imposed ignorance and humble ignorance stand as opposing worldviews.[105] Humble ignorance can "marvel at what it sees that it cannot hope to understand or control. It knows that it must question certainty and jargon."[106] Imposed ignorance is what Carson directly targets with insistent reminders of uncertainty; it is "ignorance-masquerading-as-certain-knowledge," and it often presents itself as whole systems of thought with "intellectual buffers that make its facts, claims, and practices beyond question."[107] Carson decries imposed ignorance in challenging the authorities who endeavor to soothe the public with "little tranquilizing pills of half truth," whenever concerns are raised about the safety of chemicals.[108] "This kind of ignorance is, thus, purposely imposed on many and camouflages our true state of ignorance."[109] Yet elsewhere in Carson's writing, as we have seen, the unknown takes the form of mystery that invites us in and envelops us in wonder. My claim, then, is that humble ignorance is a fellow traveler with ethical forms of wonder, while imposed ignorance thrives in an atmosphere of arrogance, inordinate certainty, and awe at human knowledge and creations. *Silent Spring* condemns the latter; Carson's sea writing cultivates the former. In all instances, the collaborative spirit of Carson's discourse and her respect for readers is apparent.

WONDER IN RELATION TO VIRTUOUS IGNORANCE

This positive appraisal of humble ignorance resonates strongly with ignorance-based worldviews endorsed by some recent commentators on science. Consciousness of ignorance not only allows a place for wonder; it may also produce better science—*better* in the sense of generating fruitful research questions, but superior too in its ethical engagement with the natural world. Take, for example, Bill Vitek and Wes Jackson's collection of essays on *The Virtues of Ignorance*.[110] At first blush, promoting ignorance, a term that typically conjures an array of vices rather than virtues, might not seem a wise strategy.[111] But these scholars are not advocating an end to knowledge-seeking. Rather, they call attention to a broad and problematic set of attitudes and beliefs that attend the standard knowledge-based worldview that is "increasingly being shown to be inadequate and dangerous."[112] They might instead celebrate any number of virtuous dispositions—prudence, humility, wisdom, precaution, reverence—closely associated with ignorance, as they define it. But *ignorance* has shock value that may help to jolt us out of our complacency, our sense of security in the steady growth and accuracy of our knowledge. As defined here, ignorance implies that "no matter how much human beings discover about the natural world or ourselves or our political and social systems, knowledge will always be dwarfed by what we do not, should not, and cannot ever know."[113] Ignorance stands as an "initial operating condition" for existence in a "living universe."[114] And as with Carson's worldview, consciousness of ignorance brings into sharper relief the need for a robust ethic of caution—an ethic of what we should *not* know and do.

The knowledge-based worldview is strongly implicated in recurring motifs of forbidden but tantalizing knowledge, such as the theft of knowledge that occurs in the Genesis story of the Fall, or in Prometheus's ambition to bring fire to humans— or twentieth-century atomic scientists' discourse of sinful, irresistible knowledge. This perspective is deeply complicit with environmental destruction because it continually fosters confidence that something more or better can always be discovered or created. More energy can be found and harvested; economic growth will be perpetual; land can be made more productive; and, above all, human ingenuity will prove unlimited. These very attitudes, I argue, fuel the delusional discourses of the "good Anthropocene." They thrive on a popular myth that makes our current environmental crisis bearable: "the belief that human knowledge is sufficient to get us out of the holes we've dug for ourselves and the world."[115] Wilson's rejoinder to God, cited above, exemplifies this mythology in action. Unfortunately, these myths make environmental problems even more intractable. Acknowledging ignorance may be the "secular mind's only way" to a more humble worldview.[116]

Many of the contributors to *The Virtues of Ignorance* are scientists and engineers whose day-to-day activities entail the creation and vetting of new knowledge. But their emphasis on ignorance disrupts the standard narrative of progress by showing how new knowledge is constructed upon older knowledge (hence, the old knowledge was far from complete), and that knowledge creation perpetually sheds light on *new* areas of ignorance as well.[117] We have encountered this portrait of science as forever turning up new "unknowns" many times before. It tends to treat wonder as primarily a function of ignorance, for *both* ignorance and wonder dwell in the places where knowledge has not yet penetrated. For those committed to the knowledge-based worldview, the two are like conjoined (and somewhat evil) twins who must be eradicated simultaneously. But this attitude of relishing mysteries for the sake of *solving* them ignores the virtuous part of virtuous ignorance. Insofar as it treats mysteries as problems, it also regards ignorance as a condition that, if it cannot be cured once and for all, can at least be managed and kept at bay. In Dawkins's view, for example, it is precisely because we do not (yet) know everything "that we should loudly proclaim those things that we do."[118] Virtuous ignorance, on the other hand, asks us to go with ignorance as our "long suit," not as something to be covered over by heroic rhetoric or shamefully acknowledged in private confessionals.[119]

My claim is that a conscious cultivation of virtuous ignorance has clear parallels with the cultivation of wonder as a potentially enduring orientation. Virtuous ignorance "invites us to resist the many abstractions we have come to take for granted and to see instead with fresh eyes."[120] Writers of a Romantic or phenomenological bent, in a similar way, call for a return to *things in themselves*. While we cannot simply rid ourselves of framing concepts, we can work harder to emend the concepts and metaphors we use.[121] A world without concepts is a world largely devoid of coherence; but by the same token, we should not become so enamored of our knowledge and the frameworks we construct to organize it that we believe it to constitute a comprehensive or sacred reality. We can become more conscious of metaphors and abstractions we deploy and "remain aware of their relation to experience."[122] Cultivating such awareness through an ignorance based worldview requires relinquishing security in what we know, or think we know. In much the same way, wonder has the power to release us "from our prison of preconceptions."[123] Ignorance does not just reveal gaps in our knowledge but potentially reconfigures the world.

A similar endorsement of ignorance is offered by Columbia neurobiologist Stuart Firestein in his book *Ignorance: How It Drives Science*.[124] Like Vitek and Jackson, Firestein intends the word ignorance as a provocation. He does not promote indifference to reason or data (as, again, climate deniers might), but advocates what he calls a *thoroughly conscious ignorance* that takes science to be fundamentally question-centered.[125] Firestein presents an alternative to the standard portrait—literally, the textbook account—of science as amassing knowledge and piling up facts. In lieu of scientific practice as puzzle-solving, which implies a final solution, or science as an onion whose layers of ignorance are peeled away to reveal the kernel of truth, he suggests the image of a magic well: no matter how many buckets of water are taken out, the well remains full. Or this: if knowledge is envisioned as an expanding sphere, the vast areas of ignorance expand right along with it. What science seeks to produce, then (or ought to), is a higher quality of ignorance in the form of good questions. Knowledge exists in the service of generating high-quality ignorance.

Conscious ignorance does not merely suggest where to look next for new puzzles to solve. It reveals that "solutions" to one puzzle simultaneously *undo* solutions to others, especially as we move across disciplinary domains (more on this below). To be sure, there are echoes in Firestein's approach of what I call serial wonder, and his particular mode of wondering has the flavor of curiosity. Nevertheless, his emphasis on ignorance is a welcome change from the glorification of science perpetrated by spokesmen like Dawkins. Genuine wonder, I believe, is more likely to thrive in a participatory mode of science than in a cult of expertise that trades in static answers. That is, an ignorance-based worldview is more democratic, more civic-minded, because it necessarily depends upon sharing observations and communication across space and time: "practitioners of ignorance admit that they cannot know or have it all. Ignorance therefore invites, indeed requires, a civic mind, a community of learners, and a time frame that stretches across, and connects, generations."[126] For his own part, Firestein clearly eschews final or totalizing solutions, even invoking Keats's "negative capability"—the ability to dwell in uncertainty—as a general orientation and the "ideal state of mind."[127] He dismisses rhetoric that elevates the "scientific method" as the rarefied activity of an elite class of transcendent beings. In doing so, he shows science to be a very human enterprise driven by careful questioning rather than authoritative answering, and, thus, an enterprise in which a humbler and more ethical form of wondering remains a vital possibility.

Significantly, these endorsements of ignorance suggest an *attitudinal* difference, a shift toward honesty about scientific endeavors, and a generosity of spirit that shows up the arrogant insecurity of Wilson's or Dawkins's parading of knowledge. There is, as Rubenstein argues, "an irreducible difference between a rigorous, investigative thinking that sustains wonder's strangeness and a rigorous, investigative thinking that endeavors to assimilate that strangeness." Wonder "keeps propositions provisional, open-ended, and incomplete."[128] I see something of this attitudinal shift in Firestein's commitment to educating students in the art of *questioning*, a teaching experiment at Columbia that prompted him to write his book. This approach contrasts with the top-down model of *education as imposition* of secure knowledge, meaning, and wonder endorsed by Epic of Evolution enthusiasts. Firestein may not have intended to make this claim, but I believe his portrait of science shows its affinity and continuity—distinct from consilient vertical integration—with other disciplinary endeavors and indeed with human creativity generally. That is to say, *all* scholars, not just scientists, seek to articulate good, rigorous questions and (ideally) they endeavor to pass this skill on to students.

A question-oriented, or *erotetic*, picture of science can be qualified in ways that make it even more compelling as a counterpoint to the image of science assumed by the mythopoeic enterprise. Philosopher of science Alan Love points out that the questioning mode is also an organizational structure. That is, ignorance "drives" science not only in the sense of motivating it, as Firestein recognizes, but in the sense of *steering* it. The erotetic structure of science "accounts for *how* ignorance drives (*guides*) science."[129] The questions science poses are multifaceted, multiple, and interrelated; they do not take the form of a single interrogative, such as "What did you do last night?" Love argues. Rather, they "exhibit a complex anatomy that is composed of historical strands of debate, a variety of question-types (empirical, conceptual), and a nested architecture among the questions in terms of their abstraction and generality."[130] This complex anatomy provides a scaffolding structure to the erotetic nature of science. Changes in the organization of scaffolding over time may be counted as progress in a given area of science, though not progress in terms of an "asymptotic [increasingly exact] approach to truth."[131] Note that this account of the different science disciplines entails that they are erotetically structured quite differently. There is no monolithic practice or structure called "science," and no overarching direction or progress to the enterprise as a whole. Appreciating this underscores the absurdity of claiming a single coherent story or consilient integration of knowledge. It may suggest that an appropriate narrative mode for science is the petite narrative style—mini-narratives loosely stitched together, if at all—that emerges in the writing of Carson and Eiseley.

The nature of scientific inquiry itself suggests that there can be no comprehensive story of the universe. The different sciences suggest their own unique and even *incommensurable* perspectives. They shed very different light on questions of who "we" are, what our nature is, or where we may be headed in the future. Knowledge is always particular to particular sciences, and its meaning is often far less clear than some might like. In this vein, environmental historian Julie Adeney Thomas argues that attention to different subdisciplines within biology—say, paleobiology, microbiology, and biochemistry—produces "radically different figures of 'the human'" and reveals radically different scales, both macro and micro.[132] Those who turn to science to craft a coherent story about who *we* are or what it means to be human, will, if they are truly paying attention, come away perplexed. In particular, projects of grounding universal ethical values and themes in "science"— human solidarity, collectivity, continuity, interconnectedness—are not likely to withstand cross-disciplinary scrutiny. From the microbiological standpoint, "we" humans differ far more than we imagine. Humans share over 99 percent of their DNA, but the shared genetic profile of our microbial cells is only around 50 percent. "If 90 percent of my cells are bacterial and half of those have a different DNA sequence than yours, then on a cellular level it is not as clear that we are 'the same species,' as other branches of biology and most recent histories define us."[133] Different biologies "produce visions of 'the human' that are incommensurable with one another . . . we must necessarily make choices about where to focus our attention."[134] Those choices will reveal our values. The visions of the human they produce will never achieve the status of objective truths or apolitical narratives, however much we insist on their "scientific" provenance. If we prefer to focus on the commonality of our DNA, we should do so with honesty and awareness of the choice we make. Thus, when the new cosmologists point us to the biggest possible picture—the *longue dureé* of cosmogenesis or the broadest strokes of natural selection—for intimations of meaningful pattern or purpose, they ignore the messiness and noise, the randomness and contingency, that reign at other scales.[135]

The point is not to discourage humanists from engaging with the sciences, or to posit a radical and unbridgeable gulf between "is" and "ought," but to call for a "careful examination of our own commitments to particular scales and values."[136] The diversity of human images produced by the sciences should not provoke dismay. It is rather a "cause for rejoicing, since myriad perspectives in the humanities and sciences give us more conceptual tools." They give us room to think creatively. To return to our abiding theme: their diversity allows us "to point with *wonder* at the incommensurable yet accurate ways in which 'the human' emerges in various disciplines." This insight has particular value in the Anthropocene, when big questions and big stories about an aggregate figure of "the human species" are taking center stage.[137]

In our search for compatibilist forms of wonder that honor science without consecrating it, we have arrived again at incommensurability—incommensurable meanings, impressions, and scales—as a vital element of human experiences of nature, and an ineradicable feature of science. We may come to apprehend this diversity through concerted scientific study, or through our relatively untutored and sensory impressions—or a combination of both. By whatever path we apprehend these contrastive realms and meanings, my claim is that wonder is not true wonder that desires to collapse the scales and erase the contrasts wherever it finds them. But I also want to stake a particular claim on the value and indispensability of the sensory realm as the locus—indeed, we might say, the *scale*—of our daily lives and deepest attachments.

IGNORANCE AND A RETURN TO OUR SENSES

A virtuous awareness of our own ignorance can facilitate reconnection with the realm of sensory experience, and with a living and unpredictable world that resists our attempts to drive it into static explanations and rigid categories. It may allow one to leave behind, even if only for a time, our "culture of abstraction."[138] Commenting on the disparagement of sensuous reality that our modern discoveries and inventions have encouraged, David Abram argues that relegating ordinary experience of the world to a secondary, derivative realm increases reliance on experts to inform us of what is real and true about the world, what is worthy of our wondering response.[139] "Since we have no ordinary experience of these realms [e.g., the cosmological Big Bang or the nuclei of our cells], the essential truths to be found there must be mediated for us by experts, by those who have access to the high-powered instruments and the inordinately expensive technologies (the electron microscopes, functional MRI scanners, radio telescopes, and supercolliders) that might offer a momentary glimpse into these dimensions."[140] Echoing Abram's lament that nature becomes a derivative, subordinate reality vis-à-vis scientific abstractions, proponents of virtuous ignorance question "the strong propensity to take abstract conceptual frameworks more seriously than full-blooded experience."[141] The modern tendency is to treat the realm of genes, black holes, molecules, neural networks, or survival and reproductive strategies as "more real" than a flower opening with the warm spring sun or the cold, crystalline light of stars on a winter night. The love a parent feels for a child is *really*, we are told, the programmed imperative of selfish genes exerting their control; the beauty we experience in the presence of a Japanese maple is best understood as an adaptive biophilic response "hardwired" by evolution; the "real" magic of the rainbow is found in grasping its physical genesis. And so on. If we forget that concepts exist in order to illuminate the world, and not the other way around, we inevitably attend more to the concepts and, consequently, experience a sense of detachment. Abstractions themselves stand in for the "reality," the very "is-ness" of things. "The apples we see and taste, the melody we hear, and the warmth we sense are all only appearances, mere subjective semblances of true physical reality."[142]

Restoring the world of genes and neurons to the background reawakens our senses to what is immediately before us. It also encourages greater intellectual modesty. This is so because when we grant these abstractions the status of "the primary realities," we often forget how it is that we arrived at concepts in the first place, regarding them as discrete "objectlike facts" about the world rather than the product of a thinking human mind interacting with the world of experience. The seemingly detached and objective stance of science, Abram argues, "is itself dependent upon a more visceral reciprocity between the human organism and its world," deeply rooted in the realm of ordinary experience.[143] In ordinary experience, "the entities that meet our senses are not quarks and protons, but rather brambles and mushrooms and slowly eroding hillsides; not DNA base pairs or neuronal synapses but rather children, and woodpeckers, and the distant sound of thunder."[144] Reclaiming this realm of experience is crucial, for how can we feel affection for and moral obligation to DNA base pairs? Why attach ourselves to the seeming world of illusion that we perceive through ordinary experience, untutored by science? We have seen that the new cosmology, and the scientific perspectives that inform it, seek to articulate for us the way things really are. Actual experience becomes a subjective phantasm. To raise these objections is, of course, to repeat charges that have often been lodged against scientism or crass reductionism. But my claim is that there is something particularly troubling in the application of these scientific worldviews, and their suspect expressions of wonder, to the realm of *environmental* ethics and values. For this worldview "disconnects us from the very world it sets out to explain."[145]

Perhaps, then, firsthand experience can provide a foundation for enduring moral and aesthetic responses to the natural world. That foundation may, in turn, inform and qualify the lines of research we choose to pursue and the technologies we deploy. A sense of reverence for life is something most of us experience through personal encounters, such as the "sudden, unexpected sight of a wild creature, perhaps some experience with a pet," as Carson suggests. These experiences are notable for their potential to take us "out of ourselves" and to thereby increase our awareness of the life all around us.[146] Firsthand engagement with the natural world can provide a framework for knowledge acquired later in life. This idea is showcased, for example, in Carson's book about children's connection to the natural world, *The Sense of Wonder* (1965). A similar approach is recommended for older students as well. The beginning student of high school biology should initially become familiar with the study of life not in classrooms or with textbooks, Carson notes, but "through observing the lives of creatures in their true relation to each other and to their environment."[147] This way of thinking "associates *truth* not with static fact, but with a quality of relationship," as Abram also perceives.[148] This true relationality is not apprehended in laboratories and textbooks. It becomes distorted and lost without that larger context, that mysterious process of life in which both the student and the organism participate.[149] The whole stream of life, as Carson calls it, is not something we can narrate with confidence and accuracy; it flows out of a "dim past" and into an "uncertain future." The student who does not grasp this mystery has missed the essence of biology. More to the point, he may never develop a sense of the *moral* relation that obtains between humans and the natural world. He will not perceive the *mysterium* that, in Eiseley's phrase, "guards man's moral nature."

My claim, then, is that decisions about the uses to which knowledge will be put are informed by a prior exposure to something deemed worthy of wonder and care. The question is not what we can do and know through science, but what we ought to do. This is what Carson means when she speaks of curbing our destructive impulses by attending to the wonders and realities of the universe. In an analogy offered by Keen, we can only be horrified by the destruction of human life on the battlefield or in concentration camps if we have had some prior experience that convinces us that human beings are of value and should not be degraded or destroyed.

> Horror or outrage logically depends upon a prior experience of wonder. . . . The experience of horror arises out of the anticipation of violation—and outrage at the actual violation—of the sense of wonder. It is important to insist upon the priority of wonder, because otherwise we lose the basis of ethics . . . . The intuition of inviolability or sacredness of objects and persons invests them with the character of mystery— which means merely that they stand out in stark outline as themselves and cannot be reshaped to fit our desires and needs.[150]

Extending this analysis beyond the realm of human relations, we see the impossibility of retaining a sense of nature's inviolability in the face of a mode of science that would banish mystery and denigrate our most powerful, personal experiences of wonder. Carson grasped this connection between inviolability, sacredness, and mystery in her sea writing and in her "unscientific" hope that the nature's meaning would never be destroyed by the probing instruments of science.

WONDER'S ETHICAL AFFINITIES

For over a century, nature study approaches have cultivated wonder, sympathy, and respect for life through indirect methods of education. Here factual information such as the names of plants and animals are subordinate to engaging sensory and emotional responses through hands-on, minimally guided encounters with nature. Carson, who was steeped in this educational philosophy as a child, recommends the following:

> If facts are the seeds that later produce knowledge and wisdom, then the emotions and the impressions of the senses are the fertile soil in which the seeds must grow. . . . Once the emotions have been aroused—a sense of the beautiful, the excitement of the new and unknown, a feeling of sympathy, pity, admiration or love—then we wish for knowledge about the object of our emotional response.[151]

Once the child's curiosity is sparked, he or she will later want to know more about names, facts, and other details. Affective and moral dimensions of the human-nature relationship help to nurture and provide context for the seeds of knowledge; factual information without strong emotional and sensory connection is not likely to encourage that moral sense, and may even interfere with its development.

Empirical research appears to support these claims that experience with nature, especially in youth, can have a lasting impact on our moral commitments and decision-making. Studies of prominent environmental activists and educators have found that commitments to environmental protection, wildlife preservation, and even concerns about land use and water quality can be traced to attachment to particular, special places in childhood. In one study, environmental psychologist Louise Chawla found that 90 percent of those she interviewed attributed their devotion and concern for nature to experiences in natural places where they played as children.[152] Also important are role models, family members, or teachers in strengthening children's attachment to nature, particularly companions who simply share their delight in nature, rather than offering instruction, as Carson also suggests in *The Sense of Wonder*.[153] The impact of formal education and (especially) "books and authors" was far less significant for developing environmental sensibilities, and in nearly all cases, these educational sources only became important later in a child or adult's life.[154]

The finding that unstructured experiences in nature foster moral commitment later in life does not, of course, necessarily entail that acquaintance with nature primarily through *science* fosters opposite sensibilities. But (unrelated) research suggests that when science functions like religion in people's lives—as purveyors of consecrated science would like it to function—it can interfere with nature-friendly attitudes and practices. The more participants in one study "believed in the power of scientific progress, the more they saw the world as orderly and controllable, and the less likely they were to act in an environmentally friendly way."[155]

Scientific progress is here defined as "a testimony to humanity's increasing ability to exert control over the world."[156] Belief in science functions like strong belief in a deity, i.e., as an external source of control that "intervenes" and exerts power in the face of disorder. Uncertainty brings greater anxiety but it is a better motivator than trust in lawlike, powerful, and order-inducing science—which is to say, science as celebrated by Wilson and Dawkins, or in media portraits of "omniscient science."[157] These findings, however tentative, are a cold bath for the new cosmologists who seek cosmic order and secure science. Passivity and complacency may result from strong belief in science, as it likely does with inordinately strong belief in "God, government, and other external agents or institutions that may provide order."[158] The study concludes that "looking more critically at the power of science and the limits of progress could—somewhat ironically—encourage people to take matters in their own hands and make environmentally friendly choices."[159] Carson, who worried about the public's tendency to "rest secure in a childlike faith that 'someone' is looking after things," seems to have intuited much of this.[160]

Children and young people are often the focus of efforts to nurture wonder because they seem uniquely open to investing nature with animacy, magic, and moral significance. But wondrous encounters are available to anyone, at any age, who remains open and creative. These encounters, as Carson puts it, belong to "anyone who will place himself under the influence of a lonely mountain top—or the sea—or the stillness of a forest; or who will stop to think about so small a thing as the mystery of a growing seed."[161] Her choice of phrase—"under the influence"— suggests a beneficial form of intoxication with nature, in contrast to giddy enchantment with techno-scientific power. It bespeaks an openness to subordinating oneself joyfully rather than grudgingly to something more powerful than ourselves. At such moments, our object of wonder exercises its authority on us; we conform ourselves to it and allow it to suggest the categories by which we will come to know it.[162] "This willingness to stand in a relaxed receptivity before an object involves a certain reverence, an epistemological humility, and a willingness to appreciate."[163] It involves us in a virtuous form of ignorance that creates new opportunities for sensory education.

I have argued that wonder, when properly oriented, can foster intellectual and moral habits also encouraged by the ignorance-based worldview and its emphasis on sensory engagement with the world. These attitudes underscore wonder's ethical affinities with empathy and humility, in particular. Wonder as an ingrained sensibility, rather than a response to a particular novel stimulus, is characterized by an open-ended mood of "receptivity rather than immediate utilitarian action."[164] A hallmark of genuine wonder is its ability to move us away from a self-protective stance toward greater openness and even vulnerability to others. Wonder's ecstatic dimensions have the power to decenter the self and its interests; it does not inspire conquest, nor does it glorify and flatter the self. An ingrained disposition of wonder may take time and effort to cultivate and, given its sometimes contemplative mood, it may not immediately translate into ethical action. Nevertheless, wonder's virtuous qualities—receptivity to difference or otherness, a nonutilitarian and nonpossessive stance—clearly land us in the terrain of environmental values. Wonder's contemplative aspect, moreover, may guard against the haste and recklessness of enchantment with scientific discovery. Contemplation counters the "tyranny of the already known."[165]

The other-acknowledging qualities of wonder and its nonexploitative, nonutilitarian dimensions suggest its resemblance to virtues like compassion, generosity, and what Hepburn calls a certain gentleness—a "concern not to blunder into damaging manipulation of another." From this wondering appreciation of others, it is "a short step to *humility*." Wonder may make us more aware of the "blinding effects of self-absorption" and the false perceptions of others that our blindness encourages.[166] Release from self-absorption is what Carson has in mind when she recommends putting oneself under the influence of the natural world, and embracing encounters that take us *outside of ourselves.*

CONCLUSION

The place of storytelling in promoting environmental sensibilities has been a focus of this book throughout. It seems appropriate to conclude with some reflections on the kinds of stories we ought to tell—or perhaps *listen* for—regarding "the human" in the Age of Humans. What stories might wonder inspire about our place in the cosmos, and what is the appropriate scale and perspective from which to tell them?

Dipesh Chakrabarty has suggested, somewhat cryptically, that a "new universal history of humans" may flash up in our present moment of collective climate crisis—a *"negative* universal" arising from a shared sense of global catastrophe. This negative universal, Chakrabarty suggests, would not subsume particularities of experience or culpability, as standard Anthropocene narratives do. It would eschew the "myth of global identity," while somehow retaining a global approach to politics.[167] We do not yet know what this universal narrative might look like or what power it might have. I think we can say, however, that species discourse has so far proven insufficiently sensitive to the particularities of environmental injustices and disparities of wealth and accountability. Alternative models and counternarratives of communal responsibility, personhood, and agency are needed beyond those that assume an aggregate, mythical human. These alternatives must not be delivered in top-down, ideological fashion, or generated solely by scientific elites and their acolytes.

Thus, my own inclination is to affirm activist and novelist Arundhati Roy's call for "small heroes" and for the "dismantling of the big": "Big bombs, big dams, big ideologies, big contradictions, big countries, big wars, big heroes, big mistakes." Perhaps, as she hopes, the twenty-first century will yet prove to be "the Century of the Small," the present infatuation with TED-talk-style "big ideas" notwithstanding.[168] To Roy's list of big ideologies to be decommissioned, I would add: "big science, big history, big story."[169] No one person, or even community of people, can provide a story for the rest of humanity, nor should they try. If indeed new stories emerge in times of crisis, as the new cosmologists (and perhaps Chakrabarty) believe, then let us listen carefully for emerging narratives, rather than resurrecting and imposing timeworn anthropic, universal, progressive, or scientistic storylines.

Consider a powerful environmental movement that is unfolding—in increasingly uncertain ways—as I write. Many indigenous people are standing up to environmental assaults on their sacred grounds, in places like Standing Rock, North Dakota, where approximately three hundred native tribes and their supporters gathered in 2016 to halt the Dakota Access Pipeline. Their cause has garnered support from a number of Christian denominations (as well as secular environmentalists who might well identify with nature spirituality). Is the story at Standing Rock about an emerging new religious movement, or are we witnessing long-held, traditional beliefs put into action? Does the strength of this movement lie in its diversity or its uniformity? These are complex questions that scholars will continue to sift through for years to come. It is possible to see in these events the coalescence of many stories into one overarching narrative, the development of a broad, quasi-religious coalition. Yet the narratives, beliefs, and rituals that animate this activism belong uniquely to the indigenous peoples themselves, in all of their diversity. Even among the many tribes who have banded together to oppose pipeline construction, no single cohesive narrative or set of beliefs binds them all. "It would be a mistake to characterize the new wave of indigenous activism as emanating from a uniform, codified theology," a journalist at Standing Rock argues.[170] Activists routinely insist that they speak only for themselves, and that "each tribe harbors its own unique spiritual traditions, practices, and customs forged over the course of centuries, if not millennia."[171] While these tribes share an earth-based orientation, each is tied to specific places—particular, familiar landscapes that can be seen, touched, and *experienced* as sacred. As one activist points out, religious groups argue among themselves about whether or not their God exists, "but I know my god exists. It's the mountain—I can *see* it."[172]

From the standpoint of the new cosmology, these myriad beliefs and practices would signal religions that remain too particular and parochial in their adherence to *somebody's* story rather than everybody's story. Haven't we moved "beyond the multiple stories of this mountain or that valley, of this or that tribe or nation or god," as Rue insists?[173] Like the so-called "earth cults" disparaged by Goodenough as problematically mystical and unscientific in orientation, these indigenous traditions and their unique knowledge systems would be judged as insufficiently grounded in a universal "cognitive reality"; lacking the "canon" of earth sciences as their central text, they have nothing to offer, Goodenough might say, but the dubious "authority of custom."[174]

Indigenous activists embrace a narrative that is both old and new, a story only they can tell. Demonstrators are actively engaged in creating new religious expressions, even as they draw on ancient beliefs and customs. Religion scholar Greg Johnson notes that younger generations of many tribal groups have adopted "a new set of chants, a new set of prayers" that are emanating from protest camps. "In this moment of crisis," he adds, "the religious tradition is catalyzed, activated, but most of all articulated—this is when it happens."[175] Crisis may indeed create new stories, songs, and forms of religious expression that help safeguard the Earth and motivate affection and action. But these forms will emerge organically and spontaneously. They will likely be—as they ought to be—the creation of religious practitioners *themselves,* not something handed down from religion scholars and scientists. Religious practitioners at Standing Rock do not experience themselves as existing in a chasm between an old story and a new story, as Thomas Berry's diagnosis uniformly assumes. They do not suffer from "amythia" and meaninglessness.

What they suffer from, principally, is climate change and colonialism. Indeed, their religious practices and environmental protests are inseparable from the experience of colonialism, as indigenous scholar Kyle Powys Whyte argues.[176] Halting the construction of pipelines is "a matter of climate justice and decolonization for indigenous peoples."[177] Because they are tied to particular places and particular species, indigenous peoples are impacted differently, and disproportionately. They are uniquely vulnerable to impacts of extractive industries because of the potential loss of their cultural, spiritual, and economic ties to specific environments and species. Their experiences and losses cannot be universalized, nor can their defense of sacred lands and traditional values be translated into—or derived from—a science-inspired story of the human-as-species.

A common story and unified, global ethic may sound appealing, particularly in times of great environmental and political upheaval. And yet, at the scale on which we live our lives—what Abram calls "the scale of our living bodies"—we encounter a world of incredible diversity, not uniformity; a world that "discloses itself to our senses not as a uniform planet inviting global principles and generalizations, but as this forested realm embraced by water, or a windswept prairie, or a desert silence."[178] A global, science-based story cannot do justice to the enormous variety of places, people, problems (and possible solutions) that are part of the richness and complexity of life on this planet. An overly strong sense of solidarity or sameness with others, such as might be engendered by a planetary perspective or anthropic cosmology, can actually obscure "the task and distinctive point of view of morality."[179] Wonder that preserves otherness makes it possible to act genuinely for the good of the other or with the other truly in mind. Nonexploitative, other-oriented dimensions of wonder create a space for genuine empathy rather than mere projection of one's own experience and perspective. Although empathy is often glossed as simply a shared point of view, virtuous empathy requires a separation of the self from another with whom one empathizes. It demands that we think or feel our way into the experience of others—human or otherwise—who are alien to us.

The sort of wonder I endorse here may not be comforting to some. It does not suggest that the universe, or even our planet, was made with our preferences in mind or that human life is inevitable in or central to its functioning. We are intimately related to a natural world that remains other and even alien, a world that operates independently of us, autonomously expressing recalcitrance and unpredictability, and behaving in ways both fascinating and inconvenient to us. All of this is fully consistent with what I believe to be a genuine sense of wonder.

Wonder is an invitation to remain open to many perspectives, experiences, and ways of knowing. We should therefore entertain and encourage a panoply of stories about this world of wonder, and its many possible meanings and truths, while recognizing that not all stories are good—for us, or for the more-than-human world—and that some are decidedly bad. Our receptivity to particular narratives will depend on what we hope to achieve. If, in the final analysis, we seek to foster intimacy, humility, and reverent care for the living world, it makes little sense to turn to the biggest possible picture, the cosmos on the largest temporal and spatial scale. We should not seek relationality in the remote recesses of space, or in a homogenized vision of the globe that shifts our focus away from where we feel ourselves to be embedded. We must not outsource our deepest values to these sweeping narratives whose abstract certainties we cannot inhabit with our senses, whose grand syntheses would negate the multifarious insights of both the sciences and human experience, and whose narrow forms of reality bar us from participation. To *make sense* of wonder is not to explain the world that engenders our awe-filled response, but to experience it in all its beauty, strangeness, and ambiguity.

NOTES

INTRODUCTION

1. Lisa H. Sideris, *Environmental Ethics, Ecological Theology, and Natural Selection* (New York: Columbia University Press, 2003).

2. Although Carson was for much of her later life not conventionally religious, there is an underlying spiritual dimension to her defense of nature and her account of nature's abiding mysteries, as scholars such as Bron Taylor, *Dark Green Religion: Nature Spirituality and the Planetary Future* (Berkeley: University of California Press, 2009), have noted. See also Lisa H. Sideris, "The Secular and Religious Sources of Rachel Carson's Sense of Wonder," in *Rachel Carson: Legacy and Challenge*," ed. Lisa H. Sideris and Kathleen Dean Moore (New York: State University of New York Press, 2008), 232–50.

3. On parallels between narrative projects in religious studies and those in environmental history (such as Big History), see Lisa H. Sideris, "'To know the story is to love it': Scientific Mythmaking and the Longing for Cosmic Connection," in *Methodological Challenges in Nature-Culture and Environmental History Research,* ed. Jocelyn Thorpe, Stephanie Rutherford, and L. Anders Sandberg (New York: Routledge, 2016).

4. The Unitarian Universalist (UU) church responds especially favorably to the new cosmology; Dowd and Barlow frequently preach to UU congregations. For an account of Unitarian Universalists' reception of the new cosmology (as well as a good overview of the connections among Dowd, Barlow, Berry, Swimme, and other thinkers) see Amy Hassinger, "Welcome to the Ecozoic Era," *UU World Magazine,* Spring 2006, www.uuworld.org/ideas /articles/2679.shtml.

5. Taylor, *Dark Green Religion.*

6. Chapters 4–6 provide a fuller account of the origins and development of the new cosmology.

7. Martin Eger, "The New Epic of Science and the Problem of Communication," in *Science, Understanding, and Justice,* ed. Abner Shimony (Chicago: Open Court, 2006), 287.

8. Exactly which cultures suffer from amythia is not always clear, but the Western industrialized world is typically implicated. Rue's work on amythia focuses specifically on Western culture.

9. Loyal D. Rue, *Amythia: Crisis in the Natural History of Western Culture* (Tuscaloosa: University of Alabama Press, 2004).

10. Thomas Berry, "The New Story: Comments on the Origin, Identification, and Transmission of Values," *Teilhard Studies* 1 (Winter 1978).

11. Edward O. Wilson, *On Human Nature* (Cambridge, MA: Harvard University Press, 1978), 201.

12. Michael Dowd, "New Theists: Knowers, Not Believers," *Huffington Post,* June 6, 2012, www.huffingtonpost.com/rev-michael-dowd/new-theists-knowers-not-believers_ b_1586301.html.

13. The majority are scholars of religion or the humanities. Even Dawkins, though trained as a professional biologist, is not a practicing scientist and has not really been for decades. Wilson, though active in biology and entomology, is by no means a typical scientist, but one who is best known for controversial, book-length pronouncements about human nature, religion and ethics, the disciplines and the nature of science, as well as his (more admirable) conservation agenda and activism. As celebrity scientists, Dawkins and Wilson in no way represent the scientific profession at large, and they are famous precisely because they engage, in fiercely polemical ways, with subject matter quite beyond their specialized knowledge.

14. See Curtis White, *The Science Delusion: Asking the Big Questions in a Culture of Easy Answers* (Brooklyn: Melville House, 2013).

15. Max Weber, "Science as a Vocation," in *Essays in Sociology,* ed. and trans. H. H. Gerth and C. Wright Mills (Oxford: Oxford University Press, 1946), 143.

16. Bruno Latour, "Telling Friends from Foes in the Anthropocene," in *The Anthropocene and the Environmental Crisis: Rethinking Modernity in a New Epoch,* ed. Clive Hamilton, Christophe Bonneuil, and François Gemenne (New York: Routledge, 2015). Latour means not just that the environmental crisis, and the Anthropocene concept, force us to confront our inextricability from "nature" but also that we cannot hope for some external, universal mode of Science to rescue us from the perspectival and socially embedded nature of our knowledge.

17. Christophe Bonneuil, "The Geological Turn: Narratives of the Anthropocene," in Hamilton et al., *The Anthropocene and the Environmental Crisis,* 29.

18. Here I have in mind the new cosmologists more narrowly construed—not necessarily Wilson or (especially) Dawkins, who occasionally *revel* in a lack of humility and celebrate what they see as the virtual omnipotence of science.

19. Donovan Schaefer, "Blessed, Precious Mistakes: Deconstruction, Evolution and New Atheism in America," *International Journal for Philosophy of Religion* 76, no. 1 (2014): 76.

20. Edward O. Wilson, foreword to *Everybody's Story: Wising Up to the Epic of Evolution,* by Loyal D. Rue (Albany: State University of New York Press, 2000), x.

21. Ursula Goodenough, *The Sacred Depths of Nature* (Oxford: Oxford University Press, 1998), xv.

22. Brian Thomas Swimme, "The New Story," www.youtube.com/watch?v = TRykk_oovIo.

23. Rue, *Everybody's Story,* 38.

24. Mary Evelyn Tucker, "Religion and Ecology," in *The Good in Nature and Humanity: Connecting Science, Religion, and Spirituality in the Natural World*, ed. Stephen R. Kellert and Timothy Farnham (Washington, DC: Island Press, 2002), 75.

25. Edward O. Wilson, *Consilience: The Unity of Knowledge* (New York: Vintage, 1998), 3. Emphasis mine.

26. Mark Gray, "Letter to the *Atlantic*," *Atlantic Online*, July 1998, www.theatlantic.com /past/docs/issues/98jul/9807lett.htm.

27. Specifically, in Keats's words, negative capability—which he believed Coleridge lacked—is present "when a man is capable of being in uncertainties, Mysteries, doubts without any irritable reaching after fact and reason." John Keats, *The Complete Poetical Works and Letters of John Keats, Cambridge Edition*, ed. Horace Elisha Scudder (New York: Houghton Mifflin, 1899), 277. Not surprisingly, Dawkins goes after Keats with both barrels in *Unweaving the Rainbow* (Boston: Houghton Mifflin, 1998).

28. Brian Thomas Swimme and Mary Evelyn Tucker, *Journey of the Universe* (New Haven, CT: Yale University Press, 2011), 5.

29. Wilson, *Consilience*, 7.

30. Philip Hefner, quoted in "Does the Epic Need Art?" ed. Ursula Goodenough, *Epic of Evolution Journal* (Fall 1998): 19, http://thegreatstory.org/Epic-Evol-Journal.html.

31. Wilson, *Consilience*, 289.

32. Jonathan Gottschall and David Sloan Wilson, eds., *The Literary Animal: Evolution and the Nature of Narrative* (Evanston, IL: Northwestern University Press, 2005); see also Edward Slingerland and Mark Collard, eds., *Creating Consilience: Integrating the Sciences and Humanities* (Oxford: Oxford University Press, 2011).

33. Loyal D. Rue and Ursula Goodenough, "A Consilient Curriculum," in *The Epic of Evolution: Science's Story and Humanity's Response*, ed. Cheryl Genet et al. (Santa Margarita, CA: Collins Foundation Press, 2009), 175–82.

34. Thomas Berry, "The Viable Human," in *The Great Work: Our Way Into the Future* (New York: Random House, 1999), 71.

35. Wilson, *Consilience*, 7.

1. SEEKING WHAT IS GOOD IN WONDER

1. Mary-Jane Rubenstein, *Strange Wonder: The Closure of Metaphysics and the Opening of Awe* (New York: Columbia University Press, 2010), 10.

2. Sam Keen, *Apology for Wonder* (New York: HarperCollins, 1973), 28.

3. See Edmund Burke, *A Philosophical Enquiry into the Origin of Our Ideas of the Sublime and the Beautiful*, ed. J. T. Boulton (London: Routledge and Paul, 1958).

4. Lorraine Daston and Katharine Park, *Wonders and the Order of Nature* (New York: Zone Books, 2001), 21.

5. Keen, *Apology for Wonder*, 30.

6. Robert C. Fuller, *Wonder: From Emotion to Spirituality* (Chapel Hill: University of North Carolina Press, 2006), 77.

7. Keen, *Apology for Wonder*, 212.

8. Philip Fisher, *Wonder, the Rainbow, and the Aesthetics of Rare Experiences* (Cambridge, MA: Harvard University Press, 2003), 17.

9. Ibid., 6.

10. Rachel Carson, *The Sense of Wonder* (1965; repr., New York: Harper, 1998), 54.

11. Ronald W. Hepburn, "Wonder," in *Wonder and Other Essays: Eight Studies in Aesthetics and Neighboring Fields* (Edinburgh: University of Edinburgh Press, 1984), 135.

12. Ibid.

13. Carson, *Sense of Wonder*, 56.

14. Carson writes of the "rush of remembered delight that" comes with the first scent of, for example, the sea at low tide. "For the sense of smell, almost more than any other, has the power to recall memories and it is a pity that we use it so little." *Sense of Wonder*, 83.

15. Keen, *Apology for Wonder*, 22.

16. Ibid., 32.

17. Ibid., 25.

18. Daston and Park, *Wonders and the Order of Nature*, 317.

19. Fisher, *Wonder, the Rainbow.*

20. Marie George, "Wonder as a Source of Philosophy and of Science: A Comparison," *Philosophy in Science* 6 (1995): 99–100.

21. George sees similarities between science and philosophy, insofar as both seek understanding (though in different ways) and are not satisfied with gaping wonder or unverifiable explanations. Silverman maintains that it is characteristic of a philosopher also merely to gape in wonder, whereas science is not content to do so. Not surprisingly, George is a philosopher, whereas Silverman, of course, is a scientist.

22. M. P. Silverman, "Two Sides of Wonder: Philosophical Keys to the Motivation of Science Learning," *Synthèse* 80, no. 1 (July 1989): 44.

23. George, "Wonder as a Source," 101.

24. Daston and Park, *Wonders and the Order of Nature*, 321.

25. Ibid., 311.

26. Ibid.

27. I rely here on Daston and Park's impressive work on this subject.

28. Ibid., 110.

29. Ibid., 120 (emphasis mine).

30. Ibid., 122.

31. Ibid., 307.

32. Ibid., 124.

33. Ibid., 125.

34. Ibid., 304.

35. Ibid., 305.

36. See for example Caroline Merchant, *The Death of Nature: Women, Ecology, and the Scientific Revolution* (San Francisco: Harper and Row, 1980).

37. Daston and Park, *Wonders and the Order of Nature*, 321.

38. Ibid.

39. Ibid., 323.

40. Quoted in Daston and Park, *Wonders and the Order of Nature*, 325.

41. Ibid.

42. Ibid., 328.

43. Rubenstein writes that wonder's multifaceted moral and aesthetic dimensions have become "decimated—or, more precisely, fervently repressed—by the modern brand of wonder that connotes white bread, lunchbox superheroes, and fifties sitcoms." *Strange Wonder,* 10.

44. Rubenstein, *Strange Wonder,* 16.

45. Daston and Park, *Wonders and the Order of Nature,* 325.

46. Jesse Prinz, "How Wonder Works," *Aeon,* June 21, 2013, https://aeon.co/essays/why-wonder-is-the-most-human-of-all-emotions.

47. Ibid.

48. Daston and Park, *Wonders and the Order of Nature,* 297.

49. Rachel Carson to Dorothy Freeman, February 1, 1958, in *Always, Rachel: The Letters of Rachel Carson and Dorothy Freeman, 1952–1964,* ed. Martha Freeman (Boston: Beacon Press, 1995), 249.

50. Fisher, *Wonder, the Rainbow,* 100.

51. Ibid., 119.

52. Bill Vitek and Wes Jackson, eds., *The Virtues of Ignorance: Complexity, Sustainability, and the Limits of Knowledge* (Lexington: University Press of Kentucky, 2008).

53. Craig Holdrege, "Can We See with Fresh Eyes? Beyond a Culture of Abstraction," in Vitek and Jackson, *Virtues of Ignorance,* 326–27.

54. Keen, *Apology for Wonder,* 24.

55. Ibid., 31.

56. Ibid., 26.

57. Caroline Walker Bynum, "Wonder," *American Historical Review* 102, no. 1 (February 1997): 3.

58. Bynum, "Wonder," 12.

59. Loren Eiseley, *The Unexpected Universe* (New York: Harcourt and Brace, 1964).

60. Rubenstein, *Strange Wonder,* 8.

2. THE BOOK OF NATURE AND THE BOOK OF SCIENCE

EPIGRAPH: Quoted in Stephen S. Hall, "Darwin's Rottweiler—Sir Richard Dawkins: Evolution's Fiercest Champion, Far Too Fierce," *Discover Magazine,* September 8, 2005, http://discovermagazine.com/2005/sep/darwins-rottweiler.

1. Hanni Muerdter, "The Wonder of Science," *Conservation Biology* 19, no. 4 (2005): 987.

2. Ibid., 988.

3. Ibid.

4. Ibid.

5. Deane-Drummond's account of wisdom is far more nuanced and multifaceted than this, but it is her focus on wisdom's powers of discernment that interests me here. Knowledge is only part of wisdom; experience and insight, combined with an awareness that knowledge is not complete and that there is much we still can learn, are important facets of wisdom as it interacts with wonder.

6. Celia Deane-Drummond, *Wonder and Wisdom: Conversations in Science, Spirituality, and Theology* (Philadelphia: Templeton Foundation Press, 2006), 14.

7. Chris Mooney, "Spirituality Can Bridge Science-Religion Divide," *USA Today*, September 12, 2010, http://usatoday30.usatoday.com/news/opinion/forum/2010–09–13-column13 _ST_N.htm.

8. Celia Deane-Drummond, "Experiencing Wonder and Seeking Wisdom," *Zygon: Journal of Religion and Science* 42, no. 3 (2007): 587.

9. Richard Dawkins, "Is Science a Religion?" *Humanist*, January/February 1997, 26–29, 27.

10. With apologies to Neil Young for the paraphrase.

11. Philip Fisher, *Wonder, the Rainbow, and the Aesthetics of Rare Experiences* (Cambridge, MA: Harvard University Press, 2003), 11.

12. Ibid., 16.

13. Richard Dawkins, *Unweaving the Rainbow* (Boston: Houghton Mifflin, 1998), xi.

14. Fisher, *Wonder, the Rainbow*, 60.

15. Dawkins, *Unweaving the Rainbow*, xi.

16. Ibid., 42.

17. Ibid., x.

18. Richard Dawkins, "Science, Delusion, and the Appetite for Wonder" (Richard Dimbleby Lecture for BBC 1 Television, November 12, 1996), www.andrew.cmu.edu/user /jksadegh/A%20Good%20Atheist%20Secularist%20Skeptical%20Book%20Collection /Science_Delusion_and_the_Appetite_for_Wonder_by_Dawkins.pdf.

19. John Grim suggested this phrase during a lengthy discussion about wonder and science.

20. Dawkins, *Unweaving the Rainbow*, 23–24.

21. Ibid., 21–22.

22. Ibid., 23.

23. Ibid.

24. Lorraine J. Daston and Katharine Park, *Wonders and the Order of Nature* (New York: Zone Books, 2001), 228.

25. Ibid., 323.

26. Ibid.

27. Dawkins, "Science, Delusion, and the Appetite for Wonder."

28. Dawkins, *Unweaving the Rainbow*, 23.

29. Richard Dawkins, *A Devil's Chaplain: Reflections on Hope, Lies, Science, and Love* (Boston: Houghton Mifflin, 2003), 43.

30. See Lisa H. Sideris, "Contested Wonder: Biological Reductionism and Children's Nature Education," *Journal of Religion and Society*, Supplement Series 11 (2015): 193–205.

31. Ibid., 242.

32. Richard Dawkins, *Unweaving the Rainbow*, 141.

33. Melvin Konner, "One Man's Rainbow," *Scientific American*, March 1999, 108.

34. Alison Flood, "Richard Dawkins Targets Teenagers with Myth-busting Illustrated Book," *Guardian*, October 23, 2009, www.theguardian.com/science/2009/oct/23/richard-dawkins-teenagers-illustrated-book.

35. Richard Dawkins, *The Magic of Reality: How We Know What's Really True* (New York: Free Press, 2011), 31.

36. Ibid., 21.

37. Dawkins, *Unweaving the Rainbow*, 29.

38. Richard Dawkins and David Attenborough, "Of Mind and Matter: David Attenborough Meets Richard Dawkins," *Guardian,* September 10, 2010, www.theguardian.com/science/2010/sep/11/science-david-attenborough-richard-dawkins.

39. Dawkins, *Devil's Chaplain,* 231.

40. Dawkins rejects the idea that public science demonstrations should be made "relevant" to ordinary people's lives, to what goes on in their own kitchen or bathroom." Dawkins, *Unweaving the Rainbow,* 22. Of course "real science," as Dawkins understands it, is hard to demonstrate publicly.

41. For example, Hepburn attributes such negative views of wonder to Adam Smith. Ronald W. Hepburn, *Wonder and Other Essays: Eight Studies in Aesthetics and Neighboring Fields* (Edinburgh: Edinburgh University Press, 1984), 132.

42. M. P. Silverman, "Two Sides of Wonder: Philosophical Keys to the Motivation of Science Learning," *Synthese* 80, no. 1 (July 1989): 44.

43. Ibid., 49.

44. Ibid. Silverman, while appearing to share Dawkins's criticism of "gaping" wonder, acknowledges that children innately display both types of wonder—the investigative type and the unscientific, stunned variety—and appreciates that children naturally see magic in the world around them.

45. Alfred North Whitehead, *Science and the Modern World* (1925; repr., New York: Free Press, 1997), 54.

46. Richard Dawkins, *The Oxford Book of Modern Science Writing* (Oxford: Oxford University Press, 2008), 138.

47. John D. Boswell, "Symphony of Science" (music video), posted October 22, 2015, www.symphonyofscience.com.

48. See for example Richard Dawkins, *The God Delusion* (Boston: Houghton Mifflin, 2006). The concern with shattering magical / religious illusions (and similar language) is displayed in another neo-atheist treatise: Daniel C. Dennett, *Breaking the Spell: Religion as a Natural Phenomenon* (London: Penguin, 2007).

49. I will not pursue this here, but Dawkins particularly considers Stephen Jay Gould a bad poet (in the sense of mis- or overusing metaphors), and he hints that Darwin was no good either, though he tried "manfully" to translate science into poetry. Many scholars, writers, and even poets would take issue with the latter assertion, if not the former, as do I.

50. Dawkins, *Unweaving the Rainbow,* 180.

51. Ibid., 181.

52. Ibid., 184.

53. Ibid., 17.

54. Ibid., 18.

55. Ibid., 17 (emphasis mine).

56. Quoted in Fisher, *Wonder, the Rainbow.*

57. Ibid., 118.

58. Richard Dawkins, *The Selfish Gene,* introduction to 30th Anniversary Edition (Oxford: Oxford University Press, 2006), xiii.

59. Edward O. Wilson, *On Human Nature* (Cambridge, MA: Harvard University Press, 1978).

60. Edward O. Wilson, *Consilience: The Unity of Knowledge* (New York: Vintage, 1998).

61. Dawkins, *Unweaving the Rainbow,* x.

62. Curtis White, *The Science Delusion: Asking the Big Questions in a Culture of Easy Answers* (Brooklyn: Melville House, 2014).

63. Mary Evelyn Tucker and Brian Thomas Swimme, *Journey of the Universe* (New Haven, CT: Yale University Press, 2011), 23.

64. CNRS, "Elliptical Galaxies Are Not Dead," *Science Daily,* June 1, 2011, www.sciencedaily .com/releases/2011/07/110726093156.htm.

65. Marie George, "Wonder as a Source of Philosophy and of Science: A Comparison," *Philosophy in Science* 6 (1995): 108.

66. Dawkins, *Unweaving the Rainbow,* 36.

67. Philip Kitcher, "Militant Modern Atheism," *Journal of Applied Philosophy* 28, no. 1 (2011): 1–13.

68. Ibid., 11.

69. Ibid.

70. Dennis Quinn, *Iris Exiled: A Synoptic History of Wonder* (Lanham, MD: University Press of America, 2002), 230.

71. Kenneth Brower, "The Danger of Cosmic Genius," *Atlantic,* December 2010, www .theatlantic.com/magazine/archive/2010/12/the-danger-of-cosmic-genius/308306/.

72. Freeman Dyson, "Progress in Religion," *Edge,* May 16, 2000, http://edge.org/conversation /progress-in-religion.

73. Quoted in Lauren Redniss, "The Beautiful Mind of Freeman Dyson," *Discover Magazine,* June 2008, http://discovermagazine.com/2008/jun/09-the-beautiful-mind-of-freeman-dyson.

74. Freeman Dyson, "Our Biotech Future," *New York Review of Books,* July 19, 2007, www.nybooks.com/articles/archives/2007/jul/19/our-biotech-future/.

75. Ibid., 12.

76. Ibid., 11.

77. Ibid.

78. It seems odd that excessive faith in progress and science would lead Dyson to *doubt* some of the science of climate change. The explanation lies, in part, in Dyson's appraisal of environmentalism as a religion, not rational, and hence something unscientific, as Brower hints. See chapter 7 for more on how faith in scientific progress undermines concern with climate change.

79. Brower, "Danger of Cosmic Genius," 12.

80. Ibid.

81. Richard Dawkins and David Attenborough, "Of Mind and Matter."

82. Ibid.

83. Ibid.

84. Ibid.

85. Dawkins, "Is Science a Religion?" 27.

86. Richard Dawkins, "Growing Up in Ethology," *Edge,* December 17, 2009, http://edge .org/conversation/growing-up-in-ethology.

87. Richard Dawkins, interview by Riz Khan, *Al Jazeera One on One,* January 9, 2010, www.aljazeera.com/programmes/oneonone/2010/01/201015101057987686.html.

88. Quoted in Hall, "Darwin's Rottweiler."

89. Dawkins, *Magic of Reality*, 147.

90. Rachel Carson, *The Sense of Wonder* (1965; repr., New York: Harper, 1998).

91. Edward O. Wilson, *Naturalist* (Washington, DC: Island Press, 1994), xii.

3. E. O. WILSON'S IONIAN ENCHANTMENT

1. See Ullica Segerstrale, "Wilson and the Unification of Science," *Annals New York Academy of Sciences* 1093 (2006): 46–73.

2. Penny Sarchet, "E. O. Wilson: Religious Faith Is Dragging Us Down," *New Scientist*, January 21, 2015, www.newscientist.com/article/mg22530050-400-e-o-wilson-religious-faith-is-dragging-us-down/.

3. Edward O. Wilson, *Half-Earth: Our Planet's Fight for Life* (New York: Liveright, 2016).

4. Peter H. Kahn and Stephen R. Kellert, eds., *Children and Nature: Psychological, Sociocultural, and Evolutionary Investigations* (Cambridge, MA: MIT Press, 2002).

5. Edward O. Wilson, *Naturalist* (Washington, DC: Island Press, 1994), 11.

6. Edward O. Wilson, *Anthill* (New York: W. W. Norton, 2010), 140, 152.

7. Wilson's comments were made to an audience in Aspen in March 2008 and are excerpted in a brief article in the online magazine *Grist*. Lisa Hymas, "E. O. Wilson Calls for Kids to be Set Free Outside, Scripted Activities be Damned," *Grist*, April 2, 2008, www.grist .org/article/aspen-envt-forum-soccer-moms-are-the-enemy-of-biological-education.

8. See for example Wendell Berry, *Life Is a Miracle: An Essay against Modern Superstition* (Washington, DC: Counterpoint, 2000); Howard L Kaye, "Consilience: E. O. Wilson's Confession of Faith," *Politics and the Life Sciences* 18, no. 2 (September 1999): 344–46; Stephen Jay Gould, *The Hedgehog, the Fox, and the Magister's Pox: Mending the Gap between Science and the Humanities* (New York: Harmony Books, 2003); Mary Midgley, "A Well-Meaning Cannibal," *Commonweal*, July 17, 1998, 23; Dale Jamieson, "Cheerleading for Science," *Issues in Science and Technology* 15, no. 1 (Fall 1998): 90; John Dupré, "Unification Not Proved," *Science* 280, no. 5368 (May 29, 1998): 1395; Richard Rorty, "Against Unity," *Wilson Quarterly* 22 (Winter 1998): 28–38.

9. Group selection is the idea that evolution is driven by differential survival of entire groups of organisms, not merely individuals. See Edward O. Wilson, *The Social Conquest of Earth* (New York: Liveright, 2013).

10. Edward O. Wilson, *The Meaning of Human Existence* (New York: Liveright, 2014), 150.

11. Some Epic of Evolution advocates trace this phrase back to Loren Eiseley and / or Julian Huxley, and in some cases Goethe.

12. "The Epic of Evolution," http://epicofevolution.com/about/about-the-epic

13. Edward O. Wilson, *Consilience: The Unity of Knowledge* (New York: Vintage, 1998), 6.

14. Mark Stoll, "Edward Osborne Wilson," in *Eminent Lives in Twentieth-Century Science and Religion*, ed. Nicolaas A. Rupke (Frankfurt am Main: Peter Lang, 2009), 333.

15. Vassiliki Betty Smocovitis, "The Tormenting Desire for Unity," *Journal of the History of Biology* 32 (1991): 385–94.

16. For a detailed discussion of the differences between Wilson's and Whewell's use of consilience, see Gould, *The Hedgehog, the Fox, and the Magister's Pox*.

17. Ibid., 192.

18. Quoted in George Levine, *Darwin Loves You: Natural Selection and the Re-Enchantment of the World* (Princeton, NJ: Princeton University Press, 2008), 117.

19. Gould, *The Hedgehog, the Fox, and the Magister's Pox*, 192.

20. Edward O. Wilson, *On Human Nature* (Cambridge, MA: Harvard University Press, 1978), 192–93.

21. Ibid., 200–201.

22. Wilson, *Consilience*, 293.

23. Ionian Enchantment refers to the ideas of Thales of Miletus, in Ionia, in the sixth century BC, Wilson explains. It entails metaphysical beliefs about the "material basis of the world and the unity of nature." Wilson, *Consilience*, 5.

24. Ibid., x.

25. Ibid., 5.

26. Ibid.

27. Ibid., 6, 11.

28. Ibid., 295.

29. Ibid., 230.

30. Ibid.

31. Ibid., 5.

32. Ibid., 291.

33. H. Allen Orr, "The Big Picture," *Boston Review*, October / November 1998, http://bostonreview.net/BR23.5/Orr.html.

34. Wilson, *Consilience*, 291 (emphasis mine).

35. Ibid., 138.

36. Ibid., 105.

37. Ibid., 237.

38. Ibid., 230–33.

39. The "discovery" of epigenetic rules, at least at the present time, is arrived at primarily by observations of human behavior, over time and across cultures. Adaptive advantages that might attend these rules are then specified. (For example, if most humans have a fear of snakes, and fear of snakes leads to avoidance of them, then there is definite survival value to this near-universal behavior.) Wilson may be right that a "complete" knowledge of the brain would lessen the circularity and ad hoc nature of these kinds of arguments.

40. Ibid., 246.

41. Ronald W. Hepburn, *Wonder and Other Essays: Eight Studies in Aesthetics and Neighboring Fields* (Edinburgh: Edinburgh University Press, 1984), 137.

42. Wilson, *Consilience*, 295.

43. Ibid., 72.

44. Edward O. Wilson, "Divisive Ideas on 'Unification,'" *Los Angeles Times*, July 9, 1998, http://articles.latimes.com/1998/jul/09/local/me-2107.

45. See Robert Wright, *Three Scientists and Their Gods: Looking for Meaning in an Age of Information* (New York: Times Books, 1988).

46. H. Allen Orr, "The Big Picture," *Boston Review*, October 1, 1998, http://bostonreview.net/BR23.5/Orr.html.

47. Wilson, *Consilience*, 9.

48. Ibid.

49. Ibid.

50. Later on, I will also touch on the role of consilient ideas in the area of religious studies and ethics; however, a sustained discussion of the impact of consilient ideas on religion / environmental ethics—in the form of the Epic of Evolution and the Universe Story—is reserved for chapters 4–6.

51. Linda Weiner and Ramsey Eric Ramsey, *Leaving Us to Wonder: An Essay on the Questions Science Cannot Ask* (Albany: State University of New York Press, 2005), 5.

52. Ibid.

53. George's work has received numerous awards from Templeton, and this particular essay was awarded a Templeton Foundation prize (1994) for "humility theology," a form of humble inquiry that is especially cognizant of human finitude and that refrains from exulting in the power and glory of science. My own take is rather different. Although George's typology of wonder is instructive—I utilize it in certain places throughout this book—I strongly disagree with many of the conclusions she draws from that typology. George is remarkably uncritical of some blatantly arrogant and unsupported claims to totalizing knowledge made by scientists. She imputes to scientists theological motives where they are not obviously present, in order to buttress the claim that humility undergirds their endeavors.

54. Marie George, "Wonder as a Source of Philosophy and of Science: A Comparison," *Philosophy in Science* 6 (1995): 102.

55. Ibid., 105.

56. Ibid., 111.

57. Richard Dawkins, A *Devil's Chaplain: Reflections on Hope, Lies, Science, and Love* (Boston: Houghton Mifflin, 2003), 6.

58. Ibid.

59. Wilson, *Consilience*, 94.

60. Ibid.

61. Ibid., 12.

62. Jon Adams, *Interference Patterns: Literary Study, Scientific Knowledge, and Disciplinary Autonomy* (New York: Bucknell University Press, 2007), 27.

63. Wilson's account of philosophy is strongly reminiscent of the "important distinction" that Mark Silverman defends between science and philosophy. Both are stimulated by wonder, but "the scientist goes beyond 'gapes and stares' employing his experimental and mathematical resources in an effort to understand in some more profound way the significance of his observations." Silverman, "Two Sides of Wonder: Philosophical Keys to the Motivation of Science Learning," *Synthese* 80, no. 1 (1989): 44.

64. See for example Brian Boyd's review essay "Literature and Science: Doomed Reduction or Evolutionary Literary Pluralism?" *Evolutionary Psychology* 6, no. 1 (2008): 80–84.

65. Mary Midgley, "Rival Fatalisms: The Hollowness of the Sociobiology Debate," in *Sociobiology Examined,* ed. A. Montagu (New York: Oxford University Press, 1980), 25.

66. For a clear account of the important differences between Wilson's form of unified knowledge and the more modest "unity of science" approach defended by philosophers such as Hilary Putnam, see Adams, *Interference Patterns,* 23–38.

67. Wilson, *Consilience*, 5

68. Philip Kitcher, "Unification as a Regulative Ideal," *Perspectives on Science* 7, no. 3 (1999): 337–48. See also John Dupré, "Unification Not Proved," *Science* 280, no. 5368 (May 29, 1998): 1395. Other critics of unity include Ian Hacking and Nancy Cartwright.

69. Adams, *Interference Patterns*, 26.

70. Ibid.

71. Edward Slingerland, *What Science Offers the Humanities: Integrating Body and Culture* (Cambridge: Cambridge University Press, 2008), 301.

72. This "second wave" of consilience entails, for example, some movement away from eliminative reductionism (English departments will not be folded into neuroscience) and a softening of scientists' chauvinism toward the humanities; it also means deemphasis of the Pleistocene brain as the reference point for interpreting human behavior and preferences. My own impression is that the second wave represents a (welcome) change in tone more than a change in actual methodology and bedrock assumptions (for example, see the chapter on "Paleolithic Politics in British Novels of the Nineteenth Century" in which the caveman brain remains central). The volume is notable for its inclusion of dissenting voices to the consilience project, and an afterword by Geoffrey Harpham—in which he equates the success of consilience with the death of all mystery—sounds a particularly ambivalent note. Edward Slingerland and Mark Collard, eds., *Creating Consilience: Integrating the Sciences and the Humanities* (Oxford: Oxford University Press, 2011).

73. Slingerland, *What Science Offers*, 301.

74. Ibid., 301.

75. Wilson, *Consilience*, 233.

76. Ibid., 231.

77. C. Gabrielle Starr, "Evolved Reading and the Science(s) of Literary Study," *Critical Inquiry* 38, no. 2 (Winter 2012): 418–25.

78. See David Barash and Nanelle Barash, *Madame Bovary's Ovaries* (New York: Delacorte Press, 2005); Jonathan Gottschall and David Sloan Wilson, eds., *The Literary Animal: Evolution and the Nature of Narrative* (Evanston, IL: Northwestern University Press, 2005). Published prior to *Consilience* but inspired by sociobiology is Robert Storey, *Mimesis and the Human Animal: On the Biogenetic Foundations of Literary Representation* (Evanston, IL: Northwestern University Press, 1996).

79. Brian Boyd, *On the Origin of Stories: Evolution, Cognition, and Fiction* (Cambridge, MA: Belknap Press, 2010).

80. E. O. Wilson, foreword to Gottschall and Wilson, *Literary Animal*, viii.

81. In an intriguing departure from usual academic practice, promotional blurbs on the back cover of *The Literary Animal* were garnered not from outside reviewers but excerpted verbatim from essays in the book itself (to be sure, the endorsements are judiciously drawn from famous contributors—McEwan, Frederick Crews, and E. O. Wilson himself). Should readers conclude that persecution of literary Darwinists is so pervasive that a fair and cool-headed appraisal from colleagues in the broader field is out of the question?

82. Orr, "Big Picture."

83. For a more thorough discussion of the pitfalls of literary Darwinism see Jonathan Kramnick, "Against Literary Darwinism," *Critical Inquiry* 37, no. 2 (Winter 2011): 315–47. In his response to Kramnick's critique, Brian Boyd rejects the label "literary Darwinism," and

identifies himself with the term "evocriticism"—a more sophisticated and nuanced version of literary Darwinism. Evocritics, he claims, take more seriously the plasticity of the brain and the way in which evolution shaped our brains to be "reshapeable." Forms of evolutionary psychology / literary Darwinism that Boyd and other evocritics reject remain too enamored of nativist conceptions and computational models of "hard mental modularity" (such as the existence of literary modules). Boyd maintains that evocritics also question the idea that the Pleistocene represents the "Prime Era of Evolutionary Adaptedness." See Boyd's (and others') responses to Kramnick's critique of literary Darwinism in *Critical Inquiry* 38, no. 2 (Winter 2012): 388–460.

84. William Deresiewicz, "Adaptation: On Literary Darwinism," *Nation*, May 20, 2009, www.thenation.com/issue/june-8-2009#.

85. Kramnick, "Against Literary Darwinism," 325.

86. Boyd, *Origin of Stories*, 121.

87. Slingerland and Collard, *Creating Consilience*, 18.

88. Travis Landry, "The Taming of *The Literary Animal*," *Evolutionary Psychology* 4 (2006): 49–56.

89. Wilson, *Consilience*, 233.

90. Joseph Carroll, "Evolutionary Studies," in *The Encyclopedia of Literary and Cultural Theory*, ed. Michael Ryan, Gregory Castle, Robert Eaglestone, M. Keith Booker (Chichester, West Sussex: Wiley Blackwell, 2011), 610.

91. See the example of scientific accounts of beauty discussed in Wiener and Ramsey, *Leaving Us to Wonder*.

92. Deresiewicz, "Adaptation."

93. Leda Cosmides and John Tooby, "Evolutionary Psychology: A Primer," University of California–Santa Barbara, January 13, 1997, www.cep.ucsb.edu/primer.html.

94. Ibid.

95. Orr, "Big Picture."

96. Ibid.

97. Wilson, *Consilience*, 34.

98. Ibid., 105. As far as I can tell, Wilson believes that science and technology will help to fill in the gaps and blind spots inherent in our evolved brains: "The mind unaided by factual knowledge from science sees the world only in little pieces" (ibid.). With the appropriate aids, the big picture will be apprehended.

99. Whether or not all literary Darwinists argue for the "hard" mental modular account of our storytelling capacities, some Epic of Evolutionist proponents clearly do, most notably Loyal Rue, whose work I discuss in detail in the next chapter.

100. Connie Barlow, *Green Space, Green Time: The Way of Science* (New York: Copernicus, 1997), 27.

101. I have found that such perceptions of the role of the humanities are fairly widespread among scientists. At a conference populated mostly by ecologists that I attended (as a representative of religion and ethics), many scientists understood the humanities to deal in some vague way with "texts" or stories, while scientists deal with data. More than once, a scientist expressed exasperation at trying and failing to get data (in this case, regarding environmental problems) out to the mainstream public; these scientists felt that the lack of public response was the fault of the *humanities,* whose job is to make information *accessible,*

to translate it or render it interesting, appealing, or digestible to the public. As one scientist said, he and his science colleagues had done their research, published their data, and were still waiting for scholars in the humanities to "pick up the baton" that science had passed to them. I left the conference with the impression that many scientists expect the humanities to function as science journalism.

102. Wilson, *On Human Nature*, 201.

103. Wilson, *Consilience*, 8.

104. Ibid., 291.

105. Ibid., 47.

106. Ibid., 13.

107. Neil Evernden, *The Natural Alien: Humankind and Environment* (Toronto: University of Toronto Press, 1993).

108. Wilson, *On Human Nature*, 204 (emphasis mine).

109. Edward Slingerland, "Who's Afraid of Reductionism? The Study of Religion in the Age of Cognitive Science," *Journal of the American Academy of Religion* 76, no. 2 (2008): 375–411, 393.

110. Ibid., 382.

111. Attributing agency to objects can confer great survival advantages: imagine our ancestors' perception that a predator in the bush had the imminent intention of attacking. Attributing agency in such situations leads to taking evasive action and thus surviving such encounters. However, when agency detection runs amok (creating what psychologists term Hyperactive Agency Detection Devices) it can foster dangerous and maladaptive illusions, such as what Dawkins calls the God delusion—the attribution of divine agency to meaningless physical forces in the world around us. In such cases, the application of an evolutionary rule of thumb—attributing agency to objects—becomes dysfunctional.

112. Slingerland, "Who's Afraid of Reductionism?" 375–411, 393.

113. Ibid., 399 (emphasis mine).

114. It is precisely this mistake that Charles Taylor falls into, according to Slingerland's analysis. "If human reality is indeed real for us, why not follow Taylor and say that it is just as real as anything studied by the natural sciences?" Ibid., 400.

115. Ibid., 400 (emphasis mine).

116. Ibid., 404.

117. Ibid.

118. Ibid., 401.

119. In their response to Slingerland, Francisca Cho and Richard K. Squier also pick up on this problem in "Reductionism: Be Afraid, Be Very Afraid," *Journal of the American Academy of Religion* 76, no. 2 (2008): 412–17.

120. Slingerland, "Who's Afraid of Reductionism?" 404 (emphasis mine).

121. Wilson, *On Human Nature*, 204.

122. Ibid., 206.

123. Ibid., 280.

124. Ibid., 207.

125. Ibid., 193.

126. Ibid., 207.

127. Wilson, *Consilience*, 289.

128. Ibid., 286.

129. Ibid., 289.

130. Wilson, *On Human Nature*, 201.

131. The phrase is in Mary Midgley, "Evolution as a Religion," *Zygon* 22, no. 2 (June 1987): 192.

132. Wilson, *On Human Nature*, 192.

133. Wilson, *Consilience*, 289 (emphasis mine).

134. Ibid., 200.

135. Wilson, *On Human Nature*, 193.

136. Wilson, *Consilience*, 290 (emphasis mine).

137. Wilson, *On Human Nature*, 203.

138. As we will see, Connie Barlow suggests something very like this possibility of human immortality through the scientific quest, in the form of what she calls the "story" of the story, or the story of how human discovery is progressively revealing a true Epic of Evolution.

139. For a discussion of Wilson's anthropocentrism, see James Gustafson, "Sociobiology: A Secular Theology," *Hastings Center Report* 9, no. 1 (February 1979): 44–45.

140. Wilson, *On Human Nature*, 204.

141. George, "Wonder as a Source of Philosophy and of Science," 111.

142. Ibid., 113.

143. Ibid.

144. Silverman, "Two Sides of Wonder," 44.

145. George, "Wonder as a Source of Philosophy and of Science," 111.

146. Lorraine J. Daston and Katharine Park, *Wonders and the Order of Nature* (New York: Zone Books, 2001), 325.

147. In Wilson's 2016 work, *Half-Earth*, he revisits the dialogue between God and Job. He still confidently asserts that humans have solved the great mysteries of life with which God challenged Job. But now—apparently chastened by the Anthropocene epoch that places humans in a godlike position—Wilson seems to perceive possible dangers of the godlike portrait in which he has been heavily invested for decades. *Half-Earth*, 11–12.

148. Wilson, *On Human Nature*, 202 (emphasis mine).

149. Stoll, "Edward Osborne Wilson," in Rupke, *Eminent Lives*, 342.

150. Howard L. Kaye, "Consilience: E. O. Wilson's Confession of Faith," *Politics and the Life Sciences* 18, no. 2 (September 1999): 134–5.

151. John Horgan, *The End of Science: Facing the Limits of Knowledge in the Twilight of the Scientific Age* (New York: Broadway Books, 1997), 147–48.

152. Wilson, *Consilience*, 13.

153. Ibid., 73.

154. Mary-Jane Rubenstein, *Strange Wonder: The Closure of Metaphysics and the Opening of Awe* (New York: Columbia University Press, 2010), 16.

155. Daston and Park, *Wonders and the Order of Nature*, 124.

156. Recall Dawkins's speculation about "whether physics itself will come to an end in a final 'theory of everything,' a *nirvana of knowledge*." "Science, Delusion, and the Appetite for Wonder" (Richard Dimbleby Lecture for BBC 1 Television, November 12, 1996).

Dawkins's language reveals the very positive associations final knowledge holds for him. Interestingly, Wilson, who is otherwise so openly enchanted with the idea—this, after all, is what Ionian Enchantment means—pulls back at times from this nirvanic vision. While science is well on its way to consilient and complete knowledge of the universe, the human brain itself remains a vast and possibly endless frontier for scientific exploration and explanation. John Horgan alludes to Wilson's "fear of a final theory," his concern about the "end of biology," *End of Science*, 148. At times Wilson seems to recognize, and even be depressed by, the way in which his project, if accomplished, would mean an end to wonder and enchantment.

157. Gustafson, "Sociobiology."

158. Wilson, *Consilience*, 7.

159. Stoll, "Edward Osborne Wilson," 14.

160. Wilson, *Consilience*, 303.

161. David Takacs, *The Idea of Biodiversity: Philosophies of Paradise* (Baltimore: Johns Hopkins University Press, 1996), 319.

162. Stoll, "Edward Osborne Wilson," in Rupke, *Eminent Lives*, 343.

163. See Lisa H. Sideris, *Environmental Ethics, Ecological Theology, and Natural Selection* (New York: Columbia University Press, 2003).

164. Stoll, "Edward Osborne Wilson," 336.

165. Edward O. Wilson, *Diversity of Life* (New York: W. W. Norton, 200), 351.

166. Wilson, *Consilience*, 12–14.

167. Wilson, *Diversity of Life*, 351.

168. Edward O. Wilson, *The Creation: An Appeal to Save Life on Earth* (W. W. Norton, 2006), 66.

169. Edward O. Wilson, *The Future of Life* (New York: Vintage Books, 2002), 131.

170. Ibid., 132.

171. Wilson, *The Creation*, 69.

172. Ibid., 29.

173. Ibid., 109 (emphasis mine).

174. Note that Wilson characterizes our ethical orientation toward nature as "the near side of metaphysics," something ennobling, suggesting that ethical responses to nature have a kind of metaphysical status, but this competes with consilience as a metaphysics and materialism as our best and noblest myth. *Diversity of Life*, 351.

175. Stoll, "Edward Osborne Wilson," in Rupke, *Eminent Lives*, 344.

176. Evernden, *Natural Alien*, 26.

177. I borrow the phrase an "earthly cosmology," from David Abram, *Becoming Animal: An Earthly Cosmology* (New York: Pantheon, 2010).

178. Wilson, *Anthill*, 124.

179. Ibid., 140.

180. Wilson, *The Diversity of Life*, 344.

181. Charles Darwin to Emma Darwin, April 28, 1858, Darwin Correspondence Project, University of Cambridge, http://darwinproject.ac.uk.gridhosted.co.uk/letter/?docId = letters/DCP-LETT-2261.xml%3bquery = %3bbrand = default.

182. Hepburn, *Wonder and Other Essays*, 139.

4. EVOLUTIONARY ENCHANTMENT AND DENATURED
RELIGIOUS NATURALISM

1. So writes Big Historian David Christian in an edited volume that includes essays by Brian Swimme, Loyal Rue, Ursula Goodenough, and many other advocates. David Christian, "Introduction: Celebrating the Birth of a New Creation Story," in *The Evolutionary Epic: Science's Story and Humanity's Response*, ed. Cheryl Genet et al. (Santa Margarita, CA: Collins Foundation Press, 2009), 11.

2. Loyal Rue, for example, argues that religious naturalists are defined in part by their common commitment to a science-based cosmology, the details of which vary hardly at all compared to the cosmologies that attend other religious traditions. See Loyal Rue, *Nature Is Enough: Religious Naturalism and the Meaning of Life* (Albany: State University of New York Press, 2011), 112.

3. Ursula Goodenough, *The Sacred Depths of Nature* (Oxford: Oxford University Press, 1998), xx.

4. Rue, *Nature Is Enough,* 135.

5. In making these claims about science, religion, and nature, I do not mean to argue that one must subscribe to one of the traditional faiths in order to have a proper sense of wonder and concern for the natural world.

6. Thomas Berry, "The New Story," *Teilhard Studies* 1 (Winter 1978).

7. Connie Barlow, *Evolution Extended: Biological Debates on the Meaning of Life* (Oxford: Oxford University Press, 1994), 287

8. Loyal Rue, "Redefining *Myth* and *Religion*: Introduction to a Conversation," *Zygon* 29, no. 3 (1994): 315–20.

9. Ibid., 319.

10. These papers are collected in *The Epic of Evolution: Science and Religion in Dialogue,* ed. James B. Miller (Upper Saddle River, NJ: Prentice Hall, 2004).

11. For a more detailed write-up of these events as they were unfolding, see Connie Barlow, "The Epic of Evolution: A Report of Current Events," *Teilhard Perspective* 30, no. 2 (Fall 1997): 1–3.

12. J. Baird Callicott, *Earth Insights: A Multicultural Survey of Ecological Ethics from the Mediterranean Basin to the Australian Outback* (Berkeley and Los Angeles: University of California Press, 1994), 188.

13. Ibid., 186.

14. Ibid., 185.

15. For example, Callicott writes that "a grand narrative that is contradicted by the fossil record or evidence of an expanding universe" is not sufficiently credible. J. Baird Callicott, "Myth and Environmental Philosophy," in *Thinking through Myths: Philosophical Perspectives,* ed. Kevin Schilbrack (New York: Routledge, 2002), 167.

16. J. Baird Callicott, "Science as Myth (Whether Sacred or Not), Science as Prism," *Journal for the Study of Religion, Nature and Culture* 9, no. 2 (2015): 155.

17. Callicott, "Myth and Environmental Philosophy," 166.

18. But see my exchange with Callicott in volume 9, number 2 of the *Journal for the Study of Religion, Nature and Culture* cited above.

19. See Connie Barlow, *Green Space, Green Time: The Way of Science* (New York: Copernicus, 1997).

20. Journal issues and articles are archived at "Articles published in the *Epic of Evolution Journal*," http://thegreatstory.org/Epic-Evol-Journal.html.

21. Press release, Collins Foundation Press, www.collinsfoundationpress.org/Press%20 Page.htm.

22. Philip Hefner, "Editorial," *Zygon* 32, no. 2 (1997): 145.

23. Edward O. Wilson, *Consilience: The Unity of Knowledge* (New York: Vintage, 1998), 6.

24. Mary Evelyn Tucker and John Grim, series foreword, in *Buddhism and Ecology: The Interconnection of Dharma and Deeds*, ed. Mary Evelyn Tucker and Duncan R. Williams (Cambridge, MA: Harvard University Press, 1998), xvii.

25. "Students of history," Martin Eger notes, "will notice that this is not an altogether new view of things. . . . [I]f we look back about one hundred years, we see clearly among leading philosophers and scientists the forerunner movement: Herbert Spencer in Britain, Ernst Haeckel in Germany, John Fiske in the United States—all produced massive works advocating a philosophy of 'cosmic evolution.' Then as now, books appeared treating astronomical, geological, biological, neurological, social and moral evolution as part of the *same narrative*. . . . [T]he most recent scientific discoveries—Darwinism, biological cell theory, astronomical spectroscopy—were cited as prime evidence that, for the most part, the story is true. Then as now, the mere disclosure of such unity, such an all-embracing drama, was expected to lead to profound philosophical reorientations." Martin Eger, "The New Epic of Science and the Problem of Communication," in *Science, Understanding, and Justice: The Philosophical Essays of Martin Eger*, ed. Abner Shimony (Chicago: Open Court, 2006), 284.

26. Bernard Lightman, *Victorian Popularizers of Science: Designing Nature for New Audiences* (Chicago: University of Chicago Press, 2010), 220.

27. Eger, "New Epic of Science and the Problem of Communication," 284.

28. Lightman and Eger both note that epic science books that appeared largely in the 1970s and 1980s include those authored by E. O. Wilson (particularly *On Human Nature*), Jacques Monod, Steven Weinberg, Douglas Hofstadter, and one of the founders of the Epic of Evolution movement, Eric Chaisson.

29. Ian Hesketh, "The Recurrence of the Evolutionary Epic," *Journal of the Philosophy of History* 9, no. 2 (2015): 196–219.

30. Ian Hesketh, "The Story of Big History," *History of the Present* 4, no. 2 (Fall 2014): 171–202, 182.

31. Hesketh, "Recurrence of the Evolutionary Epic," 219.

32. Hesketh, "Story of Big History," 174.

33. Hesketh, "Recurrence of the Evolutionary Epic," 219.

34. Ibid., 219.

35. Eger, "Hermeneutics and the New Epic of Science," in Shimony, ed., *Science, Understanding, and Justice*, 269.

36. Ibid., 266.

37. Ibid., 265–66.

38. Hesketh, "Story of Big History," 181.

39. Eger, "Hermeneutics and the New Epic," 267.

40. Chaisson quoted in Eger, "Hermeneutics and the New Epic," 273.

41. Hefner alludes to roughly this category of epic science writing in the remarks quoted above, and he goes on to acknowledge that "Carl Sagan got [the epic narrative] started in the early 1980s" with the broadcast of his popular series *Cosmos* (recently reprised by Neil DeGrasse Tyson). Hefner, "Editorial," 145.

42. When musician Cee Lo Green performed "Imagine" on New Year's Eve, 2011, he outraged Lennon fans and—especially—atheists by replacing Lennon's reference to "no religion, too" with one imagining "all religions *true.*"

43. Paul Eckstein, host, "Religion Is Not about God!: A Conversation with Dr. Loyal Rue," *Equal Time for Free Thought* (MP3 podcast), June 15, 2008, www.equaltimeforfreethought.org/2008/06/15/show-265-religion-is-not-about-god-a-conversation-with-dr-loyal-rue/.

44. Loyal Rue, *By the Grace of Guile: The Role of Deception in Natural History and Human Affairs* (Oxford: Oxford University Press, 1994).

45. It is a stretch to characterize Rue's view of religion as positive, though he does accept the likelihood that religion will continue in some form into the future. It is telling that the avid atheist blogger P. Z. Myers would "be quite content if all the reactionary religious nuts would convert to Rue's religion [as presented in *Everybody's Story*], even if they did fall shy of the perfect ideal of atheism." P. Z. Myers, "Loyal Rue vs (?) PZ Myers," *Pharyngula* (blog), February 8, 2008, http://scienceblogs.com/pharyngula/2008/02/08/loyal-rue-vs-pz-myers/.

46. Edward O. Wilson, foreword to *Everybody's Story: Wising Up to the Epic of Evolution* by Loyal Rue (Albany: State University of New York Press, 2000), x.

47. Loyal Rue, "Epic of Evolution," in *The Encyclopedia of Religion and Nature*, ed. Bron Taylor (London and New York: Continuum, 2005), 614.

48. Rue, *Everybody's Story*, 135.

49. Richard Dawkins, *The Selfish Gene* (Oxford: Oxford University Press, 1976), 192.

50. Rue, *Everybody's Story*, 88–89.

51. Rue writes that the Epic of Evolution is the product of "imaginative mythmaking under the critical and watchful eye of contemporary science." Ibid.

52. Loyal Rue, *Religion Is Not about God: How Spiritual Traditions Nurture Our Biological Nature and What to Expect When They Fail* (New Brunswick, NJ: Rutgers University Press, 2004), 116.

53. Ibid.

54. Ibid., 126.

55. Ibid., 316.

56. Rue, *Everybody's Story*, 127.

57. Ibid., 36.

58. Ibid., 130.

59. Ibid., 41.

60. Rue, "Redefining *Myth* and *Religion*," 315–20.

61. Rue, *Everybody's Story*, 90.

62. Ibid., 91.

63. Ibid., 39.

64. Rue attempts to understand the universe as a whole in terms of its utility function— asking what the universe is designed to "maximize"; this is a principle borrowed from the adaptationist explanatory framework of Dawkins (see also his similar reference to "algorithms of nature"). Rue, *Everybody's Story*, 76.

65. Rue, "Epic of Evolution," in Taylor, *Encyclopedia of Religion and Nature*, 614.

66. Ibid.

67. Rue, "Religion Is Not about God! A Conversation" (podcast).

68. Rue, "Epic of Evolution," in Taylor, *Encyclopedia of Religion and Nature*, 612.

69. Rue, *Religion Is Not about God*, 17.

70. Ibid., 16.

71. Rue, *Everybody's Story*, 42.

72. Ibid., 130–31.

73. Ibid., 131.

74. Rue, "Epic of Evolution," in Taylor, *Encyclopedia of Religion and Nature*, 615.

75. Rue, *Religion Is Not about God*, 15.

76. Ibid., 71.

77. Ibid.

78. Rue, *Everybody's Story*, 130.

79. Ibid., 100–101.

80. Ibid., 118.

81. Ibid.

82. Ibid., 121.

83. Ibid.

84. Ibid., 124.

85. Ibid.

86. Ibid., 93.

87. Ibid., 94.

88. Ibid.

89. Ibid.

90. It is not always easy to distinguish these two ways of telling the story—contingency or inevitability—because in some versions of the story, such as Swimme's or Barlow's, it is the seeming improbability or utter contingency of certain events (say the finely tuned expansion rate of the universe or the death of the dinosaurs that allowed mammals to abound) that suggests that some process is *guiding* the universe past certain obstacles, as though with foresight.

91. Rue, *Everybody's Story*, 79.

92. Ibid., 61.

93. Ibid., xiii.

94. Robert Wright, *Three Scientists and Their Gods: Looking for Meaning in the Age of Information* (New York: Times Books, 1988).

95. Rue, *Religion Is Not about God*, 14.

96. Rue, *Everybody's Story*, 134.

97. On attempts to infuse the new cosmology with phenomenological and affective dimensions, see Lisa H. Sideris, "'To know the story is to love it': Scientific Mythmaking and the Longing for Cosmic Connection," in *Methodological Challenges in Nature-Culture and Environmental History Research*, ed. Jocelyn Thorpe, Stephanie Rutherford, and L. Anders Sandberg (London: Routledge, 2016).

98. Rue, *Everybody's Story*, 134.

99. Ibid.

100. Ibid., 135.

101. Ibid.

102. Ibid., 134.

103. Ibid.

104. Ibid., 49.

105. Ibid., 95.

106. Ibid.

107. Ibid., 96.

108. Ibid., 74.

109. Ibid., 61.

110. Ibid., 132.

111. Rue, *Religion Is Not about God*, 1.

112. Rue, *Everybody's Story*, 120.

113. Poets, Dennis Quinn argues, look to nature for precisely these obscurities and difficulties. "When a poet encounters a difficulty, he contemplates it through the poem but without advancing to philosophical inquiry; he 'tells a story,' rather, about the mystery." Dennis Quinn, *Iris Exiled: A Synoptic History of Wonder* (Lanham, MD: University Press of America, 2002), 41.

114. Rue, *Religion Is Not about God*, 363.

115. Rue, *Everybody's Story*, 28.

116. Rue, *Religion Is Not about God*, 368.

117. Rue, *Grace of Guile*, 3.

118. Ibid., 367.

119. Ibid., 279, 306 (emphasis mine).

120. Ibid., 304.

121. Ibid., 306. Rue's evolutionary deception is inseparable from the logic of reciprocal altruism; ultimately it is "in my interest to place value on the interests of every other form of life. This is the logic of reciprocal altruism." Ibid., 306.

122. Rue, *Everybody's Story*, 60.

123. Rue, *Nature Is Enough*, 116.

124. Rue, *Grace of Guile*, 274.

125. Wilson, *Consilience*, 44.

126. Bron Taylor, *Dark Green Religion: Nature Spirituality and the Planetary Future* (Berkeley: University of California Press, 2009), 197 (emphasis mine).

127. Ibid., 218.

128. Rue, *Everybody's Story*, 49.

129. Ibid.

130. Ibid., 38.

131. Ibid., 37.

132. Rue, *Nature Is Enough*, 124.

133. Rue claims, in the interview cited previously, that he is merely predicting the ascendency of everybody's story, and the dissolution of traditional faiths, in the wake of disaster.

134. Ursula Goodenough, "Exploring Resources of Naturalism: Religiopoiesis," *Zygon* 35, no. 3 (September 2000): 563.

135. Goodenough, *Sacred Depths*, xi.

136. Ibid., xvi.

137. Ursula Goodenough, "My Covenant with Mystery," *13.7 Cosmos and Culture Blog*, August 27, 2010, www.npr.org/blogs/13.7/2010/08/27/129471676/my-covenant-with-mystery.

138. Ibid.

139. Dawkins, "Great Convergence," in *Devil's Chaplain*, 147.

140. Ibid., 146.

141. Goodenough, *Sacred Depths of Nature*,

142. Sam Keen, *Apology for Wonder* (New York: Harper Collins, 1973), 22.

143. At one point, Goodenough defends contingency that eschews the progressive and purposive framework of Thomas Berry's cosmic narrative, arguing that a nonprogressive, nonhierarchical account is more generative of wonder. She is correct, in my view, and this critique of Berry and his disciples deserves greater attention, though how her preference for a nonprogressive and nonpurposive narrative fits with her strong support of consilience is unclear. See Ursula Goodenough, "Progress, Purpose, and Contingency: A Response to Thomas Berry's *The Great Work: Our Way into the Future*," *Worldviews* 5 (2001): 142–47.

144. Ursula Goodenough, "What Science Can and Cannot Offer to a Religious Narrative," *Zygon* 29, no. 3 (September 1994): 321.

145. Ibid., 321.

146. The fault for this lies ultimately with *Zygon*'s editors.

147. Ibid., 321.

148. Ibid., 322.

149. Ibid., 323.

150. Ibid., 324.

151. Ibid., 325.

152. Ibid., 326.

153. Ibid., 324.

154. Ursula Goodenough, "Ecomorality: Toward an Ethic of Sustainability," in *Pivotal Moment: Population, Justice, and the Environmental Challenge*, ed. Laurie Ann Mazur (Covelo, CA: Island Press, 2009), 373.

155. Goodenough, "What Science Can and Cannot Offer," 325.

156. Ibid., 327. Interestingly, Goodenough goes on to draw an analogy between knowing about gay rights and supporting them, on the one hand, and having personal friends who are gay, on the other. She argues that caring about those rights becomes a truly *moral* concern when those rights pertain to someone we "know" directly and personally. But if this analogy with nature holds, it seems to argue for having particular, not "universal," knowledge of nature such as that proffered by the new cosmology. "Knowing" a person is not like knowing facts about the cellular structure of plants. Knowledge of persons is particular, and the affection we feel is a function of that specific experience of them, not the result of universal knowledge of human beings.

157. Ibid., 325 (emphasis mine).

158. Ibid., 328.

159. Ibid., 329.

160. Ibid., 327.

161. Ibid., 328.

162. Ibid.

163. Goodenough, "Exploring Resources of Naturalism," 565.

164. Ibid.

165. Ibid. (emphasis mine).

166. Ibid.

167. Goodenough offered this portrait of scientists *pulling back the curtain* at a conference convened by the International Society for the Study of Religion, Nature, and Culture, in Gainesville, Florida, January 16, 2016. Her comments showed little awareness that scientists construct and do not simply reveal the "epic story" and its meaning.

168. Goodenough, "What Science Can and Cannot Offer to a Religious Narrative," 329.

169. Ibid.

170. Goodenough, *Sacred Depths*, xvi.

171. Ibid., 173.

172. Goodenough, "Ecomorality," 373–74.

173. Goodenough, "What Science Can and Cannot Offer," 324.

174. Ibid., 328.

175. Connie Barlow and Michael Dowd, hosts, "Ursula Goodenough: 'The Sacred Depths of Nature,'" Inspiring Naturalism (MP3 podcast), August 27, 2010, http://inspiring-naturalism.libsyn.com/6_ursula_goodenough_the_sacred_depths_of_nature_.

176. Ibid.

177. Ibid.

178. Karl Giberson, "What's Wrong with Science as Religion," *Salon*, July 31, 2008, www.salon.com/2008/07/31/religion_science/.

179. Their skepticism does not keep them from promoting the Epic as not only compatible with but profoundly enriching for the traditional faiths. See "Meta-Religious Essays and Sermons: How the Great Story Enriches Faith and Philosophical Traditions," www.the-greatstory.org/metareligious.html.

180. Thomas Berry, *The Great Work* (New York: Random House, 1999), 84.

181. Ibid., 81–83. Berry goes on to say that the New Story would only enhance the Book of Genesis, though it is clear from his appraisal here of the New Story that Genesis does not approximate its magnificence.

182. Thomas Berry, "The American College," in *Dream of the Earth* (Berkeley: Counterpoint, 2015). Berry's essay "The American College in the Ecological Age," *Journal of Religion and Intellectual Life* 6, no. 2 (Winter, 1989): 7–28, varies slightly from the chapter of the same name in *The Dream of the Earth*.

183. Ibid., 18.

184. "First Year Experience: Big History," Dominican University, www.dominican.edu/academics/first-year-experience-big-history. See also Sharon Abercrombie, "California College Helps Place Humans in Universe Story," *National Catholic Reporter*, November 11, 2011, www.ncronline.org/news/people/california-college-helps-place-humans-universe-story.

185. Russell Merle Genet, "The Epic of Evolution: A Course Development Project," *Zygon* 33, no. 4 (1998): 635. Note the categorization of all these perspectives as "sciences."

186. Ibid., 637.

187. Course materials previously accessed at http://epsc.wustl.edu/classwork/classwork_210a/index.html, on file with author. See also Ursula Goodenough, "The Epic of Evolution:

Life, the Earth, and the Cosmos: A Course for Non-Science Majors at Washington University, www.journeyoftheuniverse.org/conference-at-yale/.

188. Loyal Rue and Ursula Goodenough, "A Consilient Curriculum," in Genet et al., *Evolutionary Epic*, 175.

189. Ibid., 181.

190. Ibid., 178

191. Ibid., 175.

192. Ibid., 181.

193. Ibid., 178.

194. Rue and Goodenough, "A Consilient Curriculum," in Genet et al., *Evolutionary Epic*," 181 (emphasis mine). This division of the core curriculum appears to be an amendment to Rue's earlier proposal, in *Everybody's Story*, for a curriculum built around four areas of knowledge or types of "natural facts" found in the universe: physical, biological, psychological, and cultural / symbolic.

195. Ibid., 180.

196. Goodenough, "Epic of Evolution: Life, the Earth, and the Cosmos."

197. Goodenough, "Exploring Resources of Naturalism," 564.

198. Barlow and Dowd, "Ursula Goodenough" (podcast).

199. Course assignments and exam questions, previously accessed at http://epsc.wustl.edu/courses/epsc210a/, on file with author.

200. Course lectures may well present "straight science," but the assigned texts—notably, Goodenough's own *Sacred Depths of Nature* and Rue's *Everybody's Story*— go much further, informing readers "how things are and which things matter." Goodenough writes in her introduction: "It is therefore the goal of this book to present an accessible account of our scientific understanding of Nature and then suggest ways that this account can call forth appealing and abiding religious responses" (xvii). The book lays out her own "credo" and profession of "Faith" (171). Students, one might presume, are permitted to disagree with these assertions, but they may well find disagreement uncomfortable when the text's author is a course instructor. The confessional tone perhaps gives some clue to what she understands the disciplinary approach of religious studies to consist of, and how students might likewise reflect religiously or philosophically.

201. In this sense, Dawkins may have a point that Goodenough misuses the word *religious*, though his reasons for objecting are different from mine, since he strongly concurs that religion and theology are not worthy of study and that science merits unlimited prestige.

202. Goodenough, "Exploring Resources of Naturalism," 563.

203. See, for example, William Nichols's response to Berry's "American College in the Ecological Age": "The Limits of Ecological Vision," *Journal of Religion and Intellectual Life* 6, no. 2 (Winter 1989): 42–47.

204. Wilson, *Consilience*, 12.

5. ANTHROPIC AND ANTHROPOCENE NARRATIVES OF THE NEW COSMOLOGY

1. Dipesh Chakrabarty, "The Climate of History: Four Theses," *Critical Inquiry* 35, no. 2 (Winter 2009): 197–222.

2. In this chapter I will follow the convention of referring to Teilhard de Chardin as "Teilhard" as is common among the new cosmologists and other enthusiasts.

3. Editors of *What Is Enlightenment?* "The Real Evolution Debate," *What Is Enlightenment?* (magazine), January–February 2007, 99.

4. Ibid.

5. Anne Marie Dalton, "The Great Work in a Sacred Universe: The Role of Science in Berry's Visionary Proposal," in *The Intellectual Journey of Thomas Berry: Imagining the Earth Community,* ed. Heather Eaton (Plymouth, UK: Lexington Books, 2014), 186.

6. Berry's biography and intellectual development and influences are discussed in detail by Mary Evelyn Tucker in a variety of sources. See www.thomasberry.org/Biography/tucker-bio.html.

7. Brian Thomas Swimme and Mary Evelyn Tucker, *Journey of the Universe* (New Haven, CT: Yale University Press, 2011), 2.

8. Ibid.

9. Thomas Berry, "The New Story: Comments on the Origin, Identification, and Transmission of Values," *Teilhard Studies* 1 (Winter 1978): 1.

10. Ibid., 2.

11. Ibid., 5.

12. Ibid., 13.

13. Kathleen Dean Moore, "A Roaring Force from One Unknowable Moment" (Conversation with Mary Evelyn Tucker), *Orion Magazine,* May / June 2015, 28. The same appraisal of wonder as a guide appears in Swimme and Tucker, *Journey of the Universe,* 113.

14. Tucker first encountered Teilhard's work in high school and later discerned affinities between his philosophy and Eastern religions. She and Grim would ultimately follow in Berry's footsteps by assuming a leadership role in the American Teilhard Association.

15. Susan Bridle, "The Divinization of the Cosmos: An Interview with Brian Swimme on Pierre Teilhard de Chardin," *What Is Enlightenment?* (magazine), September / October 2006, www.renewedpriesthood.org/ca/hpage.cfm?Web_ID = 896.

16. Ibid.

17. Ibid.

18. Pierre Teilhard de Chardin, *The Phenomenon of Man,* trans. Bernard Wall, with an introduction by Julian Huxley (New York: Harper and Row, 1959).

19. Paul R. Samson and David Pitt, eds., *The Biosphere and Noosphere Reader: Global Environment, Society, and Change* (New York: Routledge, 1999), 3.

20. Bridle, "Divinization of the Cosmos."

21. Teilhard is a popular figure among transhumanists who favor enhancement of human life and the body through technology, and some of whom advocate the rapid acceleration of technology to a Singularity (the advent of superhuman intelligence). On Teilhard's legacy for these various movements see www.teilhardproject.com/. On his transhumanist following, see Eric Steinhart, "Teilhard de Chardin and Transhumanism," *Journal of Evolution and Technology* 20, no. 1 (December 2008): 1–22.

22. Ilia Delio, *The Unbearable Wholeness of Being: God, Evolution and the Power of Love* (New York: Orbis, 2013), 171.

23. Will Steffen et al., "The Anthropocene: Conceptual and Historical Perspectives," *Philosophical Transactions of the Royal Society A* 369, no. 1938 (January 2011): 842–67.

24. Clive Hamilton and Jacques Grinevald, "Was the Anthropocene Anticipated?" *Anthropocene Review* 2, no. 1 (April 2015): 66.

25. Samson and Pitt, *Biosphere and Noosphere Reader*, 3. My emphasis.

26. Hamilton and Grinevald, "Was the Anthropocene Anticipated?" 66.

27. Ibid.

28. Julian Huxley, introduction to *Phenomenon of Man*, 84.

29. Teilhard, *Phenomenon of Man*, 226.

30. Ibid., 224.

31. Ibid., 276.

32. American Teilhard Association, "Our Mission," 2016, www.teilharddechardin.org /index.php/our-mission.

33. Ibid.

34. Mary Evelyn Tucker, "The Ecological Spirituality of Pierre Teilhard de Chardin," *Teilhard Studies* 51 (Fall 2005): 9.

35. Tucker, "Ecological Spirituality," 11.

36. Swimme and Tucker, *Journey of the Universe*, 50.

37. Tucker, "Ecological Spirituality," 11.

38. Ibid., 12.

39. See Tucker's comments in Moore, "Roaring Force from One Unknowable Moment," as well as Swimme and Tucker, *Journey of the Universe*, 2.

40. Tucker, "Ecological Spirituality," 15.

41. Mary Evelyn Tucker, "An Intellectual Biography of Thomas Berry," editor's afterword to *Evening Thoughts: Reflecting on Earth as Sacred Community*, by Thomas Berry, ed. Mary Evelyn Tucker (San Francisco: Sierra Club Books, 2006), 163.

42. Ibid., 164.

43. Julian Huxley, "The New Divinity," in *Essays of a Humanist* (London: Chatto and Windus, 1964).

44. Center for the Story of the Universe, http://storyoftheuniverse.org/. Swimme and Huxley's sentiment ignores Berry's own occasional reminders that humans should not feel "that we alone are determining the future course of events," for "geological and biological" forces continue to shape Earth's future. Thomas Berry, "The Human Presence," in *The Dream of the Earth* (San Francisco: Sierra Club Books, 1988), 23.

45. Brian Swimme and Thomas Berry, *The Universe Story: From the Primordial Flaring Forth to the Ecozoic Era* (San Francisco: Harper, 1992), 227.

46. Swimme and Berry align the Technozoic impulse with Western civilization and its commitment to commercial/industrial progress, while presenting a benign and romantic view of Eastern and Indigenous culture that renders these worldviews compatible with the Ecozoic vision.

47. Ibid., 248.

48. Ibid., 250.

49. Stephen Bede Scharper, *Redeeming the Time: A Political Theology of the Environment* (New York: Continuum, 1998), 130.

50. Samson and Pitt, *Biosphere and Noosphere Reader*.

51. Ibid., 82

52. Huxley, introduction to *Phenomenon of Man*, ibid., 82.

53. See for example Berry's discussion of education, especially college education, in *The Dream of the Earth*, "The American College in the Ecological Age," 89–108.

54. Ibid., 98.

55. Berry, *Evening Thoughts*, 121.

56. Berry, *Dream of the Earth*, 108.

57. Thomas Berry, *The Great Work: Our Way into the Future* (New York: Random House, 1999), 159.

58. Berry, "The Human Presence," in *Dream of the Earth*, 21.

59. Berry, *Evening Thoughts*, 125.

60. Berry, *Dream of the Earth*, 18.

61. Ibid., 105–6.

62. Ibid., 100.

63. Ibid., 98–99.

64. "Interdisciplinary Curriculum Design and *Journey of the Universe*," Journey of the Universe, 2016, www.journeyoftheuniverse.org/high-school-conferences/.

65. Brian Thomas Swimme and Mary Evelyn Tucker, "Journey of the Universe," *Teilhard Perspective* 44, no. 1 (Spring 2011): 2.

66. See Lisa H. Sideris, "Science as Sacred Myth? Ecospirituality in the Anthropocene Age," *Journal for the Study of Religion, Nature, and Culture* 9, no. 2 (2015): 136–53; and "The Confines of Consecration: A Reply to Critics," *Journal for the Study of Religion, Nature, and Culture* 9, no. 2 (2015): 221–39.

67. Scharper, *Redeeming the Time*, 130.

68. Ibid., 129.

69. Ibid.

70. J. Matthew Ashley, "Reading the Universe Story Theologically: The Contribution of a Biblical Narrative Imagination," *Theological Studies* 71 (2010): 881.

71. J. Baird Callicott, "Myth and Environmental Philosophy," in *Thinking through Myths: Philosophical Perspectives,* ed. Kevin Schilbrack (New York: Routledge, 2002), 167.

72. Thomas Berry, *Befriending the Earth: A Theology of Reconciliation between Humans and the Earth* (Mystic, CT: Twenty-Third, 1991), 21.

73. Neil Evernden, *The Natural Alien: Humankind and Environment* (Toronto: University of Toronto Press, 1993), 139.

74. Gretel Van Wieren, *Restored to Earth: Christianity, Environmental Ethics, and Ecological Restoration* (Washington, DC: Georgetown University Press, 2013), 186.

75. Ashley, "Reading," 890.

76. Tucker and Grim explain that Berry "was academically formed before the postmodern penchant for uncovering power dynamics and concealing rhetoric"—implying that subsequent generations of universe storytellers are alert to such dynamics and rhetoric. Yet the latest versions of the Universe Story, notably Swimme and Tucker's, also display little sensitivity to so-called postmodern concerns about the hegemonic intent and power dynamics of grand scientific narratives. See Grim and Tucker, "Thomas Berry: Reflections."

77. Swimme and Berry, *Universe Story*, 3.

78. Ibid., 268.

79. Brian Thomas Swimme, "The New Story," (video), March 2007, www.youtube.com /watch?v = TRykk_oovIo.

80. Whitney Bauman, "Planetary Journeys and Eco-justice: The Geography of Violence" (draft paper for Yale Living Cosmology conference), November 8, 2014, 3, on file with author. A revised version of this essay, with the author's critical observations noticeably softened, appears in Mary Evelyn Tucker and John Grim, eds., *Living Cosmology: Christian Responses to* Journey of the Universe (Maryknoll, NY: Orbis, 2016), 190–97.

81. Ibid.

82. Ibid., 7.

83. Tucker, "Ecological Spirituality of Teilhard," 12.

84. Willis Jenkins, "Does Evolutionary Cosmology Matter for Ecological Ethics?" (draft paper for Yale Living Cosmology conference), November 9, 2016, 3, www.academia.edu/8123931/Does_Evolutionary_Cosmology_Matter_For_Ecological_Ethics.

85. Ibid., 2. Jenkins's observation that no practical guidance flows from the empty proposition that everything in the universe is a product of the processes that made it does not take seriously enough the shift from process (cosmos) to progress (cosmogenesis) that animates the story of the universe. These stories do not merely describe a physical process of unfolding; they do not claim that humans *happened* to emerge as the universe's heart and mind or reflective self-consciousness. Rather, these developments are the *point* of the universe. This progressive reading of the universe, and of the importance of humans, does not give equal support to any number of moral sensibilities but tends to underwrite particular, problematic modes of conduct.

86. Scharper, *Redeeming the Time*, 128.

87. Jenkins grants that a certain *mood* of wonder may be kindled by *Journey's* cosmic perspective in that it commends a "restoration of the universe to the imagination of a species" that has cut itself off from the vast, starry realm beyond. Ibid., 6. Once restored to the universe, it remains to be seen what stories we will generate.

88. Scharper too worries about the new cosmology's lack of attunement to social justice concerns.

89. A weak version of the principle regards this fact as unremarkable, for if the universe were not compatible with life, we would not be here. Cosmological inquiry of the sort that motivates the Universe Story would not take place in a universe without intelligent life. Our existence, in other words, imposes a strong selection effect on cosmological observations.

90. Swimme and Tucker, *Journey of the Universe*, 11.

91. Berry, *Dream of the Earth*, 16.

92. Ibid.

93. Swimme affirms belief in a purposive universe and its movement toward sentience (though with some prodding from his interlocutor) in an interview. See Robert Wright, "Robert Wright Interviews Brian Swimme on Religion in a Global Age," MeaningofLive.TV, http://origins.meaningoflife.tv/video.php?speaker = swimme&topic = complete.

94. Brian Thomas Swimme, "Cosmology and Environmentalism," in *The Evolutionary Epic: Science's Story and Humanity's Response*, ed. Cheryl Genet et al. (Santa Margarita, CA: Collins Foundation Press, 2009), 277.

95. The strong anthropic principle is sometimes criticized as unscientific in the sense of being nonfalsifiable: there are no alternative universes against which to test the claim that the development of life within ours was an inevitable occurrence somehow built into its very structure and design.

96. Alan Lightman, *The Accidental Universe: The World You Thought You Knew* (New York: Pantheon, 2013), 7.

97. Marilynne Robinson, *The Givenness of Things* (New York: Farrar, Straus, and Giroux, 2015), 14.

98. Ibid.

99. Brian Thomas Swimme, "The Cultural Significance of the Story of the Universe," in *The Epic of Evolution: Science and Religion in Dialogue*, ed. James B. Miller (Upper Saddle River: Prentice Hall, 2004), 38–43.

100. Swimme and Berry, *Universe Story*, 236.

101. Ibid., 237.

102. Similarly, in Berry and Swimme's telling, cosmic events and "characters" are personified and invested with intentionality. The Big Bang is invoked as "the Primordial Flaring Forth"; Tiamat, a name derived from the Babylonian creation myth, is given to a special ancestral star responsible for the creation of complex elements in our bodies and in the Earth. "Tiamat knit together wonders in its fiery belly," they write, "carving its body up in a supernova explosion that dispersed this new elemental power in all directions, so that the adventure might deepen." Ibid. 8.

103. Swimme and Tucker, *Journey of the Universe*, 51.

104. Ibid., 8.

105. Ibid., 106.

106. Ibid., 87–88.

107. Ibid., 102.

108. Ibid., 113.

109. Ibid., 114.

110. *Journey of the Universe*, directed by David Kennard and Patsy Northcutt, DVD (InCA Productions, 2011).

111. Swimme and Tucker, *Journey of the Universe*, 114

112. Ibid., 115.

113. Ibid., 112.

114. Ibid., 115.

115. Kennard and Northcutt, *Journey of the Universe* (DVD).

116. Ian Hesketh, "The Recurrence of the Evolutionary Epic," *Journal of Philosophy of History* 9 (2015): 196–215, 200. My emphasis.

117. In a feature cited previously in *Orion* magazine, Kathleen Dean Moore questions Tucker about the moral implications of *Journey* for humans and other life-forms. Tucker's answers are eloquent and well rehearsed, and decidedly vague; she is unable to pinpoint how any moral direction and practical guidance—at least, guidance in new and desirable directions—is gleaned from cosmogenesis. Moore, "Roaring Force from One Unknowable Moment," 27–31.

118. Berry's vision is sometimes less sugar-coated, as when observing that "the universe, earth, life, and consciousness are all violent processes . . . . Neither the universe as a whole nor any part of the universe is especially peaceful . . . . Conflict is the father of all things." *Dream of the Earth*, 216.

119. Huxley, introduction to *Phenomenon of Man*, 16.

120. Joan Gibb Engel, "Dreaming the Universe: Contending Stories of Our Place in the Cosmos," in *Confronting Ecological and Economic Collapse: Ecological Integrity for Law,*

Policy, and Human Rights, ed. Laura Westra, Prue Taylor, and Agnès Michelot (Florence, KY: Taylor and Francis, 2013), 255–64.

121. Mary Midgley, *Evolution as Religion: Strange Hopes and Stranger Fears,* rev. ed. (New York: Metheun, 2002), 7–8.

122. Ibid., 79.

123. Ibid.

124. Gibb Engle, "Dreaming the Universe," 258.

125. Grim and Tucker, "Thomas Berry: Reflections."

126. Mary Evelyn Tucker and John Grim, series foreword, in *Buddhism and Ecology: the Interconnection of Dharma and Deeds,* ed. Mary Evelyn Tucker and Duncan R. Williams (Cambridge, MA: Harvard University Press, 1997), xxiv.

127. Christophe Bonneuil, "The Geological Turn: The Anthropocene and Its Narratives," in *The Anthropocene and the Global Environmental Crisis: Rethinking Modernity in a New Epoch,* ed. Clive Hamilton, Christophe Bonneuil, and François Gemenne (New York: Routledge, 2015), 17–31.

128. Chakrabarty, "Climate of History."

129. Bonneuil, "Geological Turn," 18–19.

130. Ibid., 23.

131. Chakrabarty, "Climate of History," for example, invokes Wilson's species concept in his analysis of the Anthropocene and the new challenges it poses for humanists.

132. Edward O. Wilson, "The Riddle of the Human Species," *New York Times Opinionator Blog,* February 24, 2013, http://opinionator.blogs.nytimes.com/2013/02/24/the-riddle-of-the-human-species/?_r = 0.

133. Edward O. Wilson, foreword to *Commonwealth: Economics for a Crowded Planet,* by Jeffrey Sachs (New York: Penguin, 2008), xii.

134. See Hamilton and Grinevald, "Was the Anthropocene Anticipated?"

135. Paul J. Crutzen and Eugene F. Stoermer, "The Anthropocene," *IGBP Global Change Newsletter* 41 (2000): 17–18. Clive Hamilton and Jacques Grinevald argue that there are no *genuine* precursors to the Anthropocene idea (defined as a radical break and rupture with the geological history of the planet). However, I would argue that there are precursors to the *good* Anthropocene idea, or aspects thereof, to be found in thinkers such as Huxley, Teilhard, and Berry; for whereas the Anthropocene might suggest—as Grinevald and Hamilton—the breakdown and rupture of Earth and evolutionary systems, the good Anthropocene (as even Grinevald and Hamilton agree) displays a linear, progressive model of evolution, with humans advancing to a higher stage and greater degree of importance on the planet. This idea has precursors.

136. Swimme and Berry, *Universe Story,* 280.

137. Ibid., 247 (emphasis mine).

138. See Tucker, "Ecological Spirituality of Teilhard," which treats unity as a central theme in Teilhard's work.

139. Bonneuil, "Geological Turn," 20 (emphasis mine).

140. Scharper, *Redeeming the Time,* 131.

141. See Bronislaw Szerszynski et al., "Why Solar Radiation Management Geoengineering and Democracy Won't Mix," *Environment and Planning A,* 45, no. 12 (December 2013): 2809–16.

142. See Mary Evelyn Tucker, "Focus on the Anthropocene: Journey of the Universe" (lecture, Carsey-Wolf Center, University of California–Santa Barbara, February 19, 2015), www.carseywolf.ucsb.edu/pollock/events/focus-anthropocene-journey-universe. Geological *eras*, it should be noted, are periods of much longer duration than epochs, which are measured in thousands of years.

143. Grim and Tucker, "Thomas Berry: Reflections."

144. See Mary Evelyn Tucker, "Overview," Journey of the Universe, www.journeyofthe-universe.org/storage/JOTU_Overview_8-28-13.pdf. Tucker presents a similar but more ambiguous association between the Anthropocene and the Ecozoic elsewhere, claiming that Berry's work "assist[s] in the transition from the last 65 million years of the Cenozoic era to what he termed a life-sustaining Ecozoic era. (Many geologists, such as Paul Crutzen, are naming our present period the 'Anthropocene' because of the immense effect of humans on Earth's ecosystems in this last 12,000 years)." Mary Evelyn Tucker, "Journey of the Universe: An Integration of Science and the Humanities," *Journal for the Study of Religion, Nature, and Culture* 9, no. 2 (2015): 209–10.

145. Tucker, "Overview."

146. Eileen Crist, "On the Poverty of Our Nomenclature," *Environmental Humanities* 3 (2013) 129–47, 132.

147. Ibid., 136.

148. Ibid., 141.

149. Ned Hettinger, "Valuing Naturalness in the 'Anthropocene': Now More Than Ever," in *Keeping the Wild: Against the Domestication of Earth,* ed. George Wuerthner, Eileen Crist, and Tom Butler (San Francisco: Foundation for Deep Ecology, 2014), 176.

150. Ibid., 179.

151. Swimme and Tucker, *Journey of the Universe,* 102.

152. Berry, *Dream of the Earth,* 16.

153. Ibid., 102 (emphasis mine).

154. Ibid.

155. Ibid., 103.

156. Ibid. (emphasis mine).

157. Ibid., 106.

158. Ibid., 109.

159. Brian Thomas Swimme, "The Current Moment" (video), March 2007, www.youtube.com/watch?v = JwoRS2Tfk74.

160. Clive Hamilton, "Human Destiny in the Anthropocene," in Hamilton et al., *Anthropocene and the Global Environmental Crisis,* 41.

161. For examples of and commentary on these new forms of conservationism, see Ben A. Minteer and Stephen J. Pyne, eds., *After Preservation: Saving American Nature in the Age of Humans* (Chicago: University of Chicago Press, 2015) and the previously cited *Keeping the Wild.*

162. Bonneuil, "Geological Turn," 31.

163. Ibid., 23.

164. My own sense is that the world would be better off without the term Anthropocene at all, and indeed without a practice of naming epochs or eras on the basis of prescriptive agendas for the (mostly human) future. But it is difficult to stuff the genie back into the bottle.

165. Clive Hamilton, *Earthmasters: The Dawn of the Age of Climate Engineering* (New Haven, CT: Yale University Press, 2014), 198–199.

166. Ibid.

167. Ibid., 201.

168. See for example Berry's essay "The Gaia Theory: Its Religious Implications," *ARC: The Journal of the Faculty of Religious Studies, McGill University* 22 (1994): 7–19.

169. I have in mind Latour's claim that the Anthropocene, understood as an encounter with this agent-filled universe, is *anti*-anthropocentric and marks the end of anthropocentrism. This message, central to Latour's Gifford lectures, "Facing Gaia," might encourage us to view the natural world as animate, alive, valuable, as new cosmologists appear to urge us to do. Bruno Latour, "Facing Gaia, Six Lectures on the Political Theology of Nature" (Gifford Lectures, University of Edinburgh, February 18, 19, 21, 25, 26, 28, 2013), www.ed.ac.uk /arts-humanities-soc-sci/news-events/lectures/gifford-lectures/archive/series-2012–2013/ bruno-latour. However Latour's rendezvous with the ecomodernists, exemplified by his essay "Love Your Monsters," undoes much of that good and shows the danger of taking post-naturalism or post-environmentalist perspectives too far. Latour's arguments in that essay seem incoherent with the thrust of his Gifford lectures. Bruno Latour, "Love Your Monsters," in *Love Your Monsters: Postenvironmentalism and the Anthropocene*, ed. Michael Shellenberger and Ted Nordhaus (Oakland: Breakthrough Institute, 2011), 19–26, www .bruno-latour.fr/sites/default/files/downloads/107-BREAKTHROUGH-REDUXpdf.pdf.

170. Swimme and Tucker, *Journey of the Universe*, 106.

171. For examples of how recognizing the active and animate quality of matter has the potential to overthrow our assumptions of human dominance and control over the natural world, see Jane Bennett, *Vibrant Matter: A Political Ecology of Things* (Durham, NC: Duke University Press, 2010); Tim LeCain, "Against the Anthropocene," *International Journal for History, Culture, and Modernity* 3, no. 1 (2015): 1–28.

172. Bronislaw Szerszynski, "The End of the End of Nature: The Anthropocene and the Fate of the Human," *Oxford Literary Review* 34, no. 2 (2012): 176.

173. See Andrew Revkin, *Global Warming: Understanding the Forecast* (New York: Abbeville Press, 1992).

174. Andrew Revkin, "Embracing the Anthropocene," *New York Times Dot Earth Blog*, May 20, 2011, http://dotearth.blogs.nytimes.com/2011/05/20/embracing-the-anthropocene /?_r = 0.

175. Andrew Revkin, "Peter Kareiva, an Inconvenient Environmentalist," *New York Times Dot Earth Blog*, April 3, 2012, http://dotearth.blogs.nytimes.com/2012/04/03/peter-kareiva-an-inconvenient-environmentalist/?_r = 0.

176. For more on the Nature Conservancy's newfound intimacy with the new conservationism, and Karieva's role in fostering it, see D. T. Max, "Green Is Good," *New Yorker*, May 12, 2014.

177. Michael Soulé, "The 'New Conservation,'" in Wuerthner et al., *Keeping the Wild*, 77.

178. John Asafu-Adjaye et al., "An Ecomodernist Manifesto," Breakthrough Institute, April 2015, www.ecomodernism.org/.

179. Michael Soulé, "The 'New Conservation,'" *Conservation Biology* 27, no. 5 (October 2013): 895.

180. See Michael Shellenberger and Ted Nordhaus, "The Death of Environmentalism: Global Warming Politics in a Post-Environmental World," 2004, http://thebreakthrough. org/archive/the_death_of_environmentalism.

181. Tom Butler, "Lives Not Our Own," in Wuerthner et al., *Keeping the Wild*, x.

182. Revkin, "Peter Kareiva."

183. Krista Tippett, "Teilhard de Chardin's 'Planetary Mind' and Our Spiritual Evolution," *On Being* transcript, December 19, 2012, Onbeing.org/program/transcript/4967.

184. Revkin, "Embracing the Anthropocene."

185. Andrew Revkin, "Remembering the Great Worker," *New York Times Dot Earth Blog*, June 4, 2009, http://dotearth.blogs.nytimes.com/2009/06/04/the-great-worker/.

186. See Andrew Revkin, "Paths to a 'Good' Anthropocene" (lecture, Association for Environmental Studies and Sciences, January 20, 2014), www.youtube.com/watch?v = VOtj3mskx5k.

187. Mary Evelyn Tucker, "Thomas Berry and the New Story: An Introduction to the Work of Thomas Berry," in *The Intellectual Journey of Thomas Berry: Imagining the Earth Community*, ed. Heather Eaton (Lanham, MD: Lexington Books, 2014), 10.

188. Berry, *Dream of the Earth*, 19.

189. Ibid.

190. Ibid., 19–20 (emphasis mine).

191. Mary Evelyn Tucker, "Thomas Berry," in *The Encyclopedia of Religion and Nature*, vol. 1, ed. Bron Taylor (New York: Continuum, 2nd edition, 2008), 165.

192. Soulé, "'New Conservation,'" 79–80.

193. Hamilton and Grinevald raise concerns about the deflationary move of seeing the current epoch as coextensive with human activity stretching back thousands of years, or more. Noospheric / Ecozoic framings treat humans' alleged rise to geological dominance as something that emerges—gradually but inevitably—out of deep time. These frameworks are impotent to critique attitudes and behaviors contributing to climate change and other Anthropocenic transformations. "Was the Anthropocene Anticipated?" 2.

194. A good example of a progressive evolutionary storyline that erodes concern for Anthropocenic changes to the planet like climate change is the David H. Koch–funded Hall of Human Origins, at the Smithsonian Museum. The Hall presents an ascendant narrative of human innovation and adaptability, positing increases in brain size and information-processing capacities in humans as direct responses to climate challenges that (according to the Smithsonian) have always plagued our resourceful species. Interestingly, the exhibit's curator, paleoanthropologist Rick Potts, and others involved in presenting the exhibit to a broad public, are inspired by Teilhard (among them is Tucker). The appeal of this storyline to libertarian climate-deniers like David Koch is obvious: changing climates drive progress and innovation, and humans have always adapted and improved themselves in response. Hence, there is little reason to worry about, and many reasons to embrace, current climate fluctuations. For more, see my essay, "Surviving the Anthropocene: Big Money and Big Brains at the Smithsonian," *Inhabiting the Anthropocene Blog*, July 5, 2016. https://inhabitingtheanthropocene.com/2016/07/05/surviving-the-anthropocene/.

195. Hamilton and Grinevald, "Was the Anthropocene Anticipated?" 9.

6. GENESIS 2.0

EPIGRAPH: Richard Dawkins, interview by *Spiegel Online*, "Religion? Reality Has a Grander Magic of Its Own," March 2, 2011, www.spiegel.de/international/world/interview-with-scientist-richard-dawkins-religion-reality-has-a-grander-magic-of-its-own-a-748673.html.

1. Michael Dowd and Connie Barlow, "Evolutionary Evangelism," in *Encyclopedia of Religion and Nature*, vol. 1, ed. Bron Taylor (New York: Continuum, 2008), 630.

2. "Michael Dowd, America's Evolutionary Evangelist," The Great Story, n.d., http://thegreatstory.org/michaeldowd.html.

3. Michael Dowd and Connie Barlow, "Evolutionize Your Life," Evolving Wisdom, 2011, http://evolutionizeyourlife.com/free-online-class.php.

4. Ibid.

5. Michael Dowd, *Thank God for Evolution: How the Marriage of Science and Religion Will Transform Your Life and Our World* (New York: Penguin, 2009), 275.

6. Dowd, "Evidential Mysticism and the Future of Earth," The Great Story, Fall 2014, thegreatstory.org/dowd-evidential-mysticism.pdf.

7. Dowd, *Thank God for Evolution*, 83.

8. Ibid., 361.

9. Ibid., 2.

10. Michael Dowd, "New Theists: Knowers, Not Believers," *Huffington Post*, June 15, 2012, www.huffingtonpost.com/rev-michael-dowd/new-theists-knowers-not-believers_b_1586301.html.

11. A creatheist (crea-*theist*) in Dowd and Barlow's usage is an atheist who "knows that the whole of reality is creative and that humans are an expression of this divine process." See Amy Hassinger, "Welcome to the Ecozoic Era," *UU World*, February 20, 2006, www.uuworld.org/articles/wonder-evolution.

12. Indeed, readers familiar with Barlow's writing may experience déjà vu as they peruse Dowd's work; entire sections of *Thank God for Evolution* are excerpted verbatim from Barlow's *Green Space, Green Time*, though Dowd is listed as sole author.

13. An exaptation is a shift in the function of a trait during its evolution. Hence a trait that evolved to have one function may be co-opted for another. An exaptation therefore is not an adaptation. The concept of exaptation is usually seen to be in tension with teleological or progressive accounts of evolution, such as that generally espoused by Dowd.

14. Dowd, *Thank God for Evolution*, 34.

15. Ibid., 25.

16. Ibid., 26.

17. Connie Barlow, "Pluto's Identity Crisis: A Great Story Parable," The Great Story, last modified March 2007, www.thegreatstory.org/Plutoscript.pdf.

18. Dowd, *Thank God for Evolution*, 36.

19. Ibid., 51–52.

20. Dowd cites this passage as one of his favorites from Berry, in a post dedicated to Berry following his death in 2009. Michael Dowd, "Thomas Berry, 1916–2009," *Thank God for Evolution Blog*, June 2009, http://thankgodforevolution.com/node/1869.

21. Dowd, *Thank God for Evolution*, 26.

22. Gould defends a far more contingent view of evolution in his *Wonderful Life: The Burgess Shale and the Nature of History* (New York: Norton, 1989), arguing that if we were able to rewind and then replay the "tape of life," entirely different life-forms would emerge. Conway Morris, by contrast, defends a convergent account of the evolution of inevitable forms in *Life's Solution: Inevitable Humans in a Lonely Universe* (Cambridge: Cambridge University Press, 2004).

23. Connie Barlow, *Green Space, Green Time: The Way of Science* (New York: Copernicus, 1997), 38.

24. Connie Barlow, "Let There Be Sight! A Celebration of Convergent Evolution," The Great Story, last modified April 2011, www.thegreatstory.org/convergence.html.

25. Celia Deane-Drummond defends an evolutionary-theological position that incorporates both contingency and convergence. She discerns (but does not necessarily endorse as accurate) certain parallels between Conway Morris's convergent account and the relative fixity of Natural Law theory. As I note below, in place of a grand and somewhat fixed "epic" of evolution, such as Dowd and Barlow celebrate, she develops a more nuanced motif of "theodrama" that captures both the contingent and convergent features of evolutionary history and processes. See Deane-Drummond, *Christ and Evolution: Wonder and Wisdom* (Minneapolis: Augsburg Fortress, 2009).

26. Dowd describes Big History as "the scholarly enterprise of discerning patterns and meaningful storylines in the 13.7-billion-year saga of everyone and everything (a.k.a. the Universe Story, the Epic of Evolution, or the Great Story)," and cites Julian Huxley's and Teilhard de Chardin's cosmologies as "important antecedents." Michael Dowd, "Big History Hits the Big Time," *Huffington Post,* May 8, 2012, www.huffingtonpost.com/rev-michael-dowd/big-news-about-big-histor_b_1477137.html.

27. Dowd, *Thank God for Evolution,* 171.

28. See Dowd's chapter on "Realizing Salvation," in *Thank God for Evolution.*

29. Brandon Keim, "Former Evangelical Minister Has a New Message: Jesus Hearts Darwin," *Wired,* December 5, 2007, http://archive.wired.com/science/planetearth/news/2007/12/dowd_qa.

30. Dowd, *Thank God for Evolution,* 15.

31. Keim, "Former Evangelical Minister."

32. Michael Dowd, "Reverend Michael Dowd Comes Out as Reverend Reality" (video, November 29, 2014), www.youtube.com/watch?v = CuqoJ_mHbNg.

33. Dowd, "Thomas Berry: 1916–2009."

34. Dowd, "Big History Hits the Big Time."

35. Ibid.

36. Ibid.

37. Michael Dowd, "Reality: God's Secular Name," *Thank God for Evolution Blog,* 2009, http://thankgodforevolution.com/node/1902.

38. Michael Dowd, "New Atheists Are God's Prophets," *Thank God for Evolution Blog,* June 4, 2010, http://thankgodforevolution.com/node/2018.

39. Michael Dowd, "The Evidential Reformation: Humanity Comes of Age," *Evolutionary Times,* September 5, 2011, http://evolutionarytimes.org/index.php?id = 1224152607589129425.

40. Michael Dowd, *Thank God for Evolution Blog,* 2012, http://thankgodforevolution.com/node/2012.

41. "Thank God for Atheists?" *Patheos*, August 15, 2010, www.patheos.com/blogs /unreasonablefaith/2010/08/thank-god-for-atheists/. For a more detailed and sermonic presentation of these ideas see Michael Dowd, "Thank God for the New Atheists!" *The Great Story*, August 2010, http://thegreatstory.org/new-atheists.pdf.

42. Connie Barlow, "Ritualizing Big History," Metanexus, March 14, 2013, www.metanexus .net/blog/ritualizing-big-history.

43. Ibid.

44. Ibid.

45. Quoted in Tom Atlee, "An Emerging Evolutionary Spirituality Project: Evolutionary Revivals!" Evolutionary Life, December 2006, www.co-intelligence.org/newsletter /EvolutionaryRevivals1.html.

46. Richard Dawkins, *The Ancestor's Tale: A Pilgrimage to the Dawn of Evolution* (New York: Houghton Mifflin, 2004), 8.

47. Interestingly, in telling the tale in reverse order—a journey into the past that leads back to our common ancestors—Dawkins's tale intentionally avoids the implication that evolution necessarily culminated in the evolution of humans. Dowd and Barlow do not appear to give much thought to this difference, though it appears at odds with their preference for a progressive evolutionary narrative.

48. Connie Barlow, "We Are All Cousins" Song, The Great Story, 2009, www.thegreat-story.org/ancestors-tale.html.

49. Jon Cleland-Host, "Ancestors Meditation," "We Are All Cousins," The Great Story, 2009, http://thegreatstory.org/ancestors-tale.html.

50. Dowd recommends a video lecture by fundamentalist Christian–turned-atheist Seth Andrews called "Get Them While They're Young," in his blog post "Inoculating Kids against Fundamentalism," *Huffington Post Religion Blog*, July 17, 2013, www.huffingtonpost .com/rev-michael-dowd/inoculating-kids-against-_b_3601229.html.

51. Connie Barlow, "Teachers Guide to 'We Are All Cousins,'" The Great Story, February 2013, http://thegreatstory.org/we-are-all-cousins-teacherguide.pdf.

52. The verses appear in Dowd, *Thank God for Evolution*, 91.

53. Richard Dawkins, *The Magic of Reality: How We Know What's Really True* (New York: Free Press, 2011), 265.

54. Michael Dowd and Connie Barlow, "*The Magic of Reality*: An Inside Look at Richard Dawkins [*sic*] First Children's Book" (video, October 9, 2011), www.youtube.com/watch?v = CcOwS8EFSoU.

55. Ibid., 23.

56. See Richard Dawkins, *A Devil's Chaplain: Reflections on Hope, Lies, Science, and Love* (New York: Houghton Mifflin, 2003), particularly his essay titled "The Great Convergence" where he takes Ursula Goodenough to task for referring to her sense of awe as religious.

57. Dowd and Barlow, "*The Magic of Reality*: An Inside Look."

58. Ibid.

59. Dowd, "Big History Hits the Big Time."

60. Dawkins has made known his disapproval of the Harry Potter series, not only in *The Magic of Reality* but frequently in public lectures and interviews. See Martin Beckford and Urmee Khan, "Harry Potter Fails to Cast Spell over Professor Richard Dawkins," *Telegraph*,

October 24, 2008, www.telegraph.co.uk/news/3255972/Harry-Potter-fails-to-cast-spell-over-Professor-Richard-Dawkins.html.

61. Dowd, *Thank God for Evolution*, 77.

62. Ibid.

63. Dowd notes that while he does not endorse everything the Church of Reality proclaims, "much of it is really good!" Michael Dowd, "Religion Is about Right Relation to Reality, Not the Supernatural," *Thank God for Evolution Blog*, http://thankgodforevolution.com/node/2012.

64. "Welcome Home," The Church of Reality, www.churchofreality.org/wisdom/welcome_home/.

65. "Registered Trademark," The Church of Reality, www.churchofreality.org/wisdom/trademark/.

66. Mark Perkel, e-mail correspondence to Church of Reality subscribers, July 25, 2012.

67. Barlow, *Green Space, Green Time*, 43.

68. Ibid., 50.

69. Ibid., 53

70. Ibid.

71. Ibid.

72. Rue quoted in ibid., 71.

73. Ibid., 59.

74. Ibid., 7.

75. Ibid.

76. Ibid., 240.

77. Ibid., 17.

78. See Wilson's endnotes to *Consilience: the Unity of Knowledge* (New York: Vintage, 1998), particularly for Chapter 3, "The Enlightenment."

79. Edward O. Wilson, *On Human Nature* (Cambridge, MA: Harvard University Press, 1978), 206.

80. Barlow, *Green Space, Green Time*, 294.

81. Peter J. Bowler, *Evolution: The History of an Idea* (Berkeley: University of California Press, 2003), 325.

82. Ibid., 310.

83. Barlow, *Green Space, Green Time*, 283, 296.

84. Ibid., 290.

85. Ibid., 291.

86. Ibid., 19.

87. Ibid., 274–75.

88. Quoted in ibid., 280.

89. Quoted in ibid., 292.

90. Eger argues that the minor epic might appropriately serve as an entry point to the grand evolutionary narrative and that this telling of the story is preferable to the standard narration, because it reveals the epic as a human construction, not a final truth closed off to public communication and interpretation. The epic that emerges may then be appropriated in various ways by those who encounter it. But Barlow resists this degree of openness, and invokes the minor epic as a way of increasing our sense of "security" and "pride" in ourselves. Ibid., 291.

91. Ibid., 292.

92. Quoted in ibid., 292.

93. The discussion originated on a listserv of the Institute for Religion in an Age of Science, and was later published in the *Epic of Evolution Journal:* Connie Barlow et al., "Forum: Epic, Story, Narrative: A Cosmogen Dialogue," *Epic of Evolution Journal* (Fall 1998): 10–16.

94. Ibid., 15.

95. Ibid., 14.

96. Ibid., 13.

97. Connie Barlow, "Science Update: The Rebirth of Philosophical Paleontology," *Epic of Evolution Journal* (Fall 1998): 31, http://thegreatstory.org/Epic-Evol-Journal.html.

98. Barlow et al., "Forum: Epic, Story, Narrative," 11.

99. Ibid., 13.

100. Ibid., 15.

101. Ibid.

102. Ibid.

103. Paul A. Harris, "To Tell a Transformational Tale: The Evolutionary Epic as Narrative Genre," in *The Evolutionary Epic: Science's Story and Humanity's Response,* ed. Cheryl Genet et al. (Santa Margarita, CA: Collins Foundation Press, 2009), 102.

104. David Christian, "The Evolutionary Epic and the Chronometric Revolution," in Genet et al., *Evolutionary Epic,* 98.

105. Harris, "To Tell a Transformational Tale," in Genet et al., *Evolutionary Epic,* 102.

106. Ibid.

107. Ibid.

108. Ibid., 105.

109. It is not clear that Harris's analysis is aimed at Tucker and Swimme's narrative, and his essay appeared prior to *Journey of the Universe.* Nevertheless, his insights are useful in thinking about the relationship between content and format in the new cosmology as a whole. Berry and Swimme sometimes move forward and backward in time in their telling of story in *The Universe Story,* though the typical telling is linear and forward-looking.

110. Celia Deane-Drummond, "Christ and Evolution: A Drama of Wisdom?" *Zygon* 47, no. 3 (September 2012): 528.

111. Ibid., 529.

112. Ibid., 530.

113. Loyal Rue, "Epic of Evolution," in Taylor, *Encyclopedia of Religion and Nature,* 614.

114. Kathy Schick and Nicholas Toth, "The 'Little Bang': The Origins and Adaptive Significance of Human Stone Toolmaking," in Genet et al., *Evolutionary Epic,* 43.

115. Barlow, *Green Space, Green Time,* 292.

116. Nancy E. Abrams and Joel R. Primack, "The Epic of Cosmic Evolution," in Genet et al., *Evolutionary Epic,* 109–13.

117. Brian Thomas Swimme and Mary Evelyn Tucker, *Journey of the Universe* (New Haven, CT: Yale University Press, 2011), 20.

118. Interestingly, Wilson actually proposes a *labyrinth* as an image that captures the consilient quest for total knowledge. Wilson hits upon the same myth suggested by Harris as a better model for the Epic's narrative form, the tale of Ariadne's thread. The labyrinth is the setting for the story of Ariadne, Harris notes, "but also may be seen as a map of the

myth's narrative logic" and more generally "a metaphor for narrative itself." Wilson suggests that the Cretan labyrinth serves as a metaphor for consilience, with Ariadne's thread representing the tortuous progress of knowledge and suggests that the peculiarities of the labyrinth render complete mastery of its terrain impossible. Taking the labyrinth metaphor seriously suggests that Wilson's ambition to find a handful of laws binding the disciplines together and explaining all of physical reality is a pipe dream, a scientist's expression of distaste for a complex, messy world. The labyrinth has a certain intuitive appeal, Harris argues, because "in several cultural traditions, it is viewed as a map of the cosmos." "To Tell a Transformational Tale," in Genet et al., *Evolutionary Epic*, 104.

119. Brian Swimme, "The Cultural Significance of the Story of the Universe," in *The Epic of Evolution: Science and Religion in Dialogue*, ed. James B. Miller (Upper Saddle River, NJ: Pearson, 2004), 38.

120. Scott Russell Sanders, "The Most Human Art" (draft conference paper, Journey of the Universe Conference, March 24–26, 2011), 4, www.journeyoftheuniverse.org/conference-at-yale/.

7. MAKING SENSE OF WONDER

EPIGRAPH: David Abram, interview by Derrick Jensen, July 2000, published in Jensen, ed., *How Shall I Live My Life?: On Liberating the Earth from Civilization* (Oakland: PM Press, 2008), available from Alliance for Wild Ethics, http://wildethics.org/essay/david-abram-interviewed-by-derrick-jensen/.

1. Ronald W. Hepburn, *Wonder and Other Essays: Eight Studies in Aesthetics and Neighboring Fields* (Edinburgh: Edinburgh University Press, 1984), 137.

2. Mary-Jane Rubenstein, *Strange Wonder: The Closure of Metaphysics and the Opening of Awe* (New York: Columbia University Press, 2010), 12.

3. Rubenstein, *Strange Wonder*, 7–8.

4. Hepburn, *Wonder and Other Essays*, 134.

5. Sam Keen, *Apology for Wonder* (New York: Harper, 1973), 26.

6. Hepburn, *Wonder and Other Essays*, 132.

7. Francis Bacon's puppet analogy, from several centuries ago, remains suggestive of the way in which gene-centered biologists seek to locate our genuine motivating forces in the actions of our genes that pull the strings.

8. Hepburn, *Wonder and Other Essays*, 139.

9. Ibid., 139 (emphasis mine).

10. Ibid., 138.

11. Loren Eiseley, "The Coming of the Giant Wasps," in *All the Strange Hours: The Excavation of a Life* (Lincoln, NE: Bison Books, 2000) 242. Eiseley's expression of wonder here straddles two closely related categories outlined by Hepburn: that which remains "perceptually wonder-evoking" (where perceptual contrasts are highlighted) and wonder at "emergent qualities" such as the "evolutionary emergence of living structures from the less ordered and less differentiated" (Hepburn, *Wonder and Other Essays*, 139).

12. Annie Dillard, *An American Childhood* (New York: Harper and Row, 1987), 161.

13. Hepburn, *Wonder and Other Essays*, 138.

14. Ibid., 139.

15. As I have noted, some mythmakers, notably Rue and Goodenough, recognize the contingency of the evolutionary process.

16. Keen refers to this as ontological wonder: "The primal source of all wonder is not an object but the fact that something exists rather than nothing . . . there is no necessary reason for the existence of the world or anything in it." Keen, *Apology for Wonder*, 22. Both Hepburn and Keen attribute the idea to Wittgenstein.

17. Hepburn, *Wonder and Other Essays*, 142–43.

18. Ibid., 33–34.

19. See Bill Vitek and Wes Jackson, eds., *The Virtues of Ignorance: Complexity, Sustainability, and the Limits of Knowledge* (Lexington: University of Kentucky Press, 2008).

20. The details of Carson's life and work and her reasons for writing *Silent Spring* can be found in a number of excellent biographies of Carson that have appeared in the last several years, including Linda Lear's *Rachel Carson: Witness for Nature* (New York: Henry Holt, 1997); Mark Lytle's *The Gentle Subversive: Rachel Carson,* Silent Spring, *and the Rise of the Environmental Movement* (New York: Oxford University Press, 2007); and William Souder's *On a Farther Shore: The Life and Legacy of Rachel Carson* (New York: Crown, 2012). Some of Carson's public lectures, previously unpublished essays, letters, and other miscellaneous writings are available in *Lost Woods: The Discovered Writings of Rachel Carson,* ed. Linda Lear (Boston: Beacon, 1998). The Beinecke Rare Book and Manuscript Library at Yale University houses Carson's papers.

21. Carson received a master's degree in marine zoology from Johns Hopkins University in 1932 and began coursework toward a PhD, but financial and family burdens prevented her from completing a doctorate.

22. Nancy K. Frankenberry, *The Faith of Scientists: In Their Own Words* (Princeton, NJ: Princeton University Press, 2008), 197.

23. In an obvious echo of Genesis, Carson writes of the early Earth: "For there was no living voice, and no living thing moved over the surface of the rocks." Rachel Carson, *The Sea Around Us* (1961; repr., New York: New American Library, 1991), 1.

24. Carson, "The Real World around Us," in *Lost Woods,* 163.

25. Michael A. Bryson, "Nature, Narrative, and the Scientist-Writer: Rachel Carson's and Loren Eiseley's Critique of Science," *Technical Communication Quarterly* 12, no. 4 (Fall 2003): 369.

26. Ibid., 386.

27. Loren Eiseley, "Using a Plague to Fight a Plague," *Saturday Review,* September 29, 1962, 18.

28. Rachel Carson, *Always, Rachel: The Letters of Rachel Carson and Dorothy Freeman, 1952–1964—The Story of a Remarkable Friendship,* ed. Martha Freeman (Boston: Beacon Press, 1994), 355.

29. Bryson, "Nature, Narrative, and the Scientist-Writer," 378.

30. Rachel Carson, "Biological Sciences," in *Lost Woods,* 165.

31. Bryson, "Nature, Narrative, and the Scientist-Writer," 380.

32. Loren Eiseley, "How the World Became Natural," in *Firmament of Time* (New York: Atheneum, 1960), 6–7.

33. Loren Eiseley, "Days of a Thinker," in *All the Strange Hours,* 201.

34. Loren Eiseley, *The Unexpected Universe* (New York: Harcourt and Brace, 1969), 31.

35. Loren Eiseley, "Strangeness in the Proportion," in *The Night Country* (New York: Scribner, 1971), 139.

36. Eiseley, *Unexpected Universe*, 31.

37. Carson, "Real World around Us," in *Lost Woods*, 161.

38. Richard E. Wentz, "The American Spirituality of Loren Eiseley," *Christian Century*, April 1984, 431, www.religion-online.org/showarticle.asp?title = 1391.

39. J. Matthew Ashley criticizes the totalizing metanarrative of the Universe Story and instead frames the results of science as a composite of 'petit narratives,' such as are found in Aldo Leopold's work, notably, *A Sand County Almanac* (1949). Leopold's writing—like Eiseley's, I would argue—offers a "more humble constellating of small stories" that help to chart "a more adequate terrain on which to engage the tableau that the sciences are opening up to us.... It does so without the dangers attendant on metanarratives like the universe story." J. Matthew Ashley, "Reading the Universe Story Theologically: The Contribution of a Biblical Narrative Imagination," *Theological Studies* 71 (2010): 899. For a response to such critiques of Berry, see Stephen Dunn, "Afterword: Postmodern Suggestions," in *The Intellectual Journey of Thomas Berry*, ed. Heather Eaton (Lanham, MD: Lexington Books, 2014), 239–46.

40. Bryson, "Nature, Narrative, and the Scientist-Writer," 381.

41. Loren Eiseley, *The Immense Journey* (New York: Vintage, 1956), 197.

42. Ibid., 13.

43. Ibid., 12.

44. Bryson, "Nature, Narrative, and the Scientist-Writer," 381.

45. Eiseley, *All the Strange Hours*, 245.

46. Eiseley, *Immense Journey*, 25.

47. Bron Taylor and Gavin van Horn, "Nature Religion and Environmentalism in North America," in *Faith in America: Changes, Challenges, New Directions*, vol. 3, ed. Charles Lippy (New York: Praeger, 2006), 182.

48. See Mary Evelyn Tucker, "Biography of Thomas Berry," Center for Humans and Nature, www.humansandnature.org/biography-of-thomas-berry.

49. Mary Evelyn Tucker, personal communication with author, July 1, 2012. Tucker and Swimme also mention the importance of Eiseley's work for their project in the introductory pages to Brian Thomas Swimme and Mary Evelyn Tucker, *Journey of the Universe* (New Haven, CT: Yale University Press, 2011), xi.

50. Mary Evelyn Tucker, "Journey of the Universe: The Lineage of a New Story," http://journeyoftheuniverse.com/.

51. Mary Evelyn Tucker, "Religion and Ecology: The Interaction of Cosmology and Cultivation," in *The Good in Nature and Humanity: Connecting Science, Religion, and Spirituality in the Natural World*, ed. Stephen R. Kellert and Timothy J. Farnham (Washington, DC: Island Press, 2002), 72.

52. Connie Barlow, "An Immense Journey: Religious Naturalism and the Great Story," *The Great Story*, December 2003, www.thegreatstory.org/ReligiousNaturalism.html. The essay is a tribute not only to Eiseley but also to "Julian Huxley, Paul Martin, Aldo Leopold, Thomas Berry, Brian Swimme, Annie Dillard," though it is difficult to imagine how Huxley and Eiseley belong in the same category, given Eiseley's persistent critique of anthropocentrism and teleology in evolutionary science and Huxley's conceit that humans are in the driver's seat of evolution.

53. See Mary Ellen Pitts, *Toward a Dialogue of Understandings: Loren Eiseley and the Critique of Science* (Bethlehem, PA: Lehigh University, 1995).

54. Bryson, "Nature, Narrative, and the Scientist-Writer," 386.

55. Eiseley, who places Darwin in the former category and Freud in the latter, describes Darwin as "infused with wonder over the clambering tree of life," while Freud dismisses all such oceanic feelings as an atavistic survival of the infant's ego. Loren Eiseley, "Science and the Sense of the Holy," in *The Star Thrower* (New York: Times Books, 1978), 191.

56. Ibid., 190.

57. Ibid., 200.

58. For more on the destructive wonder of atomic science, see Lisa H. Sideris, "Forbidden Fruit: Wonder, Religious Narrative, and the Quest for the Atomic Bomb," in *Technofutures, Nature and the Sacred: Transdisciplinary Perspectives,* ed. Celia Deane-Drummond, Sigurd Bergmann, and Bronislaw Szerszynski (Farnham, Surrey: Ashgate, 2015).

59. Barlow depicts the Epic as arising from the storytelling efforts of a range of diverse figures, including Huxley, Wilson, Swimme, Berry, Goodenough, Rue, Dawkins, Dillard, Eiseley, and Jim Lovelock. See Connie Barlow, *Green Space, Green Time: The Way of Science* (New York: Copernicus, 1997), 237.

60. Rachel Carson, *The Edge of the Sea* (New York: Mariner Books, 1998), xiv.

61. Ibid., xiii.

62. Quoted in Frankenberry, *Faith of Scientists,* 218.

63. Gary Kroll, "Rachel Carson's *The Sea Around Us,* Ocean-Centrism, and a Nascent Ocean Ethic," in *Rachel Carson: Legacy and Challenge,* ed. Lisa H. Sideris and Kathleen Dean Moore (New York: State University of New York Press, 2008), 118–35.

64. Rachel Carson, "Memo to Mrs. Eales on *Under the Sea-Wind,*" in *Lost Woods,* 55.

65. Rachel Carson, "*New York Herald-Tribune* Book and Author Luncheon Speech," in *Lost Woods,* 80.

66. Rachel Carson, "Design for Nature Writing," in *Lost Woods,* 96.

67. Carson, *Sea Around Us,* 212.

68. Rachel Carson, "*New York Herald-Tribune* Book and Author Luncheon Speech," in *Lost Woods,* 80.

69. Richard Dawkins, "Science, Delusion, and the Appetite for Wonder" (Richard Dimbleby Lecture for BBC 1 Television, November 12, 1996), www.edge.org/conversation/richard_dawkins-science-delusion-and-the-appetite-for-wonder.

70. David Abram, *The Spell of the Sensuous: Perception and Language in a More than Human World* (New York: Vintage, 1996), 70.

71. Carson, *Sea Around Us,* 3.

72. Ibid.

73. Ibid., 7.

74. Swimme and Tucker, *Journey of the Universe,* 1–5.

75. In public presentations of *Journey,* the project is presented as a mere "conversation beginner," an "offering," just a "starting point." Yet it is clearly far more ambitious. See, for example, Mary Evelyn Tucker, "*Journey of the Universe* and the World Religions" (lecture, Chautauqua Institution in New York, June 24, 2013), www.journeyoftheuniverse.org/conference-at-chautauqua/.

76. Ian Hesketh, "The Story of Big History," *History of the Present* 4, no. 2 (Fall 2014): 171–202, 181.

77. Mary H. O'Brien writes that "Rachel Carson shows profound respect for her readers. She assumes they will be able to follow scientific details, and to apply ethics that are already familiar to them in human society." See "Science, Ethics, and Changed Lives: How Did Rachel Carson Do It?" Science and Environmental Health Network, November 8–10, 2000, www.sehn.org/web2printer4.php?img = 0&lnk = 0&page = conbiocarson.html.

78. Carson, *Sea Around Us*, 7.

79. Carson, *Edge of the Sea*, 5.

80. Hepburn, *Wonder and Other Essays*, 135.

81. Carson, *Edge of the Sea*, 5.

82. Lisa H. Sideris, "The Secular and Religious Source of Rachel Carson's Sense of Wonder," in Sideris and Moore, *Rachel Carson: Legacy and Challenge*, 232–50.

83. Quoted in Paul Brooks, *House of Life: Rachel Carson at Work* (Boston: Houghton Mifflin, 1972), 129.

84. Rachel Carson to Dorothy Freeman, February 1, 1958, in *Always, Rachel*, 248–49.

85. Rachel Carson, *Silent Spring* (Boston: Houghton Mifflin, 1962), 68–69.

86. Ben Minteer, "The Perils of De-Extinction," *Minding Nature* 8, no. 1 (January 2015): 11–17, 13–14, www.humansandnature.org/the-perils-of-de-extinction.

87. For this reason, I have always thought it not quite appropriate that Wilson contributes the afterword to the fortieth anniversary edition of *Silent Spring*. Carson, I suspect, would find much in his worldview appalling.

88. Wilson, *On Human Nature* (Cambridge, MA: Harvard University Press, 1978), 202.

89. Wilson believes that biophilia is a genetic endowment, and thus environmental ethics that builds upon biophilia has an "objective" basis. "This ethic will endure [Wilson believes] because it is 'true': it is grounded in the real world that Wilson's scientific investigations have revealed to him." David Takacs, *The Idea of Biodiversity: Philosophies of Paradise* (Baltimore: John Hopkins University Press, 1996), 319.

90. Edward O. Wilson, *Consilience: The Unity of Knowledge* (New York: Vintage, 1998), 7.

91. Rachel Carson, "Design for Nature Writing," *Lost Woods*, 94.

92. Ibid., 92.

93. Lear, *Rachel Carson: Witness for Nature*, 24.

94. Mark Stoll, "Rachel Carson," in *Eminent Lives in Twentieth-Century Science and Religion*, ed. Nicolaas A. Rupke (Frankfurt am Main: Peter Lang, 2009), 54–57.

95. Carson, quoted in Lear, *Rachel Carson: Witness for Nature*, 397.

96. Carson protests against humans taking on the functions of God, though she sometimes puts the word in scare quotes.

97. Stoll, "Rachel Carson," in Rupke, *Eminent Lives*, 66–67.

98. Carson to Dorothy Freeman, *Always, Rachel*, 241.

99. Kenny Walker and Lynda Walsh, " 'No One Yet Knows What the Ultimate Consequences May Be': How Rachel Carson Transformed Scientific Uncertainty into a Site for Public Participation in *Silent Spring*," *Journal of Business and Technical Communication* 26, no. 1 (2011): 3–34.

246 NOTES TO PAGES 188–191

100. Walker and Walsh, "'No One Yet Knows,'" 21.

101. Ibid., 27.

102. Carson, *Silent Spring*, 277.

103. Walker and Walsh, "'No One Yet Knows,'" 26–27.

104. Carson, *Silent Spring*, 127.

105. Paul G. Heltne, "Imposed Ignorance and Humble Ignorance—Two Worldviews," in Vitek and Jackson, *Virtues of Ignorance*, 136.

106. Heltne, "Imposed Ignorance and Humble Ignorance," 136. Much as Ashley turns to Leopold's "petite narratives" as a counterpoint to totalizing metanarratives of the New Story, Heltne invokes Leopold's writing about forestry as a case in point of humble ignorance and a "humility-based worldview that starts from the point of admitted ignorance and leads us to continuous renewal and celebration." Ibid., 138.

107. Ibid., 135.

108. Carson, *Silent Spring*, 13.

109. Heltne, "Imposed Ignorance and Humble Ignorance," 135.

110. David Ehrenfeld's *The Arrogance of Humanism* (Oxford: Oxford University Press, 1978) might be seen as a (rather harsher and uncompromising) precursor to *The Virtues of Ignorance*. Ehrenfeld opens the book, appropriately, with a passage from Job: "Is it by your wisdom that the hawk soars, and spreads his wings toward the south?"

111. Robert Proctor and Londa Schiebinger have proposed that the study of ignorance be given its own category, akin to epistemology, namely, agnotology. There are many different varieties of ignorance, they note, "and lots of different reasons to expose it, undo it, deplore it, or seek it" (24). They trace agnotology's impact on science, politics, and public health, among other areas, and recognize that greater awareness of ignorance can powerfully challenge hubris. This category of ignorance that is deliberately sought (not imposed) gestures toward the virtuous ignorance that Vitek and Jackson have in mind. Proctor and Schiebinger allude to moral resistance or moral caution regarding certain types of knowledge—ignorance deliberately maintained or created, or knowledge intentionally *limited*, as when deciding not to use certain technologies in the future, or refusing to know about the genetic conditions of one's child. Proctor and Schiebinger, *Agnotology: The Making and Unmaking of Ignorance* (Stanford, CA: Stanford University Press, 2008).

112. Bill Vitek, "Joyful Ignorance and the Civic Mind," in Vitek and Jackson, *Virtues of Ignorance*, 213–14.

113. Bill Vitek and Wes Jackson, "Introduction: Taking Ignorance Seriously," in Vitek and Jackson, *Virtues of Ignorance*, 9.

114. Ibid.

115. Ibid., 7

116. Ibid., 5.

117. Ibid., 9.

118. Dawkins, "Science, Delusion, and the Appetite for Wonder."

119. Vitek and Jackson, "Taking Ignorance Seriously," in Vitek and Jackson, *Virtues of Ignorance*, 1.

120. Ibid., 14.

121. For an excellent discussion of the way scientific and sustainability metaphors might be more carefully (and even democratically) crafted see Brendon Larson, *Metaphors for Environmental Sustainability* (New Haven, CT: Yale University Press, 2011).

122. Craig Holdrege, "Can We See with Fresh Eyes? Beyond a Culture of Abstraction," in Vitek and Jackson, *Virtues of Ignorance,* 324.

123. Neil Evernden, *The Natural Alien: Humankind and Environment* (Toronto: University of Toronto Press, 1993), 141.

124. Stuart Firestein, *Ignorance: How It Drives Science* (New York: Oxford University Press).

125. Ibid., 7.

126. Vitek, "Joyful Ignorance and the Civic Mind," in Vitek and Jackson, *Virtues of Ignorance,* 217.

127. Firestein, *Ignorance,* 17.

128. Rubenstein, *Strange Wonder,* 8.

129. Alan C. Love, "Ignorance: How It Drives Science, Part 2," review of *Ignorance: How It Drives Science,* by Stuart Firestein, *Christianity Today,* August 2012, www.booksandculture.com/articles/webexclusives/2012/august/ignorance-part-2.html.

130. Ibid.

131. Alan C. Love, "The Erotetic Organization of Developmental Biology," in *Towards a Theory of Development,* ed. Alessandro Minelli and Thomas Pradeu (New York: Oxford University Press, 2014), 53.

132. Julie Adeney Thomas, "History and Biology in the Anthropocene: Problems of Scale, Problems of Value," *American Historical Review* 119, no. 5 (December 2014): 1588.

133. Ibid., 1595.

134. Ibid., 1589.

135. Recall in chapter 5, Mary Evelyn Tucker's discussion of the importance of the macro level of cosmic unfolding for locating meaning and purpose in the universe, a la Teilhardian cosmogenesis.

136. Thomas, "History and Biology in the Anthropocene," 1597.

137. Ibid., 1590.

138. Holdrege, "Can We See with Fresh Eyes?" in Vitek and Jackson, *Virtues of Ignorance,* 323–34.

139. J. Baird Callicott recognizes this point as well, noting that the stories science tells may be "accessible only to initiates" or "intellectual elites," though he appears confident that science can be mediated in ways that transform it into a popular mythology ("Myth in Environmental Philosophy," in *Thinking through Myths: Philosophical Perspectives,* ed. Kevin Schilbrack, New York: Routledge, 2002, 171).

140. David Abram, *Becoming Animal: An Earthly Cosmology* (New York: Pantheon, 2010), 5.

141. Holdrege, "Can We See with Fresh Eyes?" in Vitek and Jackson, *Virtues of Ignorance,* 323.

142. Ibid., 324.

143. Abram, *Becoming Animal,* 73.

144. Ibid., 76.

145. Holdrege, "Can We See with Fresh Eyes?" in Vitek and Jackson, *Virtues of Ignorance*, 325.

146. Quoted in Paul Brooks, *Rachel Carson: The Writer at Work* (San Francisco: Sierra Club, 1998), 315–17.

147. Rachel Carson, "To Understand Biology / Preface to *Animal Machines*," in *Lost Woods*, 193.

148. Abram, *Spell of the Sensuous*, 264.

149. Carson, "To Understand Biology," in *Lost Woods*, 194.

150. Keen, *Apology for Wonder*, 30.

151. Rachel Carson, *The Sense of Wonder* (1965; repr., New York: Harper, 1998), 56.

152. Julie Dunlap and Stephen R. Kellert, ed. *Companions in Wonder: Children and Adults Exploring Nature Together* (Cambridge, MA: MIT Press, 2012), 9.

153. Louise Chawla, "Childhood Experiences Associated with Care for the Natural World: A Theoretical Framework for Empirical Results," *Children, Youth and Environments* 17, no. 4 (2007): 144–70, www.colorado.edu/journals/cye.

154. Louise Chawla, "Life Paths into Effective Environmental Action," *Journal of Environmental Education* 31, no. 1 (1999): 21.

155. Piercarlo Valdesolo, "Trust in Science Reduces Concerns about Climate Change," *Scientific American*, September 24, 2014, www.scientificamerican.com/article/trust-in-science-reduces-concerns-about-climate-change/. For the original study, see Marijn H. C. Meijers and Bastiaan T. Rutjens, "The Social Psychology of Climate Change: Affirming Belief in Scientific Progress Reduces Environmentally Friendly Behavior," *European Journal of Social Psychology* 44 (2014): 487–95.

156. Ibid., 488.

157. Ibid., 494.

158. Ibid., 493–94.

159. Ibid., 494.

160. Carson, "To Understand Biology," in *Lost Woods*, 194.

161. Carson, "Real World around Us," in *Lost Woods*, 160.

162. Sam Keen, *Apology for Wonder*, 34.

163. Ibid., 35.

164. Robert Fuller, "Spirituality in the Flesh: The Role of Discrete Emotions in Religious Life," *Journal of the American Academy of Religion* 75, no. 1 (2007): 39.

165. Keen, *Apology for Wonder*, 34.

166. Hepburn, *Wonder and Other Essays*, 146.

167. Dipesh Chakrabarty, "The Climate of History: Four Theses," *Critical Inquiry* 35, no. 2 (Winter 2009): 197–222, 222.

168. Arundhati Roy, "The Greater Common Good," in *The Cost of Living*, ed. Arundhati Roy (New York: Modern Library, 1999), 7–90, 12.

169. "Synopsis" of *Journey of the Universe*, www.journeyoftheuniverse.org/synopsis/

170. Jack Jenkins, "The Growing Indigenous Spiritual Movement that Could Save the Planet," ThinkProgress, September 30, 2016, https://thinkprogress.org/indigenous-spiritual-movement-8f873348a2f5#.e3ogfe9ay.

171. Ibid.

172. Ibid.

173. Loyal Rue, *Everybody's Story: Wising Up to the Epic of Evolution* (Albany: State University of New York Press, 2000), 127.

174. Ursula Goodenough, "What Science Can and Cannot Offer to a Religious Narrative," *Zygon* 29, no. 3 (September 1994): 321–30, 329.

175. Greg Johnson, quoted in Jenkins, "Growing Indigenous Spiritual Movement."

176. Kyle Powys Whyte, "Why Native American Pipeline Resistance in North Dakota Is about Climate Justice," *Conversation*, September 16, 2016, http://theconversation.com/why-the-native-american-pipeline-resistance-in-north-dakota-is-about-climate-justice-64714.

177. Ibid., n.p.

178. Abram, *Spell of the Sensuous*, 268.

179. Hepburn, *Wonder and Other Essays*, 145.

GLOSSARY OF TERMS

Amythia (Loyal Rue):   the claim that civilization is in a state of crisis owing to the lack of a global, unifying myth or narrative that would take the place of competing and obsolete traditional religious myths

Anthropic Principle: the philosophical position that the universe is structured in such a way as to make life and consciousness possible; the strong version of the anthropic principle holds that the universe is somehow compelled to create life and consciousness

Anthropocene: the proposed current geological age in which human activity is the predominant determinant of the environment

Anthropocentric: understanding the world from a perspective that places human values and experience above other considerations

Big History: an emerging scientific approach to history that seeks to provide a *longue durée* history, grounded in scientific conclusions regarding the cosmos, the earth, life, and humanity

Biophilia (E. O. Wilson):   an evolutionarily ingrained love of and instinctive attachment to the natural world

Cephalization: the evolutionary trend in which sense organs and the central nervous system are concentrated at one end of the body; seen as a precursor to the development of large-brained animals (such as humans) and the evolutionary development of consciousness

Compatibilist Wonder: wonder at an experience of a phenomenon that continues even after a causal explanation is found

Conscious Evolution:	the concept that with the emergence of human self-awareness, evolution will henceforth be guided not only by biological processes, but by self-conscious directing by human agents or the human species
Consilience (E. O. Wilson):	a theory endorsing the unity of knowledge which posits that the world is an orderly system and therefore that all knowledge—whether derived from the sciences, the arts, or the humanities—is interrelated and can be reduced to a small number of natural laws
Cosmogenesis (Teilhard de Chardin):	a teleological theory of the evolution of the universe as a process that is moving toward a spiritual climax
Dark Green Religion (Bron Taylor):	religion or religious-like sensibility and environmentalism grounded in evolutionary theory and ecology
Ecomodernism:	a school of environmental philosophy which proposes that humans can protect nature and limit environmental degradation through technology; it embraces the concept of the Anthropocene and holds that the future of nature and humanity can be managed for the common good of both through the judicious use of technology
Ecozoic (Brian Thomas Swimme and Thomas Berry)	an emerging geological era defined by human activity and characterized by a harmonic relationship between humanity and the Earth
Epic Of Evolution:	a grand narrative that combines cosmic, biological, and sociocultural development in what is intended as an all-encompassing and universally accessible story with the potential to replace or supplement traditional religious narratives of cosmic, biological, and human development
Epigenetic:	biological development not determined by genetic makeup; in other words, the effect of influences outside the genome (such as the environment) on biological development
Erotetic:	a methodology that is guided by the asking of questions and assuming at the outset a posture of ignorance; some consider the methodology used (or which should be used) in the sciences to be driven by the asking of questions
Evolutionary Paradigm:	the set of theories, methods, and / or the worldview associated with the theory of evolution
Existential Wonder:	wonder rooted in the contingency of a phenomenon; wonder that something exists rather than nothing
Good Anthropocene:	the belief that the new geological age identified as the *Anthropocene* can be managed through science and technology for positive outcomes for both humans and nature

Hominization (Teilhard de Chardin):	the transition from instinct to thought in evolution, both individual and collective; the stage in the evolution of life on Earth marked by the emergence of *Homo sapiens,* at which point life begins to be dictated by human will
Ionian Enchantment (E. O. Wilson):	the philosophical conviction (ascribed to the ancient Ionian philosophers) that nature is a unified phenomenon which can be explained by physical laws
Literary Darwinism (or biocultural critique / evocriticism):	a branch of literary theory that examines literature through the lens of evolutionary theory by, for example, considering the success or failure of genre, style, etc., as a result of natural selection, or by considering plot, character development, etc., as exhibiting patterns of animal behavior
Materialism (in science):	the position that all phenomena (including such features as thought or spirituality) are reducible to matter and natural laws or explainable in terms of a material cause and natural laws; it is a fundamental principle of consilience and other forms of the unity of science thesis
Meme (Richard Dawkins):	the cultural analogue to biology's gene; an element of a cultural system or a behavior that passes from individual to individual by nongenetic means, namely by imitation
Metareligious / Metamythical:	the perceived relationship between the Epic of Evolution and traditional religion that understands the former as complementary to or the fulfillment of the latter with the goal of enriching or reconciling various faith traditions through a grand narrative
Mythopoeic Science:	an attitude that privileges scientific knowledge over nature and aims to use this privileged knowledge as a basis for an overarching and consecrated narrative of cosmic meaning and biological development
Neural Self (Loyal Rue):	an explanation for personal identity which argues that the brain's innate storytelling functions create narratives about external and subjective events which in turn are developed into a metanarrative of personal subjectivity
New Materialism:	a recently developed philosophical position that emphasizes the vitality and potency of matter
Noosphere (Teilhard de Chardin):	a "sphere" of the Earth ecosystem in addition to the hydro sphere, atmosphere, biosphere, etc., constituted by human thought and social phenomena; the next stage of the Earth's development after the emergence of life, it is a natural stage in cosmogenesis
Omnicompetence:	the view that human beings are capable of fully understanding (through science) the origins and development of the

cosmos and of life, and thus capable of producing a comprehensive mythopoeic science that can provide answers to transcendent questions such as the meaning of existence or the place and purpose of humanity

Ontological Wonder: see *Existential Wonder*

Physics Envy: an attitude ascribed to sciences other than physics that sees physics as a paradigmatic science with the best methodology and the most unified results, and that laments the supposed lack of rigor or unified results of other sciences

Reductionism (in science):   the position that complex phenomena can be explained by (or are *reducible* to) simpler or more fundamental phenomena; or, that complex theories are *reducible* to fundamental laws

Religiopoiesis (Ursula Goodenough):   the activity of producing, or the impulse to produce, a new religion based upon scientific and empirical worldviews

Religious Naturalism: a set of beliefs and attitudes that entail a spiritual response to the natural world without appeal to the supernatural

Scientism: the privileging of science over all other forms of inquiry

Scientize: to make scientific, as in the creation of a scientific religion

Serial Wonder: the pursuit of successive mysteries or puzzles that crop up in the wake of mysteries solved; akin to curiosity

Sociobiology (E. O. Wilson):   the science of studying human social behavior as a consequence of evolution; a form of reductionism that explains social phenomena in terms of biology

Technozoic: a postulated geological era that is an alternative to the more ecologically holistic Ecozoic, in which faith in human science and technology would dictate the future evolution of Earth's ecosystems

Triumphalism (in science):   the attitude that expresses the supposed superiority of science over other forms of human experience such as religion, or over other forms of inquiry such as the humanities

Universe Story: see *Epic of Evolution*

Viability (Loyal Rue):   a moral value ascribed to the act of living, particularly living in such a way as to achieve personal wholeness, social cohesion, and biospheric integrity

Virtuous Ignorance (Bill Vitek and Wes Jackson):   the admission that human ignorance will always outweigh human knowledge (in opposition to Enlightenment ideals of the unity of knowledge or consilience), and that appreciation of this fact is vital for forming an ethical stance toward matters pertaining to scientific knowledge

REFERENCES

Abercrombie, Sharon. "California College Helps Place Humans in Universe Story." *National Catholic Reporter*, November 11, 2011. www.ncronline.org/news/people/california-college-helps-place-humans-universe-story.

Abram, David. *Becoming Animal: An Earthly Cosmology*. New York: Pantheon, 2010.

———. *The Spell of the Sensuous: Perception and Language in a More than Human World*. New York: Vintage, 1996.

Abrams, Nancy E., and Joel R. Primack. "The Epic of Cosmic Evolution." In Genet et al., *Evolutionary Epic*, 109–13.

Adams, Jon. *Interference Patterns: Literary Study, Scientific Knowledge, and Disciplinary Autonomy*. New York: Bucknell University Press, 2007.

The American Teilhard Association. "Our Mission." 2016. www.teilharddechardin.org/index.php/our-mission.

Asafu-Adjaye, John, et al. "An Ecomodernist Manifesto." Breakthrough Institute. April 2015. www.ecomodernism.org/.

Ashley, J. Matthew. "Reading the Universe Story Theologically: The Contribution of a Biblical Narrative Imagination." *Theological Studies* 71 (2010): 870–902.

Atlee, Tom. "An Emerging Evolutionary Spirituality Project: Evolutionary Revivals!" Evolutionary Life, December 2006. www.co-intelligence.org/newsletter/EvolutionaryRevivals1.html.

Barash, David, and Nanelle Barash. *Madame Bovary's Ovaries*. New York: Delacorte Press, 2005.

Barlow, Connie. "The Epic of Evolution: A Report of Current Events." *Teilhard Studies* 30, no. 2 (Fall 1997): 1–3.

———. *Evolution Extended: Biological Debates on the Meaning of Life*. Oxford: Oxford University Press, 1994.

————. "Experiencing the Epic." *Epic of Evolution Journal* (Spring 1999). www.thegreat-story.org/ExperienceEpic.pdf.

————. *Green Space, Green Time: The Way of Science.* New York: Copernicus, 1997.

————. "An Immense Journey: Religious Naturalism and the Great Story." The Great Story. Last modified December 2003. www.thegreatstory.org/ReligiousNaturalism.html.

————. "Pluto's Identity Crisis: A Great Story Parable." The Great Story. Last modified March 2007. www.thegreatstory.org/Plutoscript.pdf.

————. "Ritualizing Big History." Metanexus, March 14, 2013. www.metanexus.net/blog/ritualizing-big-history.

————. "Science Update: The Rebirth of Philosophical Paleontology." *Epic of Evolution Journal* (Fall 1998): 31. http://thegreatstory.org/Epic-Evol-Journal.html.

————. "Teachers' Guide to 'We Are All Cousins.'" The Great Story, February 2013. http://thegreatstory.org/we-are-all-cousins-teacherguide.pdf.

————. "We Are All Cousins" Song. The Great Story, 2009. www.thegreatstory.org/ancestors-tale.html.

————, et al. "Forum: Epic, Story, Narrative: A Cosmogen Dialogue." *Epic of Evolution Journal* (Fall 1998): 10–16.

————, and Michael Dowd, hosts. "Ursula Goodenough: 'The Sacred Depths of Nature.'" Inspiring Naturalism (MP3 podcast), August 27, 2010. http://inspiringnaturalism.libsyn.com/6_ursula_goodenough_the_sacred_depths_of_nature_.

Bauman, Whitney. "Planetary Journeys and Eco-Justice: The Geography of Violence." Draft paper for Yale University Living Cosmology conference, November 8, 2014. www.journeyoftheuniverse.org/storage/Whitney_Bauman.pdf.

Bennett, Jane. *Vibrant Matter: A Political Ecology of Things.* Durham, NC: Duke University Press, 2010.

Berry, Thomas. "The American College in the Ecological Age." In Berry, *Dream of the Earth.*

————. "The American College in the Ecological Age." *Journal of Religion and Intellectual Life* 6, no. 2 (Winter 1989): 7–28.

————. *Befriending the Earth: A Theology of Reconciliation between Humans and the Earth.* Mystic, CT: Twenty-Third, 1991.

————. *The Dream of the Earth.* San Francisco: Sierra Club Books, 1988.

————. "The Gaia Theory: Its Religious Implications." *ARC: The Journal of the Faculty of Religious Studies, McGill University* 22 (1994): 7–19.

————. *The Great Work: Our Way into the Future.* New York: Random House, 1999.

————. "The Human Presence." In Berry, *Dream of the Earth,* 13–23.

————. "The New Story: Comments on the Origin, Identification, and Transmission of Values." *Teilhard Studies* 1 (Winter 1978).

————. "The Viable Human." *In The Great Work: Our Way into the Future,* 56–71. New York: Three Rivers Press, 1999.

Berry, Wendell. *Life Is a Miracle: An Essay against Modern Superstition.* Washington, DC: Counterpoint, 2000.

Bonneuil, Christophe. "The Geological Turn: The Anthropocene and Its Narratives." In Clive Hamilton et al., *The Anthropocene and the Global Environmental Crisis,* 17–31.

Boswell, John D. "Symphony of Science" (music video). Posted October 22, 2015. www.symphonyofscience.com.

Bowler, Peter J. *Evolution: The History of an Idea.* Berkeley: University of California Press, 2003.

Boyd, Brian. "For Evocriticism: Minds Shaped to be Reshaped." *Critical Inquiry* 38, no. 1 (Winter 2012): 388–460.

———. "Literature and Science: Doomed Reduction or Evolutionary Literary Pluralism?" *Evolutionary Psychology* 6, no. 1 (2008): 80–84.

———. *On the Origin of Stories: Evolution, Cognition, and Fiction.* Cambridge, MA: Belknap Press, 2010.

Bridle, Susan. "The Divinization of the Cosmos: An Interview with Brian Swimme on Pierre Teilhard de Chardin." *What Is Enlightenment?* (magazine), September / October 2006. www.renewedpriesthood.org/ca/hpage.cfm?Web_ID = 896.

Brooks, Paul. *Rachel Carson: The Writer at Work.* San Francisco: Sierra Club, 1998.

Brower, Kenneth. "The Danger of Cosmic Genius." *Atlantic,* December 2010. www.theatlantic.com/magazine/archive/2010/12/the-danger-of-cosmic-genius/308306/.

Bryson, Michael A. "Nature, Narrative, and the Scientist-Writer: Rachel Carson's and Loren Eiseley's Critique of Science." *Technical Communication Quarterly* 12, no. 4 (Fall 2003): 369–87.

Burke, Edmund. *A Philosophical Enquiry into the Origin of Our Ideas of the Sublime and the Beautiful.* Edited by J. T. Boulton. London: Routledge and Paul, 1958.

Butler, Tom. "Lives Not Our Own." Introduction to Wuerthner et al., *Keeping the Wild,* ix–xv.

Bynum, Caroline Walker. "Wonder." *American Historical Review* 102, no. 1 (February 1997): 1–26.

Callicott, J. Baird. *Earth Insights: A Multicultural Survey of Ecological Ethics from the Mediterranean Basin to the Australian Outback.* Berkeley: University of California Press, 1994.

———. "Myth and Environmental Philosophy." In *Thinking through Myths: Philosophical Perspectives,* ed. Kevin Schilbrack, 158–73. New York: Routledge, 2002.

———. "Science as Myth (Whether Sacred or Not), Science as Prism." *Journal for the Study of Religion, Nature, and Culture* 9, no. 2 (2015): 154–68.

Carroll, Joseph. "Evolutionary Studies." In *The Encyclopedia of Literary and Cultural Theory,* ed. Michael Ryan et al., 587. Chichester, West Sussex: Wiley Blackwell, 2011.

Carson, Rachel. *Always, Rachel: The Letters of Rachel Carson and Dorothy Freeman, 1952–1964—The Story of a Remarkable Friendship.* Edited by Martha Freeman. Boston: Beacon Press, 1995.

———. "Biological Sciences." In *Lost Woods,* edited by Lear, 164–67.

———. "Design for Nature Writing." In *Lost Woods,* edited by Lear, 93–97.

———. *The Edge of the Sea.* New York: Mariner Books, 1998.

———. "Help Your Child to Wonder." *Woman's Home Companion,* July 1956. http://digitalmedia.fws.gov/cdm/ref/collection/document/id/1055.1956.

———. *Lost Woods: The Discovered Writings of Rachel Carson.* Edited by Linda Lear. Boston: Beacon Press, 1998.

———. "Memo to Mrs. Eales on *Under the Sea-Wind.*" In *Lost Woods,* edited by Lear, 53–62.

———. "*New York Herald-Tribune* Book and Author Luncheon Speech." In *Lost Woods,* edited by Lear, 76–82.

_____. "'The Real World around Us." In *Lost Woods,* edited by Lear, 147–63.

_____. *The Sea Around Us.* 1961. Reprint, New York: New American Library, 1991.

_____. *The Sense of Wonder.* 1965. Reprint, New York: Harper, 1998.

_____. *Silent Spring.* Boston: Houghton Mifflin, 1962.

_____. "To Understand Biology / Preface to *Animal Machines.*" In *Lost Woods,* edited by Lear, 192–96.

Chakrabarty, Dipesh. "The Climate of History: Four Theses." *Critical Inquiry* 35, no. 2 (Winter 2009): 197–222.

Chawla, Louise. "Childhood Experiences Associated with Care for the Natural World: A Theoretical Framework for Empirical Results." *Children, Youth and Environments* 17, no. 4 (2007): 144–70. www.colorado.edu/journals/cye.

_____. "Life Paths into Effective Environmental Action." *Journal of Environmental Education* 31, no. 1 (1999): 15–27.

Cho, Francisca, and Richard K. Squier. "Reductionism: Be Afraid, Be Very Afraid." *Journal of the American Academy of Religion* 76, no. 2 (June 2008): 412–17.

Christian, David. "The Evolutionary Epic and the Chronometric Revolution." In Genet et al., *Evolutionary Epic,* 91–100.

_____. "Foreword: Celebrating the Birth of a New Creation Story." In Genet et al., *Evolutionary Epic,* 11–14.

_____, and William H. McNeill. *Maps of Time: An Introduction to Big History.* Berkeley: University of California Press, 2004.

The Church of Reality. "Registered Trademark." www.churchofreality.org/wisdom/trademark/.

_____. "Welcome Home." www.churchofreality.org/wisdom/welcome_home/.

Cleland-Host, John. "Ancestors Meditation." "We Are All Cousins." The Great Story, 2009. http://thegreatstory.org/ancestors-tale.html.

CNRS (Le Centre national de la recherche scientifique). "Elliptical Galaxies Are Not Dead." *Science Daily,* June 1, 2011. www.sciencedaily.com/releases/2011/07/110726093156.htm.

Cosmides, Leda, and John Tooby, "Evolutionary Psychology: A Primer." University of California–Santa Barbara, January 13, 1997. www.psych.ucsb.edu/research/cep/primer.html.

Crist, Eileen. "On the Poverty of Our Nomenclature." *Environmental Humanities* 3 (2013): 129–47.

Crutzen, Paul J., and Eugene F. Stoermer. "The Anthropocene." *IGBP Global Change Newsletter* 41 (2000): 17–18.

Dalton, Anne Marie. "The Great Work in a Sacred Universe: The Role of Science in Berry's Visionary Proposal." In Eaton, *Intellectual Journey of Thomas Berry,* 173–94.

Daston, Lorraine J., and Katharine Park. *Wonders and the Order of Nature.* New York: Zone Books, 2001.

Dawkins, Richard. *The Ancestor's Tale: A Pilgrimage to the Dawn of Evolution.* New York: Houghton Mifflin, 2004.

_____. *A Devil's Chaplain: Reflections on Hope, Lies, Science, and Love.* Boston: Houghton Mifflin, 2003.

_____. *The God Delusion.* Boston: Houghton Mifflin, 2006.

_____. "Growing Up in Ethology." *Edge,* December 17, 2009. http://edge.org/conversation/growing-up-in-ethology.

———. Interview by Riz Khan. *Al Jazeera One on One,* January 9, 2010. www.aljazeera.com /programmes/oneonone/2010/01/201015101057987686.html.

———. "Is Science a Religion?" *Humanist,* January / February, 1997.

———. *The Magic of Reality: How We Know What's Really True.* New York: Free Press, 2011.

———. *The Oxford Book of Modern Science Writing.* Oxford: Oxford University Press, 2008.

———. "Science, Delusion, and the Appetite for Wonder." Richard Dimbleby Lecture. BBC 1 Television, November 12, 1996. www.andrew.cmu.edu/user/jksadegh/A%20Good%20 Atheist%20Secularist%20Skeptical%20Book%20Collection/Science_Delusion_and _the_Appetite_for_Wonder_by_Dawkins.pdf.

———. *The Selfish Gene.* Oxford: Oxford University Press, 1976.

———. *Unweaving the Rainbow.* Boston: Houghton Mifflin, 1998.

———, and David Attenborough. "Of Mind and Matter: David Attenborough Meets Richard Dawkins." *Guardian,* September 10, 2010. www.theguardian.com/science/2010/sep/11 /science-david-attenborough-richard-dawkins.

Deane-Drummond, Celia. "Christ and Evolution: A Drama of Wisdom?" *Zygon* 47, no. 3 (September 2012): 528.

———. *Christ and Evolution: Wonder and Wisdom.* Minneapolis: Augsburg Fortress, 2009.

———. "Experiencing Wonder and Seeking Wisdom." *Zygon* 42, no. 3 (2007): 587–90.

———. *Wonder and Wisdom: Conversations in Science, Spirituality, and Theology.* Philadelphia: Templeton Foundation Press, 2006.

Delio, Ilia. *The Unbearable Wholeness of Being: God, Evolution and the Power of Love.* New York: Orbis, 2013.

Dennett, Daniel C. *Breaking the Spell: Religion as a Natural Phenomenon.* London: Penguin, 2007.

Deresiewicz, William. "Adaptation: On Literary Darwinism." *Nation,* May 20, 2009. www .thenation.com/issue/june-8–2009#.

Dillard, Annie. *An American Childhood.* New York: Harper and Row, 1987.

Dowd, Michael. "Big History Hits the Big Time." *Huffington Post,* May 8, 2012. www.huffin-gtonpost.com/rev-michael-dowd/big-news-about-big-histor_b_1477137.html.

———. "Evidential Mysticism and the Future of Earth." The Great Story, Fall 2014. thegreat-story.org/dowd-evidential-mysticism.pdf.

———. "The Evidential Reformation: Humanity Comes of Age." *Evolutionary Times,* September 5, 2011. http://evolutionarytimes.org/index.php?id = 1224152607589129425.

———. "Inoculating Kids against Fundamentalism." *Huffington Post Religion Blog,* July 17, 2013. www.huffingtonpost.com/rev-michael-dowd/inoculating-kids-against-_b_3601229.html.

———. "New Atheists Are God's Prophets." *Thank God for Evolution Blog,* June 4, 2010. http://thankgodforevolution.com/node/2018.

———. "New Theists: Knowers, Not Believers." *Huffington Post,* June 6, 2012. www.huffing-tonpost.com/rev-michael-dowd/new-theists-knowers-not-believers_b_1586301.html.

———. "Reality: God's Secular Name." *Thank God for Evolution Blog,* 2009. http://thank-godforevolution.com/node/1902.

———. "Religion Is about Right Relation to Reality, Not the Supernatural." *Thank God for Evolution Blog,* 2012. http://thankgodforevolution.com/node/2012.

———. "Reverend Michael Dowd Comes Out as Reverend Reality" (video). November 29, 2014. www.youtube.com/watch?v = CuqoJ_mHbNg.

———. *Thank God for Evolution: How the Marriage of Science and Religion Will Transform Your Life and Our World*. London: Viking Penguin, 2009.

———. "Thank God for the New Atheists!" The Great Story, August 2010. http://thegreatstory.org/new-atheists.pdf.

———. "Thomas Berry, 1916–2009." *Thank God for Evolution Blog*, June 2009. http://thankgodforevolution.com/node/1869.

Dowd, Michael, and Connie Barlow. "Evolutionary Evangelism." In Taylor, *Encyclopedia of Religion and Nature*, vol. 1, 629–32.

———. "Evolutionize Your Life." Evolving Wisdom, 2011. http://evolutionizeyourlife.com/free-online-class.php.

———. "*The Magic of Reality*: An Inside Look at Richard Dawkins [*sic*] First Children's Book" (video). October 9, 2011. www.youtube.com/watch?v = CcOwS8EFSoU.

Dunlap, Julie, and Stephen R. Kellert, eds. *Companions in Wonder: Children and Adults Exploring Nature Together*. Cambridge, MA: MIT Press, 2012.

Dunn, Stephen. "Afterword: Postmodern Suggestions." In Eaton, *Intellectual Journey of Thomas Berry*, 239–46.

Dupré, John. "Unification Not Proved." *Science* 280, no. 5368 (May 29, 1998): 1395.

Dyson, Freeman. "Progress in Religion." *Edge*, May 16, 2000. http://edge.org/conversation/progress-in-religion.

———. "Our Biotech Future." *New York Review of Books*, July 19, 2007. www.nybooks.com/articles/archives/2007/jul/19/our-biotech-future/.

Eaton, Heather, ed. *The Intellectual Journey of Thomas Berry: Imagining the Earth Community*. Lanham, MD: Lexington Books, 2014.

Eckstein, Paul. "Religion Is Not about God!: A Conversation with Dr. Loyal Rue." Equal Time for Free Thought (MP3 podcast), June 15, 2008. www.equaltimeforfreethought.org/2008/06/15/show-265-religion-is-not-about-god-a-conversation-with-dr-loyal-rue/.

Eger, Martin. "The New Epic of Science and the Problem of Communication." In Shimony, *Science, Understanding, and Justice*, 281–96.

———. "Hermeneutics and the New Epic of Science." In Shimony, *Science, Understanding, and Justice*, 261–80.

Ehrenfeld, David. *The Arrogance of Humanism*. Oxford: Oxford University Press, 1978.

Eiseley, Loren. *All the Strange Hours: The Excavation of a Life*. Lincoln, NE: Bison Books, 2000.

———. "Days of a Thinker." In *All the Strange Hours*, 73–206.

———. *Firmament of Time*. New York: Atheneum, 1960.

———. "How the World Became Natural." In *Firmament of Time*, 3–32.

———. *The Immense Journey*. New York: Vintage, 1956.

———. *The Night Country*. New York: Scribner, 1971.

———. "Science and the Sense of the Holy." In *Star Thrower*, 186–201.

———. *The Star Thrower*. New York: Times Books, 1978.

———. "Strangeness in the Proportion." In *Night Country*, 127–52.

———. *The Unexpected Universe*. New York: Harcourt and Brace, 1969.

———. "Using a Plague to Fight a Plague." *Saturday Review*, September 29, 1962.

Epic of Evolution. http://epicofevolution.com/.

Evernden, Neil. *The Natural Alien: Humankind and Environment*. Toronto: University of Toronto Press, 1993.

Firestein, Stuart. *Ignorance: How It Drives Science.* New York: Oxford University Press.

Fisher, Philip. *Wonder, the Rainbow, and the Aesthetics of Rare Experiences.* Cambridge, MA: Harvard University Press, 2003.

Frankenberry, Nancy K. *The Faith of Scientists: In Their Own Words.* Princeton, NJ: Princeton University Press, 2008.

Fuller, Robert C. "Spirituality in the Flesh: The Role of Discrete Emotions in Religious Life." *Journal of the American Academy of Religion* 75, no. 1 (2007): 25–51.

———. *Wonder: From Emotion to Spirituality.* Chapel Hill: University of North Carolina Press, 2006.

Genet, Cheryl. "The Epic of Evolution: A Course Development Project." *Zygon* 33, no. 4 (1998): 637.

———, et al., eds. *The Evolutionary Epic: Science's Story and Humanity's Response.* Santa Margarita, CA: Collins Foundation Press, 2009.

George, Marie. "Wonder as a Source of Philosophy and of Science: A Comparison." *Philosophy in Science* 6 (1995): 97–128.

Gibb Engel, Joan. "Dreaming the Universe: Contending Stories of Our Place in the Cosmos." In *Confronting Ecological and Economic Collapse: Ecological Integrity for Law, Policy, and Human Rights,* ed. Laura Westra, Prue Taylor, and Agnes Michelot, 255–64. Florence, KY: Taylor and Francis, 2013.

Giberson, Karl. "What's Wrong with Science as Religion." *Salon,* July 31, 2008. www.salon .com/2008/07/31/religion_science/.

———, and Mariano Artigas. *Oracles of Science: Celebrity Scientists versus God and Religion.* Oxford: Oxford University Press, 2006.

Goodenough, Ursula. "Ecomorality: Toward an Ethic of Sustainability." In *Pivotal Moment: Population, Justice, and the Environmental Challenge,* ed. Laurie Ann Mazur, 372–82. Covelo, CA: Island Press, 2009.

———. "The Epic of Evolution: Life, the Earth, and the Cosmos: A Course for Nonscience Majors at Washington University." www.journeyoftheuniverse.org/storage/Goodenough _Yale2.pdf.

———. "Exploring Resources of Naturalism: Religiopoiesis." *Zygon* 35, no. 3 (September 2000): 561–66.

———. "My Covenant with Mystery." *13.7 Cosmos and Culture Blog,* August 27, 2010. www .npr.org/blogs/13.7/2010/08/27/129471676/my-covenant-with-mystery.

———. "Progress, Purpose, and Contingency: A Response to Thomas Berry's *The Great Work: Our Way into the Future.*" *Worldviews* 5 (2001): 142–47.

———. *The Sacred Depths of Nature.* Oxford: Oxford University Press, 1998.

———. "What Science Can and Cannot Offer to a Religious Narrative." *Zygon* 29, no. 3 (September 1994): 321.

Gottschall, Jonathan, and David Sloan Wilson, eds. *The Literary Animal: Evolution and the Nature of Narrative.* Evanston, IL: Northwestern University Press, 2005.

Gould, Stephen Jay. *The Hedgehog, the Fox, and the Magister's Pox: Mending the Gap between Science and the Humanities.* New York: Harmony, 2003.

———. *Wonderful Life: The Burgess Shale and the Nature of History.* New York: Norton, 1989.

Gray, Mark. "Letter to the *Atlantic.*" *Atlantic,* July 1998. www.theatlantic.com/past/docs /issues/98jul/9807lett.htm.

The Great Story. "Articles Published in the *Epic of Evolution Journal.*" http://thegreatstory.
org/Epic-Evol-Journal.html.

———. "Meta-Religious Essays and Sermons: How the Great Story Enriches Faith and Philosophical Traditions." http://thegreatstory.org/metareligious.html.

———. "Michael Dowd, America's Evolutionary Evangelist." http://thegreatstory.org
/michaeldowd.html.

Grim, John, and Mary Evelyn Tucker. "Thomas Berry: Reflections on His Life and Thought."
Teilhard Studies 61 (Fall 2010): 1–21. http://teilharddechardin.org/old/studies/61-Thomas
_Berry.pdf.

Gustafson, James. "Sociobiology: A Secular Theology." *Hastings Center Report* 9, no. 1 (February
1979): 44–45.

Hall, Stephen S. "Darwin's Rottweiler—Sir Richard Dawkins: Evolution's Fiercest Champion, Far Too Fierce." *Discover Magazine,* September 8, 2005. http://discovermagazine.
com/2005/sep/darwins-rottweiler.

Hamilton, Clive. *Earthmasters: The Dawn of the Age of Climate Engineering.* New Haven,
CT: Yale University Press, 2014.

———. "Human Destiny in the Anthropocene." In Hamilton et al., *Anthropocene and the
Global Environmental Crisis,* 32–43.

———, Christophe Bonneuil, and François Gemenne. *The Anthropocene and the Global
Environmental Crisis: Rethinking Modernity in a New Epoch.* New York: Routledge, 2015.

———, and Jacques Grinevald. "Was the Anthropocene Anticipated?" *Anthropocene Review*
2, no. 1 (April 2015): 59–72.

Harris, Paul A. "To Tell a Transformational Tale: The Evolutionary Epic as Narrative Genre."
In Genet et al., *Evolutionary Epic,* 101–6.

Hassinger, Amy. "Welcome to the Ecozoic Era." *UU World,* February 20, 2006. www
.uuworld.org/ideas/articles/2679.shtml.

Hefner, Philip. "Does the Epic Need Art?" *Epic of Evolution Journal,* 1998.
http://thegreatstory.org/Epic-Evol-Journal.html.

———. "Editorial." *Zygon* 32, no. 2 (June 1997): 145–46.

Heltne, Paul G. 2008. "Imposed Ignorance and Humble Ignorance: Two Worldviews." In
Vitek and Jackson, *Virtues of Ignorance,* 135–50.

Hepburn, Ronald W. *Wonder and Other Essays: Eight Studies in Aesthetics and Neighboring
Fields.* Edinburgh: Edinburgh University Press, 1984.

Hesketh, Ian. "The Recurrence of the Evolutionary Epic." *Journal of the Philosophy of History*
9 (2015): 196–219.

———. "The Story of Big History." *History of the Present* 4, no. 2 (Fall 2014): 171–202.

Hettinger, Ned. "Valuing Naturalness in the 'Anthropocene': Now More than Ever." In
Wuerthner et al., *Keeping the Wild,* 174–79.

Holdrege, Craig. "Can We See with Fresh Eyes? Beyond a Culture of Abstraction." In Vitek
and Jackson, *Virtues of Ignorance,* 323–34.

Horgan, John. *The End of Science: Facing the Limits of Knowledge in the Twilight of the
Scientific Age.* New York: Broadway Books, 1997.

Huxley, Julian. Introduction to *The Phenomenon of Man.* In Samson and Pitt, *Biosphere and
Noosphere Reader,* 80–85.

———. "The New Divinity." In *Essays of a Humanist.* London: Chatto and Wyndus, 1964.

Hymas, Lisa. "E. O. Wilson Calls for Kids to be Set Free Outside, Scripted Activities be Damned." *Grist,* April 2, 2008. www.grist.org/article/aspen-envt-forum-soccer-moms-are-the-enemy-of-biological-education.

Jamieson, Dale. "Cheerleading for Science." *Issues in Science and Technology* 15, no. 1 (Fall 1998): 90–91.

Jenkins, Jack. "The Growing Indigenous Spiritual Movement That Could Save the Planet." ThinkProgress, September 30, 2016. https://thinkprogress.org/indigenous-spiritual-movement-8f873348a2f5#.e3ogfe9ay.

Jenkins, Willis. "Does Evolutionary Cosmology Matter for Ecological Ethics?" Draft paper for Yale Living Cosmology conference, November 9, 2016. www.academia.edu/8123931/Does_Evolutionary_Cosmology_Matter_For_Ecological_Ethics.

Journey of the Universe. "Interdisciplinary Curriculum Design and *Journey of the Universe.*" 2016. www.journeyoftheuniverse.org/high-school-conferences/.

Kahn, Peter H., and Stephen R. Kellert, eds. *Children and Nature: Psychological, Sociocultural, and Evolutionary Investigations.* Cambridge, MA: MIT Press, 2002.

Kahn, Urmee. "Harry Potter Fails to Cast Spell over Professor Richard Dawkins." *Telegraph,* October 24, 2008. www.telegraph.co.uk/news/3255972/Harry-Potter-fails-to-cast-spell-over-Professor-Richard-Dawkins.html.

Kaye, Howard L. "Consilience: E. O. Wilson's Confession of Faith." *Politics and the Life Sciences* 18, no. 2 (September 1999): 344–46.

Keats, John. *The Complete Poetical Works and Letters of John Keats, Cambridge Edition.* Edited by Horace Elisha Schudder. New York: Houghton Mifflin, 1899.

Keen, Sam. *Apology for Wonder.* New York: HarperCollins, 1973.

Keim, Brandon. "Former Evangelical Minister Has a New Message: Jesus Hearts Darwin." *Wired,* December 5, 2007. http://archive.wired.com/science/planetearth/news/2007/12/dowd_qa.

Kellert, Stephen R., and Timothy J. Farnham, eds. *The Good in Nature and Humanity: Connecting Science, Religion, and Spirituality in the Natural World.* Washington, DC: Island Press, 2002.

Kennard, David, and Patsy Northcutt, dirs. *Journey of the Universe.* InCA Productions, 2011. DVD.

Kitcher, Philip. "Militant Modern Atheism." *Journal of Applied Philosophy* 29, no. 1 (2011): 1–13.

———. "Unification as a Regulative Ideal." *Perspectives on Science* 7, no. 3 (1999): 337–48.

Konner, Melvin. "One Man's Rainbow." *Scientific American,* March 1999.

Kramnick, Jonathan. "Against Literary Darwinism." *Critical Inquiry* 37, no. 2 (Winter 2011): 315–47.

Krauss, Lawrence. *A Universe from Nothing: Why There Is Something Rather than Nothing.* New York: Free Press, 2012.

Kroll, Gary. "Rachel Carson's *The Sea around Us,* Ocean-Centrism, and a Nascent Ocean Ethic." In Sideris and Moore, *Rachel Carson: Legacy and Challenge,* 118–35.

Landry, Travis. "The Taming of *The Literary Animal.*" *Evolutionary Psychology* 4 (2006): 49–56.

Larson, Brendan. *Metaphors for Environmental Sustainability.* New Haven, CT: Yale University Press, 2011.

Latour, Bruno. "Facing Gaia, Six Lectures on the Political Theology of Nature." Gifford Lectures, University of Edinburgh, February 18, 19, 21, 25, 26, 28, 2013. www.ed.ac.uk/arts-humanities-soc-sci/news-events/lectures/gifford-lectures/archive/series-2012–2013/bruno-latour.

———. "Love Your Monsters." In *Love Your Monsters: Postenvironmentalism and the Anthropocene*, ed. Michael Shellenberger and Ted Nordhaus, 19–26. Oakland: Breakthrough Institute, 2011. www.bruno-latour.fr/sites/default/files/downloads/107-BREAK-THROUGH-REDUXpdf.

Lear, Linda. *Rachel Carson: Witness for Nature.* New York: Henry Holt, 1997.

LeCain, Tim. "Against the Anthropocene." *International Journal for History, Culture, and Modernity* 3, no. 1 (2015): 1–28.

Levine, George. *Darwin Loves You: Natural Selection and the Re-Enchantment of the World.* Princeton, NJ: Princeton University Press, 2008.

Lightman, Alan. *The Accidental Universe: The World You Thought You Knew.* New York: Pantheon, 2013.

Lightman, Bernard. *Victorian Popularizers of Science: Designing Nature for New Audiences.* Chicago: University of Chicago Press, 2010.

Love, Alan C. "The Erotetic Organization of Developmental Biology." In *Towards a Theory of Development*, ed. Alessandro Minelli and Thomas Pradeu, 33–55. New York: Oxford University Press, 2014.

———. "Ignorance: How It Drives Science, Part 2." Review of *Ignorance: How It Drives Science*, by Stuart Firestein. *Christianity Today*, August 2012. www.booksandculture.com/articles/webexclusives/2012/august/ignorance-part-2.html.

Lytle, Mark. *The Gentle Subversive: Rachel Carson, Silent Spring, and the Rise of the Environmental Movement.* New York: Oxford University Press, 2007.

Max, D. T. "Green Is Good." *New Yorker*, May 12, 2014.

Meijers, Marijn H. C., and Bastiaan T. Rutjens. "The Social Psychology of Climate Change: Affirming Belief in Scientific Progress Reduces Environmentally Friendly Behavior." *European Journal of Social Psychology* 44 (2014): 487–95.

Merchant, Caroline. *The Death of Nature: Women, Ecology, and the Scientific Revolution.* San Francisco: Harper and Row, 1980.

Midgley, Mary. "Evolution as Religion: A Comparison of Prophesies." *Zygon*, 22, no. 2 (1987): 179–94.

———. *Evolution as Religion: Strange Hopes and Stranger Fears.* Rev. ed. New York: Methuen, 2002.

———. "Rival Fatalisms: The Hollowness of the Sociobiology Debate." In *Sociobiology Examined*, ed. A. Montagu, 15–38. New York: Oxford University Press, 1980.

———. "A Well-Meaning Cannibal." *Commonweal*, July 17, 1998, 23.

Miller, James B., ed. *The Epic of Evolution: Science and Religion in Dialogue.* Upper Saddle River, NJ: Prentice Hall, 2004.

Minteer, Ben. "The Perils of De-Extinction." *Minding Nature* 8, no. 1 (January 2015): 11–17, on 13–14. www.humansandnature.org/the-perils-of-de-extinction.

———, and Stephen J. Pyne, eds. *After Preservation: Saving American Nature in the Age of Humans.* Chicago: University of Chicago Press, 2015.

Mooney, Chris. "Spirituality Can Bridge Science–Religion Divide." *USA Today*, September 12, 2010. http://usatoday30.usatoday.com/news/opinion/forum/2010-09-13-column13 _ST_N.htm.

Moore, Kathleen Dean. "A Roaring Force from One Unknowable Moment" (Conversation with Mary Evelyn Tucker). *Orion Magazine*, May / June 2015.

Morris, Conway. *Life's Solution: Inevitable Humans in a Lonely Universe*. Cambridge: Cambridge University Press, 2004.

Muerdter, Hanni. "The Wonder of Science." *Conservation Biology* 19, no. 4 (2005): 987–89.

Myers, P. Z. "Loyal Rue vs (?) PZ Myers." *Pharyngula* (blog), February 8, 2008. http://scienceblogs.com/pharyngula/2008/02/08/loyal-rue-vs-pz-myers/.

Nichols, William. "The Limits of Ecological Vision." *Journal of Religion and Intellectual Life* 6, no. 2 (Winter 1989): 42–47.

O'Brien, Mary. "Science, Ethics, and Changed Lives: How Did Rachel Carson Do It?" Science and Environmental Health Network, November 8–10, 2000. www.sehn.org/web-2printer4.php?img = 0&lnk = 0&page = conbiocarson.html.

Orr, H. Allen. "The Big Picture." *Boston Review*, October / November 1998. http://bostonreview.net/BR23.5/Orr.html.

Pitts, Mary Ellen. *Toward a Dialogue of Understandings: Loren Eiseley and the Critique of Science*. Bethlehem, PA: Lehigh University, 1995.

Prinz, Jesse. "How Wonder Works." *Aeon*, June 21, 2013. https://aeon.co/essays/why-wonder-is-the-most-human-of-all-emotions.

Proctor, Robert, and Londa Schiebinger. *Agnotology: The Making and Unmaking of Ignorance*. Stanford, CA: Stanford University Press, 2008.

Quinn, Dennis. *Iris Exiled: A Synoptic History of Wonder*. Lanham, MD: University Press of America, 2002.

Redniss, Lauren. "The Beautiful Mind of Freeman Dyson." *Discover Magazine*, June 2008. http://discovermagazine.com/2008/jun/09-the-beautiful-mind-of-freeman-dyson.

Revkin, Andrew. "Embracing the Anthropocene." *New York Times Dot Earth Blog*, May 20, 2011. http://dotearth.blogs.nytimes.com/2011/05/20/embracing-the-anthropocene/?_r = 0.

———. *Global Warming: Understanding the Forecast*. New York: Abbeville Press, 1992.

———. "Paths to a 'Good' Anthropocene." Lecture, Association for Environmental Studies and Sciences, January 20, 2014. www.youtube.com/watch?v = VOtj3mskx5k.

———. "Peter Kareiva, an Inconvenient Environmentalist." *New York Times Dot Earth Blog*, April 3, 2012. http://dotearth.blogs.nytimes.com/2012/04/03/peter-kareiva-an-inconvenient-environmentalist/?_r = 0.

———. "Remembering the Great Worker." *New York Times Dot Earth Blog*, June 4, 2009. http://dotearth.blogs.nytimes.com/2009/06/04/the-great-worker/.

Robinson, Marilynne. *The Givenness of Things*. New York: Farrar, Straus, and Giroux, 2015.

Rorty, Richard. "Against Unity." *Wilson Quarterly* 22 (Winter 1998): 28–38.

Roy, Arundhati. "The Greater Common Good." In *The Cost of Living*, ed. Arundhati Roy, 7–90. New York: Modern Library, 1999.

Rubenstein, Mary-Jane. *Strange Wonder: The Closure of Metaphysics and the Opening of Awe*. New York: Columbia University Press, 2010.

Rue, Loyal D. *Amythia: Crisis in the Natural History of Western Culture.* Tuscaloosa: University of Alabama Press, 2004.

———. *By the Grace of Guile: The Role of Deception in Natural History and Human Affairs.* Oxford: Oxford University Press, 1994.

———. "Epic of Evolution." In Taylor, *Encyclopedia of Religion and Nature,* 612–15.

———. *Everybody's Story: Wising Up to the Epic of Evolution.* Albany: State University of New York Press, 2000.

———. *Nature Is Enough: Religious Naturalism and the Meaning of Life.* Albany: State University of New York Press, 2011.

———. "Redefining Myth and Religion: Introduction to a Conversation." *Zygon* 29, no. 3 (2005): 315–20.

———. *Religion Is Not about God: How Spiritual Traditions Nurture Our Biological Nature and What to Expect When They Fail.* New Brunswick, NJ: Rutgers University Press, 2004.

———, and Ursula Goodenough. "A Consilient Curriculum." In Genet et al., *Evolutionary Epic,* 175–82.

Rupke, Nicolaas A., ed. *Eminent Lives in Twentieth-Century Science and Religion.* Frankfurt am Main: Peter Lang, 2009.

Samson, Paul R., and David Pitt, eds. *The Biosphere and Noosphere Reader: Global Environment, Society, and Change.* New York: Routledge, 1999.

Sanders, Scott Russell. "The Most Human Art." Draft paper for Journey of the Universe Conference, March 24–26, 2011. www.journeyoftheuniverse.org/conference-at-yale/.

Sarchet, Penny. "E. O. Wilson: Religious Faith Is Dragging Us Down." *New Scientist,* January 21, 2015. www.newscientist.com/article/mg22530050-400-e-o-wilson-religious-faith-is-dragging-us-down/.

Schaefer, Donovan. "Blessed, Precious Mistakes: Deconstruction, Evolution, and New Atheism in America." *International Journal for Philosophy of Religion* 76, no. 1 (2014): 75–94.

Scharper, Stephen Bede. *Redeeming the Time: A Political Theology of the Environment.* New York: Continuum, 1998.

Schick, Kathy, and Nicholas Toth. "The 'Little Bang': The Origins and Adaptive Significance of Human Stone Toolmaking." In Genet et al., *Evolutionary Epic,* 43–60.

Segerstrale, Ullica. "Wilson and the Unification of Science." *Annals New York Academy of Sciences* 1093 (2006): 46–73.

Shellenberger, Michael, and Ted Nordhaus. "The Death of Environmentalism: Global Warming Politics in a Post-Environmental World." 2004. http://thebreakthrough.org/archive/the_death_of_environmentalism.

Shimony, Abner, ed. *Science, Understanding, and Justice.* Chicago: Open Court, 2006.

Sideris, Lisa H. "The Confines of Consecration: A Reply to Critics." *Journal for the Study of Religion, Nature, and Culture* 9, no. 2 (2015): 221–39.

———. "Contested Wonder: Biological Reductionism and Children's Nature Education." *Journal of Religion and Society,* Supplement Series 11 (2015): 193–205.

———. *Environmental Ethics, Ecological Theology, and Natural Selection.* New York: Columbia University Press, 2003.

———. "Forbidden Fruit: Wonder, Religious Narrative, and the Quest for the Atomic Bomb." In *Technofutures, Nature and the Sacred: Transdisciplinary Perspectives,* ed. Celia Deane-Drummond, Sigurd Bergmann, and Bronislaw Szerszynski. Farnham, Surrey: Ashgate, 2015.

———. "Science as Sacred Myth? Ecospirituality in the Anthropocene Age." *Journal for the Study of Religion, Nature, and Culture* 9, no. 2 (2015): 136–53.

———. "The Secular and Religious Sources of Rachel Carson's Sense of Wonder." In Sideris and Moore, *Rachel Carson: Legacy and Challenge,* 232–50.

———. "Surviving the Anthropocene: Big Money and Big Brains at the Smithsonian." *Inhabiting the Anthropocene Blog,* July 5, 2016. https://inhabitingtheanthropocene. com/2016/07/05/surviving-the-anthropocene/.

———. " 'To know the story is to love it': Scientific Mythmaking and the Longing for Cosmic Connection." In *Methodological Challenges in Nature-Culture and Environmental History Research,* ed. Jocelyn Thorpe, Stephanie Rutherford, and L. Anders Sandberg, 200–213. London: Routledge, 2016.

———, and Kathleen Dean Moore, eds. *Rachel Carson: Legacy and Challenge.* New York: State University of New York Press, 2008.

Silverman, M. P. "Two Sides of Wonder: Philosophical Keys to the Motivation of Science Learning." *Synthese* 80, no. 1 (July 1989): 43–61.

Slingerland, Edward. *What Science Offers the Humanities: Integrating Body and Culture.* Cambridge: Cambridge University Press, 2008.

———. "Who's Afraid of Reductionism? The Study of Religion in the Age of Cognitive Science." *Journal of the American Academy of Religion* 76, no. 2 (June 2008): 375–411.

———, and Mark Collard, eds. *Creating Consilience: Integrating the Sciences and the Humanities.* Oxford: Oxford University Press, 2011.

Smocovitis, Vassiliki Betty. "The Tormenting Desire for Unity." *Journal of the History of Biology* 32 (1999): 385–94.

Souder, William. *On a Farther Shore: The Life and Legacy of Rachel Carson.* New York: Crown, 2012.

Soulé, Michael. "The 'New Conservation.' " *Conservation Biology* 27, no. 5 (October 2013): 895–97.

———. "The 'New Conservation.' " In Wuerthner et al., *Keeping the Wild,* 66–80.

Starr, C. Gabrielle. "Evolved Reading and the Science(s) of Literary Study." *Critical Inquiry* 38, no. 2 (Winter 2012): 418–25.

Steffen, Will, et al. "The Anthropocene: Conceptual and Historical Perspectives." *Philosophical Transactions of the Royal Society A* 369, no. 1938 (January 2011): 842–67.

Steinhart, Eric. "Teilhard de Chardin and Transhumanism." *Journal of Evolution and Technology* 20, no. 1 (December 2008): 1–22.

Stoll, Mark. "Edward Osborne Wilson." In Rupke, *Eminent Lives in Twentieth-Century Science and Religion,* 333–48.

———. "Rachel Carson." In Rupke, *Eminent Lives in Twentieth-Century Science and Religion,* 47–72.

Storey, Robert. *Mimesis and the Human Animal: On the Biogenetic Foundations of Literary Representation.* Evanston, IL: Northwestern University Press, 1996.

Swimme, Brian Thomas. "Cosmology and Environmentalism." In Genet et al., *Evolutionary Epic*, 273–78.

———. "The Current Moment" (video). March 2007. www.youtube.com/watch?v = JwoRS2Tfk74.

———. "The Cultural Significance of the Story of the Universe." In Miller, *Epic of Evolution*, 38–43.

———. "The New Story" (video). March 2007. www.youtube.com/watch?v = TRykk_oovIo.

———, and Mary Evelyn Tucker. *Journey of the Universe*. New Haven, CT: Yale University Press, 2011.

———, and Mary Evelyn Tucker, "Journey of the Universe," *Teilhard Perspective* 44, no. 1 (Spring 2011): 2.

———, and Thomas Berry. *The Universe Story: From the Primordial Flaring Forth to the Ecozoic Era—A Celebration of the Unfolding of the Cosmos*. San Francisco: Harper, 1992.

Szerszynski, Bronislaw. "The End of the End of Nature: The Anthropocene and the Fate of the Human." *Oxford Literary Review* 34, no. 2 (2012): 176.

———, et al. "Why Solar Radiation Management and Democracy Won't Mix." *Environment and Planning A*, 45, no. 12 (December 2013): 2809–16.

Takacs, David. *The Idea of Biodiversity: Philosophies of Paradise*. Baltimore: John Hopkins University Press, 1996.

Taylor, Bron. *Dark Green Religion: Nature Spirituality and the Planetary Future*. Berkeley: University of California Press, 2009.

———. *The Encyclopedia of Religion and Nature*. London and New York: Continuum, 2005.

———, and Gavin van Horn. "Nature Religion and Environmentalism in North America." In *Faith in America: Changes, Challenges, New Directions*, vol. 3, ed. Charles Lippy, 165–90. New York: Praeger, 2006.

Teilhard de Chardin, Pierre. *The Phenomenon of Man*. Translated by Bernard Wall. New York: Harper and Row, 1959.

Thomas, Julie Adeney. "History and Biology in the Anthropocene: Problems of Scale, Problems of Value." *American Historical Review* 119, no. 5 (December 2014): 1587–1607.

Tippett, Krista. "Teilhard de Chardin's 'Planetary Mind' and Our Spiritual Evolution." *On Being* transcript, December 19, 2012. Onbeing.org/program/transcript/4967.

Tucker, Mary Evelyn. "Biography of Thomas Berry." Center for Humans and Nature. www .humansandnature.org/biography-of-thomas-berry.

———. "The Ecological Spirituality of Pierre Teilhard de Chardin." *Teilhard Studies* 51 (Fall 2005): 1–18.

———. "Focus on the Anthropocene: Journey of the Universe." Lecture, Carsey-Wolf Center, University of California–Santa Barbara, February 19, 2015. www.carseywolf .ucsb.edu/pollock/events/focus-anthropocene-journey-universe.

———. "An Intellectual Biography of Thomas Berry." Editor's afterword to *Evening Thoughts: Reflecting on Earth as Sacred Community*, by Thomas Berry, ed. Mary Evelyn Tucker, 151–71. San Francisco: Sierra Club Books, 2006.

———. "Journey of the Universe: An Integration of Science and the Humanities." *Journal for the Study of Religion, Nature, and Culture* 9, no. 2 (2015): 206–12.

———. "Journey of the Universe: A Lineage of a New Story." http://journeyoftheuniverse. or/storage/Lineage_of_Journey.pdf.

———. "*Journey of the Universe* and the World Religions." Lecture, Chautauqua Institution in New York, June 24, 2013. www.journeyoftheuniverse.org/conference-at-chautauqua/.

———. "Overview." Journey of the Universe. www.journeyoftheuniverse.org/storage/JOTU _Overview_8–28–13.pdf.

———. "Religion and Ecology: The Interaction of Cosmology and Cultivation." In Kellert and Farnham, *Good in Nature and Humanity*, 65–90.

———. "Thomas Berry." In Taylor, *Encyclopedia of Religion and Nature*, vol. 1, 164–68.

———. "Thomas Berry and the New Story: An Introduction to the Work of Thomas Berry." In Eaton, *Intellectual Journey of Thomas Berry*, 1–16.

———, and John Grim. Foreword to Religions of the World and Ecology series. In Mary Evelyn Tucker and Duncan Ryuken Williams, eds., *Buddhism and Ecology: The Interconnection of Dharma and Deeds*, xv–xxxiii. Cambridge, MA: Harvard University Press, 1997.

———, and John Grim, eds. *Living Cosmology: Christian Responses to* Journey of the Universe. Maryknoll, NY: Orbis, 2016.

———, and Brian Thomas Swimme. *Journey of the Universe.* New Haven, CT: Yale University Press, 2011.

Valdesolo, Piercarlo. "Trust in Science Reduces Concerns about Climate Change." *Scientific American,* September 24, 2014. www.scientificamerican.com/article/trust-in-science-reduces-concerns-about-climate-change/.

Van Wieren, Gretel. *Restored to Earth: Christianity, Environmental Ethics, and Ecological Restoration.* Washington, DC: Georgetown University Press, 2013.

Vitek, Bill. "Joyful Ignorance and the Civic Mind." In Vitek and Jackson, *Virtues of Ignorance,* 213–14.

Vitek, Bill, and Wes Jackson. "Introduction: Taking Ignorance Seriously." In Vitek and Jackson, *Virtues of Ignorance,* 1–20.

———, eds. *The Virtues of Ignorance: Complexity, Sustainability, and the Limits of Knowledge.* Lexington: University of Kentucky Press, 2008.

Walker, Kenny, and Lynda Walsh. " 'No One Yet Knows What the Ultimate Consequences May Be': How Rachel Carson Transformed Scientific Uncertainty into a Site for Public Participation in *Silent Spring.*" *Journal of Business and Technical Communication* 26, no. 1 (2011): 3–34.

Weber, Max. "Science as a Vocation." In *Essays in Sociology,* ed. and trans. by H.H. Gerth and C. Wright Mills. Oxford: Oxford University Press, 1946.

Weiner, Linda, and Ramsey Eric Ramsey. *Leaving Us to Wonder: An Essay on the Questions Science Cannot Ask.* Albany: State University of New York Press, 2005.

Wentz, Richard E. "The American Spirituality of Loren Eiseley." *Christian Century,* April 1984. www.religion-online.org/showarticle.asp?title = 1391.

What Is Enlightenment? Editors. "The Real Evolution Debate." *What Is Enlightenment?* (magazine) 35 (January / February, 2007).

White, Curtis. *The Science Delusion: Asking the Big Questions in a Culture of Easy Answers.* Brooklyn: Melville House, 2013.

Whyte, Kyle Powys. "Why Native American Pipeline Resistance in North Dakota Is about Climate Justice." *Conversation,* September 16, 2016. http://theconversation.com/why-the-native-american-pipeline-resistance-in-north-dakota-is-about-climate-justice-64714.

Whitehead, Alfred North. *Science and the Modern World*. 1925. Reprint, New York: Free Press, 1997.

Wilson, Edward O. *Anthill*. New York: W. W. Norton, 2010.

———. *Consilience: The Unity of Knowledge*. New York: Vintage, 1998.

———. *The Creation: An Appeal to Save Life on Earth*. New York: W. W. Norton, 2006.

———. *The Diversity of Life*. New York: W. W. Norton, 2002.

———. "Divisive Ideas on 'Unification.'" *Los Angeles Times*, July 9, 1998. http://articles.latimes.com/1998/jul/09/local/me-2107.

———. Foreword to *Commonwealth: Economics for a Crowded Planet*, by Jeffrey Sachs (New York: Penguin, 2008).

———. Foreword to Rue, *Everybody's Story*.

———. *The Future of Life*. New York: Vintage Books, 2002.

———. *Half-Earth: Our Planet's Fight for Life*. New York: Liveright, 2016.

———. *The Meaning of Human Existence*. New York: Liveright, 2014.

———. *Naturalist*. Washington, DC: Island Press, 1994.

———. *On Human Nature*. Cambridge, MA: Harvard University Press, 1978.

———. "The Riddle of the Human Species." *New York Times Opinionator Blog*, February 24, 2013. http://opinionator.blogs.nytimes.com/2013/02/24/the-riddle-of-the-human-species/?_r = 0.

———. *The Social Conquest of Earth*. New York: Liveright, 2013.

Wright, Robert. "Robert Wright Interviews Brian Swimme on Religion in a Global Age." MeaningofLive.TV. www.origins.meaningoflife.tv/genesis-transcript.php?speaker = swimme.

———. *Three Scientists and Their Gods: Looking for Meaning in an Age of Information*. New York: Times Books, 1988.

Wuerthner, George, Eileen Crist, and Tom Butler, eds. *Keeping the Wild: Against the Domestication of Earth*. San Francisco: Foundation for Deep Ecology, 2014.

INDEX

Abram, David, 169, 183, 194–196, 201
abstraction, as part of the scientific process, 8, 26, 172, 175, 191, 193–195
adaptationism, 89–90, 221n96
agency, 69, 118–122, 132, 140, 166, 216n11
Age of Man environmentalism, 134–135, 138, 141–144
altruism, 64, 96, 101, 223n121
American Teilhard Association, 123, 227n14
amythia, 5, 90–91, 152, 157, 201, 204n8
Ancestors Meditation, 154,
The Ancestor's Tale (Dawkins), 153, 155, 166
Anthill (Wilson), 52, 80
Anthrocene, 141
anthropic, 9, 117–133, 167, 175, 180, 200–201
The Anthropic Cosmological Principle (Barrow and Tipler), 130
anthropic principle, 124, 130–131, 230n95
Anthropocene: as geological epoch, 118, 124, 134–136, 233n144, 235n193; control of nature and, 139–145, 170, 234n169; defined, 134; Ecozoic and, 136–138, 233n144; Epic of Evolution and, 2, 117–145, 184–185; good, 118, 135–145, 190, 232n135; noosphere and, 121–122, 135; positive assessment of, 9, 137–145; Wilson and, 54, 74, 217n147
anthropocentrism, 7–9, 38–41, 88, 125–145, 234n169. *See also* hubris
anthropophilia, 143

argument from design, 34, 131
Aristotle, 14, 43
arrogance. *See* hubris
arrow of evolution, 96, 122, 129, 149
astonishment, 23, 33
atheism, 31, 103, 148, 236n11. *See also* new atheists
Attenborough, David, 46, 48
Augustine, 21–22, 25, 77
authoritarian science, 3, 108, 135, 159, 179, 184, 187–189

Bacon, Francis, 18, 20, 22, 34, 44–45, 139, 171, 241n7
Barlow, Connie, 117–118, 146–167, 180–181; Epic of Evolution Society founded by, 85–87
Berry, Thomas: conscious evolution and, 118–128, 140, 157, 224n143, 228n44; Ecozoic and, 135–145; Eiseley and, 179–180; influence of, 5, 9, 12, 146–152, 157–160, 232n135, 233n144; origins of the Universe Story, 85–88; Technozoic and, 228n46; Teilhard de Chardin and, 120–124, 141–145; universe education and, 110, 114, 125–126; Universe Story and 118–130, 135–148, 225n181, 229n76, 231n102
Big Bang, 62, 145, 231n102; cosmology, 4–5, 10, 12, 111, 170
Big History. *See* Epic of Evolution
biocentric lie, 100–101
biocentrism, 89, 99–102

of Loyal Rue and, 93; Universe Story and,
11–12, 71–74, 170–171; wonder and, 68–71
Consilience (Wilson), 51, 56,-63, 72–78, 111–114
contingency, 96–98, 150, 174–175, 222n90,
224n143, 237nn22, 25
convergence: cultural. *See* convergence, noetic;
evolutionary, 150–151, 237nn22, 25; noetic,
125; of disciplines, 55, 93, 103, 110
cosmic: Communion, 153, 161; evolution. *See* evolution, cosmic; Rosary, 153; self-consciousness.
See consciousness, cosmic self-; Walk, 153
Cosmism, 144
cosmogenesis, 119–127, 132–133, 140–144, 230n85,
231n117
cosmology: as comprehensive, 71–72, 88, 164; as
story, 1–3, 5–11, 67, 87, 164–168; Big Bang. *See*
Big Bang cosmology; evolutionary, 54, 80,
99–102, 156; functional, 6, 110, 134; new, 1–12,
67, 83–88, 117–145, 162–172, 195, 200–201. *See
also* Epic of Evolution; Universe Story; scientific vs. religious, 10–11, 44, 53, 73, 108–109;
wonder and, 107–108
cosmos: humanity in relation to, 28, 54, 122–126,
170, 199, 230n85; implications of immensity
of, 12–13, 103, 128, 183–184; sentient, 183–184;
with agency, 131–141; wonder at, 8–9,
createheism, 148, 236n11
The Creation (Wilson), 51–54, 78–80
creation: knowledge. *See* knowledge creation;
myth. *See* myth, creation; myth, new cosmology as creation
creationism, 86, 154
creativity: human, 11, 65, 112–114, 124, 130–145,
192; nature's, 118, 129–131, 138–145; of matter,
100, 138; of science, 175–176, 179–181
crisis, environmental. *See* environmental crisis
Crist, Eileen, 130, 137
critique of science 7–8, 92, 177–180, 188–189
Crutzen, Paul, 134–135, 141, 233n144
cultural: coding, 114; diversity, 86, 101–102, 111,
125–127, 201; evolution as part of the curriculum, 112–113; evolution, naturalized, 94;
evolution of stories, 91–93, 104–105; evolution reducible to biology, 57, 64, 72; evolution
superseding natural selection, 132–133;
malaise. *See* amythia
culture, global, 85, 91, 97, 125–127
curiosity. *See* wonder and curiosity

dark green religion, 4, 101
Darwin, Charles, 65, 81–82, 159, 209n49, 244n55

Darwinian, 1, 40, 81, 90, 220n25
Darwinian literary criticism. *See* literary Darwinism
Deane-Drummond, Celia, 29, 30–31, 166, 207n5,
237n25
deceit, 31, 89, 99–100, 223n121
deep time, 7–8, 122, 145, 235n193
deflationary effect of good Anthropocene narratives, 145, 235n193
democracy, 90, 114, 188, 192, 247n121
Dennett, Daniel, 69, 87
Descartes, René, 14, 19–23, 32–33, 41, 138, 172
design arguments. *See* argument from design
desire, 21, 24–25, 64, 94
determinism, 5, 138, 150, 166, 180
Dillard, Annie, 173–174, 185
discernment, 19–20, 30–31, 132–133, 207n5, 237n26
disciplines, academic, 11–12, 55–69, 93, 110–114,
125–126, 192–194
disenchantment, 22, 42, 69–71, 76
diversity. *See* biological diversity; cultural diversity; religious diversity
The Diversity of Life (Wilson), 78, 81
Dominican University (California), 110, 113
Dowd, Michael, 117, 146–156, 159, 163–166, 203n4,
236nn12, 237n26
Dyson, Freeman, 44–48, 130, 210n78

earth cults, 100–101, 105–109, 131
Earth Insights (Callicott), 86, 127
earthly cosmology, 80, 105, 218n177
ecological: crisis. *See* crisis, environmental;
integrity, 151; literacy. *See* environmental
education; praxis, 119, 126
ecology, 117, 120, 142, 145, 151, 164
Ecomodernist Manifesto, 142–144, 234n169
ecomorality, 89, 101, 109
ecospiritualism, 3, 181
Ecozoic era, 121–124, 132, 135–145, 228n46,
233n144, 235n193
The Edge of the Sea (Carson), 176, 184
education, childhood, 17, 52, 149, 197–198;
environmental, 17, 52, 134; nature, 17, 81; uni-
versity/college, 93, 110–114, 125–126, 192
Eger, Martin, 4–5, 87–88, 161, 220nn25, 28,
239n90
Eiseley, Loren, 28, 173–186, 193, 196, 244n55
emergence of humans, evolutionary, 121, 130, 133,
241n11
emergent properties: of matter, 93, 126, 138–139;
of the self, 95–97

Journey of the Universe (Swimme and Tucker), 120–123, 128–134, 138–143, 165, 179–180, 183–184

Keen, Sam, 27, 175–176, 196, 242n16
Kitcher, Philip, 43–44, 62
knowledge: awareness of, 26, 178–180, 190–191; conditions, improved, 138–140; consilient. *See* consilience; creation, 7, 14, 57, 169–170, 190, 225n167; forms of, 11, 21, 93–94, 193, 226n194; limits of, 114, 204n16, 246n111; objects of. *See* knowledge, forms of; production. *See* knowledge creation; provoking wonder, 106, 161, 173–174; scientific. *See* scientific knowledge; serial wonder as productive of, 33–34; totalizing. *See* consilience; wonder as compatible with, 172–202; wonder at, 16–29, 169–170; wonder at 1, 8, 18–19, 25–28, 40–43, 77, 164, 169–172, 218n156; wonder at, marginalizing nature, 47–49; wonder at, possession of experts, 16, 75; wonder at, superior to other types of wonder, 60, 74–75, 106; wonder posterior to, as reversed dynamic, 22–25, 34, 75
knowosphere, 143

labyrinth, 165, 167, 240n118
Lamarckian evolution, 122
Latour, Bruno, 140, 204n16, 234n169
liberal religion, 109, 129, 147, 153
life: as the ultimate good, 94, 97; diversity of. *See* biological diversity; emergence of, 83, 93, 111–112, 130–133, 139; future of, 45, 121–123, 135–137; human control over. *See* nature, mastery over; more-than-human, 3, 8, 84, 169–170, 202; mystery of, 45, 165–166, 172–176, 185–187; not mysterious, 104, 186–187, 217n147; the good, science as basis for, 43; valuing, 80, 95, 106–108, 133–137, 195–197
Lightman, Alan, 116, 131
limits of knowledge. *See* knowledge, limits of
literary Darwinism, 59, 63–67, 214nn72, 81, 83, 215n99
Little Bang, 167
logical positivism. *See* positivism
Love, Alan C., 192–193

The Magic of Reality: How We Know What's Really True (Dawkins), 36, 48, 154–156
maladaption, 100, 102, 216n111
Marcel, Gabriel, 27, 171

materialism: as mythology, 6, 53–56, 72–73; as threat to meaning, 70–71; challenged by vitalism, 138–141; wonder inspired by, 68–69, 78, 93;
mathematics, 19, 45, 61–62, 74–75, 132
meaning: elusiveness of, 176, 184–185; in mystery, 168; nature as providing, 41, 78, 177–182; new cosmology as providing, 84–87, 124–129, 148–151, 184–185, 192–193; science as providing, 6–8, 41–44 72, 158; science as reducing, 172. *See also* materialism, as threat to meaning
The Meaning of Human Existence (Wilson), 52, 54
meme, 90–92, 94, 102, 158–159
memetic evolution, 159
metamyth, 150
metanarrative, 92, 96, 128, 243n49, 246n106
metaphor: as link between fact and value, 91; in new cosmology, 11, 86; used to mythologize science, 107, 131, 149
metaphysics, 10, 50, 54–56, 66–67, 71–72, 212n23, 218n174
metareligion, 110, 150
Midgley, Mary, 54, 62, 116, 133–134, 140, 150
mindsphere. *See* noosphere
minor epic, discovery of Epic of Evolution as, 161, 239n90
modules, brain. *See* brain modules
Morris, Simon Conway, 149–150, 237nn22, 25
Muerdter, Hanni, 29–30, 42
multicultural. *See* cultural diversity
music, 38, 43, 65, 112, 119, 132, 155, 221n42
mysterium, 181, 196
mystery: and wonder, 27, 165–172, 182–190; as puzzles for science, 81, 171. *See also* wonder, serial; as reality, 18, 176–177, 182–190; cosmic, 15, 102–103, 131, 165, 170; of existence. *See* mystery, cosmic; science as explaining away, 25, 32–36, 76, 171–172, 181, 196, 214n72; solution of one opens another, 33, 170–171; Universe Story reduces, 11
mysticism, 28, 105–109, 119–122, 126, 200
myth: as part of traditional religion, 48, 104–106; as product of human evolution, 72–73, 89–93, 98–99, 104–106; biocentric, 100–101; creation, 48, 75–76, 120, 165, 183; creation, new cosmology as, 151–152, 156; evolution as, 71–74, 150, 154–156; of traditional religion, 48, 104–10, 155–156; science used to eliminate, 36–37, 57; scientific, 2–12, 53–59, 71–77,

83–110, 154–172, 231n102; Wilson's use of, 81, 170. *See also* amythia

mythmaking. *See* mythopoeic science

mythopoeisis, 1–13, 84–109, 157–165; as product of evolution, 72–73, 149, 159; claims of truth and, 127–128; compatibilism vs., 180, 186–188, 192–193; defined, 5; of science at the expense of nature, 77; science, object of, 75–76, 87; *See also* religiopoiesis;

narrative: as human contrivance, 162–163, 168, 239n90; brain adapted for, 64–65, 93–96; conflation of scientific, with its objects, 97; cosmic. *See* cosmology as story; counter-, 199; evolution as, 57; labyrinth as metaphor for, 240n118; master, 86, 110–112, 124, 164, 229n76; mismatch between content and form of, 165, 170; naturalizing, 134–136, 139; of the new cosmology, 119–153; of the new cosmology, linearity of 128, 165–166; petite, 179, 193, 243n39, 246n106; religious, 10–11, 86, 91, 97, 108, 113; scientific, accessible to non-scientists, 71; scientific, superiority of, 10–11, 73, 92, 108–109, 112, 127; truth claims and, 127

natural: Law theory, 237n25; philosophy, 20–24; selection, 47, 64, 69, 91–92, 132; theology, 23–25, 34; world. *See* nature

naturalist, compared to scientist, 46–49, 52–53, 88, 178

Naturalist (Wilson), 49, 52–53

naturalizing narrative. *See* narrative, naturalizing

naturalized religion. *See* religious naturalism

nature: as reality, 48, 81, 177, 181–184, 194–195; as sacred, 93, 99–100, 106–108; as source of values, 158–161, 176–182, 195–199; as subordinate to human reason, 33, 40, 121; concern for, 6–12, 51–53, 68, 163–164, 177–188, 195–199, 224n156; concern for, sociobiological basis for, 77–81; concern for, to safeguard human existence, 98; Conservancy, 142, 234n176; education. *See* education, nature; God as, 152; human. *See* human nature; human transformation of. *See* nature, mastery over; innate attraction to. *See* biophilia; mastery over, 16, 40, 77, 132, 137–145, 170, 186, 234n171; mechanism as cause of disenchantment with, 22, 40, 76; poets and, 32–33, 38–40, 44, 48, 170, 223n113; preserves, 139–142; study movement, 13, 17, 48, 52–53, 197; value of. *See* nature, concern for; wonder at nature

Nature is Enough (Rue), 100–101

negative capability, 11, 192, 205n27

neural self, 95–98

new atheists, 31, 38, 147, 152, 209n48

new conservationism, 142, 233n161, 234n176

new cosmologists. *See* Barlow, Connie; Berry, Thomas; Christian, David; Dowd, Michael; Goodenough, Ursula; Grim, John; Rue, Loyal; Swimme, Brian; Tucker, Mary Evelyn

new cosmology. *See* cosmology, new

new naturalism, 100–101

New Materialism, 141

The New Story. *See* Epic of Evolution

new theism, 148, 151

Newton, Isaac, 32–33, 44, 138, 173

nihilism, 86, 89, 99–101

Noah, 32, 36

noble lie, 100–102

nonrealism, in religion, 91–92

noosphere, 120–125, 132, 135, 143–145, 235n193

novelty, 16–18, 24, 26–28, 171, 197

objectifying, as part of the scientific process, 56, 172

objectivity, 10–11, 64–65, 92, 100, 193, 195

objects of wonder, proper. *See* wonder, proper objects of

ocean. *See* sea

The Omega Point, 130

omnicompetence, 11, 86, 127–128, 168, 170, 186

On Human Nature (Wilson), 51, 72–74, 163

ontological wonder. *See* wonder, existential

Open Source biotechnology. *See* biotechnology, Open Source

optimism: cosmic, 133, 140, 150; techno-, 141–143; towards the Anthropocene, 117–118, 124, 139–140, 142–144, 179

Orr, H. Allen, 56, 59, 64

otherness, 27–28, 133, 172, 182, 199–202

paradigm, evolutionary. *See* evolutionary paradigm

paradigms in science, 79, 104, 125, 160, 170

passions, 14, 19, 21, 22–24,

Perkel, Marc, 146, 156

petite narratives. *See* narrative, petite

phenomenal irreducibility, 82, 173–175

phenomenology, 149, 191, 222n97

The Phenomenon of Man (Teilhard), 159

philosophy of science, 4, 7, 20, 59, 62, 87, 92, 192

physicalism. *See* materialism

factual faith, 151–152; naturalism, earth cults as insufficient for, 105–106; naturalism, education reform and, 93–94, 110–114; naturalism, evolutionary framework for, 87–93, 148–149; naturalism, provisional science implies provisional, 160; naturalism, religion as biological impulse and, 72–73, 99–101, 158–159; naturalism, simultaneously enchanting and disenchanting, 76–77; naturalism, unity of, 101–102, 109–110, 219n2; naturalism, values in, 94–98, 106–108, 158; naturalism, Wilson replaces religion with, 53–56. *See also* dark green religion; studies, 69, 104, 112–113, 118; tolerance, 101–102
responsibility: differential, for environmental crisis, 129, 136; in the Anthropocene, human, 118, 122–124, 199; nature's, 137–138; science's role in downplaying, 179
revelation: evolution as, 54; moral implications of science as, 73, 99; physicalist, 71; science as, 126, 178; science as public, 148, 161; Universe Story as, 88, 184–185
reverence: for nature, 30, 51, 84, 95, 184, 202; for science, 114, 130, 160–162, 176; for scientists, 130, 156, 160–162, 176; for the story of science, 97, 148
Revkin, Andrew, 141–144
Robinson, Marilynne, 131
Romanticism. *See* poetry, Romantic
Rubenstein, Mary-Jane, 24, 41, 77, 192, 207n43
Rue, Loyal: and amythia, 90–91; and consilience, 93–94; and the biocentric lie, 100–101; and the neural self, 95–98; on educational reform, 110–114; on evolution of religion, 10, 90–102, 221n45; on guile and deceit, 89, 99–101, 223n121; on nature, 84; and Everybody's Story, 85, 89–102, 109–110, 127, 157–158, 166, 219n2

The Sacred Depths of Nature (Goodenough), 84, 102–104, 108, 111, 226n200
sacredness. *See* consecrated science
Sagan, Carl, 38, 83, 87, 98, 153, 163, 221n41
Sanders, Scott Russell, 167–168
scale, 8, 15, 63, 136, 165, 167, 174, 193–194, 199–202
"Science and the Sense of the Holy" (Eiseley), 180–181
science: as public revelation, 148, 161; as religion. *See* religious naturalism; as revelation. *See* revelation, science as; consecrated. *See* consecrated science; demonstrations, 34, 209n40; limits of. *See* knowledge, limits of; unification of. *See* consilience;

scientific: knowledge, 92, 106, 161, 164–165, 172, 183. *See also* knowledge; materialism. *See* materialism; progress. *See* progress in science
scientific wonder. *See* wonder at science
scientist as hero. *See* epic hero, scientists as scripture, 75, 151, 156, 168, 187. *See also* revelation
sea, 53, 176–177, 182–185
The Sea Around Us (Carson), 176–177, 182–183
self-awareness, 118, 124, 139. *See also* conscious reflection; consciousness, human; consciousness, cosmic self-
The Selfish Gene (Dawkins), 41, 76, 91, 94
self-organization, 100, 123, 132, 138, 140
The Sense of Wonder (Carson), 48, 53, 177, 196–197
serial wonder. *See* wonder, serial
Silent Spring (Carson), 80, 176–178, 182, 184, 186–189, 242n20
Silverman, Mark, 19, 23, 37, 74, 206n21, 213n63
simplifying, as part of the scientific process, 55, 172
sin, 151, 187, 190
singularity, 128, 227
Slingerland, Edward, 62, 69–71, 89, 99–100
snakes, innate fear of, 57, 64, 78, 212n39
sociobiology, 5, 51, 76, 78, 107
Sociobiology (E. O. Wilson), 51, 76
solipsism, 27, 133
Soulé, Michael, 145
species unification, 135. *See also* human as species
spiritual futurists. *See* futurism
spirituality, post-apocalyptic. *See* post-apocalyptic spirituality
spiritual uplift. *See* uplift, scientific/spiritual
Standing Rock, ND, 200–201
stewardship, environmental, 79. *See also* planetary management
Stoermer, Eugene, 134
story. *See* narrative; Epic of Evolution
storytelling: as evolved, 64, 92; as socialization, 65; modules. *See* brain modules
sublime, 15, 186
supernatural, 24, 31, 100, 102, 155
Swimme, Brian, 120–131, 167, 228n46, 231n102; and Gaia, 140; optimism of, 139, 143; teleology in, 134, 222n90, 230n93
symbolic consciousness. *See* consciousness, symbolic
symbolism, 32, 39, 93–94, 97
"The Symphony of Science" (John Boswell), 38

96–98, 117–120, 132–134, 183–184, 230n87; ethical potential of, 26–28, 176–202, 207n 43; existential, 104, 174–175, 242n15; fake, 39–41; historical meanings of, 14, 18, 20–25, 32–33; humanity as object of, 2, 9, 95–96, 133–134, 169–170; imposed form of, 41; knowledge as object of, 6–12, 16, 19, 22–28, 31–48, 60, 67–80, 103–108, 162–164. *See also* knowledge, wonder at; mind as object of, 38; nature as object of, 2, 12–13, 78–79, 162, 173–189; ontological. *See* wonder, existential; proper objects of, 19–20, 27, 47, 133, 170, 186, 197–198; reality as object of wonder, 11, 36–41, 60–71;

reversed dynamic of knowledge and, 22–25, 34, 75; science as object of. *See* wonder, knowledge as object of; scientists as object of, 75–78; serial, 16, 26–27, 33, 77, 170–171, 191
wonders (as objects), 15
Wonders and the Order of Nature (Daston and Park), 14
Wright, Robert, 147

X-Files, 34

Zygon, 84–85, 87, 102